More Reviews of *We've Been Had*

We've Been Had is an American wake-up call. James R. Keena has laid out, in exquisite detail, an encyclopedic one-stop-shopping resource manual. His book shines a brilliant light on the Chicago-mob-meets-international-Marxist-regime that is systematically dismantling our constitutionally driven Republic. Get this book, read it, learn from it, know what you don't know…*we've been had*!

—Thayrone X, Host of radio's '*On the Edge with Thayrone*'

Keena has provided readers with an exhaustive compendium of the documented facts of Obama's Marxist education, training, and personal associations with radicals. *We've Been Had* should be read by everyone in the U.S. who has the legal right to vote. At this stage in history, voters cannot afford to be ignorant. This book should be required reading for every high school senior, and all college students, in the U.S. to ensure they are exposed to a balanced knowledge of Obama and his real political philosophy.

— *Dr. Gene Lebrenz*, Emeritus Professor of Economics, and Emeritus Professor of Business Administration, at Florida Southern College

"James Keena has done a superb job of reconstructing Barack Obama's carefully obscured past and documenting his network of radical connections. The result is an unsettling, detailed portrait of the first anti-American President."

— Scott Swett, author of *To Set the Record Straight: How Swift Boat Veterans, POWs and the New Media Defeated John Kerry*

"We've Been Had is an amazingly breezy read for an encyclopedic study of the President of the United States and the various influences that have shaped his character and values."

> —*Mark Hendrickson*, instructor of economics at Grove City College and a Fellow for Economic & Social Policy with the College's Center for Vision & Values.

"This book will awaken those outside of the 20 percent far-left demographic who still somehow believe the narrative that Barack Obama is a post-partisan, post-racial, all-American politician. James leaves hardly a stone unturned exposing the true identity of the man behind the lofty rhetoric. Unfortunately, it's true: *"We've Been Had."*

> —*Monte Kuligowski*, attorney and author of "Does the Declaration of Independence Pass the *Lemon* Test?"

"If a man can be judged by the company he keeps, then Barack Obama should frighten the whole nation with his associations and his own Marxist background, all concisely documented by James Keena. With each chapter, the portrait Keena paints of Obama looks less like Fairey's 'Hope' and more like Munch's 'Scream'. Truly, 'We've Been Had'."

> —*Julian Dunraven*, J.D., M.P.A. Legal & Business Editor of People's Press Collective

We've Been Had

How Obama and the Radicals Conned
Middle Class America

James R. Keena

Foreword by Trevor Loudon

Twin Creek Books

We've Been Had: How Obama and the Radicals Conned Middle Class America by James R. Keena

Twin Creek Books
PO Box 140475
Nashville, TN 37214-0475 USA
orders@twincreekbooks.com; http://twincreekbooks.com

Twin Creek Books
PO Box 140475
Nashville, TN 37214-0475 USA

Disclaimer: The views and opinions contained herein are strictly those of the author and do not necessarily represent those of the publisher. The author makes no claims, promises or guarantees about the accuracy, completeness, or adequacy of the information contained in any portion of the book.

ISBN: 978-0-9845345-0-0

Cover photo Copyright © 2010 by Joanne Michalik
Cover design by Maribeth Schmidt

Published by Twin Creek Books, Nashville, Tennessee
Printed and bound in the United States of America
Library of Congress Control Number: 2010927943

Dedication

This book is dedicated to TEA Party activists everywhere.

More than two centuries ago, we fought a military revolution over the sacred principles of individual liberty and limited government. Since then, millions of brave men and women have sacrificed their very lives to defend them. Sadly, these principles are now under assault by radicals *in our own country*. The TEA Party movement is nurturing a grass roots political uprising to retake America from the radicals in Washington.

As Thomas Jefferson said, "A little rebellion now and then is a good thing, and as necessary in the political world as storms in the physical."

Contents

Acknowledgments
Foreword by Trevor Loudon

Index
Endnotes

Acknowledgments

This book would not have been possible without the contributions and support of many people. This is my wholly inadequate attempt to recognize and thank them.

I am indebted to my lovely wife Audrey. Not only did she manage the Keena household while I was immersed in this project, she invested countless hours helping with this book. She was my toughest critic and my greatest supporter. My love for her grew as a result of—or perhaps despite—our intense and sometimes stressful collaboration.

I am indebted to *Rattle With Us, Inc.*, the remarkably effective and inspirational TEA Party organization in Plymouth, Michigan. This group of passionate fellow patriots gave me many opportunities to share my thoughts with large audiences and to hone my arguments for this book. They are the best support group an author and speaker could hope for. I will always cherish the friendships and adventures Audrey and I experienced with Maribeth, Tom, Jim, Sharon Lollio, Marco Lollio, Patrick Colbeck, and Angie Colbeck. Our political process is better for the involvement of these great Americans. This book is better for the inspiration they provided me.

I am indebted to a host of authors and journalists for their tremendous research and reporting on topics presented in this book. It is not possible to acknowledge everyone's hard work that I drew upon and synthesized, but I would be remiss if I did not offer recognition to particularly fruitful resources. The works of authors David Horowitz, Richard Poe, Jerome Corsi, Don Fredrick, David Fredosso, Pamela Geller, Trevor Loudon, Michelle Malkin, Aaron Klein, Matthew Vadum, Stanley Kurtz, Brenda Elliott, Tim Novak, Jim Simpson, Evelyn Pringle, Ed Morrissey, and Cliff Kincaid were invaluable resources for this project. Online journals and data repositories such as *Discover the Networks*, *World Net Daily*, *Newsmax*, *American Thinker*, *National Review Online*, *Front Page Magazine*, *The Obama File*, *Canada Free Press*, and *Fox News* provided a cornucopia of critical information about the radical ambitions and backgrounds of our current leaders. I encourage interested readers to explore the works of these authors and online journals, because they offer a wealth of fascinating data, history, and insight. While *We've Been Had* offers uniquely framed perspectives on how the ascendant radicals in Washington are impacting the middle class and the future of America, this book is built on the foundation of the unflagging investigative efforts of the resources mentioned above.

I am indebted to Kit and Brook Babcock of Twin Creek Books for their faith in this project and their aggressive efforts to bring this book to market as rapidly and effectively as they did. Their collaboration and friendship are truly appreciated.

I am indebted to Maribeth Schmidt for her creative and technical wizardry designing and laying out the cover of the book. She invested considerable time and energy developing an outstanding product.

I am indebted to Sharon Lollio for her tireless efforts to arrange speaking opportunities for me at various TEA party events. Her friendship and passionate advocacy will always be remembered.

I am indebted to my son Patrick Keena for his generous technical assistance with my website, *Pathlessland.net*, and with my Facebook page, *Wevebeenhad*.

I am indebted to Thayrone X, host of the outstanding conservative radio talk show *On the Edge* at WAAM in Ann Arbor, Michigan. Thayrone and the team at WAAM have been passionate and vocal supporters of this project.

I am indebted to Kim Richardson for her tireless assistance with proofreading, editing, and footnoting. She was also a prolific font of topical material and reference resources.

Finally, and most importantly, I am indebted to all of the brave men and women who have ever served in the American Armed Forces. Without their courage and sacrifice over the centuries, our freedom would be nothing but a forlorn and distant memory. They have bought and paid for our liberty with their blood and lives on American battlefields called Yorktown and Gettysburg, on Normandy beaches called Omaha and Utah, on Pacific islands called Iwo Jima and Guadalcanal, and in dangerous theaters called Korea, Vietnam, Afghanistan, and Iraq. There are no words sufficient to thank them. While I cannot match their sacrifice, I can offer the power of my pen to complement the might of their swords in defense of our liberty.

Foreword by Trevor Loudon

We've Been Had.

Just as citizen journalist and pamphleteer Tom Paine contributed mightily to the first American Revolution with his classic "Common Sense" and other tracts, a new generation of citizen journalists are stepping forward to fight the second.

There is no doubt that the United States of America is in the throes of a second revolution, or perhaps a third if you are willing to grant the Obama Administration's headlong march to socialism that noble title. I prefer to call it a "putsch" or simply a power grab.

"America", as we admiring foreigners know you, stands on the brink of destruction. President Obama and the radicals have swept through your country's institutions, purging all that made you different in the world.

On the sidelines, we, who were brought up to appreciate the good that America has done for the world, stand in horror as your "1960s generation" seems hell bent on transforming your country into a corrupt, politically correct, bankrupt, shadow of its former glory.

But that's not the worst of it. Poverty has its upside, it builds character, and political correctness can be overthrown. Given enough time, America could recover.

But, do we have time? Will America's enemies in Moscow, Havana, Beijing, Tehran, Pyongyang and Caracas, stand idly by while the American economy grinds to a halt and your country is forced to retreat militarily from all corners of the globe?

When Roman military power collapsed, as a result of government excess and massive debt, did the Goths and

Vandals patiently wait for Rome to recover? Our modern barbarians won't either.

America IS the world's last best hope for mankind. If you falter, we will all fail.

Therefore, as a New Zealander, I am grateful that citizen journalist Jim Keena has written this book.

We've Been Had is not just another Obama biography. It is a clearly written and concise overview of the movement that put Barack Obama in power. I can very confidently say that Barack Obama did not build a movement, a movement built Barack Obama.

Jim Keena has laid it all out for you. From his earliest days Barack Obama has been groomed to do big things. From his radical family to his childhood communist mentor Frank Marshall Davis, to his radical friends at Occidental and Columbia, and in Chicago, Barack Obama has been anointed by the political left to enact their agenda.

Jim Keena's book gives you the facts, but much more importantly, it makes the connections. From the streets of South Chicago to the court of Emperor Soros the First, armies of dedicated leftists have worked tirelessly to put Barack Obama and his henchmen in the White House. Now they work tirelessly to irrevocably change your country and eventually our world, for the worse, much much worse.

America needs a change, a real change, a return to its constitutional roots.

That change is a brewing in "tea" pots across the land. It is a race against time now. Either the TEA Party movement and the constitutionalists and patriots take America back and restore your Republic back to and beyond its former glory, or your country will sink into a black hole of poverty, fear and tyranny. That is the choice before you.

Change is needed. Hope is on the horizon. Millions of Americans are demanding the restoration of their Republic.

Schedule Change / Time Off Request

This is a request for: ☐ Schedule change ☐ Time off

Name: _____ Job Title: _____

Department: _____ Employee #: _____

Please check one: ☐ CTO ☐ Float Holiday ☐ Other _____

Time Off:

First Choice: _____ to _____ Return to work: _____
            Date/Time   Date/Time

Second Choice: _____ to _____ Return to work: _____
            Date/Time   Date/Time

Schedule Change:

I agree to work: _____ For _____ _____ _____ _____
            Day   Date   Shift/Time   Signature/Date

I agree to work: _____ For _____ _____ _____ _____
            Day   Date   Shift/Time   Signature/Date

Comments:

_____

Signature of Employee: _____ Date Submitted: _____

Management Approval: ☐ Granted ☐ Denied Reason: _____

Management Signature: _____ Date: _____

210201 Rev. 7/09   White Copy - Manager   Yellow Copy - Employee

What is needed is for even more Americans to awaken. Read Jim Keena's book and make sure your friends and relatives do the same.

The American Revolution would have failed without its Tom Paines. People will only become engaged when they understand the consequences, when they know full well what's at stake.

The second American Revolution will succeed or fail by similar means. If enough information can get into enough hands, quickly enough, America will have a fighting chance.

Jim Keena's book is a valuable contribution to that cause.

Trevor Loudon

New Zeal Blog, Obama Files and <u>KeyWiki.org</u>
Christchurch
New Zealand

Chapter One

Meet the Enemies of the Middle Class

> *"A government big enough to give you everything you want is a government big enough to take from you everything you have."*
>
> Ronald Reagan

We've been had.

Democrats have been had. Republicans have been had. Independents have been had. If you are in the middle class, you've *really* been had.

Radicals have leeched onto the aorta of our political system. They have succeeded, after 50 years of effort, to take control of our country. Socialists and anti-Western ideologues have duped the American middle class into electing extremist politicians who are changing our Constitutional Republic into a European-style socialist democracy. Government bureaucrats are rapidly replacing private individuals as the sovereigns of our nation.

For decades, the radicals quietly won small skirmishes in the courts, the legislatures, and over tax code. They gradually snuck up on the middle class, camouflaged with high-minded slogans like "change", "economic justice", and "fairness". But the radicals are no longer lurking furtively in the dark shadows of fringe organizations. Now that they control Congress and the White House, they are openly devouring our freedom, our wealth, and our security.

The radical forces behind this assault on America are political parasites that have hijacked mainstream party organizations to fool the middle class into electing the agents of their own destruction. We are witnessing the opening acts of the most profound restructuring of our political system since 1776. This reformation will include the biggest wealth redistribution in our history, along with a massive expansion in government control of our economy and our lives.

Let's begin with an obvious paradox. Isn't it surreal that Barack Hussein Obama is President of the United States? Set aside any emotional affinity and political support that you might have for Mr. Obama. How is it possible that he holds the most important executive office in the world, and is now Commander-in-Chief of the most powerful armed forces in history? If this doesn't yet seem surreal or improbable to you, consider the following highlights of Obama's biography:

- He was born the son of a Kenyan Marxist, allegedly in Hawaii, although no one has seen any documents that identify corroborating information, such as the name of his delivery physician or the hospital where he was born.

- Prior to becoming President, he had no executive leadership experience, aside from supervising other community organizers like himself, and handing out other people's money from philanthropic foundations.

- His only foreign policy experience was described by Hillary Clinton as "a speech he made in 2002"[1]. She was referring to an anti-war speech he delivered when he had no official role in deciding our strategy in Iraq.

- He is responsible for the biggest economy in the world during a time of tremendous economic turmoil, but he has zero business experience or training.

- He was a junior U.S. Senator for only 143 working days before forming an exploratory committee for a presidential run.

- He won his U.S. Senate seat only because his two strongest competitors bowed out of the election due to messy divorce situations that spilled over into the tabloids. He lost a run for the U.S. House of Representatives by a landslide to a former Black Panther.

- He was an Illinois State Senator for only eight years. He achieved this position by hiring a lawyer to disqualify all four of his opponents, including his political mentor, on technical grounds. As a state Senator, he voted "present" with remarkable frequency, to avoid taking stands on difficult issues.

- He was rated as the most liberal senator in 2007 (further left than Ted Kennedy, Barbara Boxer, Harry Reid, and socialist Bernie Sanders).

- Five of his campaigns for public office were financially supported by Antoin Rezko, a Syrian national recently convicted of 16 felonies, including bribing public officials.

- His father and stepfather were Muslims, he was raised in Indonesia as a Muslim, and he received two years of training in the Qur'an.

- He was a congregant in a virulently anti-American church for almost two decades, and supported it with tens of thousands of dollars. He and his children were baptized into this Marxist congregation, and he and his wife were married in it.

- His political career was nurtured by a staunch Communist (Alice Palmer), former Weather Underground terrorists (Bill Ayers and Bernardine Dohrn), an anti-Western Hungarian financier (George Soros), and a spurious vote-gathering machine (ACORN) that was investigated in 14 states for voter registration fraud.

- He received financial contributions and official endorsements from the Black Panthers, various Communist and Socialist organizations, and groups that support radical Islamic terrorists.

- He was heavily influenced, according to his own autobiography, by the writings of militant Black Nationalists, including Malcolm X.

- He went through a protracted period in his life during which he was alienated and directionless. He admitted to using cocaine and marijuana.

This is not a typical résumé of an American president. Obama's résumé might not even warrant a security clearance by the National Security Agency, if someone else's name was on it. It is almost inconceivable that a person with such a radical background, with a career almost entirely localized to Illinois, with a long litany of shady associations, with a history of unscrupulous political shenanigans, and with microscopic experience in economic and international affairs, could leap to the top of the American political pyramid so rapidly. The only reasonable explanation is that he is just a media-protected figurehead, an effusive Manchurian candidate for a powerful and influential political network.

This book is not a personal diatribe against Barack Obama. It is pointless to attack Obama per se, for two reasons. First, he is charming, affable, and eloquent, which means that ad hominem attacks are easily deflected. He and his sycophantic legions in the media are adept at parsing, isolating, and minimizing such attacks. They will surely close ranks and attempt to parse, isolate, and minimize this book. Second, attacking him personally does not really illuminate the bigger picture. His ascendance to the Presidency and to near godliness did not happen in a vacuum. Examining his past and his philosophy, without studying the power brokers and organizations surrounding and supporting him, actually leaves one quite puzzled as to how he got where he is. He is just a fresh smiley face camouflaging a much deeper and enduring radical movement. He is a gift-wrapped Trojan horse with deadly provocateurs lurking inside. He is the product of a media-abetted "Immaculate Conception" that began in 2004 to obscure his radical, tawdry background.

This book will demonstrate that a deceptively cultish mythology of Obama was constructed by his handlers and was propagated by the mainstream media. This mythology is part of the con being perpetrated on America. It is intended to artfully conceal the radicalism and brute force "Chicago Way" politics that truly define Obama. A useful analogy is the media-created illusion of Tiger Woods as a perfect role model of golfing excellence and blemish-free character that corporate sponsors lusted after. This deceptive mythology persisted for many years, until it collapsed amid a sudden flurry of revelations that Woods was really a prolific philanderer who was immersed in multiple extramarital affairs, dozens of lurid trysts with high-priced prostitutes, wild gambling sprees, drunkenness, and performance-enhancing drugs. Likewise, Barack Obama's hidden life as a socialist, an unethical bare-knuckled politician, a radical outsider from mainstream American culture, and a hypocritical shill for Wall Street tycoons will eventually explode into public awareness and burst the magical bubble of his mythological purity. This book will help burst that bubble.

To a large degree, Obama won the election in 2008 because of this magical bubble. No one really knew anything substantive about him. He suddenly appeared on the national political scene in 2004 as if the first four decades of his life belonged to someone else. Obama is a talented con man able to charm naïve middle-class citizens into handing over their wealth for promised security that will never actually materialize. *American Thinker* editor J.R. Dunn wrote, "Liberals see their leaders as transcendent beings, someone more than human, someone with a touch of the divine....Leaders don't handle tasks, they lead movements, they embody the spirit of the age. They transform. Leaders, to put it simply, are fuehrers."[2] Obama donned such a mantle, even if facetiously, by declaring in New Hampshire in 2008, "A light will shine through that window, a beam of light will come down upon you, you will experience an epiphany...and you will suddenly realize that you must go to the polls and vote for Obama."[3]

Ironically, he told a southern crowd during the campaign that they had been "hoodwinked" and "bamboozled" by Republicans, paraphrasing Nation of Islam spokesman Malcolm X's declaration that "You've been hoodwinked. You've been had. You've been took. You've been led astray, led amok. You've been bamboozled." [4] [5] Essentially, the master charlatan Obama was disingenuously warning America to beware of charlatans! When Obama's political façade implodes, it will become clear that the middle class of America has indeed been had, not by Republicans or other bogeymen of the left, but by the radicals themselves.

This book does not suggest that Obama is the mastermind of a vast left-wing conspiracy. To argue that he is the organizing force that coordinated a radical change in our government is to miss the point entirely. It is the other way around. The organizing force of various radical movements brought him to where he is, almost by happenstance. He is just a very charismatic, eloquent proxy for a powerful and ruthless political machine that has been gaining momentum for decades.

Obama was elevated to the presidency by powerful "change" agents who are perverse mirror images of the revolutionary triumvirate that championed the American Revolution. Two centuries ago, Thomas Jefferson was the "Pen", with his timeless Declaration of Independence. Patrick Henry was the "Voice", with his passionate calls for revolution from taverns and town halls. George Washington was the "Sword", with his bold leadership of the American military.

Compare these heroes with the radicals responsible for the rising socialist revolution in America. Saul Alinsky is the "Pen", defining the methods of this new revolution with his book *Rules for Radicals*. George Soros is the "Voice", with his influence over the media and his surreptitious usurpation of the Democratic Party. Socialists, Black Nationalists, and radical Islamists have aligned forces to become the "Sword", providing the organized foot soldiers for the battle that is already raging to redistribute wealth and destroy capitalism.

This book examines these radical forces in detail. It documents their direct influence on the career of Barack Obama and on the political transformation of America. Here is a brief introduction to them.

Saul Alinsky was a socialist and the philosophical guru of the radicals who hijacked the modern Democratic Party. Alinsky created the blueprint that radicals used to wrest power from moderates and conservatives in the United States. He catalyzed the labyrinthine network of organizations, foundations, training camps, media influences, and cultural trend setters who are collectively moving the American political center to the left. A key facet of Alinsky's strategy was to deceive the middle class into supporting a socialist revolution that will eventually devour them. Not many in the middle class will recognize Alinsky's name, but nearly every leftist organization today counts him in its genealogy. Obama's rise to the Presidency is a direct result of the clout and influence of the Alinsky legacy.

George Soros is a rogue Hungarian-born billionaire who broke the Bank of England to enrich himself, supported regime changes in Eastern Europe to amuse himself, and spent a fortune trying to remove George W. Bush and the Republicans from office. He is the de facto puppet master of the Democratic Party. He has established more than 30 shadow organizations, such as Media Matters and MoveOn.org, which have become the real party machinery of the DNC. He is a frustrated philosopher who abhors Western principles, hates the United States, and wants to establish a borderless "Open Society" that rejects the U.S. Constitution. He has invested $5 billion over three decades to support radical programs and politicians, including Barack Obama.

Socialists, Black Nationalists, and radical Islamists have worked for decades to instigate a revolution against capitalism and Western values. They have quietly established footholds in urban America, public schools and universities, labor unions, news media, pop culture, environmental organizations, and many fringe political groups that orbit the Democratic Party. Militant Black Nationalist leaders and organizations, such as Elijah Muhammad, Malcolm X, Louis Farrakhan, the Black Panthers, and the Nation of Islam have collaborated with socialist and communist groups to fight perceived oppression by a capitalistic, Eurocentric culture. This radical alliance lusts after middle-class wealth, jobs, and benefits. Their lust does not involve a desire to earn these perquisites, but rather to plunder them.

The synergy among Alinsky, Soros, the socialists, the Black Nationalists, and the radical Islamists is found in their antagonism toward the Western principles of political freedom, limited government, and the sovereignty of the individual. These bedrock Western principles contradict the socialist vision of collective societal action. These principles frustrate "Have-nots" in their quest to siphon wealth from the "Haves". These principles interfere with the Islamic mandate that all secular laws be derived from Allah. All of these radical forces are consequently united in a common hatred of capitalism and Jeffersonian liberalism.

These radical forces found in Obama an extraordinary fulcrum for aligning and leveraging their efforts to wrest power from mainstream, middle-class Americans. Obama is the perfect radical foil. He is an African-American connected with militant Black Nationalists, a leftist politician trained by Saul Alinsky's Industrial Areas Foundation, a former Muslim with extensive ties to radical Muslims, and the son of a Marxist father with lifelong connections to Marxist organizations and mentors. He is the perfect figurehead for a brutally effective coalition that has not only mobilized the usual cadre of radical activists; it has also deceitfully co-opted large swaths of the middle class.

Alinsky's model for achieving socialism in America has been adopted by this radical coalition. The battle plan includes setting in motion a subtle revolution. The goal of this revolution is to transfer power and wealth from the upper and middle classes to the underclass and to the government bureaucrats and financial oligarchs who will administer America after the destruction of capitalism.

"Change" was Alinsky's code word for using professional community organizers to quietly nurture socialism. To Alinsky, the end justified any means, including outlandish deception. He needed to deceive the middle-class into embracing a leftward shift, because without the millions of middle class voters, his stealth revolution could not succeed. His strategy was to make the middle class fear that our institutions were crumbling and a radical change was therefore necessary. In his words, "There's a revolution seething beneath the surface of middle class of America—the revolution of a bewildered, frightened, and as-yet-inarticulate group of desperate people groping for alternatives—for hope." [6] Alinsky's mantras of "Change" and "Hope" are the tantalizing hooks that today's radical vanguard have used to con the middle class.

Community organizers trained by Alinsky and his foundations seek to "disorganize" society to stir up sufficient insecurity for revolution to occur. But, instead of candidly talking about revolution, they use disingenuous slogans like "A new kind of politics" and "Change we can believe in" to stupefy the middle class into believing that government power and taxes must grow, while middle-class freedom and wealth must shrink. Their mission is to con the middle class into believing that "sacrifice" and "collective action" are the only possible paths to the future.

This deceptive strategy to make the middle class feel insecure is augmented by a media onslaught of "economic crisis," "banking crisis," "war crisis," "climate change crisis," "infrastructure crisis," "social security crisis," "health care crisis," and "global poverty crisis." After frightening the middle class with these crises, the socialists vilify capitalist institutions such as banks and global corporations as the evil straw men responsible for the mess. This lends credibility to their grand deception, because Wall Street and Big Business are often resented by the middle class.

This fertile ground of crises sets the stage for the inevitable big-government solutions, which invariably involve broad new bureaucratic powers, which always lead to confiscating wealth from citizens. Thus, the death of capitalism and the rise of socialism results, not from violent revolution, but from a thousand bureaucratic paper cuts.

The strategy that the radicals are using for this gradual transition toward socialism is outlined below. It is essentially Saul Alinsky's model. It instructs radicals to constantly destabilize mainstream society, and then to use the resulting disequilibrium to gradually move the country closer to socialism. It is nothing more than 19th Century Marxian dialectics, window-dressed for a gullible middle class in a modern democracy:

1) Target a subgroup of society that is being "victimized" by capitalism and Eurocentric culture.

2) Agitate this subgroup into anger, resentment, and political action.

3) Instigate a crisis involving this subgroup, so that the status quo is somehow destabilized or overwhelmed.

4) Create deceptive popular momentum behind the manufactured crisis with highly visible activism and media exposure.

5) Leverage this manufactured momentum to win political concessions. These concessions will include redistribution of wealth to the "victimized" subgroup, along with increased funding and influence for the activists who helped agitate for the "change".

6) Repeat steps one through five, until enough "victimized" subgroups have been mobilized to achieve sufficient political power to effect a radical transformation of America, resulting in massive redistribution of wealth and power from the upper and middle classes to the underclass and their "representatives".

7) During steps one through six, continuously deceive the middle class into being sympathetic to the cause, because without their votes and support, systemic

"change" is not possible. Play heavily upon their guilt, fear, and sense of obligation.

We've Been Had thoroughly explains how the radicals have used this model to orchestrate the structural transformation of America that is now underway. Radicals have a dagger pointed at the heart of the American economic system, the U.S. Constitution, and Western culture. With socialism as their goal, anarchic destabilization as their weapon, theft and deceit as their morality, and an army of venomous anti-American "organizers" as their vanguard, they are launching an unparalleled attack on our society.

We've Been Had introduces readers to key figures in this radical coalition. You will meet veteran socialists from the Students for a Democratic Society, including Wade Rathke, the founder of ACORN, and Aryeh Neier, head of George Soros's Open Society Institute. You will meet Black Nationalists like Jeremiah Wright, Malcolm X, and Louis Farrakhan. You will meet Bill Ayers and Bernardine Dohrn of the Weather Underground domestic terrorist group. You will also be introduced to a host of organizations that are allies in the war on American capitalism and the U.S. Constitution, including the Democratic Socialists of America (DSA), the New Party, the Woods Fund, the Apollo Alliance, the Industrial Areas Foundation, the Gamaliel Network, the Black Panthers, and the Nation of Islam.

Obama and our left-leaning legislators will assure us that they are not socialists or radicals. They will feign indignation and call us alarmists if we apply these labels to them. But, if something looks like a duck, walks like a duck, and quacks like a duck, it's probably a duck. The politicians running our government may try to evade the labels of "socialist" and "radical", but let's briefly examine the early initiatives of the Obama administration to see if they apply:

- They essentially nationalized a number of banks and investment firms by forcing companies to accept TARP funds, whether they wanted them or not. In the process, the government took equity positions in these companies and influenced their policies. While much of the TARP money has been paid back, Obama's administration is now considering permanent TARP-like legislation to establish perpetual control over the banking industry.

- They essentially nationalized General Motors by underwriting the company with debtor-in-possession financing, firing the CEO, taking control of their restructuring efforts, eliminating unwelcome dealers, positioning the United Auto Workers (UAW) as a major equity holder, closing independent dealerships, and influencing what types of vehicles they should build.

- They began setting executive compensation levels for private companies and determining which private workers can be paid bonuses.

- They passed legislation to nationalize health care, which will lead to waiting lists, rationing, and the government ultimately deciding who gets which procedure.

- They declared land containing valuable natural resources "off-limits" for exploration.

- They are further nationalizing our education system with an enormous increase in federal funding for local schools and expansion of state-funded education to include ages zero to five.

- They are pushing for the Employee Free Choice Act, which is just an Orwellian political cover to allow union thugs to easily unionize any company.

- They are proposing to essentially nationalize our energy industry with a cap-and-trade carbon emission program that will discourage traditional fossil fuel sources of energy and force conversion to expensive, government-subsidized alternative energy sources.

- They have approved a $3.7 trillion budget with a deficit that dwarfs all previous deficits in history. Most of the spending growth is for programs that transfer wealth from the "Haves" to the "Have-Nots" and their caretakers. The Obama administration will accumulate more government debt in four years than the 43 previous presidents accumulated across a span of 233 years.

- They are preparing to crack down on freedom of speech with proposals such as "diversifying" local media content, purchasing failing newspapers in exchange for control over "editorial content," and regulating internet blogging. Mainstream news providers are devolving into a captive fourth branch of the federal government.

- They have made our country less safe by neutering our secret services, reducing military spending, failing to police illegal immigration, and projecting an image of American weakness and passivity abroad.

- They are abdicating the independence and sovereignty of the U.S. political and economic system in favor of United Nations and International Monetary Fund authority. They are laying the foundation for the "One World Government" that the socialists have hoped for decades to achieve. This will make us not only slaves to the elitists in Washington and the underclass in America, but also slaves to every international "victim" that wants to lay claim to our wealth.

When government leaders begin nationalizing the financial, automotive, energy, health care, information, and education industries, and then audaciously claim that they are not moving us toward socialism, they are simply lying. With the mass media, pop culture, and public educators as complicit wing men, the Obama administration is proceeding as if everyone in the middle class is uninformed or gullible. The future of our country depends on whether their assessment is right or wrong. The radicals are betting that they can continue to deceive the middle class with the "hope" of cradle-to-grave security that is allegedly the benefit of their "change".

When Obama declared, "We are the ones we have been waiting for,"[7] it was an incestuous political allegory to the 50-year-old radical dream to control America. Now that the radicals are in power, they will first come for the rich, to reinforce the deception that they are fighting for the common man. Unfortunately, the rich don't have nearly enough money to conquer all of the "crises" that the radicals have manufactured, nor to fulfill all of the needs and wants of the underclass. Some of the rich, particularly the Wall Street oligarchs and the professional bureaucrats who feed at the public trough, are the *recipients* of taxpayer money and government bailouts. The middle class is ultimately going to pay for the spending, borrowing, and money-printing orgy of the Obama administration, one way or another.

Margaret Thatcher said, "The problem with socialism is that you eventually run out of other people's money."[8] Your middle-class standard of living is about to deteriorate. You will become a slave to government solutions for exaggerated or imagined "crises". You will pay taxes or fees for carbon emissions to combat the global warming hoax. You will pay higher utility and fuel costs as energy markets are circumvented in favor of expensive alternative energy sources. You will be saddled with either higher taxes or dramatic inflation in order to bail out banks, mortgage deadbeats, auto companies, state and local governments, pension funds, unions, foreign countries, and the International Monetary Fund. Social Security and Medicare taxes will skyrocket as the reality of our Ponzi-scheme retirement system becomes apparent. Your access to quality health care will decline as more and more non-paying consumers, including illegal immigrants, are covered by government-run health care.

If this transition to socialism is not derailed in the coming elections, the middle class can wave goodbye to its wealth, its security, its culture, its liberty, and its future. Instead, the middle class can welcome its new masters: the pillaging underclass horde and the elitist radicals who have ridden them into power.

We've been had.

"We must reject the idea that every time a law's broken, society is guilty rather than the lawbreaker. It is time to restore the American precept that each individual is accountable for his actions."

Ronald Reagan

Chapter Two

Meet Barack Hussein Obama

"What is our community, and how might that community be reconciled with our freedoms? How far do our obligations reach?"[1]

Barack Obama, *Dreams from My Father*

Barack Obama is still a mystery to most Americans.

Yes, he is President of the United States. Everybody knows his name, even in foreign countries. Magazine racks are littered with his omnipresent smiling face. He is a regular fixture on the cover of *Time* magazine. There are millions of bumper stickers with his "O" logo and vapid slogans. The media bombards us with his ubiquitous cries of crisis and the need for us to sacrifice. Artwork is being commissioned of him and his programs. Indoctrinated public school children sing his praises, like chirpy little North Korean group thinkers.

But how much do we truly know about Obama, other than a media-polished sketch of his life? He is very recent to the national scene. His ascendance to messianic stardom was remarkably rapid. His biography and philosophy have not been properly vetted, mostly because the media has formed partisan ranks around him. A *New York Times* columnist titled an article about Obama "The 46-Year-Old Virgin."[2] Another columnist observed, "We know less about Senator Obama than about any prospective president in American history."[3]

In the Illinois Senate, he voted "present" almost 130 times. He was mostly absent from his U.S. Senate post during his run for the Presidency, so he missed many Senate votes. Voting "present", or neglecting to vote at all, effectively veiled his positions on issues.

But it is not just a careless voting record and a protective media shell that have obscured our view of Obama. There just aren't that many people who know him intimately. He lived in Indonesia and on the remote island of Hawaii for nearly two decades. His parents and his grandparents are deceased. His siblings didn't grow up with him, and they have spent most of their lives overseas. His children are not old enough to share useful insights. For half of his life, he was just another alienated, anonymous youth drifting on the radical fringes of society.

Obama has also refused to share documentation that would remove the clouds hiding his past, including his original long-form birth certificate, his adoption records, his college and university transcripts, his test scores, his selective service records, his passport records, his employment records, his legislative records, and even his medical history. He has spent a lot of money on legal fees to *prevent* access to these records. He wrote a memoir called *Dreams from My Father*, but the vaguely autobiographical docudrama was surprisingly devoid of objective information. It rarely referenced dates, it used many aliases, it glossed over major life events, and it was written non-sequentially. It begs more questions than it answers.

Even Obama's public pronouncements are fuzzy and omni-directional. He is a consummate politician who tries to take both sides of every issue. A law school classmate said that he was like a "kind of human Rorschach test...people see in him what they want to see."[4] Obama once said, "I serve as a blank screen on which people of vastly different political stripes project their own views."[5] Biographer David Mendel described his "ingenious lack of specificity."[6] His speeches, though eloquent and sometimes stirring, are all read from a teleprompter. They pour forth in a torrent of amorphous words. His rhetoric is the political equivalent of Marshall McLuhan's "Deep Out" poetry. He sounds transcendent, but there is rarely anything tangible in his message.

It is time to shine the harsh light of day on Barack Obama. This chapter begins our exploration of what the mainstream media should have told us about Obama, but chose not to, opting instead for misinformation, deceit, and outright cover-up. This chapter outlines his biography and highlights the key milestones in his life. It establishes the context and the chronological framework of the radical forces that made him who he is. The rest of the book will flesh out the skeletal outline presented in this chapter with the meat of his résumé, connecting all of the dots and coloring in all of the pixels, so that the breadth and depth of his suppressed radical background will become apparent and unmistakable.

Barack Obama's story began in exotic places. His father, Barack Hussein Obama, Sr., was an Arab-African Muslim born in Kenya in 1936. He was a member of the Luo tribe near Lake Victoria. Obama Sr. enrolled at the University of Hawaii in 1959 after receiving a scholarship from the Kenyan government. He graduated in three years with a degree in Econometrics.

In 1960, Obama Sr. met an 18-year-old Caucasian woman named Stanley Ann Dunham in a Russian language class. Stanley Ann, who was given her unusual name because her father was hoping for a boy, was born in Kansas in 1942. Obama Sr. and Ann (as she shall be called henceforth) appear to have gotten married, although there is no documentation of a wedding. According to Barack Jr. in *Dreams from My Father*, "...how and when the marriage occurred remains a bit murky, a bill of particulars that I've never quite had the courage to explore. There's no record of a real wedding, a cake, a ring, a giving away of the bride. No families were in attendance...."[7] Subsequent divorce records referred to a civil marriage on February 2, 1961, when Ann would have been three months pregnant.[8]

Ann presumably gave birth to Barack Hussein Obama, Jr. on August 4, 1961 in Honolulu. He allegedly was born at the Kapi'olani Maternity and Gynecological Hospital, although his half-sister Maya claimed that he was born at the Queens Medical Center. According to researchers, neither hospital will confirm that it hosted Barack Jr.'s birth, because he refuses to sign a simple form authorizing release of the information. Relatives in Kenya claimed that they attended his birth in Mombasa. Strangely, Kenyan authorities declared that all records regarding Barack Jr. are sealed, implying that there are records to seal.[9]

These divergent accounts of Barack Jr.'s birth could be easily resolved if he were to relent and authorize the State of Hawaii to release his long-form birth certificate for public view. A short-form Certificate of Live Birth (COLB) for Barack Jr. was posted online by his supporters. But, even if that short-form COLB is legitimate, it doesn't identify his birthplace. Such COLB's were routinely and legally issued by Hawaii for children not actually born in the state (including Barack Jr.'s Indonesian-born half-sister, Maya).[10] More information about the birth certificate controversy is available on the internet (see especially Pamela Geller's *atlasshrugs.com*) and in many books (see especially Don Fredrick's *The Obama Timeline*).

This book will not dwell on the controversy, other than to note it as one of the many forensic curiosities of Barack Jr.'s early life that presents a consistent pattern of deceit and cover-up.

After a brief marriage, Ann and Obama Sr. divorced in 1964. According to *Dreams from My Father*, Ann told Barack Jr., "It wasn't your father's fault that he left, you know. I divorced him. When the two of us got married, your grandparents weren't happy with the idea. But they said okay—they probably couldn't have stopped us anyway, and they eventually came around to the idea that it was the right thing to do. Then Barack's father—your grandfather Hussein—wrote Gramps this long, nasty letter saying that he didn't approve of the marriage. He didn't want the Obama blood sullied by a white woman, he said. Well, you can imagine how Gramps reacted to that. And then there was a problem with your father's first wife...."[11]

The "problem with the first wife" was that when Obama Sr. married Ann, he was already married to an African woman named Kezia. He abandoned his pregnant wife Kezia and a young son named Abongo, in order to attend the University of Hawaii. Discovery of this bigamy probably contributed to his divorce from Ann. It is also possible that the "free love" mentality of the times contributed. There are nude photos on the internet of a woman who looks like Ann that were allegedly taken by Frank Marshall Davis, who was a Marxist writer and an amateur pornographer.[12] There are even suggestions that Davis was actually Barack Jr.'s father. More will be said about the curious relationship between Davis and the Obama family later on.

Ann left Obama Sr. shortly after Barack Jr. was born. She abruptly departed Hawaii to attend the University of Washington in the fall of 1961.[13] There are conflicting reports as to whether she brought newborn Barack Jr. along with her, or left him behind to be cared for by her parents. She returned to the University of Hawaii in 1963, eventually earning a degree in Mathematics in 1967. There is no evidence that Obama Sr. and Ann ever lived together.

Obama Sr. left Hawaii in 1962 to study at Harvard. His decision showed remarkable disinterest in his purported family. As Ann later told Barack Jr., "When your father graduated from UH, he received two scholarship offers. One was to the New School, here in New York. The other one was to Harvard. The New School agreed to pay for everything—room and board, and a job on campus, enough to support all three of us. Harvard just agreed to pay tuition."[14] Obama Sr. chose the fellowship to Harvard. A story in a local newspaper said that Obama Sr. planned to tour the mainland before attending Harvard.[15] It did not mention his wife and infant son.

After graduating from Harvard, Obama Sr. returned to Africa with fellow Harvard student Ruth Nidesand, whom he later married. He returned to Hawaii once, for a school reunion in 1971. He briefly visited 10-year-old Barack Jr. The only pictures of Obama Sr. and Barack Jr. together were taken at the airport on this visit. They would never see each other again.

Obama Sr.'s undistinguished career included a failed effort to establish communism in Kenya. He became a chronic alcoholic and a philanderer. He fathered two more children named Bernard and Abo by Kezia, and two children named Mark and David by Ruth Nidesand. He also fathered a child named George by a woman named Jael. George lives in a hut outside of Nairobi, according to the Italian edition of *Vanity Fair*. George told the magazine, "If anyone says something about my surname, I say we (Barack Jr. and he) are not related."[16] He is seemingly as indifferent to his famous half-brother as Barack Jr. is to George's poverty.

Obama Sr. lost both legs in a 1982 car accident. Shortly after that, he killed himself while drunk in a car accident in Nairobi. He was buried in accordance with Muslim practices at age 46. Barack Jr. was 21 at the time.

Barack Jr.'s mother Ann met Lolo Soetoro after she returned to Hawaii from Washington in 1963. Lolo was a Muslim who lived most of his life in Indonesia. The two married in 1966. Barack Jr. began his education at Noelani Elementary School in 1966. Strangely, the Hawaii Department of Education can't find his school records, even though Barack Jr. appears in a kindergarten class photo. It is tempting to speculate that the missing documentation contains information about his birthplace or citizenship.

When Indonesian President Suharto seized power in 1967, all Indonesian students studying overseas were compelled to return home. So, Lolo moved back to Jakarta, and Ann and Barack soon followed. Lolo served in the Indonesian army for a year. Barack described their life in his second book, *The Audacity of Hope*: "Our family was not well off in those early years; the Indonesian army didn't pay its lieutenants much. We lived in a modest house on the outskirts of town, without air-conditioning, refrigeration, or flush toilets. We had no car—my stepfather rode a motorcycle, while my mother took the local jitney service every morning to the U.S. embassy, where she worked as an English teacher."[17]

Barack lived in Jakarta for more than four years. His name was changed to Barry Soetoro. According to his half-sister Maya, he was adopted by Lolo, thus making him an Indonesian citizen. Circumstantial evidence suggests that Maya's account is correct. School records in Jakarta show his citizenship as Indonesian.[18] Indonesia does not allow dual citizenship, so he would have had to relinquish his U.S., British, or Kenyan citizenship, depending on which he actually held at that time. Obama's questionable citizenship triggered a major debate in the 2008 election about his legal right to be president. Depending on complex legal interpretations, it is possible that he was at various times a citizen of the U.S., of Kenya, of Britain, and of Indonesia.

Obama studied at the St. Francis of Assisi Catholic School for three years. He registered as a Muslim. Then he studied for two years at Sekolah Dasar Negeri Besuki, a public elementary school with a mandatory Islamic curriculum. Tine Hahiyary, the principal of Besuki, confirmed that Barack was registered as a Muslim and actively took part in Islamic religious lessons.[19] In the third grade, he wrote in an essay that he wanted to be president some day.[20]

Barack's half-sister, Maya Soetoro-Ng, was born to Ann and Lolo on August 15, 1970. By 1971, however, Ann and Lolo's marriage deteriorated. Barack was sent back to Hawaii in 1971, to be raised by his maternal grandparents. Grandfather Stanley Armour Dunham was a salesman. Grandmother Madelyn Lee Payne Dunham was a bank executive.[21] It appears that Ann traveled with Maya and Barack to return him to Hawaii and to register Maya's birth. She promptly returned to Indonesia with just Maya.

Ann came back to Hawaii with Maya between 1974 and 1977 to study anthropology at the University of Hawaii. Barack took a hiatus from living with his grandparents to live with his mother for three years. When Ann returned once again to Indonesia with Maya, Barack chose to stay behind with his grandparents.[22] Ann rarely saw her son after that.

In Indonesia, Ann worked for the U.S. Agency for International Development and the Ford Foundation, arranging microcredit for rural poor people. Ann and Lolo officially divorced in November 1980. Lolo died of a liver ailment in 1987. Ann returned to Hawaii for the last time in 1994. She died of ovarian cancer in 1995 at the age of 52.

While Barack lived with his grandparents, Frank Marshall Davis reentered his life. Davis worked in Chicago for many years as a community organizer and as a writer for socialist publications. He moved to Honolulu in 1948. Davis hung out with Barack and his grandfather, Stanley Dunham. In *Dreams from My Father*, Barack wrote: "I was intrigued by old Frank, with his books and whiskey breath and the hint of hard-earned knowledge behind the hooded eyes. The visits to his house always left me feeling vaguely uncomfortable, though, as if I were witnessing some complicated, unspoken transaction between the two men, a transaction I couldn't fully understand."[23] Perhaps this subliminal confusion was related to the speculation that Davis was really his father.

Davis became a mentor for Barack during his teens. He may also have been a source of drugs for Barack. He sold marijuana and cocaine from a hot dog stand.[24] Davis held a dim view of mainstream America. Before Barack left for college, Davis warned him, "They'll train you so good, you'll start believing what they tell you about equal opportunity and the American way and all that shit…you may be a well-trained, well-paid nigger, but you're a nigger just the same."[25] He also told him, "Black people have a reason to hate."[26]

Davis also allegedly supplied drugs to Stanley Dunham, and chaired Marxist meetings in Stanley's apartment. Davis was a pornographer who wrote of sexual encounters with a 13 year old girl, coincidentally named Anne. He wrote a pornographic book in 1968 titled *Sex Rebel: Black*, using the pseudonym Bob Greene.[27] His sexual fetishes included bondage, simulated rape, and being urinated on. One of his poems was titled "Christ is a Dixie Nigger."[28] He died in 1987 at the age of 81. The impact of Davis's Marxism and Black Nationalism on Obama will be discussed in later chapters.

Barack attended a private prep school named Punahou from the fifth grade until he graduated in 1979. He was an undistinguished student, who compiled a B- average and was noted for his basketball skills. He played on Punahou's 1979 state championship team.

While at Punahou, Obama evolved into an alienated outsider. In *The Audacity of Hope*, he wrote that his "rejection of authority spilled into self-indulgence and self-destructiveness."[29] In other words, he became involved with alcohol and drugs. "Pot had helped, and booze; maybe a little blow when you could afford it…could push questions of who I was out of my mind."[30] His high school yearbook picture featured "Zig-Zag" rolling papers and a caption thanking the "Choom Gang", a slang reference to fellow marijuana smokers, "for all the good times."[31] Bryon Leong, a former classmate, said that Obama "…was known as a partier, as a guy looking for a good time, but not much more."[32] Between the alcohol and drugs, he found time to carve "King Obama" into wet concrete outside the school cafeteria.[33]

Obama's alienation evolved into a fascination with his racial identity. He read African-American authors with extreme views on Black Nationalism. Keith Kakugawa, a high school friend, later said that Obama "...made everything out like it was all racial...Barry's biggest struggles then were missing his parents. His biggest struggles were his feelings of abandonment. The idea that his biggest struggle was race is bull shit."[34]

In 1979, Obama went to Occidental College in Los Angeles, where he played basketball. Even though he had a scholarship, he continued down the path of alienation and drug use. He later wrote, "To avoid being mistaken for a sell-out, I chose my friends carefully. The more politically active black students. The foreign students. The Chicanos. The Marxist professors and structural feminists and punk-rock performing poets. We smoked cigarettes and wore leather jackets....When we ground out our cigarettes in the hallway carpet or set our stereos so loud that the walls began to shake; we were resisting bourgeois society's stifling constraints. We weren't indifferent or careless or insecure. We were alienated...most of the other black students at Oxy didn't seem all that worried about compromise. There were enough of us on campus to constitute a tribe, and when it came to hanging out many of us chose to function like a tribe, staying close together, traveling in packs."[35]

Obama increasingly identified himself as a black man, despite the mixed marriage of the parents who abandoned him. After reading Joseph Conrad's *Heart of Darkness*, he told a friend, "...the book teaches me things. About white people, I mean. See, the book's not really about Africa. Or black people. It's about the man who wrote it. The European. The American. A particular way of looking at the world. If you can keep your distance, it's all there, in what's said and what's left unsaid. So I read the book to help me understand just what it is that makes white people so afraid. Their demons. The way ideas get twisted around. It helps me understand how people learn to hate."[36]

Barack's alienation and racial angst evolved into action. He wrote, "It was around that time that I got involved in the divestment campaign (as a protest against South African apartheid). It had started as something of a lark, I suppose, part of the radical pose my friends and I sought to maintain, a subconscious end run around issues closer to home. But as the months passed and I found myself drawn into a larger role—contacting representatives of the African National Congress to speak on campus, drafting letters to the faculty, printing up flyers, arguing strategy—I noticed that people had begun to listen to my opinions. It was a discovery that made me hungry for words."[37]

Obama has not released his records from Occidental College. Perhaps this is because his grades were poor, his classes were radical, or they contained clues about his birthplace or citizenship. Perhaps all three are pertinent.

Obama transferred to Columbia University in New York after two years. He wrote, "When I heard about a transfer program that Occidental had arranged with Columbia University, I'd been quick to apply. I figured that if there weren't any more black students at Columbia than there were at Oxy, I'd at least be in the heart of a true city, with black neighborhoods in close proximity."[38] His transfer to Columbia was unusual, because he presumably did not know anyone there, and he already had a scholarship to Occidental. This transition is examined more deeply in later chapters. This important fork in the road led him to powerful forces that would heavily influence his development and career.

In New York, Obama did odd jobs and explored the city's radical subculture. He wrote, "I spent three months working for a Ralph Nader offshoot up in Harlem, trying to convince the minority students at City College about the importance of recycling. Then a week passing out flyers for an assemblyman's race in Brooklyn—the candidate lost and I never did get paid. In six months I was broke, unemployed, eating soup from a can. In search of some inspiration, I went to hear Kwame Toure, formerly Stokely Carmichael of SNCC and Black Power fame, speak at Columbia. At the entrance to the auditorium, two women, one black, one Asian, were selling Marxist literature and arguing with each other about Trotsky's place in history. Inside, Toure was proposing a program to establish economic ties between Africa and Harlem that would circumvent white capitalist imperialism."[39]

Obama graduated without honors from Columbia in 1983 with a Bachelor of Arts degree in Political Science. It was a remarkably undocumented period of his life. According to *The New York Times*, Obama "declined repeated requests to talk about his New York years, release his Columbia transcript, or identify even a single fellow student, co-worker, roommate or friend from those years."[40]

After graduating, he worked for a year at the Business International Corporation, which introduced him to the "coldness of capitalism."[41] His disappointment with the business world and his emerging passion for political activism triggered a career change. He wrote, "I decided to become a community organizer. There wasn't much detail to the idea; I didn't know anyone making a living that way. When classmates in college asked me just what it was that a community organizer did, I couldn't answer them directly. Instead, I'd pronounce on the need for change. Change in the White House, where Reagan and his minions were carrying on their dirty deeds. Change in the Congress, compliant and corrupt. Change in the mood of the country, manic and self-absorbed. Change won't come from the top, I would say. Change will come from a mobilized grass roots."[42]

Obama got his community organizing opportunity via a help-wanted ad in *The New York Times* in 1985. The Calumet Community Religious Conference (CCRC), a group working to radicalize black churches in Chicago, was seeking an African-American to help with its inner-city Developing Communities Project (DCP).[43]

Obama took the job and worked three years for the DCP. His boss was Gerald Kellman, who was trained by socialist agitator Saul Alinsky. Kellman got the money to hire Obama from the Woods Fund, a Chicago foundation. The Woods Fund was supported by Thomas Ayers and other prominent philanthropists. It would eventually become a critical cog in Obama's absorption into the radical politics of Chicago. Thomas Ayers and his domestic terrorist son, William Ayers, would also become influential in Obama's career. Obama's relationship with these radicals and other notorious cohorts in the Ayers network will be explored more deeply in Chapter Six.

Kellman taught Obama Saul Alinsky's thuggish community organizing methods. Obama later taught these methods to new organizers joining Saul Alinsky's Industrial Areas Foundation and the radical community organizing group ACORN.

Obama thrived as an Alinsky-style community organizer. In *Dreams from My Father*, he wrote, "Issues, action, power, self-interest. I liked these concepts. They bespoke a certain hardheadedness, a worldly lack of sentiment; politics, not religion."[44] He later said that his experience as an organizer was "the best education I ever had...,"[45] which is a compelling statement from a graduate of Columbia and Harvard.

Saul Alinsky was deceased by the time Obama arrived in Chicago, but his legacy permeated Chicago politics. Kellman, Obama, and many other community organizing leaders were trained through Alinsky's Industrial Areas Foundation (IAF). Alinsky's book *Rules for Radicals* was iconic in radical spheres. Through various legacy organizations, the socialist Alinsky profoundly influenced Obama's career. Alinsky's influence is the subject of Chapter Three, because it is critical for understanding the methods that Obama and other radicals have used to achieve political power.

Obama applied Alinsky's principles for three years while assisting the residents of the Roseland community and the tenants of Altgeld Gardens, a public housing development. One of his key projects, removing asbestos from Altgeld, was never completed. He tried to work with public officials, but an important meeting with the Chicago Housing Authority degenerated into scuffles between tenants and officials.[46] Kellman, Obama's boss, judged Obama's efforts to be a failure, saying, "It is clear that the benefit of those years to Mr. Obama dwarfs what he accomplished....On issues, we made very little progress, nothing that would change poverty on the South Side of Chicago."[47]

Barack continued his fascination with Black Nationalism while working as a community organizer. In *Dreams from My Father*, he wrote, "Among the handful of groups to hoist the nationalist banner, only the Nation of Islam had any significant following. Minister Farrakhan's sharply cadenced sermons generally drew a packed house, and still more listened to his radio broadcasts...the physical presence of the Nation in the neighborhoods was nominal, restricted mainly to the clean-cut men in suits and bow ties who stood at the intersections of major thoroughfares selling the Nation's newspaper, *The Final Call*. I would occasionally pick up the paper from these unfailingly polite men, in part out of sympathy to their heavy suits in the summer, their thin coats in winter; or sometimes my attention was caught by the sensational, tabloid-style headlines (Caucasian Woman Admits: Whites are the Devil)."[48] Obama's long association with militant Black Nationalists will be examined in Chapter Five.

Obama "found" religion while working as a community organizer in Chicago. Until then, he was generally apathetic about spiritual matters. He was raised as a Muslim during his youth, but he drifted away from Islam when he lived with his grandparents, who were also apathetic about religion. Barack's mother was likely an

quoted

agnostic. Here's how Obama described his religious upbringing: "I was not raised in a religious household....For my mother, organized religion too often dressed up closed-mindedness in the garb of piety, cruelty and oppression in the cloak of righteousness."[49]

However, Kellman told Obama that if he wanted to succeed as a community organizer, he needed to become active in the African-American church.[50] Similarly, a black minister told Obama, "It might help your mission if you had a church home....It doesn't matter where, really."[51] In Chicago, the black churches were important community and political focal points. In *The Audacity of Hope*, Obama wrote, "It was because of these newfound understandings — that religious commitment did not require me to suspend critical thinking, disengage from the battle for economic and social justice, or otherwise retreat from the world that I knew and loved — that I was finally able to walk down the aisle of Trinity United Church of Christ one day and be baptized. It came about as a choice and not an epiphany...."[52]

Obama recognized the pragmatism of fusing religion and community organizing: "I was drawn to the power of the African American religious tradition to spur social change."[53] Thus, his conversion to Christianity, which was prodded by his boss Kellman, was a political tactic. He saw faith, including the faith of others, as a means for spurring social change, rather than as a path to personal salvation.

Obama needed to pick a church to join. He wrote, "When I asked for other pastors to talk to, several gave me the name of Reverend Wright....Toward the end of October, I finally got a chance to pay Reverend Wright a visit and see the church (Trinity United Church of Christ, or TUCC) for myself....Afterward, in the parking lot, I sat in my car and thumbed through a silver brochure that I'd picked up in the reception area. It contained a set of guiding principles—a 'Black Value System'—that the congregation had adopted in 1979...the principles in Trinity's brochure were articles of faith no less than belief in the Resurrection...."[54]

This was a watershed moment for Obama. Nothing articulates the innate character of a person as thoroughly as the choice of religious expression. Before Obama joined TUCC, Wright warned him that the church was viewed as "too radical."[55] But Obama became a parishioner anyway. Thus, his association with the radical parish was not an accident, but a conscious choice designed to bolster his credibility in the realm of community organizing and politics. The choice also echoed the radical tapestry of his entire life.

Obama's chosen spiritual community at TUCC was oriented around Black Liberation Theology (BLT), a Marxist doctrine alien to mainstream religious experience. Most middle-class church-goers receive pontification on the golden rule, the power of forgiveness, and the need to love all of God's children. Obama received from his church a steady anti-American and racist pontification that was brutally consistent with his radical political orientation.

According to TUCC's website, "The vision statement of Trinity United Church of Christ is based upon the systematized liberation theology that started in 1969 with the publication of Dr. James Cone's book, *Black Power and Black Theology*."[56] The church made Cone's writings required reading for parishioners who wanted to understand its theology and mission.[57] Black Liberation Theology likely resonated with Obama, who wrote in *Dreams from My Father* that he frequently read the works of black civil rights figures, including Nation of Islam leader Malcolm X.[58]

TUCC's formal Black Value System reflected the spirit of BLT. It included a disavowal of "middleclassness", in order to prevent seduction into a socioeconomic system based on competition rather than cooperation. TUCC's Black Value System also urged members to support black institutions and all black leaders who shared similar views.[59]

Jeremiah Wright's writings, public statements, and fiery sermons echoed Dr. Cone's philosophy, which permeated the church's culture. Wright's vitriolic rants reflected his conviction that America was a nation infested with racism and injustice. Here are examples of Wright's incendiary comments:

- "Racism is how this country was founded and how this country is still run!...We (Americans) believe in white supremacy and black inferiority and believe it more than we believe in God."[60]

- "White supremacy undergirds the thought, the ideology, the theology, the sociology, the legal structure, the educational system, the healthcare system, and the entire reality of the United States of America and South Africa!"[61]

- "The government gives them (blacks) the drugs, builds bigger prisons, passes a three-strike law and then wants us to sing 'God bless America?' No, no, no! Not 'God bless America!' God damn America!"[62]

In *Dreams from My Father*, Obama documented a sermon by Wright in 1988 titled "The Audacity of Hope." The sermon assessed the modern world harshly: "It is in this world, a world where cruise ships throw away more food in a day than most residents of Port-au-Prince see in a year, where white folks' greed runs a world in need, apartheid in one hemisphere, apathy in another hemisphere....That's the world! On which hope sits!"[63] Obama claimed that this sermon inspired a fundamental revelation, and that he cried while listening to it.

Obama participated in the Trinity congregation for two decades, before resigning under political duress in 2008. He claimed he attended the 11:00 a.m. Sunday mass at TUCC as often as he could. Major events in his life involved Wright and Trinity. He was baptized at TUCC, as were daughters Malia (born in 1998) and Natasha (born in 2001). Barack and Michelle were married there. Wright blessed the Obama's new home. The title of Wright's emotional "The Audacity of Hope" sermon eventually became the title of Obama's second book published in 2006. The synergistic impact of Reverend Wright, Trinity Church, and Black Liberation Theology on Obama's life and career will be studied further in later chapters.

Shortly before Obama launched his presidential campaign, here's how a reporter described a TUCC service: "On this particular Sunday, the sea of black worshippers is dotted with a few white folks up in the balcony, clutching copies of *The Audacity of Hope* they've brought for Obama's book-signing later. Obama, sitting in the third row with his wife and two daughters, Malia and Natasha, stands, claps, prays, and sways along with the rest of the congregation. During the sermon, he watches the preacher carefully and writes notes. When asked by Wright to say a few words, Obama grabs the microphone and stands. 'I love you all,' he says. 'It's good to be back home.' The 150-person choir breaks into a chorus of 'Barack, Hallelujah! Barack, Hallelujah!'"[64]

Here's a snippet from a TUCC bulletin: "On Sunday, January 28th, immediately following the 11:00 a.m. worship service, meet Senator Barack Obama, author of the best-selling book, *Audacity of Hope*. Purchase your copy of *Audacity of Hope* in the Akiba Bookstore (TUCC's bookstore) and have it personally signed by Senator Obama. You do not want to miss this monumental experience!"[65]

Obama tithed $22,500 to TUCC in 2006 alone.[66] Such a large contribution suggests a strong commitment to TUCC's mission and leader. Obama described Wright as his "spiritual advisor", his "mentor", and "one of the greatest preachers in America." He said the radical minister was his "sounding board" and that he received "day-to-day political advice" from him.[67]

It was remarkably disingenuous for Obama to claim multiple times during the 2008 presidential campaign that he was unaware of Wright's racist, anti-American radicalism. Not only was he warned about it before he chose to join the parish, he certainly heard it during 20 years of weekly sermons. If he was magically oblivious to hundreds of sermons, the church's weekly bulletins highlighted its radical orientation. They included blurbs about the terrorist group Hamas and local Islamic activist groups.[68] The church also published a periodical called *Trumpet*, which chronicled the history and philosophy of Wright and TUCC. Wright's rhetoric in the magazine was as strident as his incendiary sermons. Since Obama was featured on the covers of at least three issues of *Trumpet*, he must have been familiar with their content.[69] Thus, his plea of ignorance regarding TUCC's radical doctrine suggests that he either does not possess the cognition required of a President of the United States, or that he was lying to American voters.

Lying to voters is the likely explanation. Obama spoke with forked tongue about the depth of his experience at TUCC. In 2004, when no one was concerned about his relationship with the radical parish, he said he attended church "Every week. 11 o'clock service. Ever been there? Good service."[70] In July 2008, when contamination by TUCC threatened his campaign, he said that he "didn't hear a lot of sermons at Trinity."[71]

Interestingly, in *The Audacity of Hope*, Obama derided politicians who disingenuously milked their religious résumés. He wrote: "...nothing is more transparent than inauthentic expressions of faith—such as the politician who shows up at a black church around election time and claps (off rhythm) to the gospel choir or sprinkles in a few biblical citations to spice up a thoroughly dry policy speech."[72] It is fair to infer from this derision of other politicians that Obama thinks he is better than them. In other words, his religious experience at the radical anti-American parish that he attended for 20 years was an authentic one that represented core values rather than political window dressing.

Controversy erupted during the presidential campaign when excerpts of Wright's sermons splashed across the airwaves in March 2008. At first, Obama denounced the excerpts, but not Reverend Wright. After critics continued to challenge his relationship with Wright, Obama delivered a speech titled "A More Perfect Union," which attempted to place Wright's radicalism in historical and sociological context.

The issue refused to fade. Under increasing pressure, Obama said he was "outraged" and "saddened" by Wright's behavior.[73] In May 2008, he resigned from TUCC. Ironically, despite his public pretensions, Obama knew all along that his relationship with Wright would be poisonous to his campaign. On the day he announced his candidacy, he abruptly cancelled Wright's supporting speech. Wright said Obama got "some bad advice from some of his own campaign people who thought it would not be a good idea for me to be in front of the cameras on the day he announced."[74] When the Obama campaign heard that Wright was upset afterward, they said "Senator Obama is proud of his pastor and his church."[75]

At one point during the controversy, Obama said of Wright: "I can no more disown him than I can disown the black community."[76] However, Obama soon disowned him anyway, after Wright publicly declared: "Politicians say what they say and do what they do based on electability, based on sound bites, based on polls."[77] In other words, he accused Obama of deceiving the public in order to get elected. Obama replied, "That's a show of disrespect to me. It's – it is also, I think, an insult to what we've been trying to do in this campaign."[78]

So, when Wright espoused the anti-American Black Liberation Theology of Dr. James Cone, when he blamed America for the 9/11 tragedies, when he ranted "God damn America" from the pulpit at Trinity, and when he equated capitalism with systemic slavery, Obama considered him "an old uncle who says things I don't always agree with."[79] But when Wright "disrespected" Obama (ironically, by saying something that was probably true), that was too much.[80] Most middle-class Americans would have had their fill of Wright decades sooner, for reasons more significant than "disrespect".

Wright has generally avoided the public spotlight since retiring in 2008. However, during a June 2009 interview, he said that he and Obama have not had contact because "Them Jews aren't going to let him talk to me. I told my baby daughter, that he'll talk to me in five years when he's a lame duck, or in eight years when he's out of office."[81]

Despite Obama's attempt to fuse religion with his secular work, he became disenchanted with community organizing, so he returned to college to study law. In *Dreams from My Father,* he wrote, "I had things to learn in law school, things that would help me bring about real change. I would learn about interest rates, corporate mergers, the legislative process; about the way businesses and banks were put together; how real estate ventures succeeded or failed. I would learn power's currency in all its intricacy and detail, knowledge that would have compromised me before coming to Chicago but that I could now bring back to where it was needed, back to Roseland, back to Altgeld; bring it back like Promethean fire."[82]

Obama enrolled at Harvard Law School in 1988. It is unclear how he earned admission, given his pedestrian academic performance prior to that. It is also unclear how he was able to afford Occidental, Columbia, and Harvard, all expensive private institutions. There is evidence that some of the funding for his Harvard education was coordinated by a member of the Black Panthers, who was a business agent for a wealthy Muslim in Saudi Arabia.[83] This question, and the depth of Obama's relationships with Black Nationalists and Middle Eastern operatives, will be explored in greater detail in Chapter Five.

Despite Obama's marginal qualifications for admission to Harvard, he was an editor of the *Harvard Law Review* in his first year. In his second year, he was selected the first African-American president of the *Harvard Law Review.*[84]

Strangely, though, he never published any attributed work. As Matthew Franck discovered, "A search of the *HeinOnline* database of law journals turns up exactly nothing credited to Obama in any law review anywhere at any time."[85]

It's possible that Obama's *Law Review* presidency was abetted by racial tension at Harvard. When Obama was a candidate for the position, Harvard professor Derrick Bell was agitating for the Law School to appoint a black woman to the faculty. Bell's histrionics led to protests by supportive students. Obama himself absurdly compared Bell to Rosa Parks.[86] The *Harvard Law Review* editors may have selected their first African-American president to ease the pressure on campus.

His selection as President of the *Harvard Law Review,* however it came about, reinforced the mythology that Obama is one of the smartest presidents ever, even though no evidence is available to support this mythology. He has yet to release his college transcripts or his SAT and LSAT scores. He has never published an article in a legal journal, even though he was president of such a journal. The only sketchy information available about his academic performance is that he was a B- student in high school and did not achieve honors at Columbia. He struggles to deliver polished commentary without the aid of his omnipresent teleprompter. Without a teleprompter, his public utterances are characterized by stammering, half sentences, uncomfortable pauses, and regrettable misstatements.

Obama's notoriety at Harvard earned attention in *The New York Times* and led to a contract for a book about race relations. He received a $125,000 advance from Simon and Shuster in 1992.[87] The project evolved into a personal memoir, which was published in 1995 as *Dreams from My Father.* The project was a struggle for him. Even though the University of Chicago Law School gave him a fellowship and an office to work on the book, he failed to produce a viable manuscript. His contract with Simon and Shuster was cancelled. He then signed a less lucrative contract with Times Book.[88] When he finally delivered a manuscript, there were allegations that he used domestic terrorist William Ayers as a ghost writer, based on analyses of writing styles. Ayers frequently helped struggling writers in the area.

Obama graduated magna cum laude from Harvard with a Juris Doctor degree in 1991. Despite this pedigree, he did not immediately go to work for a law firm. David Axelrod said of his client Obama that "he could have gone to the most opulent of law firms....Obama could have done anything he wanted."[89] Abner Mikva, a Chief Judge of the U.S. Court of Appeals, tried to recruit Obama to a position considered a stepping stone to clerking on the Supreme Court. Obama turned him down.[90]

Instead, Obama went to work for Sandy Newman, a civil rights activist at Project Vote, an ACORN affiliate. Obama was hired as the director of its Chicago branch. His assignment was to lead a team to register voters in support of Clinton's 1992 presidential race. The T-shirts and posters that supplemented the Project Vote campaign proclaimed "It's a power thing!"[91]   His team registered 150,000 minority voters in Illinois, many of them culled from welfare offices and unemployment lines.   As a result, *Crain's Chicago Business* named Obama to its 1993 list of "40 under Forty" powers to be.[92]

In 1993, Obama joined the law firm of Davis Miner Barnhill & Galland as a civil rights attorney.[93] [94] Coincidentally, this firm served as legal counsel to the Woods Fund, which was the group that financed Obama's earlier foray into community organizing.   The law firm employed Obama as an associate from 1993 to 1996, and then as a counsel from 1996 to 2004.

Allison S. Davis, the lead partner in the firm, was a business associate of Syrian national Antoin Rezko.   Davis's law firm represented Rezko's company in various actions that were politically and morally tainted.[95]   Obama's relationship with both Davis and convicted felon Rezko became significant as his political career unfolded.   The remarkably unscrupulous nature of these relationships will be examined in Chapter Seven.

When Obama worked at the law firm, he also worked as a part-time lecturer teaching constitutional law at the University of Chicago Law School.   He was a lecturer from 1992 to 1996, and then a senior lecturer from 1996 to 2004.[96]

Obama was also active in numerous civic and philanthropic organizations during the same time frame.   He was a founding member of the board of directors of Public Allies in 1992.   He served from 1999 to 2002 on the board of directors of the Woods Fund of Chicago.   He served from 1994 to 2002 on the board of directors of the Joyce Foundation.   He was the Chairman of the Board of the Chicago Lawyers' Committee for Civil Rights under Law.

Intertwined with these career activities was a continuous 20-year professional relationship with socialist William Ayers, who will be the subject of deeper examination in Chapter Six.   For now, brief highlights of Obama's relationship with the Ayers family will be presented.   His career in Chicago politics would not have happened as it did without the support of the former Weather Underground terrorist Bill Ayers and his influential father, Thomas Ayers.

In 1995, Bill Ayers, who had won a $50 million grant to assist the Chicago Public Schools, hired Obama to serve as the founding president and chairman of his project, the Chicago Annenberg Challenge (CAC).[97]   Ayers served with Obama on the board of the CAC.   Obama was chairman until 1999 and a board member until 2001. While Obama chaired the CAC, Bill Ayers ran a subgroup called the Small Schools Workshop, to which Obama incestuously directed $1 million of CAC grant money.[98] Despite being hired by Ayers and collaborating with him at the CAC for six years, Obama later asserted that he barely knew Ayers, when scrutiny of his relationship with the domestic terrorist threatened his presidential campaign.

Obama met his future wife, Michelle, at the Chicago branch of the law firm of Sidley & Austin, where he worked as a summer intern between semesters at Harvard. Michelle, an attorney at Sidley, was assigned to mentor Barack. She was politically connected in her own right. Her father, Fraser Robinson, was a precinct captain for the Democratic Party. Michelle babysat Jesse Jackson's children, and she worked on Mayor Daley's staff as an economic development coordinator. Michelle and Barack began dating during the summer of 1989. They became engaged in 1991, and were married on October 3, 1992.

Bernardine Dohrn, who was the wife of William Ayers, worked as a paralegal at Sidley & Austin, from 1984 through 1988. She was hired despite her criminal record as a domestic terrorist in the Weather Underground and despite having been on the FBI's Ten Most Wanted list. She likely got the job through the influence of her father-in-law, Thomas Ayers, who was CEO of Commonwealth Edison, a major client of Sidley & Austin. Bernardine Dohrn and Michelle Robinson worked together at Sidley.

Obama began his political career in 1995. To energize Obama's Illinois state senate bid, incumbent state Senator Alice Palmer coordinated a meet-and-greet for influential liberals at the home of former Weather Underground terrorists Ayers and Dohrn.[99] Palmer, who was vacating the state senate position to seek higher office, introduced Obama, her hand-picked successor, to potential campaign benefactors.[100]

Unfortunately, after Palmer positioned Obama as her heir-apparent, she lost the special election for the U.S. Congressional seat she was seeking. So, she decided to seek reelection to her old state senate seat, which her protégé Obama was now also seeking. To stop Palmer from running, Obama hired an election law expert to convince the Chicago Board of Election Commissioners to disqualify almost 900 of the 1,600 signatures on the petition supporting her candidacy.[101] As a result, she could not run in the primary, even though she was a five-year incumbent.[102] He used this same tactic to get the other three Democratic primary challengers forced off the ballot too, essentially winning the primary unopposed.[103] Palmer, perhaps mindful of Obama's back-stabbing, eventually supported Hillary Clinton in the 2008 Democratic primaries. She apparently was not impressed by her former protégé's "new kind of politics."

Obama approached Antoin Rezko to help fund his campaign, perhaps because of Rezko's relationship with Obama's law firm employer, Allison Davis. Rezko raised $10,000 to $15,000 of the $100,000 Obama received for the race.[104] Rezko, who would eventually be convicted of 16 felonies, including bribery of public officials, bankrolled five of Obama's campaigns for public office, contributing a total of approximately $250,000.[105] In return, Obama helped Rezko and Allison Davis gain government subsidies to develop low-income housing.

Investigative reporter Tim Novak revealed that state Senator Obama sent letters to government officials supporting Rezko's and Davis's successful bid to get more than $14 million from taxpayers to build apartments for senior citizens.[106] At the time Obama wrote these letters, he was also working at Davis Miner Barnhill & Galland. In other words, he was getting paid by the law firm that represented Rezko's company, he was getting money from Rezko through campaign contributions, and he was using his state senate office to lobby for taxpayer money for Davis and Rezko. Despite lofty rhetoric like "change we can believe in," Obama wallowed in many such shady deals and associations. Later, when political pressure mounted regarding his scurrilous relationship with Rezko, Obama claimed that he barely knew him. Chapter Seven will disprove this absurd claim.

After winning the state senate seat in 1996, Obama accomplished almost nothing of note during his eight-year State Senate career. All of his legislation died in committee, if only because the Republicans controlled the Senate. The most notoriety he received was for his remarkable propensity to vote "present" on controversial issues. This enabled him to avoid the political liability that comes with definitive "yea" or "nay" votes. During his stint in the Illinois Senate, he voted "present" 129 times.[107]

The documentation covering his State Senate career is missing. Tom Fitton of Judicial Watch sought access to these documents, but the Illinois State Archives told him that they did not receive a request from Senator Obama to archive his records, which is unusual.[108] Obama told broadcast journalist Tim Russert that he did not keep any records of his appointments, schedules, calendars, or meetings.[109] It is hard to imagine a modern government official failing to do this.

Obama's political career was aided by the Association of Community Organizations for Reform Now (ACORN), a controversial community organizing group. His relationship with ACORN took many forms over the years, including the work he did for Project Vote after graduating from Harvard. He trained ACORN members in Saul Alinsky's philosophy and tactics. He represented ACORN in various lawsuits related to minority voter registration and the practice of redlining. He hired an ACORN front group to work on his presidential campaign, which resulted in a messy conflict-of-interest scandal. He used his board membership at various charitable foundations to direct tens of millions of grant dollars to ACORN.

ACORN was investigated for widespread voter registration fraud in 14 states.[110] They were accused of contaminating the U.S. electoral process with fraudulent voter registrations. ACORN boasted that it played a key role in several of Obama's election campaigns. According to ACORN Chicago leader Toni Foulkes, "...it was natural for many of us to be active volunteers in his first campaign for state senate and then his failed bid for U.S. Congress....by the time he ran for the U.S. Senate, we were old friends."[111] Obama's incestuous relationship with this renegade organization will be examined more deeply in Chapter Eight.

In 2000, Obama ran for a U.S. House of Representatives seat. He was slaughtered in the Democratic primary by Bobby Rush, a former Black Panther. Rush characterized Obama as "inauthentic" and said of Obama that "[h]e went to Harvard and became an educated fool. We're not impressed with these folks with these Eastern elite degrees."[112] The people of Illinois were not impressed either, because Obama only received 31% of their votes.

In *The Audacity of Hope*, Obama wrote of his defeat, "...bad luck or lack of money—it's impossible not to feel at some level as if you have been personally repudiated by the entire community, that you don't quite have what it takes, and that everywhere you go the word 'loser' is flashing through people's minds."[113]

Undeterred, Obama geared up in 2002 to run for the U.S. Senate. He hired political strategist David Axelrod, a former lobbyist of Tom Ayers's company and the son of New York leftist Myril Axelrod. In October 2002, Obama delivered a speech in downtown Chicago opposing the notion of a U.S. attack on Iraq. This speech was later derided by Hillary Clinton as being Obama's "only foreign policy experience."[114]

Obama formally announced his U.S. Senate candidacy in January 2003. Since Republican incumbent Peter Fitzgerald was not running, the race was wide open. In the March 2004 Democratic primary election, Obama won an unexpected landslide victory, with 53% of the vote in a seven-candidate field.

However, his primary victory was not as impressive as it seemed. Here's how Obama described the election in *The Audacity of Hope:* "There was just one problem: My campaign had gone so well that it looked like a fluke. Political observers would note that in a field of seven Democratic primary candidates, not one of us ran a negative TV ad. The wealthiest candidate of all—a former trader worth at least $300 million—spent $28 million, mostly on a barrage of positive ads, only to flame out in the final weeks due to an unflattering divorce file that the press got unsealed. My Republican opponent (Jack Ryan), a handsome and wealthy former Goldman Sachs partner turned inner-city teacher, started attacking my record almost from the start, but before his campaign could get off the ground, he was felled by a divorce scandal of his own. For the better part of a month, I traveled Illinois without drawing fire, before being selected to deliver the keynote address at the Democratic National Convention—seventeen minutes of unfiltered, uninterrupted airtime on national television. And finally the Illinois Republican Party inexplicably chose as my opponent former presidential candidate Alan Keyes, a man who never lived in Illinois and who proved so fierce and unyielding in his positions that even conservative Republicans were scared of him. Later, some reporters would declare me the luckiest politician in the entire fifty states....there was no point in denying my almost spooky good fortune. I was an outlier, a freak; to political insiders, my victory proved nothing."[115]

The "wealthy candidate" in the Democratic primary that Obama referred to was Blair Hull. At one point, Hull led 27% to 17% over Obama in the crowded race. But just weeks before the primary, Hull's sealed divorce files were made public. The files alleged that his ex-wife called him "a violent man" who "hung on the canopy bar of my bed, leered at me and stated 'Do you want to die? I am going to kill you....'"[116] Hull's wife subsequently asked for a personal protection order.

Coincidentally, David Axelrod, Obama's advisor, had once considered working for Hull and was aware of Hull's divorce issues.[117]   Axelrod's former employer, the *Chicago Tribune*, pressed the courts to release Hull's divorce files, even though such information was normally kept private to protect the minor children involved. The *Tribune* reporter who originally broke the story said that the Obama camp had "worked aggressively behind the scenes" to get the files opened.[118] As a result of the damaging publicity, Obama soundly defeated Hull. Hull's collapse was described as "the most inglorious campaign implosion in Illinois political history."[119]

Amazingly, the same thing happened in the general election. Obama ran against Republican Jack Ryan, whose sealed divorce file was made public by a California judge, after the *Chicago Tribune* and an *ABC* affiliate pressed to have the confidential records released.[120] This happened even though the couple had mutually agreed to keep portions of the file private to protect their son.[121] The file revealed that Ryan's wife, former actress Jeri Lynn Ryan, accused Jack of taking her to deviant sex clubs. He allegedly pressured her to have sex with him in public.[122]

Ryan was a handsome and charismatic former investment banker with three Ivy League degrees.   Prior to the damning revelations, he was considered a political golden boy. But, he was forced to withdraw in disgrace from the race in June 2004. In his place, the Republicans hastily recruited African-American Alan Keyes, a Maryland resident, to run in Illinois. Obama wrote that Keyes was "an ideal opponent; all I had to do was keep my mouth shut and start planning my swearing-in ceremony."[123] Keyes was prone to making inflammatory remarks like "Christ would not vote for Barack Obama."[124] He also publicly suggested that Obama was not a natural born citizen. Keyes lost the race by the largest margin in Illinois history.

It is ironic that Obama, who has been dubbed a political Wunderkind, actually had an undistinguished political career up until 2004. He won his Illinois State Senate seat by hiring a lawyer to disqualify all of his primary opponents on technical grounds. He was annihilated in his only run for the U.S. House of Representatives. He won his U.S. Senate seat only because his two toughest opponents were devastated by messy divorces and ugly publicity. Up until 2004, his career was mostly characterized by secrecy, radicalism, limited accomplishments, and political shenanigans. In this context, his sudden rise to national superstardom is surprising.

Or is it? Enter rogue financier George Soros, who stepped in to support Obama's Senate campaign. The support of Soros, an international pariah responsible for the Black Friday assault on the British currency, was crucial for Obama's rapid political ascendancy from 2004 onward. The shadowy influence of Soros on the media, the Democratic Party, and the 2008 presidential elections will be explored further in Chapter Nine. Soros's empire transformed Obama's obscure and sometimes tawdry political career into an immaculately conceived national juggernaut.

In July 2004, Obama wrote and delivered the keynote address at the Democratic National Convention in Boston. His speech was a highlight of the convention and showcased him to a national audience. It was an incredible and surprising opportunity for a state Senator whose career had thus far been localized to Chicago and Illinois.

Obama was sworn in as a U.S. Senator on January 4, 2005. He was the fifth African-American Senator in U.S. history, and the third to have been popularly elected. He was also, by most accounts of his voting record, one of the most liberal senators in Washington. He moved further left over the years, until there was no more left to go. In 2005, he was ranked as the 16th most liberal senator by the *National Journal*. In 2006, he was ranked the tenth most liberal. In 2007, he was ranked the most liberal of all 100 senators.[125]

Life was good for the Obamas at this point. Barack received $1.9 million for his book *The Audacity of Hope*. Their 2005 income included Michelle's $300,000 salary at the University of Chicago Hospital and $101,083 for her role on the board of Tree House, an anti-union Wal-Mart supplier. They purchased a mansion in Hyde Park. By 2008, their wealth grew to $7 million. Michelle accumulated an impressive collection of diamond jewelry, designer outfits, and expensive shoes. They employed a full-time housekeeper. They enrolled their children in exclusive private schools.

Ironically, despite their wealth and privilege, Michelle occasionally unmasked her contempt for America and Americans. In January 2008, she said, "…sometimes it's easier to hold on to your own stereotypes and misconceptions. It makes you feel justified in your own ignorance. That's America."[126] In February 2008, she said, "For the first time in my adult life, I am proud of my country."[127] In March 2008, she said, "…we're a divided country, we're a country that is just downright mean."[128]

This hypocrisy was apparent even in Michelle's token job as Vice President of Community Affairs at the University of Chicago

Hospital. Her job included "patient dumping," which involved redirecting indigent care-seekers away from the hospital's emergency rooms toward less-desirable clinics in rougher neighborhoods.[129] Despite her rhetorical solidarity with African-Americans, part of her job was to make sure that her employer was not burdened with the cost of uninsured medical care for her less-fortunate neighbors.

Coincidentally, Michelle's salary, which was $121,910 in 2004, jumped to $316,962 in 2005 when Barack was elected U.S. Senator. Coincidentally, when she left the hospital, management did not replace her position.[130] Coincidentally, the position did not exist before it was created for her, which was shortly after Obama became the Democratic nominee for Illinois State Senator in 1996.[131] Coincidentally, even after she went on leave in 2007 to help her husband's presidential campaign, the hospital still paid her $62,709 in 2008.[132] Coincidentally, Barack requested $1 million of federal earmark money to help pay for the construction of a new pavilion at the hospital.[133]

Obama stirred up controversy during his career with his extreme position on abortion. While an Illinois State Senator, he opposed a bill requiring hospitals to give medical assistance to babies born alive during botched abortions.[134] He said in March 2008 that he didn't want his two daughters "punished with a baby" if they made a "mistake".[135] When asked during an August 2008 interview when human life begins, he said, "...answering that question with specificity, you know, is above my pay grade."[136] In July 2007, he said, "The first thing I'd do as President is sign the Freedom of Choice Act."[137] This bill would reduce regulation of abortion and expand government funding for abortions.[138]

In January 2007, with zero executive experience and only two years' experience as a national politician, Obama announced his candidacy for President of the United States. The crowded Democratic primary field narrowed to a contest between Obama and Hillary Clinton. Coincidentally, Clinton was also an acolyte of Saul Alinsky, who was the subject of her senior thesis at Wellesley College and a personal acquaintance. The primary race was very close, with much political intrigue and controversy, including a squabble over delegates from Michigan and Florida. In June 2008, with all states more or less counted, Obama was named the presumptive nominee of the Democratic Party.

Obama then campaigned against Senator John McCain, the presumptive Republican nominee. David Axelrod formulated a campaign strategy that focused on Obama's personality and lofty vision, while hiding his radicalism by avoiding hard positions on the issues. His campaign was centered on amorphous but catchy slogans.[139] His slogan "Yes, we can" was derived from "Si, se puedo," which Alinskyite Cesar Chavez used to organize Hispanic farm workers in the 1960's. "Change we can believe in" was derived from Saul Alinsky's hijacking of the word "change" as code for gradual socialist revolution. "Hope" was morphed from Jeremiah Wright's "Audacity of Hope" sermon, which became the title of Obama's second book.

Axelrod artfully nurtured Obama's contagious personality into the realm of messianic stardom. Believers interpreted this as an indication that Obama was above the issues. Skeptics interpreted it as a tacit admission that Obama's radical political positions and his suppressed biography would not resonate with voters. Obama was physically attractive, he could read a teleprompter with dramatic flair, and nobody really knew anything about him, which made him perfect raw material for a master like Axelrod. Adoring throngs, fainting witnesses, and awe-struck media fawns fed the mythos. As the Axelrod-orchestrated Kabuki Theater reached a crescendo, *MSNBC* anchor Chris Matthews drooled that he got "a thrill going up his leg" when he saw Obama.[140] Matthews also drooled, "I've never seen anything like this. This is bigger than Kennedy. [Obama] comes along, and he seems to have the answers. This is the New Testament."[141]

At the Democratic National Convention in Denver, Obama delivered his acceptance speech while flanked by gargantuan Greek columns, as if he had just joined the pantheon of mythological heroes. The hyperbolic convention pageantry was consistent with the style of his campaign, in which he often spoke in grandiloquent terms that unavoidably devolved into a parody of narcissism. For example, he said, "I have become a symbol of the possibility of America returning to our best traditions" and "This is the moment…that the world is waiting for."[142]

In June 2008, Obama became the first major-party presidential candidate to decline public financing since the system began in 1976. This move directly contradicted his 2007 filing to the Federal Election Commission, in which he wrote, "If I am the Democratic nominee, I will aggressively pursue an agreement with the Republican nominee to preserve a publicly financed general election….I have been a long-time advocate for public financing of campaigns combined with free television and radio time as a way to reduce the influence of moneyed special interests....".[143]   But when Obama's campaign began reeling in record-breaking contributions, including significant benefaction from "moneyed special interests" like Goldman Sachs and Citigroup, he greedily abandoned his pledge.

Obama also received a treasure chest of small donations, many from undocumented and perhaps illegal overseas sources, which became a concern to election monitors. The surprising sources of Obama's campaign funding, which say much about who he really owes his allegiance to, will be examined in more detail in later chapters.

Obama also snubbed presidential campaign protocol by refusing to release his medical records. John McCain released 1,200 pages of health records in 2008. George W. Bush released 400 pages in 2000 and 2004.   John Kerry released his full records in 2004.   Al Gore released his medical records in 1999.   Obama, on the other hand, released only a six-paragraph "summary" of 21 years of medical information.[144]   For a man in obvious good health, it is unclear what he was reluctant to reveal. This makes it tempting to speculate that his medical records reflect compromising information about birthplace, citizenship, or perhaps drug abuse.

Three debates were held between Obama and McCain during September and October 2008. Neither candidate excelled, but Obama successfully tainted McCain as representing a third term of the immensely unpopular George W. Bush.   With daily reports of casualties in Iraq, with economic troubles weighing heavily, and with the implosion of the banking system in mid-September, the contest was essentially over.   In November, Obama won 52.9% of the popular vote, to McCain's 45.7%.   He won 365 electoral votes to McCain's 173, to become the first African-American president.   In his victory speech, Obama proclaimed that "change has come to America."[145]

The inauguration of Obama as the 44th President, and Joe Biden as Vice President, took place on January 20, 2009. The theme of his inauguration was "A New Birth of Freedom," commemorating the 200th anniversary of Lincoln's birth. Gala celebrations were held, duly recognizing the historic nature of his election, although their unprecedented opulence seemed improper, given the recession sweeping over America.

But, even after Obama's election as President, we are left with haunting questions about his murky background. Despite his highly public profile, how much do we really know about his philosophy? What kind of leader did we really elect? What really is his vision for America? The rest of this book will answer these and many other questions. To close this chapter, let's examine an excerpt from *Dreams from My Father* for some insight about his philosophy:

> "'We hold these truths to be self-evident.' In those words, I hear the spirit of Douglass and Delany, as well as Jefferson and Lincoln; the struggles of Martin and Malcolm and unheralded marchers to bring these words to life. I hear the voices of Japanese families interned behind barbed wire; young Russian Jews cutting patterns in Lower East Side sweatshops; dust-bowl farmers loading up their trucks with the remains of shattered lives. I hear the voices of the people in Altgeld Gardens, and the voices of those who stand outside this country's borders, the weary, hungry bands crossing the Rio Grande. I hear all of these voices clamoring for recognition, all of them asking the very same questions that have come to shape my life, the same questions that I sometimes, late at night, find myself asking the Old Man (Obama's deceased father). What is our community, and how might that community be reconciled with our freedom? How far do our obligations reach? How do we transform mere power into justice, mere sentiment into love? The answers I find in law books don't always satisfy me—for every Brown v. Board of Education I find a score of cases where conscience is sacrificed to expedience or greed."[146]

These are lofty words, indeed. But what do you suppose he is pondering when he asks, "How far do our obligations reach?" Perhaps we are finding out as he increases government spending by trillions of dollars to bail out irresponsible individuals and failed businesses, as if the brute force of government wealth redistribution can somehow erase life's necessity for earning sustenance. The Soviet Union, Cuba, and North Korea have already shown us how poorly this works.

What do you suppose he is pondering when he asks, "How might our community be reconciled with our freedoms?" Perhaps we will find out as he attempts to implement mandatory "volunteer" programs for our children, gives unions the power to intimidate workers to publicly "vote" for union representation, establishes 32 new government departments to regulate our lives, and gives grants to "community organizing" groups like ACORN and Organizing for America to disrupt our communities, harass our businesses, and pervert the electoral process. Perhaps the "new birth of freedom" he celebrated on inauguration day is really a new birth of socialist collectivism, "freeing" us from the evils of individual rights, private property, and capitalism.

What do you suppose he is pondering when he asks if our laws are too focused on "sacrificing conscience to expedience or greed"? Perhaps we are finding out as he exercises his own "conscience" by taking control of businesses, taxing away profits, setting pay scales, hiring and firing CEO's, and imposing government-run health care to ration medical services. Perhaps "conscience" means to him that the state gets to ignore the Constitution and impose its will on free individuals and businesses.

What do you suppose he is pondering when he asks about "the voices of those who stand outside this country's borders, the weary, hungry bands crossing the Rio Grande"? Perhaps we will find out when he attempts to change immigration laws to give driver's licenses to illegal aliens, access to free education and health care, and a free pass across our borders. Perhaps Obama, who has associated with anti-American groups and mentors his entire career, is willing to give our country away to anybody.

Ronald Reagan once said, "A government big enough to give you everything you want is a government big enough to take everything you have."[147]   As we examine Barack Obama's background, actions, and relationships more deeply in the chapters to come, let's keep Reagan's postulation in mind. Perhaps we will see how dangerously close Obama and his radical allies are to proving it.

Readers may have sensed during this chapter that Obama's biography is like a movie contained on three reels of film. The first reel documents his alienated life as a youth and his early career as an obscure community organizer and neophyte politician localized to Chicago. The third reel documents his startlingly rapid, messianic rise to the presidency of the United States. But the second reel, the one that really explains the transition from reel one to reel three, is missing from the public movie theater. The rest of this book documents what is in reel two, which should have already been shown to America, if Obama and the pandering media had any sense of honor and fealty to truth.

Once this second reel of film is exposed for all to see, the middle class of America will develop a much different perspective than the illusion that Obama and the left-leaning media have propagated thus far. Contrary to their deceptions, we have not arrived on the doorstep of a glorious future bubbling with effervescent "hope" and "change". The next chapter, which examines Saul Alinsky's life, philosophy, and impact on Obama, will show that we have instead arrived on the doorstep of socialism.

Ominously, socialism has no place for a middle class.

We've been had.

"Democracy and socialism have nothing in common but one word, equality. But notice the difference: while democracy seeks equality in liberty, socialism seeks equality in restraint and servitude."

Alexis de Tocqueville

Chapter Three

Meet Saul "The Red" Alinsky

> *"Lest we forget at least an over-the-shoulder acknowledgment to the very first radical: from all our legends, mythology, and history (and who is to know where mythology leaves off and history begins—or which is which), the first radical known to man who rebelled against the establishment and did it so effectively that he won his own kingdom—Lucifer."[1]*

Saul Alinsky , *Rules for Radicals*

Amen

Saul Alinsky was a prolific gardener. Deep in the heartland of America, he plowed under the roots of capitalism and sowed the seeds of the socialist revolution that are blossoming today. The radical seeds took decades to germinate and sprout, but in today's media-fertilized ground of exaggerated crises and Big Government apologetics, Alinsky's toxic weeds are choking what remains of the middle class out of the garden of American politics.

Despite Alinsky's approving nod to the fallen angel Lucifer, he never advocated a cataclysmic war between the forces of good and evil, or between capitalism and socialism. Instead, he gave birth to the concept of "community organizing" as an alternative to the violent class warfare that other communists of his time embraced. He developed a persistent, step-by-step strategy for ushering in a socialist paradise.

According to Alinsky, radical transformation of America would begin with slow, steady agitation of public discontent, moral confusion, and systemic chaos.[2] Once his legions of "community organizers" sufficiently "disorganized" enough local communities to the point where these communities felt sufficiently dissatisfied with the current structure, a majority of Americans would conclude that capitalism was fundamentally flawed and unfixable. When enough people became that dissatisfied about the current system, charismatic community organizers and visionary political leaders advocating "change" would experience little resistance to their transitional steps toward socialism. It would be inevitable and perhaps even peaceful.

Saul Alinsky was born in Chicago in 1909 to Benjamin and Sarah Alinsky, both Russian Jewish immigrants. Saul graduated with a degree in Criminology from the University of Chicago. Ironically, he immersed himself in the Chicago mob after he graduated. He became friends with Al Capone's lieutenant, Frank Nitti, known as the Enforcer. Alinsky later told *Playboy* magazine, "I joined their social life of food, drink, and women...it was heaven...I learned a hell of a lot about the uses and abuses of power from the mob, lessons that stood me in great stead later on, when I was organizing."[3] According to Alinsky, he referred to Nitti as "the Professor" and himself as the "student".[4]

After his stint with the mob, Alinsky learned a different kind of heavy-handed organizing. He worked for the CIO labor union, as an aide to renowned labor leader John L. Lewis. He learned from Lewis many of the confrontational union organizing tactics that he later used while organizing communities.

Alinsky became famous as a community organizer in the 1930's trying to improve conditions in the same wretched Chicago slums that Upton Sinclair immortalized in *The Jungle*. He created the Back of the Yards Neighborhood Council, an alliance of Catholic churches and labor unions. The alliance successfully confronted a corrupt collaboration of city councilors and local meatpacking plants. This success earned Alinsky a large grant in 1940 from liberal millionaire Marshall Field III. Alinsky used this money to establish the Industrial Areas Foundation (IAF). He called the IAF's training arm a "school for professional radicals."[5]

Alinsky's notoriety grew from there. According to David Horowitz and Richard Poe in their book *The Shadow Party*, "In 1944, the *University of Chicago Press* signed Alinsky to write a book promoting his vision of a new American radicalism. Six months before its publication, Agnes Meyer, who co-owned the *Washington Post* with her husband Eugene, lionized Alinsky and his movement in a six-part series titled 'The Orderly Revolution.' President Truman ordered 100 reprints of Meyer's series. By the time Alinsky's manifesto, *Reveille for Radicals*, hit the bookstores in January 1946, he was already famous. *Reveille* became a national bestseller, and Mrs. Meyer began funding Alinsky's Industrial Areas Foundation."[6]

During the ensuing decades, Alinsky created a radical network of colleagues and organizations that permeated American culture and politics. He died in 1972 as one of the most influential forces in the 20th Century. His 1971 book, *Rules for Radicals*, became a ubiquitous textbook for radicals seeking to transform America along the lines of Alinsky's vision. The book resonates with politicians even today, including America's "Organizer-in-Chief," Barack Obama. Obama described his training as an Alinsky-style community organizer as "the best education I ever had, better than anything I got at Harvard Law School."[7] He said it was an education that was "seared into my brain."[8] One-third of his memoir, *Dreams from My Father*, was about his years as a community organizer.

The rest of this chapter examines Alinsky's philosophy and the strategies for revolution that he pioneered. It also examines his impact on American politics, especially on the modern Democratic Party and Barack Obama.

The first credo of Alinsky's philosophy is that you need power to impose your will. In *Rules for Radicals*, he wrote: "*The Prince* was written by Machiavelli for the Haves on how to hold power. *Rules for Radicals* is written for the Have-Nots on how to take it away."[9] The mafia taught him that power transcends everything. In his words: "This liberal cliché about reconciliation of opposing forces is a load of crap. Reconciliation means just one thing: When one side gets enough power, then the other side gets reconciled to it. That's where you need organization — first to compel concessions and then to make sure the other side delivers. If you're too delicate to exert the necessary pressures on the power structure, then you might as well get out of the ball park. This was the fatal mistake the white liberals made, relying on altruism as an instrument of social change. That's just self-delusion. No issue can be negotiated unless you first have the clout to compel negotiation."[10]

If Alinsky's students said that they wanted to be community organizers to altruistically help others, he corrected them by saying, "You want to organize for *power*!"[11] In *Rules for Radicals* he wrote, "From the moment an organizer enters a community, he lives, dreams, eats, breathes, and sleeps only one thing, and that is to build the mass power base of what he calls the army."[12]

This forcefulness resonated with Barack Obama. In *Dreams from My Father,* he wrote: "Issues, action, power, self-interest. I liked these concepts. They bespoke of a certain hardheadedness, a worldly lack of sentiment; politics, not religion."[13] Thus, it is easy to understand Obama's "I won, you lost" trump card that he played when bullying Senate Republicans to back his stimulus plan in 2009.[14] Such tactics are pure Alinsky. Ignore the other side's perspective. Believe you are 100% right. Do not be a unifier. Obama's virtual exclusion of the Republicans from the health care reform debate was another example of this Alinsky tactic.

There are two kinds of power, according to Alinsky: Organized Money and Organized People. He was a master of both. His successful blueprint has been adopted by today's masters of organizing, such as George Soros, ACORN, labor unions, and Barack Obama. In Alinsky's words, "My aim here is to suggest how to organize for power: how to get it and how to use it....We are concerned with how to create mass organizations to seize power...."[15]

[16] Author Jim Rooney, who attended an IAF training session, summarized his impressions: "There is no nice way to bring about change. All change comes through pressure and threats....IAF leaders are brazenly explicit about their appetite for power."[17] In *Rules for Radicals*, Alinsky wrote, "Change comes from power, and power comes from organization."[18]

According to Alinsky, the best way to organize money and organize people is to infiltrate institutions like churches, unions, and political parties. These entities already have a pipeline to money and foot soldiers, so they just need to be reoriented toward the revolution. In *Rules for Radicals* he wrote, "So you return to the suburban scene of your middle class with its variety of organizations from PTAs to League of Women Voters, consumer groups, churches, and clubs. The job is to search out the leaders in these various activities, identify their major issues, find areas of common agreement...."[19] Accordingly, Alinsky cozied up to power brokers, including church, labor, and organized crime leaders.

Gregory Galluzzo, a former Jesuit priest who described himself as Alinsky's "St. Paul" and "his best disciple,"[20] wrote the manual that has been used for decades by the Industrial Areas Foundation and other community organizing groups to train new recruits. It has chapters titled: "Power Analysis," "Elements of a Power Organization," and "The Path to Power." It bluntly states: "We are not virtuous by not wanting power. We are really cowards for not wanting power." It also says, "Get rid of do-gooders in your church and your organization."[21] In Alinsky's view, the community organizer's yen for power should stand above everything: "The

Organizer is in a true sense reaching for the highest level for which man can reach—to create, to be a 'great creator,' to play God."[22]

The second major credo of Alinsky's philosophy is to use stealth to advance the socialist revolution. According to Jerome Corsi in his book *The Obama Nation*, Alinsky cagily used the word "change" as a euphemism for promoting socialism and redistribution of wealth.[23] Stealth radicals were encouraged to "...cut their hair, put on business suits, and run for political office..." to quietly nudge the system toward socialism.[24] In Corsi's words, "Alinsky taught organizers to hide their true intentions in the words they spoke. Denying the truth or just plain lying were both acceptable tactics, as long as the cause was advanced."[25]

Alinsky said: "It would be great if the whole system would just disappear overnight, but it won't, and the kids on the New Left sure as hell aren't going to overthrow it. Shit, Abbie Hoffman and Jerry Rubin couldn't organize a successful luncheon, much less a revolution. I can sympathize with the impatience and pessimism of a lot of kids, but they've got to remember that real revolution is a long, hard process. Radicals in the United States don't have the strength to confront a local police force in armed struggle, much less the Army, Navy and Air Force; it's just idiocy for the Panthers to talk about all power growing from the barrel of a gun when the other side has all the guns."[26]

Alinsky cautioned his followers that the "change" they sought could take decades to mature as they flew under the radar: "America isn't Russia in 1917 or China in 1946, and any violent head-on collision with the power structure will only ensure the mass suicide of the left and the probable triumph of domestic fascism. So you're not going to get instant nirvana — or any nirvana, for that matter — and you've got to ask yourself, 'Short of that, what the hell can I do?' The only answer is to build up local power bases that can merge into a national power movement that will ultimately realize your goals. That takes time and hard work and all the tedium connected with hard work."[27]

Obama must have been attracted to this mindset, because he chose to work as an organizer for the Developing Communities Project (DCP), an organization spawned by Alinsky's Industrial Areas Foundation. "He wanted to make that kind of contribution and didn't know how to do it," said Gerald Kellman, an Alinsky trainee who hired Obama into the DCP. "There's that side of him that's strongly idealistic, very much a dreamer, and this kind of work

Amen

attracts that kind of person. It isn't just that we're going to change things, but we're going to change things from the grass roots."[28] In Alinsky's view, community organizing is just a camouflage good socialists use to mobilize the "Have-Nots" to take power.

The third major credo in Alinsky's political philosophy is that community organizing really means community *disorganizing*, at least at the beginning of the process. The stealth "change" toward socialism will never get legs until discontent and outrage are stirred up. In his words, "The disruption of the present organization is the first step toward community organization. Present arrangements must be disorganized if they are to be displaced by new patterns. All change means disorganization of the old and organization of the new....When those prominent in the status quo turn and label you an 'agitator' they are completely correct, for that is, in one word, your function—to agitate to the point of conflict."[29]

A community organizer gathers momentum for "change" by cozying up to a community, creating tension, and then rubbing salt in their wounds. Alinsky wrote, "Any revolutionary change must be preceded by a passive, affirmative, non-challenging attitude toward change among the mass of our people. They must feel so frustrated, so defeated, so lost, so futureless in the prevailing system that they are willing to let go of the past and change the future. This acceptance is the reformation essential to any revolution."[30]

Once people get so frustrated with their current situation that they abandon their attachments to the past, the stage is set for the stealth revolution. As Alinsky put it, "A reformation means that the masses of our people have reached the point of disillusionment with past ways and values. They don't know what will work but they do know that the prevailing system is self-defeating, frustrating, and hopeless. They won't act for change but won't strongly oppose those who do. The time is then ripe for revolution."[31]

The catalyst for the actual "change" will come from "crises" that are intentionally manipulated or exaggerated. This will cause the current system to appear overwhelmed or fundamentally broken, so that "change" *must* happen to avoid cataclysm. Of course, the only change recommended by the radicals is a transition to socialism.

Here are some ways that modern radicals have gradually introduced crises into our society. They created an "immigration crisis" by relaxing immigration enforcement, and then allowing the immigrants to overwhelm schools, social services, and other infrastructure. They created an "environmental crisis" by exaggerating threats of global catastrophe from CO^2 emissions. They created a "war in Iraq crisis" by bombarding citizens with stories of torture and daily body counts. They created a "financial system crisis" by forcing banks to give subprime mortgages to risky borrowers, and then stirring up hysteria when the financial system inevitably failed. They created a "health care crisis" by demonizing insurance companies and exaggerating the number of uninsured. They used groups like ACORN to create an "electoral system crisis" by registering millions of undocumented or nonexistent voters. They are creating an "energy crisis" by preventing exploration of domestic sources, pricing coal-burning plants out of the market with expensive cap-and-trade programs, and preventing new refineries from being built due to environmental restrictions. They also used the British Petroleum oil spill in the Gulf of Mexico as a reason to suspend offshore drilling and to push for further restrictions on fossil fuel consumption. They created a "Social Security crisis" by spending all of the trust fund surpluses on current government programs, and then announcing that there is no money left as Baby Boomers begin to retire.

Modern radicals stirred mass hysteria by relentlessly using the word "crisis" in every news story, speech, and press conference. Our institutions thus appeared overwhelmed; therefore, it was only logical that "change" was needed. The radicals pointed to the crises, blamed Big Oil, Wall Street, and Greedy Capitalists, and reassured citizens that the evil establishment would be replaced with a "fair" and "just" administration. People fear change, so they must be made to see it as necessary, unavoidable, and even attractive. They must be made to see it as their only "hope". After decades of pump-priming by the radicals, a majority of Americans finally voted for "hope" and "change" in 2008.

The fourth major credo in Saul Alinsky's philosophy is that the middle class is *the* critical faction in the battle between the underclass and the rich establishment. Alinsky's simple math told him that the initial target of his organizing efforts, the underclass of America, was not a big enough demographic to take over the political system of the United States. He concluded that the only way to successfully implement his stealth socialist revolution was to con the middle class into jumping on board.

Understanding this lynchpin of Alinsky's philosophy is extremely important. The recognition that the middle class was critical for the revolution is what convinced radicals to abandon their old strategy of attacking at the fringes of society. They decided to move stealthily into the heartland of America and to gently co-opt the passive middle class into their revolution. In *Rules for Radicals*, Alinsky wrote: "...any positive action for radical social change will have to be focused on the white middle class, for the simple reason that this is where the real power lies."[32]

Alinsky wrote: "When more than three-fourths of our people from both the point of view of economics and of their self-identification are middle class, it is obvious that their action or inaction will determine the direction of change."[33] The middle class was a pawn. In Alinsky's view, good socialists should swallow their disdain for the middle class at least long enough to lead it to its own destruction. In his words: "Our rebels have contemptuously rejected the values and the way of life of the middle class. They have stigmatized it as materialistic, decadent, bourgeois, degenerate, imperialistic, war-mongering, brutalized and corrupt. They are right; but we must begin from where we are if we are to build power for change, and the power and the people are in the big middle class majority."[34]

He also wrote, "Many of the lower middle class are members of labor unions, churches, bowling clubs, fraternal, service, and nationality organizations....To reject them is to lose them by default. They will not shrivel and disappear. You can't switch channels and get rid of them."[35]

Alinsky was convinced that the middle class was ripe for the picking. "Right now they're nowhere....Right now they're frozen, festering in apathy, leading what Thoreau called 'lives of quiet desperation.' They're oppressed by taxation and inflation, poisoned by pollution, terrorized by urban crime, frightened by the new youth culture, baffled by the computerized world around them. They've worked all their lives to get their own little house in the suburbs, their color TV, their two cars, and now the good life seems to have turned to ashes in their mouths. Their personal lives are generally unfulfilling, their jobs unsatisfying, they've succumbed to tranquilizers and pep pills, they drown their anxieties in alcohol, they feel trapped in long-term endurance marriages or escape into guilt-ridden divorces. They're losing their kids and they're losing their dreams. They're alienated, depersonalized, without any feeling of participation in the political process, and they feel rejected and hopeless. Their utopia of status and security has become a tacky-

tacky suburb, their split-levels have sprouted prison bars and their disillusionment is becoming terminal."[36]

"They're the first to live in a total mass-media-oriented world, and every night when they turn on the TV and the news comes on, they see the almost unbelievable hypocrisy and deceit and even outright idiocy of our national leaders and the corruption and disintegration of all our institutions, from the police and courts to the White House itself. Their society appears to be crumbling and they see themselves as no more than small failures within the larger failure. All their old values seem to have deserted them, leaving them rudderless in a sea of social chaos. Believe me, this is good organizational material."[37]

Even though he needed their cooperation, Alinsky was condescending toward the middle class: "Seeking some meaning in life, they (the middle class) turn to an extreme chauvinism and become defenders of the 'American' faith….Insecure in this fast-changing world, they cling to illusory fixed points….The 'silent majority', now, are hurt, bitter, suspicious….Their fears and frustrations at their helplessness are mounting to a point of a political paranoia which can demonize people to turn to the law of survival in the narrowest sense. These emotions can go either to the far right of totalitarianism or forward to Act II of the American Revolution."[38]

Compare the above to Obama's words recorded surreptitiously by journalist Mayhill Fowler at a fundraiser in San Francisco: "You go into these small towns in Pennsylvania and, like a lot of small towns in the Midwest, the jobs have been gone now for 25 years and nothing's replaced them. And they fell through the Clinton administration, and the Bush administration, and each successive administration has said that somehow these communities are going to regenerate and they have not. And it's not surprising that they get bitter, they cling to guns or religion or antipathy to people who aren't like them or anti-immigrant sentiment or anti-trade sentiment as a way to explain their frustrations."[39] Clearly, the star pupil learned his condescending rhetoric well from the Master.

It took decades to unfold, but radicals have finally realized Alinsky's dream. Influenced by relentless coercion from the public education system, mass media, and cultural elite, the middle class has gradually moved leftward. In the 2008 elections, the candidate with the most liberal voting record in the Senate was elected President, and both the House of Representatives and the U.S. Senate were populated with a solid majority of left-leaning politicians. Obama promised to give tax cuts to 95% of Americans, even the ones who don't actually pay Federal income taxes. Even though he can't possibly keep that promise in the long term, he temporarily bought off the middle class, numbing them into quiescence so that he could implement Alinsky-style "change".

With radicals wielding nearly complete control over the entire U.S. Government, the transition to socialism in America has begun. For those in the middle class, this is a good time to study how socialism ruined countries like the Soviet Union, Cuba, East Germany, and North Korea. It is also a good time to study how the middle classes fared in those "socialist paradises." Here's a sneak peek: Wherever socialism has been broadly implemented, the middle class has disappeared.

The credos described above – Grabbing power, disguising the socialist revolution as "change", organizing communities by first disorganizing them, and conning the middle class into joining the revolution – are a concise summary of Alinsky's tactical vision. In addition to these credos, Alinsky's guideline for achieving socialism included rules that he popularized in his book, *Rules for Radicals*. A few of these rules are discussed below.

Rule #2: *"Never go outside the experience of your people."*[40] Unless your policy positions are universally accepted, avoid mentioning them. Radicals are professional contrarians. They are not so much advocates for specific, defendable, and executable solutions as they are naysayers against the totality of the current situation. When pressed to communicate their vision, they defer to vague, non-specific pabulum such as "hope", "change", "justice", "fairness", and "the children." It is not possible for enemies to attack these "visions". Enemies can only attack facts and specific policy positions. David Axelrod successfully executed this rule with his deft management of Obama's campaign of vacuous slogans in 2008.

Rule #3: *"Wherever possible go outside the experience of the enemy."*[41] Hurl arguments and accusations at your enemies, even if they are irrelevant or baseless. Take them out of their comfort zone and force them to defend phantom allegations. Characterize them as extremist, mean-spirited, greedy, selfish, and religious nuts. This will disorient them and consume their resources. With a little luck, people who are not well informed will believe your allegations, no matter how ridiculous they are or how strenuous the opposing denials are.

An example of this is when the Obama campaign painted John McCain as Bush III. No matter how much time and energy McCain invested in trying to counter with his "maverick" message, he was forever tainted by the Bush III allegory. When the mainstream media is in the bag, and when potential voters are shallowly informed at best, the mere pronouncement of something is often sufficient to make it real.

Rule #5: *"Ridicule is man's most potent weapon."*[42] There is no defense against ridicule, because fighting it just draws even more unwelcome attention. This rule is often used effectively in combination with Rule #13, which says to "Pick the target, freeze it, personalize it, and polarize it."[43] An example of these rules used in combination was the merciless onslaught of ridicule against Sarah Palin by the mainstream media. Every day brought a new torrent of trick questions by moderators, spoofs and caricatures by comedians, and vivid dissection by media pundits of every misstatement she made. In the course of just a few weeks, Obama's campaign staff and their allies in the media magically transformed Palin from a successful and popular state Governor into polarizing and knuckle-dragging white trash.

Rule #8: *"Keep the pressure on."*[44] Seize every word, every event, and every action of your enemy, and turn these to your advantage. Relentlessly hammer away at your adversary. Attack from all sides, and never let the enemy gather its wits or strength. Eventually, you will wear down your opponent and win. An example of this rule in action was when the mainstream media published at least one headline every day for years with the general grammatical structure of "Bush (frightening verb) (evil outcome)". Productive people are usually vulnerable to attack simply because they are busy achieving something. Radicals, on the other hand, are usually outsiders who are not responsible for anything. Therefore, they can focus all of their energy on attack. If they keep up the attack long enough, they will eventually win a protracted war of attrition against institutional leaders. This rule has been used relentlessly to discredit conservatism in America.

Alinsky had a powerful philosophy and clearly defined tactics for seizing power. However, Alinsky knew that revolutions also require money. Therefore, he smooth-talked some of America's wealthiest philanthropists into underwriting his Industrial Areas Foundation, an organization dedicated to waging class warfare in America.

Convincing rich capitalists to fund a revolution against capitalism is a challenge steeped in irony. But this didn't stop Alinsky. He prided himself on his ability to use the strength of the enemy against itself, a strategy he called "mass jujitsu." In *Rules for Radicals*, he wrote, "The basic tactic in warfare against the Haves is a mass political jujitsu: the Have-Nots do not rigidly oppose the Haves, but yield in such planned and skilled ways that the superior strength of the Haves becomes their own undoing. For example, since the Haves publicly pose as the custodians of responsibility, morality, law, and justice (which are frequently strangers to each other), they can be constantly pushed to live up to their own book of morality and regulations. No organization, including organized religion, can live up to the letter of its own book."[45]

Much of Alinsky's financial support came from the business world, because he used his "mass jujitsu" against their presumed guilt to support his social justice agenda. He once boasted, "...I feel confident that I could persuade a millionaire on Friday to subsidize a revolution for Saturday out of which he would make a huge profit on Sunday even though he was certain to be executed on Monday."[46]

Since Alinsky's IAF was formed, it has trained thousands of organizers, many of them who became very influential, including Barack Obama.

A critical lesson taught to community organizers during IAF workshops was Saul Alinsky's perspective on ethics that the end justifies the means. In his words: "The end is what you want, and the means is how you get it. Whenever we think about social change, the question of means and ends arises. The man of action views the issue of means and ends in pragmatic and strategic terms. He has no other problem; he thinks only of his actual resources and the possibilities of various choices of action. He asks of ends only whether they are achievable and worth the cost; of means, only whether they will work....The real arena is corrupt and bloody."[47]

Alinsky was essentially amoral, with no attachment to principles. In his words: "...I'm free to be loose, resilient and independent, able to respond to any situation as it arises without getting trapped by articles of faith."[48] He also wrote, "An organizer working in and for an open society is in an ideological dilemma. To begin with, he does not have a fixed truth—truth to him is relative and changing....To the extent that he is free from the shackles of dogma, he can respond to the realities of the widely different situations...."[49] Alinsky never broadcast an ideology more specific than "social justice."

Alinsky did not let moral considerations get in the way of the socialist revolution. In his words: "The means-and-ends moralists, constantly obsessed with the ethics of the means used by the Have-Nots against the Haves, should search themselves as to their real political position. In fact, they are passive – but real – allies of the Haves."[50] He also said, "The most unethical of all means is the non-use of any means....The standards of judgment must be rooted in the whys and wherefores of life as it is lived, the world as it is, not our wished-for fantasy of the world as it should be."[51] Michelle Obama used Alinsky's "world as it is, not the world as it should be" line frequently in her 2008 campaign speeches.[52]

Any means is justified in pursuit of revolution, according to Alinsky in a 1972 *Playboy* interview: "...when you're hungry, anything goes...the right to eat takes precedence over the right to make a profit."[53] The ethical context for Alinsky was the "Chicago Way" politics of corruption and the mafia tactics of intimidation and extortion. "In those days, they didn't even bother to count the votes, they weighed them," Alinsky said, "And every cemetery in town voted."[54] He claimed that "...in war the end justifies almost any means"[55] and "...morality is rhetorical rationale for expedient action and self-interest."[56]

Here's more from Alinsky on ethics: "In a fight almost anything goes. It almost reaches the point where you stop to apologize if a chance blow lands above the belt."[57] He also said, "To fuck your enemies, you've first got to seduce your allies."[58] Alinsky admired ruthless leaders like Soviet dictator Vladimir Lenin, remarking once that "Lenin was a pragmatist...he said that the Bolsheviks stood for getting power through the ballot but would reconsider after they got the guns!"[59]

This amorality was a critical component of Alinsky's community organizing strategy. He believed that people who are otherwise good can be seduced into accepting that the transcendental importance of the socialist cause trumps their normal sense of right and wrong.

Alinsky taught college students to turn their consciences upside down in his workshops. He persuaded thousands of young students that it is moral to be immoral. He taught them that a community "disorganizer" had to be prepared to break the moral rules of the community. He wrote, "Rousseau noted the obvious, that 'Law is a very good thing for men with property and a very bad thing for men without property.'"[60]

Alinsky summarized his own moral pathology in *Rules for Radicals*: "The practical revolutionary will understand Goethe's 'conscience is the virtue of observers and not of agents of action'; in action, one does not always enjoy the luxury of a decision that is consistent both with one's individual conscience and the good of mankind."[61] In his view, the naked purpose of a politician is to get votes, by any means necessary. Principles are not required. In fact, they often get in the way.

The desired end state of Alinsky's revolution is socialism, where "the means of production will be owned by all of the people instead of just a comparative handful."[62] His vision included creating an army of radical community organizers who would help society "advance from the jungle of laissez-faire capitalism to a world worthy of the name of human civilization."[63]

Saul Alinsky's role in the revolution included being a fund raiser for the Communists early in his career. In his words, "Anybody who tells you he was active in progressive causes in those days and never worked with the Reds is a goddamn liar....I was in charge of a big part of fund raising for the International Brigade and in that capacity I worked in close alliance with the Communist Party."[64]

Alinsky's profound influence on key leaders of the Democratic Party continues to the present day. The two top contenders for the Democratic nomination in the 2008 presidential election, Hillary Clinton and Barack Obama, were admirers of Alinsky. One way or another, an acolyte of Alinsky was going to be nominated for President. We will examine Obama's extensive connections with Alinsky's legacy organizations shortly. For now, let's take a quick look at Clinton's relationship with Alinsky.

According to Horowitz and Poe, "Hillary met the Chicago radical through a leftwing church group to which she belonged in high school. They stayed close in touch until Alinsky's death."[65] In 1969, she hosted Alinsky at a Wellesley College student dinner. Her senior thesis at Wellesley was a 75-page tribute to Alinsky and his methods titled "There is Only the Fight...An Analysis of the Alinsky Model."[66] According to Horowitz and Poe, "It contained excerpts of his forthcoming book, *Rules for Radicals*, which he had allowed

Hillary to read before the book's publication in 1971."[67] In her thesis, Hillary ensconced Alinsky on the same lofty social justice pedestal as Martin Luther King. She wrote, "If the ideals Alinsky espouses were actualized, the result would be social revolution."[68]

According to Clinton's memoir, *Living History,* Alinsky offered her a job with his Industrial Areas Foundation.[69] She chose instead to attend Yale Law School. After law school, she was appointed to the Congressional Watergate investigative team on the recommendation of mentors Peter and Marian Wright Edelman. *New Republic* editor Martin Peretz called Marian "Hillary's closest sister and ideological soul mate".[70] Coincidentally, Marian was a trustee of Alinsky's IAF. She also provided commentary for the cover of Obama's *Dreams from My Father.* According to the *Washington Post,* Hillary supported the IAF even from the White House: "As the first lady, Clinton occasionally lent her name to projects endorsed by the Industrial Areas Foundation (IAF), the Alinsky group that had offered her a job in 1968."[71]

Long before Clinton and Obama, Alinsky influenced Democratic presidents and their top advisers. For example, we saw earlier that Harry Truman was so infatuated with the six-part series titled *The Orderly Revolution,* written in praise of Alinsky, that he ordered 100 reprints of it. Alinsky's influence temporarily waned during the eight-year Eisenhower presidency. But, when Democrats regained control of the White House in 1960, the Alinskyites reemerged as key players.

According to Horowitz and Poe, "The infiltration began in 1961, when Robert Kennedy appointed Columbia University sociologist Lloyd Ohlin to direct the newly formed Office of Juvenile Delinquency. Ohlin had learned the Alinsky model of orderly revolution at its source, the University of Chicago sociology department, where Ohlin earned his Ph.D....In 1964, Johnson declared war on poverty and appointed Sargent Shriver to the post of 'poverty czar.' Ohlin and his radical colleagues slipped comfortably into Shriver's new Office of Economic Opportunity, which funded such programs as VISTA, Head Start, Job Corps, and the Community Action Program (CAP). Now the Alinskyites had their hands on the federal money spigot. Ohlin and his colleagues directed the very first CAP grant into a program at Syracuse University through which Alinsky personally trained community activists. The federal government spent more than $300 billion on War on Poverty programs in the first five years. Much of this money went to street radicals such as Alinsky."[72]

Senator Robert Kennedy collaborated with United Farm Workers co-founder Cesar Chavez, an Alinsky disciple, in order to bolster his presidential ambitions. Chavez had worked for the IAF for ten years and received his early training from it. After race riots shook Rochester, New York, Alinsky pressured Eastman-Kodak to hire more blacks. Robert Kennedy supported Alinsky's shakedown. The two men had an "understanding", Alinsky later wrote.[73]

Alinsky also wielded influence with organized religions. Thomas Pauken, a former Director of VISTA, said that "the radicalization of elements of the Catholic clergy turned out to be one of Saul Alinsky's most significant accomplishments."[74]   Bernard J. Sheil, Auxiliary bishop of Chicago, called *Reveille for Radicals* "a life-saving handbook for the salvation of democracy."[75]   Chicago's Cardinal Stritch hired the IAF to advance various social projects.[76] French Catholic philosopher Jacques Maritain called *Reveille for Radicals* "epoch making."[77]   In 1958, Maritain arranged for Alinsky to meet Archbishop Montini, the future Pope Paul VI, so that Alinsky could give him "organizational tips for stopping the Italian Communist Party from making further inroads among Catholic workers."[78]

The Catholic Church's Campaign for Human Development (CHD) donated $100 million to various Alinsky-type organizations between 1972 and 1995. The largest recipient was the IAF.   The CHD also contributed more than $7 million to ACORN.[79]   The CHD helped fund the Developing Communities Project, where Obama worked for three years. Alinsky-style "community organizing" is now part of the culture of many Christian churches in America. The IAF's training manual, written by former Jesuit priest Gregory Galluzzo, is included in the syllabi of some Catholic seminaries.

In *Rules for Radicals*, Alinsky described his interaction with Catholic seminarians: "Each year, for a number of years, the activists in the graduating class from a major Catholic seminary near Chicago would visit me for a day just before their ordination, with questions about values, revolutionary tactics, and such. Once, at the end of such a day, one of the seminarians said, 'Mr. Alinsky, before we came here we met and agreed that there was one question we particularly wanted to put to you. We're going to be ordained, and then we'll be assigned to different parishes, as assistants to-frankly-stuffy, reactionary, old pastors. They will disapprove of a lot of what you and we believe in, and we will be put into a killing routine. Our question is: how do we keep our faith in true Christian values, everything we hope to do to change the system?' That was easy. I answered, 'When you go out that door, just make your own personal decision about whether you want to be a bishop or a priest, and everything else will follow.'"[80]

With influence over seminarians, bishops and Pope Paul VI, with influence over Harry Truman, Lyndon Johnson, Robert Kennedy, Hillary Clinton, and Barack Obama, and with influence over organizations and initiatives like the War on Poverty, ACORN, and the United Farm Workers, Saul Alinsky was one of the most influential unelected social and political leaders of the 20th Century. *Time* magazine wrote, "American democracy is being altered by Alinsky's ideas".[81]   William F. Buckley, Jr. said that Alinsky was "very close to being an organizational genius."[82]   *The New York Times* wrote that Alinsky is "a major force in the revolution of powerless people—indeed, he is emerging as a movement unto himself."[83]

The rest of this chapter documents Barack Obama's involvement with the people Saul Alinsky trained and with the organizations Alinsky spawned. Even though Alinsky died before Obama arrived in Chicago, the people who mentored Obama's community organizing career, including George Kellman, Mike Kruglik, John McKnight, and Gregory Galluzzo, were all disciples trained by Alinsky's Industrial Areas Foundation. Obama worked for several community organizing groups that traced their lineage to the IAF, including the DCP, Gamaliel, and ACORN.

From 1985 to 1988, Obama was a community organizer and director of the Developing Communities Project (DCP), a subsidiary of the Calumet Community Religious Conference (CCRC). Obama was hired by Gerald Kellman, who was trained by the IAF, to learn and apply "Alinsky's philosophy of street-level democracy."[84] Obama became very proficient at this. Mike Kruglik, a mentor of Obama at the DCP, said Obama "was a natural, the undisputed master of agitation, who could engage a room full of recruiting targets in a rapid-fire Socratic dialogue, nudging them to admit that they were not living up to their own standards. As with the panhandler, he could be aggressive and confrontational. With probing, sometimes personal questions, he would pinpoint the source of pain in their lives, tearing down their egos just enough before dangling a carrot of hope that they could make things better."[85]

The Developing Communities Project and the Calumet Community Religious Conference were associated with the Gamaliel Foundation, which taught the methods of Saul Alinsky to community organizers. Gamaliel is a church-based group partially supported by some of the Thomas Ayers's philanthropic foundations. It also gets funding from George Soros's Open Society Institute and other radical groups. Gamaliel, which has operations in many states, is similar to ACORN, although it has a religious rather than a secular orientation. It organizes churches for radical activism, while ACORN organizes neighborhoods.

The Gamaliel Foundation likens its mission to that of the biblical apostle Paul. According to the Foundation, "In Corinthians, Paul states, 'I am Paul, a disciple of Gamaliel.' Saul Alinsky made all of his organizers read the letters of Paul because he regarded his namesake to be one of the greatest organizers of all time."[86] Gamaliel wants "to be a powerful network of grassroots, interfaith, interracial, multi-issue organizations working together to create a more just and more democratic society."[87] Its vision includes Marxist notions such as "Collective transformation of our society is necessary to bring about justice locally, nationally, and globally"; "The sacred community is valued over individualism"; and "There should be shared, sustained abundance for all."[88] Alinsky's *Rules for Radicals* is recommended reading for Gamaliel members.

Gregory Galluzzo was the Executive Director of Gamaliel in the 1980's. He mentored Obama when Barack worked for the DCP.[89] Galluzzo said, "I tell people I'm a mentor, but an organizer is like a musician. A musician has to play music. Somebody listens and points a few things out. But nobody teaches a jazz musician jazz. This man (Obama) was gifted. An older musician would know if a young musician was practicing, and Barack was always practicing."[90] Galluzzo also said, "I met with Barack on a regular basis as he incorporated the Developing Communities Project, as he moved the organization into action and as he developed the leadership structure for the organization."[91]

Obama eventually became a trainer for the Industrial Areas Foundation and Gamaliel after graduating from Harvard.[92] Obama is an Alinsky-style community organizer to the core. He even described his concept of politics as being rooted in community organizing. His Big Government policies of today were foreshadowed by his community-organizing activity more than two decades ago. According to Jerome Corsi, "the proposed solution to every problem on the South Side was a distribution of government funds...."[93] Obama's trillion-dollar wealth-transfer programs of today had their genesis in his South Chicago community organizing activities.

The Gamaliel Foundation is associated with many politically active churches. For example, Jeremiah Wright, pastor of Trinity United Church of Christ (TUCC), was a speaker at Gamaliel conferences. Obama spent 20 years at TUCC because he embraced Alinsky's precept that the church is a powerful vehicle for community organizing, especially in black enclaves. In 1990, he wrote, "Should a mere 50 prominent black churches, out of the thousands that exist in cities like Chicago, decide to collaborate with a trained organized staff, enormous positive changes could be wrought in the education, housing, employment, and spirit of inner-city black communities...."[94] Reverend John C. Welch, a Gamaliel acolyte, said this about Obama after the presidential election: "He is Gamaliel. He is African American. He is one of us. He is the 44th President of the United States of America!"[95] Obama has retained the class warfare worldview of Jeremiah Wright and Saul Alinsky while publicly projecting the image of a young and hip Cliff Huxtable.

After three years of community organizing for the DCP, Obama wrote an article titled, "After Alinsky: Community Organizing in Illinois." In this article, he called for more "power" to establish a "systematic approach to community organization." He praised Northwestern Professor John L. McKnight and his organizing strategies, which he considered very influential.[96]

John McKnight was a disciple of Saul Alinsky. He was a director of the ACLU and a member of the Gamaliel Foundation board. He helped train Obama in Alinsky's methods when Obama worked for the DCP.[97] He also helped launch the radical youth service group Public Allies, which Barack and Michelle were leaders of.[98] McKnight was approached by Obama to write a letter of recommendation for admittance into Harvard.[99]

Before writing the letter, McKnight advised Obama not to compromise his principles.[100] Apparently Obama took his advice, because he wrote in *The Audacity of Hope*, "My views...are not so much more refined than they were when I labored in obscurity as a community organizer."[101] In other words, what he learned from Alinsky's disciples and organizations is still a core part of his ideology.

Another Alinskyite organization that abetted Barack Obama's career was ACORN. This organization was so influential in Obama's career during a span of 16 years that it is the subject of Chapter Eight. For now, here are brief highlights of his involvement with ACORN.

Obama was employed by ACORN through its subsidiary, Project Vote. He was an attorney for ACORN during Illinois "Motor Voter" litigation and also litigation related to subprime mortgages and redlining. He helped train ACORN members in community organizing tactics. He helped fund ACORN through various philanthropic foundation boards that he served on. ACORN endorsed him during various political campaigns. He employed ACORN workers to help with his 2008 presidential campaign. He also increased funding for ACORN after he became President.

The seeds for ACORN were planted in the 1960's when two Columbia University professors, Richard Andrew Cloward and Frances Fox Piven, developed a strategy of orchestrated chaos, which was based on one of Saul Alinsky's key principles. Alinsky's *Rules for Radicals* instructed organizers to "Make the enemy live up to their own book of rules. You can kill them with this, for they can no more obey their own rules than the Christian church can live up to Christianity."[102] Cloward and Piven, inspired by this Alinsky concept, proposed overwhelming the government with demands for welfare and public services. Their intent was to induce a crisis that would trigger a popular call for structural "change", with socialism as the ultimate goal. This became known as the Cloward-Piven Strategy, which spawned the National Welfare Rights Organization (NWRO).

The mission of the NWRO was to destabilize local governments with overwhelming demands on welfare agencies. After a series of victories, the NWRO eventually faded away. Some former members, including Wade Rathke, went on to form ACORN, where they trained civil rights workers to become community organizers in the mold of Saul Alinsky.

Some of the legislation that Obama sponsored as an Illinois State Senator was drafted in collaboration with ACORN and the Gamaliel Foundation.[103] Part of his vision was to merge his political activities with his community organizing genetic code. As Michelle Obama put it, "Barack is not a politician first and foremost. He's a community activist exploring the viability of politics to make change."[104]

From 1999 through 2002, Obama was on the board of directors of the Woods Fund, a philanthropic foundation headquartered in Chicago. It was the Woods Fund back in 1985 that granted Gerald Kellman the $25,000 needed to hire Obama at the DCP.[105] The Woods Fund supported the usual set of left-wing initiatives, including redistribution of wealth. The fund granted more than $200,000 to ACORN.[106] The Woods Fund also granted money to the Gamaliel Foundation and the Midwest Academy, an organization run by disciples of Alinsky who trained young radicals.[107] The Woods Fund granted money to Jeremiah Wright while Obama was on its board.[108]

When he was a lecturer at the University of Chicago, Obama taught Alinsky's methods to students. Obama's website pictured him writing on a blackboard in a classroom. The blackboard was chalked with the words "Power Analysis" and "Relationships Built on Self Interest," phrases straight out of Alinsky's *Rules for Radicals*.[109]

During the 2008 presidential race, Obama's campaign team coordinated a number of Camp Obamas. These were intensive training sessions for his volunteers and supporters. Mike Kruglik, an Alinsky acolyte who mentored Obama at the DCP, was one of the organizers for these camps. The camps taught tactics derived from Alinsky's *Rules for Radicals*. Volunteers were instructed to follow the traditional Alinsky formula that included personally connecting with prospective voters, finding out what really concerned them, and then promising that all of their "hopes" would be fulfilled by the Obama administration. It's unlikely that these encounters with voters included a discussion about who would pay for fulfilling their hopes.

In closing, let's revisit a critical tenet espoused by Alinsky. He taught that radicals need to conceal their radicalism. He encouraged his community organizing protégés to stealthily infiltrate institutions and to conceal their agenda for radical change by appearing to work within the system, rather than by appearing to tear it down. In this context, it is not surprising that Obama has said little about his relationships with Alinsky-style radicals, despite his lifelong involvement with them.

But, Obama's collaboration with Alinskyites isn't the only part of his background that he has remained stealthily silent about. For example, even though he was mentored by Frank Marshall Davis of the Communist Party, even though he was endorsed by the Democratic Socialists of America, even though his early political mentor Alice Palmer was a Communist, even though he briefly aligned himself with the socialist New Party, even though he campaigned for socialist U.S. Senator Bernie Sanders, even though he co-sponsored a U.N. global poverty initiative supported by the Party of European Socialists, even though he had a long relationship with William Ayers and Bernardine Dohrn of the socialist Weather Underground, even though many of his financial supporters were members of the socialist Students for a Democratic Society, and even though his Marxist pastor Jeremiah Wright routinely condemned capitalist America, you will never hear Barack Obama mention socialism, other than to *deny* accusations that he's a socialist.

But, this book *will* mention socialism. It is the subject of the next chapter. In it, we will learn that Obama's association with Saul "The Red" Alinsky was just the tip of a very large iceberg of lifelong affiliations with prominent socialists and their organizations. Obama's extremist agenda is building toward socialism, one collectivist chain link at a time. His career has been so intertwined with socialists that he could have run for president as a socialist as easily as he ran as a Democrat. At one point in his career, he did run as socialist, when he was aligned with the socialist New Party. The New Party was a pioneer of "fusion" ballots, which involved simultaneously running the same candidate on Socialist and Democratic tickets. Obama was one of the candidates that did this in Illinois.

Obama faithfully applied Alinsky's tactics during his 2008 presidential campaign. He built his campaign around "change", the code word for movement toward socialism. He stirred up fear and dissatisfaction with the current system by attacking big business, big oil, Wall Street, and the war in Iraq. He successfully disguised his radicalism, with the help of an accommodating media that ignored his past. He conned the middle class into supporting his agenda by offering tax cuts to 95% of Americans, to be paid for by villainous rich capitalists. He enlisted his old accomplices like ACORN to work as the foot soldiers in his campaign. His campaign surrogates used Alinsky's rules for radicals to ridicule and polarize his opponents. He was the archetypal charismatic leader that Alinsky predicted would someday lead the revolution.

L. David Alinsky, Saul's son, described how Obama deployed Alinsky's tactics at the Democratic Convention in 2008: "All the elements were present: the individual stories told by real people of their situations and hardships, the packed-to-the rafters crowd, the crowd's chanting of key phrases and names, the action on the spot of texting and phoning to show instant support and commitment to jump into the political battle, the rallying selections of music, the setting of the agenda by the power people, the Democratic National Convention had all the elements of the perfectly organized event, Saul Alinsky style. Barack Obama's training in Chicago by the great community organizers is showing effectiveness. It is an amazingly powerful format, and the method of my late father always works to get the message out and get the supporters on board. When executed meticulously and thoughtfully, it is a powerful strategy for initiating change and making it really happen. Obama learned his lesson well. I am proud to see that my father's model for organizing is being applied successfully beyond local community organizing to affect the Democratic campaign in 2008. It is a fine tribute to Saul Alinsky as we approach his 100th birthday."[110]

Obama is treading in the footsteps of the fallen angel Alinsky. Like Alinsky, Obama has no enduring interest in the middle class. Just as Alinsky's disciples trained him, the middle class is merely a pawn, an annoying set of pixels cluttering a much larger picture. He needed middle-class votes to win the presidency, but now that he has achieved the office, and now that both Houses of Congress are firmly in the radical camp, the middle class will fall victim to the real agenda of transitioning to socialism.

The middle class will become a casualty, just like the middle class in every other country that has fallen under the spell of Marxism. The middle class will be taxed more, it will be regulated more, it will be squeezed out by the American underclass and by illegal immigrants, its wealth will be diminished by inflation, its healthcare will be rationed, the industries that employ it will be hounded out of business, and the golden retirement presumably waiting on the horizon will have mysteriously vanished into the nothingness of a bankrupt socialist state.

We've been had.

"Guard against the impostures of pretended patriotism."

George Washington, Farewell Address, September 19, 1796

Chapter Four

Meet the Socialists

> *"Democracy will cease to exist when you take away from those who are willing to work and give to those who would not."* [1]

Thomas Jefferson

A cover of *Newsweek* magazine declared, "We are all Socialists Now." [2] The *National Review* featured Obama on its cover with the headline, "Our Socialist Future." [3]

While these declarations are slightly premature, they do illustrate an undeniable movement in American government toward socialism. Government is getting bigger, industry is becoming more controlled, more wealth is being transferred to the underclass, and individual liberty and accountability are diminishing. America's drift toward socialism was turbocharged with the election of Barack Obama to the Presidency. This chapter will demonstrate that Obama has been immersed in a continuous socialist milieu since his birth. He has no significant experience in the private sector. His professional experience has been primarily rooted in the public sector. Accordingly, the early initiatives of his administration are moving us further down the socialistic path of wealth redistribution and government control of the economy.

Let's begin with a brief definition of socialism. Socialism is a system of social organization in which the means of producing and distributing goods are either owned collectively or by a centralized government that plans and controls the economy. In Marxist theory, it is the intermediate stage between capitalism and communism, in which the proletariat has not yet achieved full collective ownership of the economy. The Marxist phrase, "From each according to his abilities, to each according to his needs," succinctly defines socialism and communism. [4]

This chapter uses the terms socialism, communism, collectivism, and Marxism interchangeably. While these terms have specific technical definitions that distinguish one from another, it is sufficient for our purposes to recognize them as similar points bunched near the end of the political spectrum where the state controls the economy and the distribution of wealth. At the opposite end of this spectrum is capitalism and constitutional republicanism, where the role of the state is primarily to protect individual rights and private property.

The interchangeable use of these Marxist terms is necessary, partly because many of the sources referenced in this chapter use the terms loosely, and partly because certain disingenuous people who are trying to avoid these labels for political reasons rely on definitional loopholes to dodge around them and between them. In the end, these terms all represent the same politico-economic intent. No matter their precise definition, socialism, communism, Marxism, and collectivism all define a desire to transform society away from individual rights and private property toward collective rights and collective property.

Socialists are not new to America. They have tried to gain a foothold here for more than a century. Their attempts have historically not fared well, because socialism is anathema to America's founding principles. Until recently, socialism has been generally contrary to the spirit of Americans. The election of Obama and a radical Congress may represent a fundamental shift in the American political and economic paradigm. In contrast, the TEA Party movement and the resurgence of conservatism represent a fundamental affirmation of America's founding principles. It remains to be seen which movement will ultimately hold sway. The future of our country depends heavily on which direction the middle class leans.

The Socialist Party in America was born at the turn of the 20th Century and grew rapidly in its early years. From 1900 to 1920, charismatic leader Eugene Debs ran for President on the Socialist ticket. During those two decades, membership in the Socialist Party increased dramatically. In 1912 alone, Debs was marked on 900,000 ballots, which equated to six percent of the presidential votes cast. Also that year, hundreds of state and local officials and legislators were elected as socialists around the country. At the time, there were at least 300 socialist periodicals with hundreds of thousands of subscribers. Much of this momentum was a reaction to the coercive influence of large, monopolistic corporations.

During this era, the 16th Amendment to the Constitution was ratified. This amendment empowered the Federal Government to levy income taxes on individual taxpayers, initially at a maximum tax rate of 7%. As the decades unfolded, the ability to directly tax citizens enabled the drift toward Big Government and socialism. Other building blocks for the future expansion of Federal Government power were established during this period, including the Interstate Commerce Commission, the Federal Reserve System, and the Federal Trade Commission. Several presidents during this era classified themselves as Progressives, a term that indicated sympathy with initiatives of the socialist movement.

The Socialist Party's popularity waned after WWI because of government suppression and public disapproval. The 1917 Bolshevik revolution in Russia, bombings in the United States, and a series of labor strikes led to the Red Scare in 1919. Citizens suspected of being Marxists were jailed. Meanwhile, the wild economic expansion of the Roaring Twenties seemed to validate capitalism and render socialism irrelevant.

Even when the stock market collapsed in 1929 and the nation plunged into the Great Depression, socialists struggled to regain their clout. During the election of 1932, the Socialist and Communist parties, despite arguing that capitalism had failed, pulled less than one million votes combined. It is likely that Roosevelt, with his proto-socialistic New Deal, co-opted any momentum that the Marxists would have otherwise enjoyed.

Even though the socialists were not successful politically, they had an impact culturally. Elements of Roosevelt's New Deal, such as Social Security and widespread public works programs, were actually significant steps toward socialism. In FDR's words, "Throughout the nation, men and women, forgotten in the political philosophy of the government of the last years, look to us here for guidance and for more equitable opportunity to share in the distribution of national wealth."[5]

F.A. Hayek, in his 1944 book *The Road to Serfdom*, coined the term "creeping socialism" to describe America's drift toward a socialistic society during the New Deal.[6] Hayek warned that governmental controls on society and on the means of production did not deliver on their promises, and actually delivered dismal economic results. According to Hayek, socialism strips man of his desire to succeed, and therefore robs society of the benefit of efficiency and accountability. In contrast, the success that results from a person's desire to get ahead simultaneously improves the lives of others.

Socialism temporarily stopped creeping in America after WWII. Post-war prosperity fed a middle-class explosion, and the Cold War fed paranoia of Marxist influences. Paid vacations and 40-hour work weeks were common. Average income doubled compared to the prior economic boom in the 1920's. Many activists left the Socialist Party, believing that they could have more of an impact through the relatively mainstream Democratic Party than through radical organizations. Membership in formal Marxist organizations dried up in the 1950's. Party membership was a considerable risk due to the aggressive efforts of Senator Joseph McCarthy and FBI leader J. Edgar Hoover to root out suspected espionage during the Second Red Scare.

While this older generation of Marxists slowly ebbed into obscurity, a younger and more radical generation emerged to reenergize the socialist movement during the 1960's. This new generation of socialists was inspired by the Civil Rights movement, opposition to the Vietnam War, and the methods of Saul Alinsky.

At the vanguard of this movement was a radical organization called the Students for a Democratic Society (SDS). This Marxist group aimed to overthrow America's entrenched political, economic, and military establishment. A specific objective was to end the war in Vietnam. The group evolved from the youth branch of the socialist League for Industrial Democracy, which was formed in 1905 by Norman Thomas and Upton Sinclair, among others.[7] Many SDS members were "red-diaper babies," children of parents who were Marxist activists in preceding decades.

The SDS held its first formal meeting in Ann Arbor, Michigan in 1960. It gained notoriety when it released its 1962 Port Huron Statement, drafted principally by Tom Hayden. The statement denounced U.S. racism, American abundance, materialism, industrialization, and the threat of nuclear war, among other grievances.[8] It declared, "[The] allocation of resources must be based on social needs. A truly 'public sector' must be established, and its nature debated and planned. At present the majority of America's 'public sector', the largest part of our public spending, is for the military. When great social needs are so pressing, our concept of 'government spending' is wrapped up in the 'permanent war economy.'"[9]

The anti-war fervor of the SDS resonated at universities across the country. Hundreds of new SDS chapters were formed when Lyndon Johnson abolished student draft deferments in 1966. The SDS staged draft card burnings and harassed military recruiters.[10] During the 1968 Democratic Convention in Chicago, SDS protestors rioted as a challenge to Hubert Humphrey's support of the war in Vietnam. Hayden and several instigators were arrested. They became celebrated by the Left as the Chicago Seven.

In 1969, the SDS began fragmenting. One of the factions was a group called the Weatherman. The Weatherman advocated launching a race war in the U.S. They eventually morphed into a terrorist cult called the Weather Underground. The Weather Underground orchestrated a series of bombings around the country. This anti-American cult will be studied in Chapter Six, where we meet the Ayers family and explore the influence that veterans of the Weather Underground had on Barack Obama.

Another socialist movement that emerged in the 1960's was called Black Liberation Theology (BLT). This was a radical theology that Black Nationalists embraced. BLT was an amalgamation of Marxist principles, civil rights activism, and Christianity. It was derived from the broader Marxist Liberation Theology movement that was a growing presence in Christian America. James Cone, a professor at Union Theological Seminary, was a strong proponent of BLT. In Chapter Two, we examined the impact that Cone's vitriol had on Barack Obama through his disciple, Jeremiah Wright. Later in this chapter, we will explore the specific impact of Wright's Marxism on Obama.

By the late 1960's, the remnants of the SDS, Saul Alinsky's various legacy organizations, and militant Black Nationalists had found common ground. They share a belief in socialism, support for black civil rights, opposition to the Vietnam War, hatred of capitalism, and disdain for American wealth. Remarkably, this new generation of socialists embraced these viewpoints despite the obvious failures of applied Marxism in the Soviet Union and elsewhere.

As David Horowitz explained in his book, *Unholy Alliance: Radical Islam and the American Left*, the implosion of Soviet Communism and other Marxist states around the globe "ought to have thrown the Left into a profound crisis of faith. It should have caused radicals to rethink their Marxist critiques of democratic capitalism and socialist ideas about the revolutionary future. It should have caused them to reevaluate their opposition to American policy and their support for regimes that had murdered tens of millions and oppressed tens of millions more."[11]

But it didn't. The new generation of socialists ignored the disastrous results of Marxism in action. They simply discounted the real-world examples of the Soviet Union, Cuba, China, East Germany, Albania, North Korea, and an atlas full of other failed socialist countries. Instead, they aligned with other activists, including environmentalists, feminists, black nationalists, radical Islamists, and anyone else opposed to America, capitalism, and Western principles. Perhaps ashamed of the practical failure of Marxism around the world, these radicals camouflaged their support for redistribution of wealth and government control of the economy as "civil rights," "social justice," "change," and "global warming."

None of these will-o'-the-wisps had any practical value unless they could be attached to political power. In the United States, socialism never became a serious political force per se. However, American socialists gradually embraced Saul Alinsky's philosophy that the revolution could only be achieved by co-opting the vast middle class. So, they began collaborating with the progressive wing of the Democratic Party, which was a political force the American middle class had historically embraced. The once venerable Democratic Party was thus gradually hijacked by radicals.

Among the hijackers was Barack Obama, a red-diaper baby in his own right. Let's explore his lifelong involvement with socialism. A professor at the University of Chicago, where Obama was a lecturer, reportedly said that Obama was "…as close to a full-out Marxist as anyone who has ever run for president of the United States."[12] That is a bold statement, especially since a number of other Marxists have run for President. But, as we shall see, it may not be far from the mark.

Obama's father, Barack Hussein Obama, Sr., was a Marxist. In 1965, the *East Africa Journal* published one of his papers titled "Problems Facing Our Socialism."[13] Obama Sr. had at this point returned to Africa and was involved in Kenyan politics. His paper argued that communal ownership of land was better than private property for achieving the desired classless society. He also argued that an extremely progressive tax rate was necessary to avoid concentration of wealth and power.[14] He wrote: "Theoretically, there is nothing that can stop the government from taxing 100 percent of income so long as the people get benefits from the government commensurate with their income which is taxed….What is more important is to find means by which we can redistribute our economic gains to the benefit of all. This is the government's obligation."[15] He demonized corporations and suggested that the government should nationalize foreign businesses operating in Kenya.[16]

Some argue that Barack Obama, Jr. barely knew his father, and therefore wasn't influenced by him. However, Barack Jr.'s first book, *Dreams from My Father*, was precisely *about* his desire to understand the father who abandoned him. He maintained correspondence with his father until Obama Sr. passed away in 1982. Furthermore, Barack Jr. had a curious interest in his father's socialist ambitions in Kenya. When he was a U.S. Senator, he spent time helping Kenyan presidential candidate Raila Odinga achieve power on a platform of Marxism and Islam. Barack Jr. may have felt that a victory by Odinga would bring closure to his father's own aborted political ambitions. Perhaps it is just coincidence, but Obama Sr.'s socialism is consistent with the agenda that Barack Jr. is pushing today as President: demonizing corporations, government takeover of businesses, massive tax increases, and redistribution of wealth. Barack Jr.'s peculiar entanglement with the Marxist Odinga in Kenya will be examined in Chapter Five.

Barack Jr.'s mother, Ann Dunham, was also infatuated with Marxism. Classmates at the University of Hawaii said, "When Dunham arrived in Hawaii, she was a full-fledged radical leftist…."[17] Ann met Barack's father in a Russian language course at the University of Hawaii. At the time, the Soviet Union was the iconic Marxist state in the world, so there is some poetic irony that the language of the communists is what brought Barack's parents together.

Ann's radicalism likely came from her parents. Madelyn Payne Dunham and Stanley Dunham were linked to communist organizations in the U.S. In 1956, when Ann was a teenager, the family moved to Seattle, Washington, which had an active radical community. Ann attended Mercer Island High School, which employed some radical teachers who had been investigated by the House Un-American Activities Committee (HUAC). John Stenhouse, a school board member who was raised in China, told the HUAC that he belonged to the Communist Party USA and that there were other Marxists on Mercer's staff. He was the subject of a 1955 *Time* magazine discussion about his fitness to remain on the Mercer school board.[18] Val Foubert and Jim Wichterman were two of the

Marxist teachers at Mercer. They taught a curriculum that included attacks on Christianity and readings by Karl Marx. The hallway between them was called "anarchy alley."[19]

Wichterman said of Ann: "As much as a high-school student can, she'd question anything: What's so good about democracy? What's so good about capitalism? What's wrong with communism?"[20] Her best friend, Maxine Box, said of Ann: "She touted herself as an atheist….She was always challenging and arguing and comparing. She was already thinking about things that the rest of us hadn't."[21]

In Seattle, the Dunham's attended East Shore Unitarian Church, which was a radical congregation the locals called "the little red church on the hill." According to its website, the church acquired its nickname because of "well-publicized debates and forums on such controversial subjects as the admission of 'Red China' to the United Nations…."[22] Coincidently, Stenhouse was the president of this "church".

Obama was also influenced by a man whom some allege was his *real* father, communist Frank Marshall Davis (1905-1987). Davis, a black anti-capitalist, was a poet and a journalist for various socialist publications. He lived in Chicago for many years, and moved to Honolulu in 1948. When Barack returned from Indonesia to live with his grandparents in Hawaii, Davis established a relationship with him and became his mentor, according to *Dreams from My Father*.

Early in his career, Davis was an executive editor for the *Chicago Star*, the communist newspaper of Chicago.[23] In the mid-1940's, he joined the CPUSA, although he never publicly admitted it. However, a book by Professor John Edgar Tidwell included a letter Davis wrote confirming that he had joined the Communist Party.[24]

In Hawaii, Davis wrote a weekly column called "Frankly Speaking" for the *Honolulu Record*, a labor paper published by the International Longshore and Warehouse Union.[25] One article he wrote in 1950 was titled "Free Enterprise or Socialism?" In it, he speculated that America was at a turning point that might possibly lead to socialism. He wrote: "Before too long, our nation will have to decide whether we shall have free enterprise or socialism…at the present rate, either the giant corporations will control all our markets, the greatest share of our wealth, and eventually, our government, or the government will be forced to intervene with some form of direct regulation of business."[26]

One of Davis's poems is titled, "To the Red Army". Its concluding stanzas read: [27]

Smash on, victory-eating Red warriors!
Show the marveling multitudes
Americans, British, all your allied brothers
How strong you are
How great you are
How your young tree of new unity
Planted twenty-five years ago
Bears today the golden fruit of victory!

Drive on, oh mighty people's juggernaut!
Hear in your winning ears
Shadow songs of your departed comrades
Telling you, "Be avengers and kill our killers"
And when you have struck the last foe to the ground
Then drop their fascist dreams below hell!

The HUAC investigated Davis for his ties to CPUSA, and accused him of involvement in several communist front organizations.[28] For 19 years, he was under FBI investigation.[29] A 1951 report to the Hawaii Legislature pegged him as a CPUSA member.[30] He lived across the street from the University of Hawaii, where Ann Dunham attended college. Between 1975 and 1979, he mentored teenaged Barack, sharing his radical perspectives and his general distrust of the American establishment.

Obama was influenced by this tutelage, because he described in *The Audacity of Hope* how he automatically "slipped into the cant: the point at which the denunciations of capitalism or American imperialism came too easily...and the role of victim was too readily embraced as a means of shedding responsibility...."[31]

Obama left Hawaii in 1979 to attend Occidental College in California. There, he gave his first public speech to protest South African apartheid. The event was organized by the Students for Economic Democracy (SED), the student branch of the socialist Campaign for Economic Democracy (CED). The CED was chaired by Tom Hayden, one of the founders of the SDS.[32] Hayden received information about the rally from organizer David Peck. It is possible that Hayden, given his protest activity and relationships at Columbia University, helped convince Obama to transfer from Occidental to

Columbia in 1981. Hayden may also have introduced Obama to fellow SDS radical Bill Ayers, who went to college only a quarter mile from Columbia.

Dr. John C. Drew, a college professor who knew Obama while he was enrolled at Occidental, also helped organize the anti-apartheid rallies that Obama spoke at. Dr. Drew, a Marxist at the time, met with Obama in December 1980 specifically to discuss Marxism. In a video interview about this meeting, he claimed that Obama embraced Marxism and praised the Soviet Union, describing it as a superior model. He also claimed that Obama believed wealth in America needed to be distributed and that he looked forward to a revolution in America that would overturn the existing structure.[33]

While at Columbia University in New York, Obama went to the Socialist Scholar Conferences sponsored by the Democratic Socialists of America.[34] According to libertarian writer Trevor Loudon, guest speakers at these conferences included "members of the Communist Party USA and its offshoot, the Committees of Correspondence, as well as Maoists, Trotskyites, black radicals, gay activists, and radical feminists."[35] Later, when Obama's half-sister Maya visited Obama in New York, she expressed concern that he'd become "one of those freaks you see on the streets around here," according to *Dreams from My Father*.[36]

Another influence on Obama was Dr. James Cone, a professor at Union Theological Seminary, which is adjacent to, and affiliated with, Columbia University. Cone was a professor at Union while Obama was a student at Columbia. Cone published a book in 1970, *Black Theology of Liberation*, which fueled the Black Liberation Theology (BLT) movement. In it, he wrote: "Insofar as this country is seeking to make whiteness the dominating power throughout the world, whiteness is the symbol of the antichrist....Black theology seeks to analyze the satanic nature of whiteness and by doing so, prepare all nonwhites for revolutionary action."[37]

BLT politicizes the Christian New Testament by teaching that it can only be understood in the context of social activism and Marxist class struggle. BLT's goal is to encourage the poor to revolt and replace capitalism with socialism. If the poor accomplish this, they would become liberated from their material, and therefore their spiritual, deprivations.

Obama essentially embraced BLT by spending two decades at Reverend Wright's Trinity United Church of Christ and donating tens of thousands of dollars to it. The church's website states: "The vision statement of Trinity United Church of Christ is based upon the systematized liberation theology that started in 1969 with the publication of Dr. James Cone's seminal book *Black Power and Black Theology*."[38] During Wright's ministry, TUCC embraced Black Liberation Theology (BLT) as official church doctrine. Jeremiah Wright is considered one of the North American leaders of BLT.

Black Liberation Theology's anti-capitalist tone resonated with the Saul Alinsky activism prevalent in TUCC's local community. TUCC's "10-Point Vision" included "a congregation working towards ECONOMIC PARITY (emphasis in original)" and toward fixing "America's economic mal-distribution!"[39] Wright believed capitalism was inherently unjust. He declared, "Capitalism as made manifest in the 'New World' depended upon slave labor, and it is only maintained by keeping 'Two-Thirds World' under oppression."[40]

Wright launched a signature Marxist rant in September 2009 at an event celebrating a socialist publication called *Monthly Review*. He was introduced by Robert W. McChesney, a co-founder of Free Press, an extremist organization that has been linked to the Obama administration. In an earlier article in the *Monthly Review*, McChesney wrote, "Our job is to make media reform a part of our broader struggle for democracy, social justice, and, dare we say it, socialism."[41]

In his speech, Wright said *Monthly Review* offers "no-nonsense Marxism." He praised the publication, saying, "You dispel all the negative images we have been programmed to conjure up with just the mention of that word socialism or Marxism." He called America the "land of the greed and the home of the slave." He said, "My work with liberation theology, with Latin American theologians, with the Black Theology Project and with the Cuban Council of Churches taught me 30 years ago the importance of Marx and the Marxist analysis of the social realities of the vulnerable and the oppressed who were trying desperately to break free of the political economics undergirded by this country that were choking them and cutting off any hope of a possible future where all of the people would benefit."[42] Obama listened to rants like this from Wright for 20 years.

It is likely that Obama first met Weather Underground terrorist and socialist William Ayers while at Columbia. Ayers took education courses at Bank Street College, which was less than a quarter mile from Columbia, before earning his doctorate at Columbia's Teachers College in 1987. Obama and Ayers had mutual friends. One was Edward Said, a left-wing Columbia professor who taught Obama, according to the *LA Times*. Said wrote this dust-jacket testimonial on Ayers's 2001 Weather Underground memoir, *Fugitive Days:* "What makes *Fugitive Days* unique is its unsparing detail and its marvelous human coherence and integrity. Bill Ayers's America and his family background, his education, his political awakening, his anger and involvement, his anguished re-emergence from the shadows....For anyone who cares about the sorry mess we are in, this book is essential, indeed necessary, reading."[43]

Another likely influence on Obama at Columbia was Sociology Professor Richard A. Cloward, who, along with Frances Fox Piven, helped establish the National Welfare Rights Organization. They proposed to add new burdens on government by encouraging poor people to become dependent on taxpayers. Cloward and Piven's intent was not to help the disadvantaged, but rather to subtly conscript them in an effort to overwhelm and collapse America's capitalist society. When the NWRO eventually disbanded, ex-members formed ACORN, the radical organization that used the Cloward-Piven Strategy to create electoral chaos and to abet America's housing-related financial collapse in 2008. Obama's extensive relationship with the socialists at ACORN will be examined in Chapter Eight.

Obama has refused to release any transcripts or records regarding his activities and associations at Columbia. Both of his books are also surprisingly silent about this period of his life. It is tempting to presume that this is because a thorough airing of his Columbia years would reveal a deep immersion in radical circles that would contradict the synthetic Obama mythos that got him elected to the U.S. Senate and the Presidency.

After Columbia, Obama worked for three years as a community organizer for the Developing Communities Project, an Alinskyite organization. As outlined in the previous chapter, Saul Alinsky was a Chicago Marxist who trained activists in how to agitate for "change", in order to methodically transform America into a socialist nation.

Obama then went to Harvard Law School. After graduating, he worked for Project Vote, a subsidiary of ACORN. He then worked at the law firm of Davis Miner Barnhill & Galland. Judson

IN SHORT

Miner, a name partner in this firm, was a former college classmate and fellow anti-war activist with SDS member and Weather Underground terrorist Bernardine Dohrn.[44]

In 1995, Obama ran for the Illinois State Senate seat that was being vacated by Alice J. Palmer, who was running for the U.S. Congress. Palmer arranged for Obama, her hand-picked successor, to meet potential supporters at the home of Ayers and Dohrn.[45] Palmer also helped him gather signatures to get his name on the ballot. One of the attendees at the party was Dr. Quentin Young, who was a rumored member of the CPUSA and a recipient of the socialist Debs Award.[46][47] He became an Obama supporter and contributor.

Palmer was a socialist. In the 1980's she was a board member of the U.S. Peace Council, which the FBI identified as a front organization of the Communist Party USA and also as an affiliate of the Soviet World Peace Council.[48]

A June 1986 article titled, "An Afro-American Journalist on the USSR" appeared in the Communist Party USA's newspaper *People's Daily World*. The article said Alice Palmer had recently attended the 27th Congress of the Communist Party of the Soviet Union. Here's what Palmer had to say about the event: "The Soviets plan to provide people with higher wages and better education, health, and transportation, while we in our country are hearing that cutbacks are necessary....We Americans can be misled by the major media. We're being told the Soviets are striving to achieve a comparatively low standard of living compared with ours, but actually they have reached a basic stability in meeting their needs and are now planning to double their production."[49]

During his State Senate run, Obama obtained the endorsement of the socialist New Party (NP) in Chicago. According to *New Ground*, the Chicago newsletter of the Democratic Socialists of America (DSA), the New Party endorsement came with a price: "Once approved, candidates must sign a contract with the NP. The contract mandates that they must have a visible and active relationship with the NP."[50]

Not only did Obama have a "visible and active relationship," the New Party claimed him as their candidate on the ballot, even though Obama also ran as a Democrat. In Illinois, candidates could run under the banner of multiple parties on a ballot. The New Party announced after the Democratic primary: "Three NP-members won Democratic primaries last spring and face off against Republican opponents on election day: Danny Davis (U.S. House), Barack

Obama (State Senate) and Patricia Martin (Cook County Judiciary)."[51] [52] After the general election, the *Progressive Populist* magazine reported, "New Party member Barack Obama was uncontested for a State Senate seat from Chicago."[53] [54]

The New Party, self-described as "socialist democratic," was co-founded in 1992 by union activist Sandy Pope and University of Wisconsin Professor Joel Rogers.[55] It used the political strategy of electoral "fusion", nominating candidates from other parties (usually Democrats), so that its candidates could occupy two ballot lines and tally votes cast for both parties. In 1998, the U.S. Supreme Court declared electoral fusion unconstitutional.

The New Party was an alliance of labor unions, Marxist organizations, and black activists. Most of its members came from the Democratic Socialists of America, the Communist Party USA, and ACORN.[56] Cloward-Piven Strategy co-author Frances Fox Piven was a New Party member.[57] Another member was Carl Davidson, who was a leader in the Students for a Democratic Society and a supporter of Obama's State Senate campaign. His declassified FBI file says that he went to Cuba and worked with them to sabotage America's Vietnam War effort.[58] Davidson helped organize the October 2002 anti-war demonstration where Obama made his now-famous speech against the Iraq War.[59] The event was sponsored by the Committees of Correspondence for Democracy and Socialism.[60]

Davidson belonged to a group called Progressives for Obama during the 2008 election.[61] This group included Mark Rudd, who was in the Weather Underground.[62] It included Tom Hayden, the SDS activist who organized riots at the 1968 Democratic Convention in Chicago and whose wife, actress Jane Fonda, collaborated with the Viet Cong during the Vietnam War.[63] It included actor Danny Glover, a supporter of Venezuela's Hugo Chavez.[64] It also included Barbara Ehrenreich, who is an Honorary Chairwoman of the Democratic Socialists of America.[65]

Other socialist supporters of Obama included William Ayers and Bernardine Dohrn. As recently as 2007, these former terrorists from the SDS and the Weather Underground publicly praised communist heroes and described America as a monster. The socialist pedigree of these two radicals will be examined in greater detail in Chapter Six.

Another socialist supporter of Obama was Mike Klonsky, a former chairman of the SDS. In 1971, his SDS splinter group formed a pro-Chinese sect called the October League, which morphed into the Communist Party (Marxist-Leninist).[66] In 1977, he was one of the first westerners to visit the People's Republic of China. Chinese leaders recognized Klonsky's group as the semi-official U.S. Maoist party.[67]

When Obama chaired the Chicago Annenberg Challenge, he earmarked over $1 million for a group founded by Ayers and run by Klonsky called the Small Schools Workshop.[68] Ayers, Obama, and Klonsky shared office space during the mid-to-late 1990's while they collaborated on various projects. Klonsky maintained a blog on Obama's MyBarackObama.com until June 2008. His blog "disappeared" after Obama's presidential campaign turned toward the political center when the Democratic primaries were over.[69] Klonsky, whose parents were members of the CPUSA, said in 2007, "I was born into the Communist Party."[70]

When Obama ran for the U.S. Senate in 2004, he hired David Axelrod as his campaign advisor. Axelrod's mother, Myril, was a writer in New York City from 1940 to 1948 for *PM*, a leftist tabloid that featured a number of writers involved in the Communist Party.[71] *PM* was financed by Marshall Field III, who helped underwrite Alinsky's Industrial Areas Foundation, where Obama was trained to be a community organizer.[72]

The Democratic Socialists of America (DSA) supported at least two of Obama's political campaigns. The DSA described itself as "the principal U.S. affiliate of the Socialist International."[73] The DSA boilerplate reads: "We are socialists because we reject an international economic order sustained by private profit, alienated labor, race and gender discrimination, environmental destruction, and brutality and violence in defense of the status quo....To achieve a more just society, many structures of our government and economy must be radically transformed...."[74][75]

The DSA endorsed Obama for his 1996 State Senate campaign.[76] It also endorsed him for the Presidency in 2008 and provided campaign workers. Here is their official 2008 endorsement: "While recognizing the critical limitations of the Obama candidacy and the American political system, DSA believes that the possible election of Senator Obama to the presidency in November represents a potential opening for social and labor movements to generate the political momentum necessary to implement a progressive political agenda."[77]

The DSA's collectivist agenda includes "massive redistribution of income from corporations and the wealthy to wage earners and the poor and the public sector....Free markets or private charity cannot provide adequate public goods and services."[78] According to the DSA: "Like our friends and allies in the feminist, labor, civil rights, religious, and community organizing movements, many of us have been active in the Democratic Party. We work with those movements to strengthen the party's left wing, represented by the Congressional Progressive Caucus."[79]

In 1999, *World Net Daily (WND)* exposed the DSA's direct link with the U.S. Congressional Progressive Caucus, which included roughly 33% of all House Democrats.[80] Until 1999, the DSA hosted the website of the Congressional Progressive Caucus. After the *WND* revelation, the DSA edited its website, removing the links between the two organizations. It also removed some rather damning song lyrics that espoused hard-core Marxist thoughts.

The Communist Party USA (CPUSA) also endorsed Obama in 2008: "A broad multiclass, multiracial movement is converging around Obama's 'Hope, change, and unity' campaign because they see in it the thrilling opportunity to end 30 years of ultra-right rule and move our nation forward with a broadly progressive agenda. This diverse movement combines a variety of political currents and aims in a working coalition that is crucial to social progress at this point....The struggle to defeat the ultra-right and turn our country on a positive path will not end with Obama's election. But that step will shift the ground for successful struggles going forward."[81]

Frank Chapman, a CPUSA supporter, wrote a letter to the party newspaper celebrating an Obama victory in 2008: "Obama's victory was more than a progressive move; it was a dialectical leap ushering in a qualitatively new era of struggle. Marx once compared revolutionary struggle with the work of the mole, who sometimes burrows so far beneath the ground that he leaves no trace of his movement on the surface. This is the old revolutionary 'mole', not only showing his traces on the surface but also breaking through."[82]

The following table, adapted from a compilation by Jim Simpson on the American Daughter website, compares the positions of Obama, the CPUSA, and the DSA on key issues contested in the 2008 Presidential election:[83]

Issue	CPUSA Positions	DSA Positions	Obama Positions
Financial Crisis	-Nationalize Banks -Moratorium on Foreclosures -Extend Unemployment Benefits	-Reregulate financial institutions.	-Reregulate financial institutions -Low income tax "cuts" -Huge public works programs
Environment	-Massive public works -Renewable energy -Ratify Kyoto	-"Green" jobs investment -Massive public works -Renewable energy -Ratify Kyoto	"-Green" jobs -Massive public works -Renewable energy -Re-engage on Kyoto
Unions	-Enact Employee Free Choice Act -Renegotiate NAFTA	-Enact Employee Free Choice Act -Renegotiate NAFTA	-Enact Employee Free Choice Act -Renegotiate NAFTA
Fairness Doctrine	-Reimpose	-Reimpose	-Supports local "diversity"
Healthcare	-Universal Single-Payer Insurance	Universal Single-Payer Insurance	-Single-Payer insurance and tax credits
Immigration	-Amnesty -No guest worker program -No border security enhancements	Amnesty -No guest worker program -No border security enhancements	-Amnesty -Driver's licenses for illegals -Silent on guest worker -Increase border patrol and technology

Voting	-Public finance of elections -same day registrations -felons vote	-Public finance of elections	-Public finance of elections – except his -same day registrations -felons vote
Foreign policy	-Withdrawal from Iraq -Abolish nuclear weapons -Massive defense cuts -Strengthen UN	-Withdrawal from Iraq -Abolish nuclear weapons -Massive defense cuts -Strengthen UN	-Withdrawal from Iraq -Abolish nuclear weapons -Massive defense cuts -Strengthen UN
Taxes	-Increase rates on top income levels -Remove SS cap -Global tax	-Increase rates on top income levels -Remove SS cap -Global tax	-Increase rates on top income levels -Increase SS on top income levels -Global tax

While there are some differences, this table makes it clear why both Marxist organizations chose to endorse Obama.

Rogue financier George Soros, a major supporter of quasi-socialist organizations, backed Obama for his U.S. Senate seat and the Presidency. Soros's right hand man, Aryeh Neier, is president of Soros's Open Society Institute and the Soros Foundation Network. Earlier in his career, Neier was the director of the socialist League for Industrial Democracy. He also worked with Tom Hayden and others to found the Students for a Democratic Society in 1959. We will explore the massive involvement of Soros and Neier in Obama's political career in Chapter Nine.

Obama formed a Black Advisory Council to support his 2008 presidential run. Cornel West, a Marxist professor from Princeton, was a member. West was a member of the Democratic Socialists of America, an admirer of Jeremiah Wright, and an advocate of the Black Liberation Theology of James Cone.[84] West once said: "Free-market fundamentalism trivializes the concern for public interest. It puts fear and insecurity in the hearts of anxiety-ridden workers. It also makes money-driven, poll-obsessed elected officials deferential to corporate goals of profit—often at the cost of the common good."[85]

Obama selected Reverend Jim Wallis to oversee drafting of the party's platform at the 2008 Democratic national convention.[86] Wallis is a Marxist Liberation Theologian whom Obama calls a "good friend."[87] Like Obama, he got his start with community organizing in Chicago. Wallis once called the U.S. "the great power, the great seducer, the great captor and destroyer of human life, the great master of humanity and history in its totalitarian claims and designs."[88]

Obama's lifelong immersion in socialism is driving him to replace free and independent citizens with government servants as the foundation of American society. Here's what he told graduating students at the University of Notre Dame in May 2009: "Make it (service) a way of life. Because when you serve, it doesn't just improve your community, it makes you a part of your community….If nothing else, that knowledge should give us faith that through our collective labor…and our willingness to shoulder each other's burdens, America will continue on its precious journey towards that more perfect union."[89] Obama has suckled off from the public teat almost his entire career. Because of his Marxist parents, mentors, and associates, he has essentially lived a socialist life. So, we should not be surprised that his vision of a "more perfect union" is collectivist in nature. Collectivism is all that he knows.

Obama and the radicals in charge of our government are leading us to a statist existence founded on servitude and dependency fit for helpless children rather than self-sufficient adults. Humorist P.J. O'Rourke once said, "It takes a village to raise a child. The government is the village, and you're the child."[90] Chapter Ten provides a detailed assessment of Obama's policies and how they are leading us to a sheltered existence of childlike dependence on Washington in a socialist America.

Obama and the radicals in Washington demonize the private sector and laud the public sector. In a *Time* magazine article, Obama confessed that he questioned "the idolatry of the free market."[91] The radicals are punishing successful individuals and businesses by stealing their wealth and transferring it to failing enterprises and irresponsible individuals. They believe that private property is a vice, and that theft of it by the collective is a virtue. They believe that individual rights protected by a constitution are selfish, and that group rights protected by special interest coercion in Washington are morally superior. They believe that government bureaucrats are somehow smarter than the rest of us, and magically know better what is good for us. In other words, Obama and the radicals in charge of our government are socialists.

Socialism has been a catastrophic failure wherever it has been tried. Marxist governments yield nothing but millions of murdered citizens, poverty, deprivation, and Big Brother control of private lives. Once the state becomes the guarantor of your basic needs, it eventually becomes the regulator of your behavior and the rationing agent of scarce resources. Once the state becomes the Master, you are by definition the Slave. Once you cede your political independence in favor of government succor, you cede protection from all assaults on your wealth and freedom.

After Cuba's communist revolution, its economy collapsed from being one of the best in Latin America to being one of the worst. After the Soviet Union's revolution, tens of millions of peasants starved to death. Similar tragedies occurred in other countries that embraced Marxism, such as China, Vietnam, Cambodia, Ethiopia, Angola, Zimbabwe, Zambia, Congo, Nicaragua, and Venezuela. These social disasters are well-documented in other sources, and interested readers are invited to study them.

However, there is one particular story that is worthy of further discussion here. The remarkable clarity of this story cuts through the propaganda of both sides in the debate between capitalists and socialists, who both vigorously defend their respective philosophies. Each side has clever arguments explaining why the other side is illogical, why the other side is basing their arguments on faulty assumptions, and why the other side's data is flawed or misrepresented. For many in the middle class, this centuries-long argument is confusing and overwhelming. Thus, it is not surprising that the political leanings of the middle class have been recently skewed by tantalizing social programs offered by charismatic radical leaders like Obama. In times of stress, people naturally reach for their security blankets and dip into the cookie jar for comfort food. Socialism is a gingerbread house on a societal scale.

Fortunately, the effects of socialism and capitalism can be compared side-by-side under almost identical circumstances. Two countries offer a clear, objective, and unmistakable comparison

Great Comparison

between the two philosophies. These two countries are the perfect politico-economic laboratories.

During WWII, Germany was completely devastated by Allied forces. Its infrastructure was bombed to smithereens, it had lost nearly a whole generation in deadly warfare, it was financially ruined, its social systems were in chaotic disarray, and it was considered an international pariah. From this brutal concoction, two separate countries were carved out after the war ended: East Germany, based on socialism, and West Germany, based on capitalism.

Each of the newly created countries had the same starting point in this laboratory experiment. East and West Germany were formed from the exact same culture, the exact same ethnicity, the exact same average level of education, the exact same wealth and resources, the exact same geography and climate, at the exact same time. The only difference was their political and economic systems. So, let's flash forward four decades, to just before the Berlin Wall came down, to examine the results of the experiment.

Socialist East Germany's lab results were tragic. By all measures, East Germany had not progressed much beyond their disastrous starting point. Their standard of living had fallen well below European standards, their education system was focused more on indoctrination than on development, their environment was filthy, their citizens were hounded by secret service spies, and their national spirit was in shambles. Perhaps the most telling scorecard of all was that the East German government had to build a wall to entrap its own citizens and prevent them from fleeing the horrors of applied socialism.

Capitalist West Germany's lab results were spectacular. From the rubble of war and the chaos of a destroyed nation, the capitalist society of West Germany yielded a wealthy, satisfied culture that can be considered the envy of most of the world. West German products were desired by consumers around the globe, its standard of living was the highest in Europe, its citizens were among the freest on earth, and its schools and universities were internationally recognized. Perhaps the most telling scorecard of all was that East Germans would occasionally risk their lives by dodging sniper fire, climbing through the razor wire atop the Berlin Wall, and leaping to the Western side. Socialist countries theorize about paradise on earth. Capitalist countries actually create it.

The German experience is a dramatic real-world demonstration of the superiority of a system based on individual rights, individual responsibility and free markets, over a system based on government rights, communal responsibility, and state-controlled economy. The beauty of the German example is that you don't even need to know economics or political philosophy in order to understand the message. You just need to be able to visualize a destitute, frightened East German risking his life to get from one side of the Berlin Wall to the other. There is no more powerful or visceral understanding to be had. An identical story can be told about North and South Korea, if readers are interested in studying another real-world laboratory comparison between socialism and capitalism.

If you are wondering how the middle class fared in East Germany and North Korea, the answer is chilling: Neither country had one. There won't be a middle class in a socialist America, either. Marxist economies don't have middle classes. As Vladimir Lenin put it, "The way to crush the bourgeoisie (middle class) is to grind them between the millstones of taxation and inflation."[92] The Marxists do not even approve of private property. According to Lenin, "The goal of socialism is communism. The theory of communism may be summed up in one sentence: Abolish all private property." [93] This leads to the end game of Marxism. When you don't own your own income, and when you don't own your own home or property, you do not own yourself. The state owns you. And it's all downhill from there.

The reasons for the repeated failures of Marxism are obvious. As David Horowitz explained, socialism "provided no rational method for allocating resources and no effective work incentives, and no guarantees of individual rights."[94] It simply doesn't work, and when it fails, it takes whole civilizations down with it. The "equality" that socialism promises does not mean everyone ends up being equally wealthy. It means everyone ends up being equally poor, except for those special apparatchiks working for the government who mysteriously are more equal than everyone else, and who mysteriously have access to resources and privileges that the rest do not. Instead of a middle class, there will only be a massive class of state dependents standing in long lines waiting for rationed resources that everyone has lost the will and the means to produce. Shepherding these long lines and orchestrating the rationing will be those government elites who strangely don't have to stand in a line.

The good news is that almost all former socialist countries, whether full-fledged socialist nations like Russia, China, and the countries of Eastern Europe, or the moderately socialist nations in Western Europe, have all realized that socialism is flawed. They are shifting back toward capitalism and electing more conservative leaders. The bad news is that we in America have not yet learned their lessons. Given the results of the 2008 elections, we seem determined to learn them the hard way. We will regret electing the radicals, not just as the four-year mistake of a disastrous presidential term or the six-year mistake of a disastrous Senate term, but as the multi-generational mistake of a disastrous shift in the direction of our society.

The Democratic Party is no longer the party of Johnson and Kennedy looking out for the common working American. It is now the party of Alinsky and Soros and a host of other socialists. It is now the party of wealth redistribution, government-run health care, government-controlled industries, centralized bureaucracy, and anti-free market zealots. It is now the party of chronic dependents, radicals, illegal immigrants, and victims who are not invested in the American dream and who are not interested in being responsible for producing it. It is now the party of bailing out Wall Street, automotive companies, and other corporate welfare gluttons.

It is time for middle-class Democrats to recognize that their party is not what it used to be. The venerable Democratic Party of years gone by is dead. Likewise, the venerable Republican Party also appears to be mortally afflicted with the same collectivist disease. The Republicans have been only slightly less inclined than the Democrats to increase government spending and broaden social entitlement programs. As a result, we are left with an increasingly socialistic government propped up by two feckless political parties that masquerade as champions of the middle class, but in fact are devouring it.

There is nothing middle class about the anti-capitalist sermons that Obama heard from Jeremiah Wright for 20 years, nor the anti-capitalist philosophies he absorbed from the rest of his socialist mentors throughout his life. Perhaps it is even fair to say that there is nothing American about Obama's worldview, either. To Obama, the America that the rest of us live in is an unwelcome place of strange disproportion on the opposite side of his collectivist looking glass. The America of free and independent citizens guided by a Constitution that protects inalienable rights and strictly limits government is a universe altogether unlike Obama's purple-skied world of racial angst, economic injustice, redistribution of wealth, and Big Government.

Sam Webb, the leader of the Communist Party USA, wrote of Obama: "We now have not simply a friend, but a people's advocate in the White House."[95] Unfortunately, "the people's advocate in the White House" is not a friend of the middle class, but rather an ally of parasites looking to sink their teeth into the middle class.

In closing, here are two pearls of wisdom for the middle class from Barack Obama. First pearl: According to Pennsylvania Governor Ed Rendell, Obama told him, "We don't need the people. We just need the checks."[96] Translation: "As Saul Alinsky trained us, middle-class people are just pawns to be used for achieving socialism by the ballot box. Once they vote us into power, taking their money is all we care about." Second pearl: Obama, who was explaining to self-employed Joe "the Plumber" Wurzelbacher why Joe must pay higher taxes for everyone else's benefit: "I think when you spread the wealth around it's good for everybody."[97] Translation: "We're going to take your wealth and spread it around to the underclass of America and to Wall Street bankers. That'll be good for everybody but you."

Hey you, in the middle class…are you listening?

We've been had.

Chapter Five

Meet Radical Islam and Black Nationalism

> *"To be clear, Senator Obama has never been a Muslim, was not raised a Muslim, and is a committed Christian."*[1]
>
> Obama campaign statement, January 24, 2007

The mainstream media was so committed to electing Obama President that the most glaring falsehoods were glossed over. Contrary to Obama's campaign statement referenced above, he was in fact born a Muslim. He was in fact raised a Muslim. This chapter will document that his entire life has been immersed in personal and political relationships with Islamic radicals and Black Nationalists. It will show that his professed Christianity is a political expedient, not a core philosophy. It will also examine his executive decisions in the first year of his presidency. His decisions reflect a fundamental bias toward Islamic interests internationally and Black Nationalist interests domestically.

We will begin with a brief history of Black Nationalism and radical Islam. We will then establish Obama's ideological affinity and lifelong association with these movements.

Black Nationalism was nurtured in the U.S. by the Nation of Islam. The NOI was founded in Michigan by Wallace D. Fard Muhammad in 1930. Their main religious belief is that Allah is the only God. Their main political belief is that African-Americans are victims of systemic white oppression.

One of Fard's first disciples was Elijah Muhammad, who led the NOI from 1935 through 1975. Elijah believed African-Americans were "born righteous and turned to unrighteousness," and whites were "made unrighteous by the god who made them."[2] The NOI believed blacks were the first people on Earth, and that they had been conned out of their power by white supremacists.

Black Nationalism was popularized by Malcolm X, who was born Malcolm Little in 1925. His father died when he was a teenager, and his mother was confined to a mental institution. After living in foster homes, he consorted with criminals in Boston and New York. In 1946, he went to prison, where he joined the Nation of Islam. After his release in 1952, he connected with Elijah Muhammad and became a spokesperson for the NOI. For more than a decade, he was the Nation of Islam's most visible advocate.

Malcolm X leveraged the media to spread the NOI's message across America. He was a powerful orator who energized audiences on college campuses. He became noted for his inflammatory pronouncements. He said that nonviolence was the "philosophy of the fool."[3] He even derided Martin Luther King, the icon of the civil rights movement, by saying, "While King was having a dream, the rest of us Negroes are having a nightmare."[4] He called for a "black revolution."[5] He warned there "would be bloodshed" if racism persisted.[6] He said Islam was the "true religion of black mankind" and "Christianity was the white man's religion."[7] He wrote, "We're not Americans, we're Africans who happen to be in America. We were kidnapped and brought here against our will from Africa."[8]

In 1963, the Nation of Islam muzzled Malcolm X, allegedly because he likened President Kennedy's assassination to "chickens coming home to roost."[9] He left the NOI in 1964. Also that year, he traveled to Africa and the Middle East, where he made a pilgrimage to Mecca.

During his travels, Malcolm X encountered Muslims who professed a more peaceful version of Islam. This inspired him to reject the divisive racial agitation preached by the NOI. When he returned to America, he announced his conversion to orthodox Islam. In 1965, he was assassinated, allegedly by a group of NOI members. Shortly afterward, Elijah Muhammad said that "Malcolm X got just what he preached."[10]

When Elijah Muhammad died in 1975, the Nation of Islam was dissolved. It was reconstituted by Louis Farrakhan in 1978 and it returned to its radical roots. As an example of this radicalism, Dr. Abdul Muhammad, head of the NOI mosque in Washington, said in 1992: "Everybody has to die some time, don't they? So why shouldn't your slave master die now? They got to die anyhow! If you're white today, it ain't worth living anyhow. Would you shoot a dog and put it out of its misery? Or a horse? Well, certainly white people is equal to dogs and horses."[11]

Another militant group that advocated Black Nationalism was the Marxist Black Panther Party, formed in 1966 by Bobby Seale and Huey Newton. The Black Panthers' *Ten Point Program* included demands for free health care, an immediate end to all wars of aggression, an end to the robbery by capitalists, educational programs that expose American decadence, and release of all African-Americans from prison.[12]   The group also advocated violent revolution and payment of reparations to African-Americans.   J. Edgar Hoover called the Black Panthers "the greatest threat to the internal security of the country."[13]

While Black Nationalism was taking root in America, Islamic radicalism was erupting around the world. A major catalyst for this was Israel's creation after WWII. The state of Israel was established by the victorious Allied powers on land that belonged to the Ottoman Turks for the previous 400 years.[14] This was part of a broader Allied effort to redraw national boundaries in the Middle East after the war.[15] Several other countries were also created out of the remnants of the Ottoman Empire, including Jordan and Iraq.[16]

Islamic Arabs in the Middle East were vehemently opposed to the creation of an Israeli state in their midst. But, since they had supported the defeated Axis powers during the war, they had little political influence. So, they launched a war against Israel in 1948.[17] Arabs and Palestinians refer to the creation of Israel as the "Catastrophe."[18] Egyptian dictator Gamal Abdel Nasser declared, "The existence of Israel is in itself an aggression."[19]   Such intransigence has translated into an Islamic Arab refusal to accept any Middle East solution that does not include Israel's demise.

The 1948 war never formally ended.[20] In 1964, the Palestine Liberation Organization (PLO) was created by Palestinian refugees, in order to continue the conflict with Israel. Yasser Arafat became the chairman of the PLO in 1968. Arafat, an Egyptian, was trained by the radical Egyptian Muslim Brotherhood.

The Muslim Brotherhood was founded in 1928 to establish the Qur'an as the "sole reference point for…ordering the life of the Muslim family, individual, community…and state."[21] Sayyid Qutb, author of *Social Justice in Islam*, had a major impact on the movement.[22] According to David Horowitz, his writings "have been described as the 'main ideological influence' on the emerging radical Islamic movement, including its principal leaders, the Ayatollah Khomeini and Osama bin Laden, and its terrorist organizations— Hizbollah, Hamas, and al-Qaeda."[23]

According to Horowitz, "In 1948, the Egyptian Ministry of Education sent Qutb on a study mission to the United States, which he came to regard as the embodiment of worldly decadence, the *distruction*

antithesis of the purified Islamic state clerical radicals like himself were seeking to achieve."[24] America, a capitalistic, secular superpower that constitutionally separated church from state, stood in the way of the mission of the Egyptian radicals to impose Islamic law on the entire world.[25] Thus, Islamic radicals identified the U.S. as "The Great Satan."[26] Their hatred of America was partly ideological, and partly a practical result of American support for the Israeli state and secular leaders in the region, such as the Shah of Iran.[27]

In 1979, the Ayatollah Khomeini overthrew the Shah of Iran and installed an Islamic government.[28] Iran began exporting their revolution by sponsoring Hezbollah, an Islamic terrorist organization. Hezbollah collaborated with the PLO and the Syrians to destroy Lebanon's democracy, thereby opening a northern front against Israel.[29]

When the Soviets invaded Afghanistan in 1979, the resistance by Islamic forces attracted militants from throughout the Arab Middle East. The militants included Osama bin Laden, a Saudi converted to radical Islam by the Muslim Brotherhood. His al-Qaeda terror network was born during this war.[30]

A Hezbollah suicide bombing in Lebanon killed 243 U.S. Marines in 1983. When the Marines withdrew without retaliating, bin Laden sensed weakness.[31] In 1998, he told reporter John Miller: "We have seen in the last decade the decline of the American government and the weakness of the American soldier, who is ready to wage cold wars and unprepared to fight long wars. This was proven in Beirut when the Marines fled after two explosions."[32]

The Muslim Brotherhood drafted an internal 1991 memorandum that described its efforts against the U.S. as "a kind of grand jihad in eliminating and destroying the Western civilization from within and 'sabotaging' its miserable house by their hands and the hands of the believers so that it is eliminated and Allah's religion is made victorious over all other religions."[33]

In 1993, Islamic terrorists detonated a bomb underneath the World Trade Center in New York, in an attempt to topple the twin towers. Six people were killed, and over 1,000 were injured. The terrorists were traced to an al-Qaeda cell.

In 1996, leaders of the Islamic jihad movement issued a manifesto calling on all Muslims to expel Jews and Christians from the two holy Islamic sites in Saudi Arabia, and authorizing Muslims to kill Americans.[34] These Islamic jihad leaders included Osama bin Laden and Ayman al-Zawahiri. In 1998, al-Qaeda issued a Fatwa that declared, "We—with God's help—call on every Muslim who believes in God and wishes to be rewarded to comply with God's order to kill the Americans and plunder their money wherever and whenever they find it."[35]

In 2000, Yasser Arafat and the Palestinians abandoned peace talks at Camp David and unconditionally rejected a plan to establish a Palestinian state.[36] Two months later, Arafat escalated the war against Israel.[37]

On September 11, 2001, the World Trade Center was attacked again by radical Islamists in hijacked airplanes. This time, the towers collapsed. As a result of this attack and others on the same day, 2,977 American civilians were murdered. The attackers were traced to al-Qaeda cells.

Hamas, a terrorist organization created by the Muslim Brotherhood, issued an "Open Letter to America" explaining the reasons for the attacks: "You will face the mirror of your history for a long time to come. Thus you will be able to see exactly how much you have oppressed, how corrupt you are, how you have sinned— how many entities you have destroyed, how many kingdoms you have demolished! America, Oh sword of oppression, arrogance, and sin...Do you remember how the blacks lived under your wing?....Your white son bound their necks with the fetters of slavery, after hunting them in the jungles and on the coasts of Africa....Have you asked yourself about your actions against your 'original' inhabitants, the Indians, the Apaches? Your white feet crushed them and then used their name, Apache, for a helicopter bearing death, demolition, and destruction for anyone with rights who dared to whisper in his own ear that he has those rights....We stand in line and beg Allah to give you to drink from the cup of humiliation—and behold, heaven has answered."[38]

Since the attacks, the United States has waged an overt and covert war against Islamic terrorism. Military campaigns have been carried out against states that harbored terrorists, including Afghanistan and Iraq. Al-Qaeda has carried out additional attacks against American and Western targets worldwide. The centuries-old conflict between Islam and the West continues to this day.

Barack Obama's involvement with Black Nationalism and radical Islam *cannot* be summarized in the dishonest and dismissive way the Obama campaign attempted in 2007. Let's examine the detail of his lifelong involvement with these extremist anti-American ideologies.

Barack Hussein Obama Jr. was born a Muslim. His father was a Muslim; therefore, Obama was Muslim by birth, according to Islamic law.[39] "Barack" is an Arabic name, and "Hussein" is a common Muslim name.[40] Some of Barack Jr.'s siblings were Muslims.[41] Libyan dictator Muammar Qaddafi called Obama "a Muslim."[42] *Al-Jazeera,* an Arabic media outlet, said, "Obama may not want to be counted as a Muslim but Muslims are eager to count him as one of their own."[43]

Barack Jr.'s father was raised as a Muslim, according to Obama Sr.'s brother Sayid.[44] Obama Sr. came to America on a scholarship paid jointly by the Kenyan government and the Laubach Literacy Institute (LLI).[45] LLI's Pan-African philosophy was embraced by Malcolm X and the Nation of Islam. It was also preached at Reverend Wright's Trinity Church in Chicago.[46]

Barack Jr.'s stepfather, Lolo Soetoro, was a Muslim.[47] When Lolo returned to Indonesia in 1967, he took young Barack and his mother with him. Indonesia is the world's largest Muslim nation. In January 1968, Barack entered Franciscus Assisi Primary School in Jakarta. He was registered under his adoptive name, Barry Soetoro.[48] School documents listed his citizenship as Indonesian and his religion as Islam.[49]

Maya Soetoro-Ng, Barack's Indonesian-born half-sister, said in an April 2007 *New York Times* interview: "My whole family was Muslim, and most of the people I knew were Muslim."[50] Observers recalled that Lolo and Barack attended a prayer room called Musholla Al-Rahman for Friday prayers.[51] In a February 2007 interview with the *New York Times*, Obama said the Muslim call to prayer was "one of the prettiest sounds on Earth at sunset."[52] During the interview, he recited it "with a first-class (Arabic) accent."[53]

> Allah is supreme!
> Allah is supreme!
> Allah is supreme! Allah is supreme!
> I witness that there is no god but Allah
> I witness that there is no god but Allah
> I witness that Muhammad is his prophet....[54]

After three years at Franciscus Assisi, Obama transferred to Sekolah Dasar Negeri Besuki Primary School and was again registered as a Muslim.[55] He studied there for two years. Classmate Emirsyah Satar, now CEO of Garuda Indonesia, said, "He (Obama) was often in the prayer room wearing a 'sarong', at that time."[56] Classmate Rony Amiris, now a bank manager in Jakarta, said, "We previously often asked him (Barry) to the prayer room close to the house. If he was wearing a sarong, he looked funny."[57]

According to Tine Hahiyary, principal of Sekolah Dasar Negeri Besuki Primary School at the time, Obama participated in government-mandated Islamic religious lessons.[58] This included reading and writing Arabic, reciting from the Qur'an, and studying Islamic law. Hahiyary recalled Obama studied "mengaji", which involves reciting the Qur'an in Arabic.[59] Perhaps this mandated study prompted Obama's curious mention of "57 states" during the 2008 campaign.[60] There are 57 member states in the Organization of the Islamic Conference. It might also explain why Obama inadvertently referred to his "Muslim faith" during an interview.[61] The interviewer had to prompt him to correct himself and say "Christian faith."

It is questionable how strongly Obama embraces the Christianity he currently professes, based on a mocking quote in *The Audacity of Hope*: "Which passages of scripture should guide our public policy? Should we go with Leviticus, which suggests slavery is all right and eating shell fish is an abomination? How about Deuteronomy, which suggests stoning your child if he strays from the faith? Or should we just stick to the Sermon on the Mount—a passage so radical that it's doubtful that our Defense Department would survive its application?"[62]

When the marriage between Ann Dunham and Lolo Soetoro fell apart in 1971, Barack was sent back to Hawaii to live with his grandparents. He spent his adolescence at the elite Punahou college preparatory school. In *Dreams from My Father,* Obama described his years at Punahou as a period of growing racial sensitivity and victimhood. He wrote that he sought refuge in drugs and the writings of extreme Black Nationalists such as Malcolm X and Frantz Fanon.[63] [64] Here is how Fanon described America: "Two centuries ago, a former European colony decided to catch up with Europe. It succeeded so well that the United States of America became a monster, in which the taints, the sickness, and the inhumanity of Europe have grown to appalling dimensions."[65]

Obama wrote in his memoir that he had more affinity with Malcolm X than other black civil rights activists: "Only Malcolm X's autobiography seemed to offer something different. His repeated acts of self-creation spoke to me; the blunt poetry of his words, his unadorned insistence on respect, promised a new and uncompromising order, martial in its discipline, forged through sheer force of will….And yet, even as I imagined myself following Malcolm's call, one line in the book stayed with me. He spoke of a wish he'd once had, the wish that the white blood that ran through him, there by an act of violence, might somehow be expunged."[66]

Before leaving Punahou for Occidental College, Obama's mentor, Frank Marshall Davis, told him that college represented "an advanced degree in compromise." He said that the price of admission was "Leaving your race at the door. Leaving your people behind. Understand something, boy. You're not going to college to get educated. You're going there to get trained….They'll train you to manipulate words so that they don't mean anything anymore….They'll train you so good, you'll start believing what they tell you about equal opportunity and the American way and all that shit…they'll yank on your chain and let you know that you may be a well-trained, well-paid nigger, but you're a nigger just the same."[67]

It is not surprising, given his Muslim upbringing in Indonesia, and his fascination with Malcolm X, that Obama had many Islamic friends in his teens and his twenties. Two of them, Mohammed Hasan Chandoo and Wahid Hamid, were wealthy Pakistanis.[68] Chandoo later operated a radical anti-Semitic website (chandoo.com). Hamid and Chandoo both contributed $2,300 to Obama's presidential campaign and were listed on his website as being two of his most active fundraisers.[69]

In 1981, Obama transferred from Occidental to Columbia. During the intervening summer, he traveled with Hamid and Chandoo to Pakistan.[70] He stayed with Chandoo's family while he was in Karachi.[71] Obama began this trip by visiting his mother and half-sister Maya in Indonesia. It is curious how a poor student, transferring from one expensive private college to another, could afford such extensive worldwide travel. It is even more curious that he did not mention this exotic trip in his memoir.

Obama returned to America to attend Columbia University in New York. According to his memoir, he met up with the only man he knew there, a drug-addicted Pakistani immigrant named Sohale Siddiqi ("Sadik"). Sadik was a friend of Hamid and Chandoo. Obama and Sadik became roommates in an apartment on East 94th Street.[72]

In New York, Obama encountered many Black Nationalists and radical Islamists. For example, he wrote in his memoir, "In search of some inspiration, I went to hear Kwame Toure…."[73] Toure was Prime Minister of the Black Panther Party and was involved with the PLO and NOI. According to the *LA Times,* one of Obama's instructors at Columbia was Professor Edward Said, who was noted for cavorting with Hezbollah terrorists, throwing rocks at Israelis, and being an official apologist for the PLO.[74] Said was called the "Professor of Terror" by the magazine *Commentary.*[75] In May 1998, Barack and Michelle were photographed sitting with Edward Said and his wife Miriam at an Arab American community dinner.[76]

After graduating from Columbia, Obama moved to Chicago, which he described as "the capital of the African-American community in the country."[77] Chicago was the base for Jesse Jackson's presidential campaigns and it was the headquarters of the Nation of Islam. Harold Washington had recently become the city's first African-American mayor.

After three years of community organizing work in African-American neighborhoods in Chicago, Obama decided to pursue a law degree. The popular mythology is that he was an academic wizard destined for coronation at Harvard as the President of the *Harvard Law Review.* The real back story, however, is not quite so uplifting. It is laced with unseemly relationships and implied quid pro quos that are unsettling.

Obama did not do well enough at Columbia to justify admission to Harvard. He graduated in 1983 with a Political Science degree, but without honors.[78] The details of his academic record there remain a secret. The *New York Times* reported that "he declined repeated requests to talk about his New York years, release his Columbia transcript or identify even a single fellow student, co-worker, roommate or friend from those years."[79] Surprisingly, after a five-year hiatus from an apparently undistinguished academic career at Columbia, Obama somehow landed at Harvard Law School.

Harvard Law School is exceptionally difficult to get into. Thousands of highly qualified applicants scramble for a limited number of openings. If Obama's test scores and grades merited admission, we would know about them from sycophants eager to validate his purported status as the "the smartest guy ever to become president."[80] However, his test scores and grades have never been released.

So, how did Obama get into Harvard with his pedestrian academic record? Enter Dr. Khalid al-Mansour, a friend of Obama's radical instructor at Columbia, Edward Said. Al-Mansour, formerly Don Warden, was a radical Muslim who changed his name after converting to Islam. In one of his speeches he declared, "White people don't feel bad, whatever you do to them, they deserve it, God wants you to do it and that's when you cut out the nose, cut out the ears, take flesh out of their body, don't worry because God wants you to do it."[81] One of his books was titled *The Destruction of Western Civilization as Seen through Islam*. Al-Mansour said he "longs for the day when Islam takes over the world."[82]

Al-Mansour was well-connected. He was a friend of Louis Farrakhan, the leader of the Nation of Islam. As a lawyer, he represented OPEC in a famous 1981 Los Angeles trial. He was a mentor of Black Panthers Huey Newton and Bobby Seale.[83] He was an adviser for many years to Saudi Prince Alwaleed bin Talal.[84] He co-founded the international law firm Al-Waleed, Al-Talal & Al-Mansour.[85] He told *Newsmax* that he personally introduced Prince Alwaleed to most of the leaders of Africa.[86] He managed investments for Kingdom Holdings, the prince's company.

Prince Alwaleed bin Talal, a Muslim and one of the richest men in the world, is the nephew of King Abdullah of Saudi Arabia. He was nicknamed the "Arabian Warren Buffet" by *Time* magazine.[87] He became infamous when New York Mayor Rudy Giuliani spurned his $10 million gift to help rebuild Manhattan after 9/11.[88] Giuliani rejected the offer after learning that the Saudi prince had blamed America's pro-Israel policies for the attack.

The final piece of this puzzle is Percy Sutton, a former Harlem borough president who was formerly an attorney for Malcolm X and who had been a business partner with Khalid al-Mansour.[89] Sutton told a reporter in March 2008 that al-Mansour had told him about Obama two decades before. Sutton suggested that al-Mansour first met Obama at Columbia while doing a speech on campus.[90]

Sutton told the reporter: "I was introduced to (Obama) by a friend who was raising money for him. The friend's name is Dr. Khalid al-Mansour, from Texas….He wrote to me about him. And his introduction was there is a young man that has applied to Harvard. I know that you have a few friends up there because you used to go there to speak. Would you please write a letter in support of him?"[91] Sutton also said, "I wrote a letter of support of him to my friends at Harvard, saying to them I thought there was a genius that was going to be available and I certainly hoped they would treat him kindly."[92] According to *Newsmax*, other sources confirmed that Sutton wrote a letter of recommendation for Obama to Harvard Law professor Charles Ogletree.[93]

Why did Black Panther al-Mansour help Barack Obama? A potential answer is one that is common to many mysteries surrounding Obama's political career. Weather Underground terrorists Bill Ayers and his wife Bernardine Dohrn were supporters of the Black Panther Party. The police killing of Black Panther Fred Hampton was allegedly one of the reasons the Weather Underground declared war on the U.S. Government.[94] Dohrn and her cohorts allegedly firebombed the home of a New York judge who heard a Black Panther case.[95] Bill Ayers's father, Thomas Ayers, had business and philanthropic relationships with al-Mansour.

So what were the likely quid pro quos in this complex set of relationships? Consider the following hypothesis. Thomas Ayers, who likely met Obama when Barack worked for the DCP in Chicago, facilitated Obama's Harvard education, according to testimony that will be detailed in the next chapter. In exchange, Obama returned to Chicago after Harvard to become involved in Ayers's community organizing philanthropies and to prepare for a political career that eventually succeeded beyond everyone's wildest dreams. Coincidentally, Obama passed up many lucrative career opportunities after serving as President of the *Harvard Law Review*, choosing instead to do low-paid, obscure work for ACORN's Project Vote in Chicago. Al-Mansour, acting as a broker between Ayers, Obama, and various wealthy and influential patrons that included Percy Sutton and Prince Alwaleed, improved the standing of the Black Panther organization and helped a dynamic young African-American man gain traction and clout in the political world. Coincidentally, the website for the Black Panthers was later linked from Obama's presidential campaign website.[96] Prince Alwaleed used the arrangement to advance his own cause, which was the establishment of Islam in the United States. Coincidentally, Harvard now has a Prince Alwaleed Bin Talal Islamic Studies Program, endowed by a $20 million gift from Alwaleed, which was one of the 25 largest in Harvard history.[97] Coincidentally, Obama's paternal grandmother, Sarah Obama, made the Hajj (pilgrimage to Mecca) as a guest of Prince Alwaleed's uncle, King Abdullah, in May 2009.

Shortly after Obama graduated from Harvard, he began a long professional relationship with Antoin Rezko, a Syrian national who was eventually convicted of 16 felonies, including bribing public officials. Rezko, a business associate of Prince Alwaleed, was a major fundraising patron for five of Obama's political campaigns. Rezko was a major client of the law firm that employed Obama as an attorney. He was also a business partner of Jabir Herbert Muhammad, the son of Nation of Islam leader Elijah Muhammad. Rezko was general manager of Crucial Concessions, Muhammad's food services company. Jabir Herbert Muhammad was the manager of boxing champion Muhammad Ali. Rezko eventually became executive director of the Muhammad Ali Foundation.[98] Ali was revered among Black Muslims for going to prison rather than joining the American armed forces when he was drafted.[99] Ali collaborated with the Nation of Islam to solicit funding from Libya's Muammar Qaddafi for the NOI's national center on Chicago's South Side, near Obama's future home.[100] We will examine the tainted relationship between Obama and Rezko in greater detail in Chapter Seven.

Obama used his role as a State Senator in Illinois to help Muslims. In 1997, he introduced an "Islamic Community Day" bill.[101] In 2001, he sponsored the "Halal Food Act," which established inspection protocol for commercially prepared Islamic food.[102] He publicly supported the Palestinian cause and its activists in the Chicago area.

One such activist was Ali Abunimah, a Palestinian-American who was a leader of the Arab American Action Network. Abunimah once declared: "Zionist leaders, academics, and propagandists are actually professional, malicious liars as much as they are violent, merciless murderers."[103]

Abunimah said in March 2007: "Over the years since I first saw Obama speak, I met him about a half a dozen times, often at Palestinian and Arab-American community events in Chicago, including a May 1998 community fundraiser at which Edward Said was the keynote speaker. In 2000, when Obama unsuccessfully ran for Congress I heard him speak at a campaign fundraiser hosted by a University of Chicago professor (Rashid Khalidi)...(Obama) came to that fundraiser with his wife. That's where I had a chance to really talk to him. It was an intimate setting. He convinced me he was very aware of the issues (and) critical of U.S. bias toward Israel and lack of sensitivity to Arabs....He was very supportive of U.S. pressure on Israel."[104]

In January 2008, Abunimah told a reporter: "I knew Barack Obama for many years as my state Senator—when he used to attend events in the Palestinian community in Chicago all the time. I remember personally introducing him onstage in 1999, when we had a major community fundraiser for the community center in Deheisha refugee camp in the occupied West Bank. And that's just one example of how Barack Obama used to be very comfortable speaking up for and being associated with Palestinian rights and opposing the Israeli occupation."[105]

Abunimah also declared: "The last time I spoke to Obama was in the winter of 2004 at a gathering in Chicago's Hyde Park neighborhood. He was in the midst of a primary campaign to secure the Democratic nomination for the United States Senate seat he now occupies. But at that time polls showed him trailing. As he came in from the cold and took off his coat, I went up to greet him. He responded warmly, and volunteered, 'Hey, I'm sorry I haven't said more about Palestine right now, but we are in a tough primary race. I'm hoping when things calm down I can be more up front.' He referred to my activism, including columns I was contributing to the *Chicago Tribune* critical of Israeli and U.S. policy, 'Keep up the good work!'"[106]

After Obama's election, Abunimah wrote an article about Israel's demise that suggested the end of Zionism "...is within reach, in our lifetimes."[107] He also wrote that "...the other pillar of Israeli power – Western support and complicity – is starting to crack. We must do all we can to push it over."[108]

Abunimah's recollections suggest that Obama was duplicitously more reserved toward Islamic causes when speaking to the general public than he was when speaking to "friendly" Palestinian audiences.

Such duplicity seems normal for Obama. Let's examine his questionable claim that he is a mainstream Christian. When he joined Jeremiah Wright's Trinity United Church of Christ (TUCC), he knew that Reverend Wright had dabbled with "liquor, Islam and Black Nationalism"[109] and that TUCC embraced Black Liberation Theology. In college, Wright earned a Masters Degree in Religious History, with a focus on Islam.[110] His studies included a thesis about the Tijaniyya, a 19th Century Islamic sect in West Africa. He studied with Islamic professor Dr. Fazlur Rahman.[111]

Reverend Wright even warned Obama before he joined TUCC that the church was viewed as "too radical," but Obama joined anyway. Furthermore, it appears that Obama pursued the nominal Christianity of Wright's church out of political expediency. His decision to become a Christian "came about as a choice and not an epiphany,"[112] nudged along by his community organizing mentors who believed that an effective organizer had to belong to a church to have credibility in African-American neighborhoods. Prior to his politically-motivated "conversion" at the age of 27, Obama had virtually nothing to do with Christianity.

TUCC was an informal fusion between Christianity and Islam, partly because of its Black Nationalist philosophy, and partly because many parishioners were Muslims. Services at TUCC visually reinforced its Afro-centric orientation. A pan-African flag was prominently displayed. Some parishioners wore African-style clothing. Reverend Wright usually dressed in brightly colored dashikis, as did members of the choir. The church offered courses in Swahili. Its youth programs, Intoniane and Isuthu, took their names from Swahili words for coming into manhood and womanhood. The nominally Christian congregation celebrated the non-Christian Kwanzaa holiday.[113]

Wright and TUCC launched an Afro-centric elementary school, Kwame Nkrumah Academy. Describing the need for the school, Wright said, "We need to educate our children to the reality of white supremacy."[114]

TUCC's canon was Black Liberation Theology, as much as it was the New Testament. When Wright took over the Church in 1972, he used James Cone's book, *Black Liberation Theology and Black Power*, as the formal church doctrine. According to David Freddoso, Cone's book contained this gem: "Insofar as this country is seeking to make whiteness the dominating power throughout the world, whiteness is the symbol of the antichrist. Whiteness characterizes the activity of deranged individuals intrigued by their own image of themselves and thus unable to see that they are what is wrong with the world. Black theology seeks to analyze the satanic nature of whiteness and by doing so, prepare all nonwhites for revolutionary action."[115] Cone also wrote, "Liberal whites…want to be white and Christian at the same time; but they fail to realize that this approach is a contradiction in terms – Christianity and whiteness are opposites."[116] He also wrote, "There will be no peace in America until whites begin to hate their whiteness, asking from the depths of their being: 'How can we become black.'"[117]

Here was how Dr. Cone defined Black Liberation Theology: "Black theology refuses to accept a God who is not identified totally with the goals of the black community. If God is not for us and against white people, then he is a murderer, and we had better kill him. The task of black theology is to kill gods who do not belong to the black community.…Black theology will accept only the love of God which participates in the destruction of the white enemy. What we need is the divine love as expressed in Black Power, which is the power of black people to destroy their oppressors here and now by any means at their disposal. Unless God is participating in this holy activity, we must reject his love."[118]

According to Cone, his racial identity trumped his Christianity: "The fact that I am black is my ultimate reality...it is impossible for me to surrender this basic reality for a 'higher, more universal' reality. Black theology knows no authority more binding than the experience of oppression itself. This alone must be the ultimate authority in religious matters."[119]

Here are a few more quotes from Cone that defined his world view:

- "What we need is the destruction of whiteness, which is the source of human misery in the world."[120]

- "Theologically, Malcolm X was not far wrong when he called the white man 'the devil.'"[121]

- "Whiteness as revealed in the history of America, is the expression of what is wrong with man. It is a symbol of man's depravity...in white racist society, Christian obedience can only mean being obedient to blackness, its glorification and exaltation."[122]

Joining TUCC required accepting its guiding principles, the "Black Value System."[123] TUCC's website declared: "Our roots in the Black religious experience and tradition are deep, lasting, and permanent. We are an African people and remain 'true to our native land,' the mother continent, the cradle of civilization. God has superintended our pilgrimage through the days of slavery, the days of segregation, and the long night of racism."[124]

TUCC published a Hamas Islamic Terrorist Manifesto in one of its church bulletins. The manifesto defended terrorism and compared the Hamas Charter to the U.S. Declaration of Independence.[125] As an indication of TUCC leader Jeremiah Wright's Afro-centrist world view, he called Christianity's Holy Land "Northeast Africa."[126]

Obama's church gave its highest honor, the "Dr. Jeremiah A. Wright, Jr. Trumpeter Award", to Nation of Islam leader Louis

Farrakhan in 2007.[127] Wright's *Trumpet* magazine said Farrakhan "truly epitomized greatness."[128] Farrakhan was featured on the cover of this TUCC periodical. According to reports, Wright was a member of Farrakhan's Nation of Islam for a time.[129] Wright admitted in his sermon *Anything but Christian*, "I was influenced by Martin King, yes, but there was this other guy named Malcolm, and I tried one brief time being a Muslim: 'As salaam alaikum' (Peace be with you)."[130]

In Wright's view, white oppression was at the root of African American problems at home and anti-American xenophobia overseas. In his words: "In the 21st Century, white America got a wake-up call on 9/11/01. White America and the Western world came to realize that people of color had not gone away, faded into the woodwork or just 'disappeared' as the Great White West kept on its merry way of ignoring Black concerns."[131]

On September 16, 2001, five days after nearly 3,000 Americans were murdered by Islamic terrorists, Jeremiah Wright sermonized to his congregation: "We bombed Hiroshima, we bombed Nagasaki, and we nuked far more than the thousands in New York and the Pentagon, and we never batted an eye. We have supported state terrorism against the Palestinians and the black South Africans, and now we are indignant because the stuff we have done overseas is now brought right back into our own front yards. American's chickens are coming home to roost."[132] TUCC sold videos of this sermon, and others like it.

Wright copped the "chickens" analogy from Nation of Islam spokesman Malcolm X. In December 1963, Malcolm X delivered a speech titled "God's Judgment of White America." After the speech, he responded to a question about John Kennedy's recent assassination by saying, "the President's death was a case of 'chickens coming home to roost', that the violence that Kennedy had failed to stop had come back to him, this resulted in Elijah Muhammad (Nation of Islam leader) silencing him."[133] He added, "Chickens coming home to roost never made me sad, it only made me glad."[134]

According to Jerome Corsi, "Malcolm X believed in Elijah Muhammad's teaching that white America must suffer a doomsday calamity and feel the full fury of God's wrath for unjustly inflicting a host of social and political ills on blacks, including slavery, segregation, poverty, and racial inequality….Malcolm X embraced the idea that white people were devils and he rejected the United

States as an oppressive society controlled by a white establishment."[135]

"No, I am not an American. I'm one of the 22 million black people who are the victims of Americanism," Malcolm X declared in April 1964.[136] "I am not standing here speaking to you as an American, or a patriot, or a flag-saluter, or a flag-waver—no, not I!"[137] He also said: "Even those Americans who are blinded by childlike patriotism can see that it is only a matter of time before White America too will be utterly destroyed by her own sins, and all traces of her former glory will be removed from this planet forever."[138]

Despite ministering a nominally Christian church, Wright was a Nation of Islam sympathizer and supporter. In April 2008, he said of NOI leader Louis Farrakhan: "How many other African-Americans or European-Americans do you know that can get one million people together on the mall? He (Farrakhan) is one of the most important voices in the 20th and 21st Century….Louis Farrakhan is not my enemy. He did not put me in chains. He did not put me in slavery. And he didn't make me this color."[139]

Here are some more testimonials from Wright about Farrakhan: "(He is) one of the 20th and 21st Century giants of the African-American religious experience," a man who's "integrity and honesty have secured him a place in history as one of the nation's most powerful critics," and who's "love for Africa and African American people has made him an unforgettable force."[140]

Barack Obama participated in Louis Farrakhan's 1995 Million Man March organized by the NOI in Washington. Jeremiah Wright also participated by delivering a prayer. Farrakhan said during the event, "The real evil in America is the idea that undergirds the setup of the Western world, and that idea is called white supremacy."[141] A biography.com entry on Louis Farrakhan claimed, "In 1995, along with other prominent black leaders such as Al Sharpton and Barack Obama, Farrakhan helped lead the Million Man March…."[142] Wright co-authored a book on the event that included a series of sermons describing how the march affected him.[143]

Shortly after the NOI march, Obama said: "Historically, African-Americans have turned inward and towards Black Nationalism whenever they have a sense, as we do now, that the mainstream has rebuffed us, and that white Americans couldn't care less about the profound problems African-Americans are facing."[144]

Louis Farrakhan was prone to making inflammatory remarks about America, Jews, and white people. In 1984, he said: "Hitler was a very great man."[145] In 2000, he said: "White people are potential humans - they haven't evolved yet."[146] In 1985, he warned Jews: "You can't say 'Never Again' to God, because when he puts you in the ovens, you're there forever."[147]

In 1997, Farrakhan said: "A decree of death has been passed on America. The judgment of God has been rendered and she must be destroyed."[148] He also said: "I want to be one of the flame-throwers of God, break white folks' backs. I want to give you hell all the way to your graves. I ain't scared to die and I'm ready to kill."[149]

Farrakhan said in South Africa: "I say give 'em (whites) 24 hours to get out of town. If they don't, kill everyone white in sight. Kill the men, kill the women, kill the children, kill the blind, kill the crippled. God damn it, kill them all."[150] He also said: "Black Muslims consider themselves in a perpetual 'jihad' or holy war against the Satanic white race."[151]

More from Farrakhan: "The Nation of Islam is consistently anti-American. This is why Mahmoud Abdul-Rauf would not stand during the National Anthem at Denver Nuggets' basketball games. According to him, the United States' flag symbolized only 'oppression and tyranny.'"[152] Perhaps that is why Obama didn't put his hand on his heart during the National Anthem at a 2007 event in Iowa.

Wright's relationship with Farrakhan and the Nation of Islam spanned decades. In 1984 and 1987, he accompanied Farrakhan to visit Libyan dictator Muammar Qaddafi, who had previously helped fund the Nation of Islam.[153] During the 2008 Presidential campaign, Wright told the *New York Times*, "When (Obama's) enemies find out that in 1984 I went to Tripoli…with Farrakhan, a lot of his Jewish support will dry up quicker than a snowball in hell."[154]

In 1996, Qaddafi offered $1 billion to help Farrakhan develop a political lobby in America. He announced: "We agreed with Louis Farrakhan and his delegation to mobilize in a legal and legitimate form the oppressed minorities—and at their forefront the blacks, Arab Muslims, and Red Indians—for they play an important role in American political life and have a weight in U.S. elections."[155] He also said: "Our confrontation with America was (previously) like a fight against a fortress from outside, and today (with the NOI alliance) we found a breach to enter into this fortress and confront it."[156] Qaddafi once told Nation of Islam followers that he wanted to foment a black revolution in America.[157]

During an overseas trip to visit leaders of nations considered state sponsors of terrorism, Farrakhan called America "the Great Satan" and said, "God will destroy America by the hands of the Muslims....God will not give Japan or Europe the honor of bringing down the U.S.; this is an honor God will bestow upon Muslims."[158]

Farrakhan was a vocal supporter of Obama's 2008 presidential bid. He said of Obama to thousands of Nation of Islam conventioneers: "We are witnessing the phenomenal rise of a young man of color in the country that persecuted us...this young man is the hope of the entire world, that America will change and be made better...."[159] In an interview with his own publication, *Final Call*, Farrakhan said, "He (Obama) has been groomed, wisely so, to be seen more as a unifier."[160]

During the 2008 campaign, Farrakhan said, "You are the instruments that God is going to use to bring about universal change, and that is why Barack has captured the youth....That's a sign. When the Messiah speaks, the youth will hear, and the Messiah is absolutely speaking....Barack Obama to me, is a herald of the Messiah."[161]

Reverend Jim Wallis told a reporter: "If you want to understand where Barack gets his feeling and rhetoric from, just look at Jeremiah Wright."[162] A reporter observing a service at TUCC saw Obama nod in apparent agreement when Wright blamed "white arrogance" for the problems of the world and referred to the "United States of White America."[163]

For 20 years, Obama listened to Wright's vitriolic sermons on racism, anti-Americanism, socialism, and Black Nationalism. Obama duplicitously claimed that 20 years of these sermons had no impact on him, but two things should be considered. First, not only did he listen to these sermons week after week, he was married in Wright's church, his kids were baptized in it, he contributed a lot of money to it, he used it for political gain, and he titled his second book after a Wright sermon. Second, everything that he heard in Wright's bombastic sermons reinforced the philosophical tenor of his other radical relationships. The statements by Dr. James Cone, by Jeremiah Wright, and by Malcolm X mentioned in this chapter echo sentiments that we've already encountered when we studied Obama's involvement with Frank Marshall Davis, the cult of Saul Alinsky, and various socialists. They echo sentiments that we will encounter when we study his involvement with the Ayers family in Chapter Six and with ACORN in Chapter Eight. This suggests that he not only heard Wright's sermons, they resonated with his core values.

Another radical Muslim that Obama associated with was Rashid Khalidi. Obama worked with Professor Khalidi for 10 years when he was a lecturer at the University of Chicago. In 1995, Khalidi and his wife Mona founded the Arab American Action Network (AAAN), a group that chronicled a history project on the great "catastrophe" of Israel's founding.[164] When Obama and Bill Ayers were on the Woods Fund board, they authorized $75,000 in grants for the AAAN.[165]

Khalidi reportedly was the director of the PLO's exiled press agency WAFA for six years. He was a spokesperson for Yasser Arafat's Palestinian delegation during peace negotiations with Israel.

The Khalidi's lived in Hyde Park near the Obamas. Barack and Michelle were regular dinner guests at the Khalidi's, and the Khalidis frequently babysat the Obama children.[166] The Khalidis organized a fundraiser for Obama's congressional bid in 2000.[167] Michelle Obama attended the wedding of a Khalidi daughter, along with former Weather Underground terrorists Ayers and Dohrn.[168]

In 2003, the Obama's attended a farewell dinner for the Khalidis, who were headed to Columbia University.[169] Obama expressed gratitude for Khalidi's "consistent reminders to me of my own blind spots and my own biases....It's for that reason that I'm hoping that, for many years to come, we continue that conversation— a conversation that is necessary not just around Mona and Rashid's dinner table, but around this entire world."[170] Khalidi told the largely pro-Palestinian dinner guests that they should support Obama in his run for the U.S. Senate, stating, "You will not have a better senator under any circumstances."[171] The *LA Times* reportedly has a videotape that includes provocative footage of this dinner, but refuses to make it public. It is believed that there was considerable anti-Israel sentiment expressed at the dinner.

At Columbia, Khalidi became the Edward Said Professor of Middle Eastern studies, a new position at the school. He also became the director of the school's Middle East Institute.[172] The backers of Khalidi's endowed chair at Columbia included the United Arab Emirates and the Saudi Olayan Group. Arab and American media outlets use him regularly as an authority on the Middle East.

Obama was also involved with radical Islamists overseas. In 2006 and 2007, he assisted a movement to convert Kenya to Islam and establish Sharia law. On a visit to Kenya, he helped the campaign of Raila Odinga, who was running for President as a Muslim and a communist sympathizer.[173] Jerome Corsi has an excellent account of Obama's involvement in this affair in his book *The Obama Nation.*

Raila Odinga was educated in East Germany and named his oldest son Fidel, after Castro.[174] A core of his tribal supporters called themselves the Taliban. Odinga allied with radical Muslims in Kenya whose agenda was to establish an Islamic Africa.[175] He signed an agreement with the National Muslim Leaders Forum of Kenya promising to recognize Islamic Sharia law as the only sanctioned law for Muslim regions if he was elected.[176] He also agreed to require daily Madrassa classes in Muslim regions, to outlaw gospel radio programs, and to ban clothing for women considered offensive to the Muslim faith.[177]

When Obama visited Kenya to support Odinga, government spokespersons denounced his daily criticisms of the incumbent President Kibaki's administration and his public appearances with opposition candidate Odinga.[178] During a speech to university students in Nairobi, Obama accused the pro-American Kibaki government of corruption and talked of the need for "change."[179] [180] CBS's Chicago news team, who followed Obama to Africa, noted that criticizing the government was "something he's (Obama) done almost every day since arriving (in Kenya) last week."[181] [182]

Obama's actions were denounced by the U.S. State Department.[183] A Kenyan government spokesman said Obama appeared to be Odinga's stooge. Obama frequently gave advice to Odinga over the phone, and contacted Condoleeza Rice for help.[184] [185] [186] Odinga even flew to the U.S. to hold talks with Obama three times, once each in 2004, 2005, and 2006.[187]

Essentially, Obama was campaigning for a foreign politician, sometimes with taxpayer dollars. Obama's tribal relationship to Odinga made the situation even more inappropriate. By supporting Raila Odinga, Obama entered a decades-old Kenyan political conflict that destroyed his father's career.[188] Obama's support of Odinga indirectly linked him to financial backers of Islamic terrorism. When Odinga was Minister of Energy in Kenya, he was connected to the al Bakri Group, which was on the infamous Golden Chain, a captured al-Qaeda list of Saudi financial sponsors.[189] Saudi billionaire Abdulkader Al Bakari (aka al Bakri) was a defendant in the lawsuit brought by American insurance companies against al-Qaeda after the 9/11 attacks.

In December 2007, President Kibaki defeated Raila Odinga, despite Obama's involvement. Afterward, Odinga made good on a threat he had made before the election to instigate genocide if he lost. Claiming that Kibaki stole the election, he incited riots that killed 1,500 Kenyans and displaced a half million people from their homes. He declared, Kibaki "must step down or there must be a re-election – in this I will not be compromised."[190] During the rioting, 50 parishioners were burned to death inside of a church.[191] Odinga was subsequently given the position of Prime Minister in a power-sharing arrangement to stop the rioting.[192]

After the 2007 Kenyan election, a list of 72 top contributors to Odinga's presidential campaign surfaced. The list included $1 million from "Friends of Senator B.O." Presumably, "Senator B.O." was a reference to Barack Obama.[193] There is notable similarity between the "change" theme of Obama's presidential campaign and the "Real Change for Africa" theme of Raila Odinga's presidential campaign.[194] Sometimes the dots don't even need a connecting line.

Obama appointed Robert Malley as a foreign policy advisor to his presidential campaign in 2007. Malley's father, Egyptian-born Simon Malley, belonged to the Egyptian communist party and was linked to Yasser Arafat.[195] Robert Malley resigned from Obama's team after word leaked out that he had met several times with the terrorist group Hamas.[196] After the election, Obama rehired Malley as a foreign policy advisor, suggesting that the earlier dismissal was just for political show.

The Obama campaign team worked hard at political show to obscure his background with radical Islamists and Black Nationalists. At a gathering where Theresa Heinz Kerry was about to introduce Michelle Obama, event organizers scrambled to rearrange the crowd seated behind Michelle. A coordinator shouted, "Get me more white people, we need more white people."[197] Another coordinator told an Asian girl, "We're moving you, sorry. It's going to look so pretty, though."[198]

Mazen Asbahi, the Muslim Outreach Director of Obama's campaign team, resigned when news leaked out that he served on the board of a group linked to the Egyptian Muslim Brotherhood and Hamas.[199] Asbahi was President of the Great Lakes Muslim Students Association Council, which had distributed the propaganda of Osama bin Laden on its website.

When Minha Husaini replaced Asbahi as Obama's Muslim liaison, *Fox News* revealed that Husaini also met with groups tied to the Muslim Brotherhood and Hamas.[200] The meetings included members of the Council on American-Islamic Relations (CAIR). Several CAIR officials have been convicted of terror-related charges. Prince Alwaleed bin Talal, who Percy Sutton hinted was one of Obama's college benefactors, donated $500,000 to CAIR after 9/11.[201]

Cornel West, a member of Obama's Black Advisory Council, once said "the accumulated effect of the black wounds and scars suffered in a white-dominated society is a deep-seated anger, a boiling sense of rage, and a passionate pessimism regarding America's will to justice. It goes without saying that a profound hatred of African people...sits at the center of American civilization."[202]

An upcoming events calendar on Obama's 2008 campaign website listed events hosted by the Islamic Circle of North America (ICNA) and the Muslim American Society (MAS), both of which have ties to Islamic terrorist organizations.[203] Four people from the ICNA-related "Houston Taliban" were arrested on terrorism conspiracy charges. In April 2004, MAS's Communications Director, Randall Royer, was imprisoned for his activities in the "Virginia Jihad Network", a group that was conspiring to attack Americans. The MAS website displayed a photo and a short bio of Obama; along with those it called other prominent Muslims, such as Malcolm X and Muqtada al-Sadr.[204]

It is likely that radical Islamists from around the world helped fund Obama's presidential campaign. He received money from more than 50 different countries. Pamela Geller provides an excellent account of this issue on her website *atlasshrugs.com*.

A Federal Election Commission (FEC) employee reportedly warned for months that the Obama campaign had received as much as $223 million in amounts less than $200.[205] Unlike McCain and Clinton, Obama did not identify donors contributing $200 or less. An FEC spokesman said, "Contributions that came under $200 aggregated per person are not listed. They don't appear anywhere, so there's no way of knowing who they are."[206]

The Federal Election Campaign Act "prohibits any foreign national from contributing, donating, or spending funds in connection with any federal, state or local election in the United States, either directly or indirectly."[207] According to Pamela Geller, Obama received a $33,000 contribution from some Palestinian brothers based in a Hamas-controlled refugee camp in Gaza.[208] Geller confirmed dozens of foreign cities from which illegal contributions to Obama originated. In many cases, the donors' names and contact information were nothing more than random arrangements of letters.[209] Obama's campaign received numerous contributions in unusual amounts that were perhaps foreign contributions that became uneven after currency exchange.[210]

Coincidently, Libyan dictator Muammar Qaddafi said after the election: "All the people in the Arab and Islamic world and in Africa applauded this man. They welcomed him and prayed for him and for his success, and they may have even been involved in legitimate (sic) contribution campaigns to enable him to win the American presidency."[211]

An auditor at the FEC requested a formal investigation into the Obama campaign, stating, "I believe we are looking at a hijacking of our political system that makes the Clinton and Gore fundraising scandals pale in comparison."[212] According to the Puma PAC blog, "Obama spent a record $744 million on his campaign but has disclosed donors for only $485 million of his windfall."[213]

Middle East activists supported Obama's campaign in other ways. *Al-Jazeera* ran video of Obama phone banks being operated in Gaza. The videos showed students and young professionals gathering nightly to phone random people in America to urge them to vote for Obama. The calls were organized by a 23-year-old student at Al Aqsa University in Gaza.[214]

Obama's connections with radical Islamists will be of greater concern if they influence his actions as President. So, let's examine his record during his first year in office in this context.

In March 2008, Obama said, "An Obama presidency would work to regain the trust of Muslims worldwide with Washington-led aid programs in Muslim countries."[215] In the middle of America's own financial crisis, Obama gave $900 million to the Palestinian Authority to rebuild Gaza after Israeli bombings, even though Israel was just retaliating against an earlier attack.[216] To make matters worse, Gaza's "government" is now the terrorist group Hamas. The $900 million aid package thus made America Hamas's second largest financial supporter.

Obama earmarked an additional $20 million for "migration assistance" to the Palestinian refugees and "conflict victims" in Gaza.[217] Secretary of State Hillary Clinton announced a new scholarship program, the Middle East Partnership Initiative, to help Palestinian students.[218] In contrast, when an earthquake in Italy

√5

killed 130 and left thousands homeless, the administration pledged a paltry $50,000 in emergency relief.[219]

Obama's first call to any head of state after his inauguration was to Mahmoud Abbas, leader of the PLO.[220] His first formal one-on-one television interview with any news organization was with Dubai-based Arabic TV network *Al-Arabiya*, where he talked about the Muslim part of his family background and described America as a nation of "Muslims, Christians, and Jews", which is an unnatural ordering.[221] [222]

When asked about his views on the Israeli-Palestinian issue, Obama said if America "is ready to initiate a new partnership (with the Muslim world) based on mutual respect and mutual interest…my job is to communicate the fact that the United States has a stake in the well-being of the Muslim world, that the language we use has to be a language of respect."[223] He showed respect to the Muslim world by bowing to King Abdullah of Saudi Arabia, perhaps because of an implied debt to the King's nephew, Prince Alwaleed bin Talal, who perhaps helped fund Obama's Harvard education.

Obama ordered the Guantanamo Bay detention facility closed and all military tribunals of captured Islamic enemy combatants halted. He ordered overseas CIA interrogation centers closed. He ordered Miranda Rights to be read to captured terrorists. He withdrew all charges against the mastermind behind the October 2000 USS Cole attack.[224] He ordered General Electric Capital Corporation, a recipient of government bail-out funds, to become the first Western multinational to issue an Islamic bond. He dictated that all government security documents eliminate the words "Islamic extremism" and "jihad."[225] He called the Iraq war "a botched and ill-advised U.S. military incursion into a Muslim country."[226] His Secretary of Homeland Security stopped using the word "terrorism", substituting the smarmy euphemism "man-caused disasters."[227]

In June 2009, Obama delivered a seminal speech from Egypt about America's new approach to the Muslim world. In the speech, he declared that America was not a Christian country, and in some ways could be considered a Muslim country, given the size of our Muslim population.[228] An April 2009 Obama address in Turkey included the statement, "We do not consider ourselves a Christian nation or a Jewish nation or a Muslim nation."[229] He also said that the U.S. offers "deep appreciation for the Islamic faith, which has done so much over the centuries to shape the world—including in my own country."[230]

Obama also stated, "The United States is not and will never be at war with Islam,"[231] which clearly ignores a very long list of attacks on the U.S. by Islamic terrorists. This includes atrocities committed during Obama's Presidency, such as the Fort Hood massacre, the Christmas Day bombing attempt aboard an airliner bound for Detroit, and the failed car bombing in Times Square.

Obama sent envoy Scott Gration to the Sudan to establish a relationship of "friendship and cooperation."[232] According to Don Fredrick, author of *The Obama Timeline*, "It is not clear why Obama now seeks relations with a regime that has engaged in an Islamic jihad and killed over two million innocent people in Sudan and Darfur. On March 4 (2009), the International Criminal Court issued a warrant for the arrest of Sudan's President, Omar al-Bashir, for his war crimes. Obama nevertheless wants to establish normal relations with the al-Bashir regime."[233]

Also according to Fredrick, "Obama's State Department says it will not accept Israel's demand that Palestinians accept the Jewish state's right to exist as a pre-condition to peace talks."[234] Obama backed a Saudi peace initiative that would require Israel to make major security concessions regarding its border, Palestinian immigrants, and Iran's nuclear program, while getting nothing substantive in return.[235] Obama told Jeffrey Goldberg from the *Atlantic* that the situation with Israel is a "constant sore" that "does infect all of our foreign policy."[236]

In May 2010, the Israeli Navy confronted six ships that were attempting to run an Israeli naval blockade of Gaza. The ships were allegedly on a humanitarian mission sponsored by a leftist activist group called the Free Gaza Movement. When the six ships refused to be diverted to an Israeli port for inspection, a violent clash occurred, resulting in the deaths of at least ten activists and injuries to scores more. The brutal event triggered harsh condemnation of Israel from leaders around the world, including the Obama administration and the U.N. However, the saga has a curious back story. The Free Gaza Movement is supported by former Weather Underground terrorists Bill Ayers and Bernardine Dohrn, who were in Egypt on behalf of the movement in April 2010 in an attempt to coordinate aid for Gaza, which is now run by the terrorist group Hamas. Ali Abunimah, a Palestinian associate of Obama who was introduced earlier in this chapter, was also in Gaza with Ayers and Dohrn assisting Hamas. Furthermore, the naval clash caused the cancellation of a meeting scheduled between Obama and Israel's Prime Minister Benjamin

Netanyahu. Relations were already strained between the two leaders before this episode, largely because Obama consistently snubbed Netanyahu in favor of Arab and Islamic leaders. This invites speculation that the naval clash was intentionally provoked by activists like Ayers and Dohrn in order instigate a public relations nightmare for Israel and further erode its relations with the Obama administration.

In closing, this chapter documented Barack Obama's lifelong relationships with mentors, associates, financiers, professors, political organizations, and foreign agents who all shared the following perspectives and goals:

- Disdain for western political philosophy

- Weakening the power and influence of capitalism

- Blaming America for worldwide poverty, racism, and inequality

- Transferring wealth from white middle and upper class America to their "victims"

- Opposing American militarism, especially the war on terror

These are similar to the perspectives that we encountered when we discussed Barack Obama's immersion among socialists in the previous chapter. This is not surprising, because socialists, radical Islamists, and Black Nationalists view the U.S. as a common enemy that must be destroyed. The American principles of limited government, sovereignty of the individual, and the rule of law based on a secular Constitution are anathema to Marxists and Muslims. The Marxian view of world hegemony via the dictatorship of the proletariat cannot co-exist with the U.S. Constitution. The Islamic view of world hegemony via Sharia law cannot co-exist with the U.S. Constitution. Socialists and radical Islamists recoil from the concept of a citizen free to choose economically and religiously.

America is the Great Satan to both Marxists and radical Islamists. One group plots to destroy us with taxation, transfers of wealth, large bureaucracies, confiscation of private property, and infringement on individual rights. The other group plots to destroy us with sleeper cells, hijacked airplanes, illegal immigration, blending of church and state, and creeping intrusion of Sharia law into our culture. The Marxist and Islamist visions for the end state of America are quite different, but they are united in a conviction that the America of capitalism and limited government must die.

The socialists and radical Islamists will have to sort out their differences when they finish destroying the America of Jefferson and Adams. One outcome, however, is assured. Every Islamic government is dictatorial. Every Marxist government is dictatorial. They will just have to decide which group gets to be the dictators when our Constitutional republic is extinguished.

Barack Hussein Obama sits at the epicenter of this national and international radical alliance. He did not create the movement toward socialism in America. He did not create the assault on America by radical Islamists. He is, however, their perfect front man. His rise to power is an extension of their concerted attack on capitalism and traditional Western principals. As we have seen in this chapter and in the previous one, Obama has been immersed in their movements, their ideology, and their agents for his entire life. And he is now the President of the United States of America.

To achieve that lofty perch, he deceived the American people. Let's review one more time the fable that the Obama campaign attempted to foist on the American public. It is a fable so intrinsically dishonest that it causes one to question the motivation. In December 2007, he said, "I've always been a Christian. The only connection I've had to Islam is that my grandfather on my father's side came from that country (Kenya). But I've never practiced Islam."[237] What an incredible falsehood! First of all, he was baptized as an adult in Reverend Wright's church, so he couldn't have been a Christian all of his life. Second, there are very clear documents and witness accounts that indicate he was a practicing Muslim in his youth. His father was Muslim, his stepfather was a Muslim, and he was a Muslim. Third, he has collaborated with Islamists his entire life.

As the anti-American alliance between socialism and radical Islam becomes ascendant in the U.S., the middle class will find that it is losing its freedom, that its wealth is being transferred to countless "victims", that its interests are being subordinated to the United Nations, and that people described by the Obama administration as terrorists are no longer those assaulting us from the Middle East, but rather those who cling to their guns, religion, and conservative political principles here in America.

We've been had.

"Concentrated power has always been the enemy of liberty."

Ronald Reagan

Chapter Six

Meet the Ayers Family

Bill Ayers is just "a guy who lives in my neighborhood...."[1]

Barack Obama, during April 2008 debate

Barack Obama asserted during a Democratic primary debate in April 2008 that Pentagon bomber Bill Ayers was just a guy who lives in his neighborhood. Bill Ayers did indeed live just three blocks from Obama in an upscale Hyde Park neighborhood. However, Obama disingenuously left out the rest of the story. This is another case of appalling dishonesty and deception that characterized his entire political career.

Here's what Obama left out. Barack and Michelle had a complex 20 year relationship with the Ayers family. The patriarch of the family, Thomas Ayers, was one of the most powerful political brokers in Chicago. Bill Ayers, his son, is a socialist, a terrorist, and a political activist who leveraged his father's influence to advance the cause of Marxism. Bernardine Dohrn, Bill's wife, is a socialist and a terrorist who helped lead the violent Weather Underground to riot and murder. All three of them nurtured Barack Obama's career for two decades.

This chapter documents the entangled relationship between the President of the United States and a dangerous family that has blood on its hands and a frothing commitment to destroy capitalism and the middle class of America. We will begin with a brief biography of the Ayers clan, and then we will explore their involvement with Barack and Michelle Obama.

Thomas Ayers was a wealthy businessman, philanthropist, and social activist. He had so much local clout that he was sometimes referred to as the godfather of Illinois politics. As CEO of Commonwealth Edison (later known as Exelon), he was tightly connected to many powerful figures in Chicago. His influence or support could help elect a mayor, a governor, or a senator.

Tom Ayers served on the boards of philanthropies that had combined assets exceeding $5 billion. He helped direct how they spent their money. He leveraged this powerful network to manipulate political outcomes in Chicago.

The résumé of Tom Ayers is a testament to his connections with the sociopolitical elites of Chicago. He became President of the giant utility, Commonwealth Edison, in 1964, and was Chairman and CEO from 1973 to 1980. He continued to exert influence over the utility until his death in 2007. He served on numerous corporate boards, including Sears, G.D. Searle, Zenith, Northwest Industries, General Dynamics, First National Bank of Chicago, the Chicago Cubs, and the Tribune Company. He was Chairman of several boards, including the Chicago Urban League, the Chicago Symphony Orchestra, the Chicago Chamber of Commerce and Industry, Bank Street College of Education in New York, the Chicago Community Trust, and Northwestern University Board of Trustees.

He was also connected with the Daley political machine in Chicago, and was Vice President of the Chicago Board of Education. He used these and other corporate and philanthropic connections to nurture the career of his radical son, and then the career of Barack Obama. He was steadfastly protective of the destructive political activities of his prodigal son, his criminal daughter-in-law, and their radical associates. John Ayers, Bill's brother, said, "Our father always stood by us. He was an establishment guy, but he believed in us. He believed in change."[2] As we shall see shortly, Bill Ayers is a man that only a father or fellow radicals could love.

William Ayers was born in 1944 in Glen Ellyn, Illinois. He went to the University of Michigan, Bank Street College of Education, and Teachers College of Columbia University. He earned an M.Ed and an Ed.D, and now works as a professor at the University of Illinois at Chicago.

At the University of Michigan, his career took a radical turn toward violence and crime when he joined the socialist Students for a Democratic Society (SDS). As the conflict in Vietnam deepened, the anti-war SDS grew quickly. By 1968, it had 300 chapters on college campuses with a combined membership of 100,000. Ayers became increasingly influential in the SDS as the group engaged in anti-war violence in Chicago and on college campuses. During the 1969 "Days of Rage" riots accompanying the trial of the Chicago Seven, 287 SDS protesters were arrested and 59 police officers were injured.

Ayers and wealthy girlfriend Diana Oughton became leaders of a militant regional faction of the SDS called the "Jesse James Gang." Ayers described the Gang as "the arms of liberation inside the monster," and said, "We are tired of tiptoeing up to society and asking for reform. We're ready to kick it."[3] The Detroit-based faction eventually morphed into the Weatherman, a name taken from the Dylan song Subterranean Homesick Blues ("You don't need a weatherman to know which way the wind blows").[4] During the June 1969 SDS national convention in Chicago, the Weatherman surreptitiously took control of the group, even though they were the smallest faction. They snuck off to a separate location and essentially declared their faction to be in charge of the SDS.

In December 1969, the Weatherman declared "war on AmeriKKKa" at a War Council in Flint, Michigan.[5] They believed that the American system was irredeemable and that revolutionary war against the U.S. Government and capitalism should begin immediately. They wanted to create a "white fighting force" to collaborate with the "Black Liberation Movement" to accomplish the "destruction of U.S. imperialism and the achievement of a classless world: world communism."[6] Ayers called the group "an American Red Army."[7] John Jacobs, a Weatherman leader, said, "We're against everything that is 'good and decent.'"[8] They likened themselves to the barbarians who destroyed decadent Rome.

FBI informant Larry Grathwohl reported that the Weatherman planned to build reeducation camps in the American Southwest, with the assistance of foreign communist regimes. "Diehard capitalists" who resisted the revolution would be murdered.[9] According to Grathwohl, they estimated that 25 million Americans would have to be killed. Ayers declared, "Kill all of the rich people. Break up their cars and apartments. Bring the revolution home; kill your parents...."[10] Ayers was called "one of the chief theoreticians of the Weatherman" by the *New York Times* in 1970.[11]

The group became fugitives after being indicted for the "Days of Rage" riots, and changed their name to the Weather Underground. They went on a bombing spree to foment their revolution. During a three year span, they bombed the New York City Police Headquarters, the Capitol Building, and the Pentagon. When the spree was over, they were responsible for 30 bombings at government sites. The human toll included five fatalities and scores of injuries. Three Weather Underground terrorists were killed when a nail bomb they were assembling for an attack on Fort Dix exploded in a Greenwich Village townhouse. Ayers's girlfriend, Diana Oughton, was one of the casualties.

Ayers was a cold, calculating terrorist. In his words, "Everything was absolutely ideal on the day I bombed the Pentagon. The sky was blue. The birds were singing. And the bastards were finally going to get what was coming to them."[12] During the planning for a bombing in San Francisco, FBI informant Grathwohl objected to the proposed placement of the bomb because it would kill innocent people. Ayers replied, "We can't protect all the innocent people in the world. Some will get killed. Some of us will get killed. We have to accept that fact."[13] He dismissed Grathwohl's sentimentality as "unrevolutionary."[14] According to Grathwohl, Ayers "seemed self-important, a controller of subordinates, the type who loved to give orders."[15]

Grathwohl also reported that the Weather Underground considered kidnapping politicians such as Spiro Agnew and Henry Kissinger to facilitate their communist revolution.[16] The group helped spring narcotics guru Timothy Leary from prison and arranged for his transport to Algiers.[17]

During his fugitive years with the Weather Underground, Ayers lived in 15 states. He hid in safe houses and experimented sexually as the radicals tried "smashing monogamy." His sexual partners included his best male friend.[18] Drug use, including LSD, was prevalent in the Weather Underground.

While a fugitive, Ayers coauthored the book *Prairie Fire* with Bernardine Dohrn and other Weather Underground members. The book was dedicated to, among others, Sirhan Sirhan, the convicted assassin of Robert F. Kennedy.[19] In the book, the authors wrote, "We are a guerrilla organization. We are communist men and women, underground in the United States...."[20]

Bernardine Dohrn became Ayers's girlfriend after Oughton's brutal death. The two fugitives changed locations, changed jobs, adopted multiple aliases, and eventually got married. They came out of hiding and surrendered to police in 1980. However, the charges against them were dropped because of wiretapping improprieties.[21] A reasonable suspicion is that Thomas Ayers used his influence to clear the way for his son and daughter-in-law to surrender without consequences. At the end of the saga, Bill Ayers declared, "Guilty as sin, free as a bird, America is a great country."[22]

After rejoining mainstream society, Ayers prepared himself to work within the system to achieve socialism in America. He enrolled at Bank Street College of Education in New York, and then Teachers College at Columbia University, eventually earning a Master's degree and a Doctorate in Education. He began working for the University of Illinois at Chicago and is now a Distinguished Professor of Education and Senior University Scholar.

Ayers specializes in public school reform in Chicago, which is unfortunate for middle-class Chicago school children and their parents. It may have been safer for America when he was bombing buildings rather than perverting the minds of a new generation. Ayers is a strong proponent of radicalizing schools. According to Sol Stern of the Manhattan Institute, "Instead of planting bombs in public buildings, Ayers now works to indoctrinate America's future teachers in the revolutionary cause, urging them to pass on the lessons to their public school students."[23]

Ayers has a six-figure income and lives in a lavish Hyde Park home. This is an incredible turn of fortune for a bomb-setting terrorist who was a fugitive from the FBI for eleven years. His remarkable rehabilitation would have been impossible without his powerful father. For example, Tom Ayers was a board member of Bank Street College of Teaching where Bill began his rehabilitation and prepared for his career in education. For all of Bill's professed Marxist hatred of wealth in America, he is a spoiled beneficiary of it. In spite of this, he did not lose his radical edge. He still publicly defends his Weather Underground bombing spree, and he has suggested that they didn't do enough.[24]

Bernardine Rae Dohrn was born in Milwaukee, Wisconsin in 1942. She graduated from the University of Chicago in 1963 and from the University of Chicago School of Law in 1967. She met Bill Ayers in 1967 in Ann Arbor, Michigan. She was a member of the SDS who spoke and dressed flamboyantly. She worked for the National Lawyers Guild, a group that was accused by the FBI of being a communist front.[25]

During the Vietnam War, Dohrn connected with Castro's Cuban delegation at the U.N. She arranged for SDS groups to visit Havana as part of the infamous "Venceremos Brigade" to help Cubans with sugar harvests and to learn revolutionary tactics.[26] [27] The FBI reported that the "Brigade" assisted the Vietnamese and Cubans to "bring war home" to America.[28] Some "brigadistas" learned how to assemble bombs, a skill they later employed with great effect. Dohrn and others met with Viet Cong representatives in

Hungary to discuss antiwar strategy.[29] Her influence grew in the SDS and she organized the October 1969 "Days of Rage" riots in Chicago.

At the December 1969 Weatherman War Council meeting in Flint, Michigan, Dohrn uttered some of the most disturbing comments imaginable. Actress Sharon Tate, who was 8½ months pregnant, had recently been murdered by the Manson cult. Tate was found with a carving fork protruding from her swollen abdomen. Dohrn celebrated the slaughter by shouting, "Dig it! First they killed those pigs, then they ate dinner in the same room with them. They even shoved a fork into a victim's stomach! Wild!"[30] She praised the psychopath Manson as a true "revolutionary", giving him a three-fingered "fork salute."[31] Echoing Manson's "Helter Skelter" call for a race war, she declared, "the best thing that we can be doing for ourselves, as well as for the Panthers and the Revolutionary Black Liberation Struggle, is to build a fucking white revolutionary movement."[32] She and the War Council issued a declaration of war against "AmeriKKKa", which she frequently spelled with three K's to highlight U.S. racism.[33]

During the War Council, the 400 participants sang songs like "Communism is What We Do," "I'm Dreaming of a White Riot," and "We Need a Red Party." They also chanted "Sirhan Sirhan power!", "Charlie Manson power!", and "Red Army power!" The meeting hall was adorned with large banners of Che Guevara, Ho Chi Minh, Fidel Castro, and Malcolm X. One wall was papered with posters of murdered Black Panther Fred Hampton. An enormous cardboard machine gun dangled from the ceiling.[34]

Dohrn broadcast the group's declaration of war against America on KPFK radio, declaring: "If you want to find us, this is where we are. In every tribe, commune, dormitory, farmhouse, barracks and townhouse where kids are making love, smoking dope, and loading guns."[35] In another communiqué, Dohrn warned, "Guard your planes. Guard your colleges. Guard your banks. Guard your children. Guard your doors."[36]

In 1970, after the explosion at the Greenwich Village townhouse, Dohrn skipped her "Days of Rage" trial. She participated in the Weather Underground spree of bombings in the early 1970's. According to FBI informant Grathwohl, Dohrn planted a shrapnel-filled pipe bomb in a San Francisco Police station in February 1970 that killed one officer and partially blinded another.[37] No one was formally charged with the crime, although the FBI was reportedly close to indicting Ayers and Dohrn before the couple surrendered. J.

Edgar Hoover called Dohrn "la Pasionaria of the Lunatic Left" and put her on the FBI's *Ten Most Wanted* list. [38]

When Ayers and Dohrn surrendered in 1980, the federal charges against them were dismissed. Dohrn pled guilty to state charges related to the "Days of Rage" riots. She was fined $1,500 and given three years probation. [39] This was remarkably weak punishment for a woman who J. Edgar Hoover described as "the most dangerous woman in America." [40] When she surrendered, she declared, "I remain committed to the struggle ahead. I regret not at all our efforts to side with the forces of liberation." [41]

However, Dohrn's legal troubles did not end there. She was later jailed for seven months when she stonewalled a federal grand jury investigating a 1981 armored-car robbery that was carried out by remnants of the Weather Underground. [42] The grand jury demanded a handwriting sample from her, because she was suspected of renting the getaway cars. Two police officers and a security guard were killed during the crime. Weather Underground members Kathy Boudin, David Gilbert, and Susan Rosenberg eventually went to prison for their roles in it. The robbery took place in New York City, where Ayers, Boudin, Gilbert, Dohrn, and Barack Obama were living at the time.

Dohrn has been unable to practice law since she returned to normal society because of her criminal record. She is, however, a Clinical Associate Professor at Northwestern School of Law, and an adjunct faculty member of the University of Illinois at Chicago, where Bill Ayers works. Coincidentally, Thomas Ayers was at one time the Chairman of the Northwestern University Board of Trustees, which might explain how Dohrn landed her associate professorship there. Tom Ayers was a gift that kept on giving for his son and daughter-in-law.

Ayers and Dohrn adopted and raised Chesa Boudin, the son of terrorists Kathy Boudin and David Gilbert, who were unable to parent because of their incarceration for the armored-car robbery and related murders. Today, both Chesa Boudin and Bill Ayers are working with Venezuelan dictator Hugo Chavez, a Marxist, to "improve" the education system there. [43] Ayers and Dohrn named their first biological son "Malik" after Malcolm X and their second son "Zayd" after Zayd Shakur. Shakur was a Black Panther who was killed in a firefight with police that left an officer dead. [44]

It is important to note that Ayers and Dohrn were avowed Marxists. Presented below are quotes from them that originated in the book *Prairie Fire* and a Dohrn article titled *Our Class Struggle* that she wrote for a Weather Underground newsletter.

> "We are building a communist organization to be part of the forces which build a revolutionary communist party to lead the working class to seize power and build socialism....The struggle for Marxism-Leninism is the most significant development in our recent history....We discovered thru our own experiences what revolutionaries all over the world have found — that Marxism-Leninism is the science of revolution, the revolutionary ideology of the working class, our guide to the struggle."[45]
>
> "We are a guerrilla organization. We are communist women and men...deeply affected by the historic events of our time in the struggle against U.S. imperialism....Our intention is to disrupt the empire, to incapacitate it, to put pressure on the cracks, to make it hard to carry out its bloody functioning against the people of the world, to join the world struggle, to attack from the inside....We need a revolutionary communist party in order to lead the struggle, give coherence and direction to the fight, seize power and build the new society....The only path to the final defeat of imperialism and the building of socialism is revolutionary war."[46]

Mark Rudd, a fellow SDS member with Ayers and Dohrn, wrote a pamphlet titled *Columbia* that described the SDS takeover of the Columbia University campus in 1968. In it, he wrote, "It was no accident that we hung up pictures of Karl Marx and Malcolm X and Che Guevara and flew red flags from the tops of two buildings."[47] The pamphlet quoted Communist Chinese leader Mao Tse-tung: "Dare to struggle, dare to win."[48]

In a 1995 interview, Ayers said: "I am a radical, Leftist, small 'c' communist....Maybe I'm the last communist who is willing to admit it."[49] According to Ayers, "Socialism is the total opposite of capitalism/imperialism. It is the rejection of empire and white supremacy. Socialism is the violent overthrow of the bourgeoisie, the establishment of the dictatorship of the proletariat, and the eradication of the social system based on profit....Socialism means control of the productive forces for the good of the whole community instead of the few who live on hilltops and in mansions. Socialism means priorities based on human need instead of corporate greed."[50]

Ayers has a memento from his days as an anti-war terrorist. Vietnamese communists gave him a ring made from an American plane shot down over North Vietnam. He was so moved that he "left the room to cry."[51] According to Ayers, he realized then that America was evil.

Let's examine the 20-year relationship between Barack Obama and the Ayers family. From the outset, it is difficult to imagine Obama describing a suspected murderer, a terrorist, a communist, and an anti-American radical as "just another guy in the neighborhood," but I suppose that depends on what kind of neighborhood you frequent. Let's look inside Mr. Obama's neighborhood.

Obama was first exposed to the radical world of Bill Ayers at Occidental College in California. He mingled with the Students for Economic Democracy (SED), a group headed by former SDS founder and compatriot of Ayers, Tom Hayden. Obama's first public speech, a critique of South African apartheid, was at an event sponsored by SED.[52]

It is unclear when Obama, Ayers, and Dohrn first met, but there were numerous opportunities for these three socialists to link up when Obama transferred to Columbia University in New York City in 1981.

According to Obama, he continued to protest South African apartheid through the Black Students Organization at Columbia. At roughly the same time, remnants of the Weather Underground were also involved in protests against apartheid around New York City. When Obama was living in New York, Ayers was at Bank Street College of Education and at Teachers College of Columbia University. Bank Street College is 371 yards from Columbia, where Obama studied. Weather Underground terrorists David Gilbert and Kathy Boudin lived in the same part of New York as Obama. Dohrn lived four blocks away. Weather Underground terrorists Dianne Donghi, Jeff Jones, and Mark Rudd were all former members of the Columbia University SDS chapter. Weather Underground members were captured after a dramatic Brinks armored car robbery and chase that ended in three deaths right in the city. Bill Ayers would likely have attended the annual Socialist Scholars Conference at nearby Cooper Union College, which Obama said he attended in *Dreams from My Father*. It is reasonable to assume that the politically active Obama, already familiar with Hayden's SED, would have been keenly aware of the highly visible SDS and Weather Underground presence in and around his home and university.[53][54]

Perhaps Frank Marshall Davis connected Obama with Bill Ayers. Davis was allegedly acquainted with Thomas Ayers from his own radical days in Chicago. Davis certainly had a connection to the Ayers family via the family of Valerie Jarrett, who has been a close friend of Barack and Michelle for at least two decades and who is now a senior adviser to the President.

The Jarrett family and the Ayers family were connected over the course of two generations. Jarrett's mother, Professor Barbara Taylor Bowman, co-founded the Erikson Institute in Chicago. The board Chairman of the institute was Thomas Ayers. Bernardine Dohrn was a board member. Valerie Jarrett's father-in-law, Vernon Jarrett, was a noted *Chicago Sun-Times* columnist. According to political activist Trevor Loudon, Vernon worked in the late 1940's in the South Side Community Art Center and on the *Chicago Defender* newspaper, a journal sympathetic to communist causes. Frank Marshall Davis also worked at the Art Center and the *Chicago Defender*.[55] Davis and Jarrett collaborated as officials of a citizens' sub-committee supporting a CIO labor union strike. The Davis-Jarrett-Ayers connection was a possible catalyst for the relationship between Obama and Bill Ayers.

Obama refuses to release his Columbia University records. Perhaps they indicate that he was in a seminar that Ayers or Dohrn presented at, or that he and Ayers attended the same class as students (Bank Street College collaborates with Columbia). Obama studied under Edward Said, the left-wing Columbia professor who was friends with Ayers and Dohrn, so perhaps Obama's records point to something there.[56]

It is clear, though, that Obama met Ayers and Dohrn at this point, based on later events that would make no sense unless they had previously connected. For example, Obama eventually interned at the same Chicago law firm, Sidley & Austin, where Dohrn had worked.[57] One of Sidley's major clients was the utility company that Thomas Ayers ran. Out of all of the law firms in the U.S., it is an almost impossible coincidence that Obama would end up interning at the same one that Dohrn and Thomas Ayers were involved with, unless there was already some relationship between Obama and the Ayers family.

From 1984 to 1988, Dohrn worked as a legal clerk at Sidley & Austin in their New York and Chicago offices (she transferred

Describes the steps under ground took ground obama

when she and Bill Ayers moved from New York to Chicago in 1987).[58] Howard Trienens, a managing partner of the law firm, said that he hired Dohrn as a favor to his fellow Northwestern University trustee and classmate, Tom Ayers.[59] He said, "We often hire friends."[60] Trienens succeeded Ayers as the Chairman of the Board of Trustees for Northwestern University. Ayers's firm, Commonwealth Edison, used Trienens at Sidley as a legal counsel for years.[61]

Sidley & Austin was the law firm where Michelle Robinson, Obama's future wife, began work in 1988.[62] Michelle worked in the area of entertainment law and intellectual property at the law firm.[63] She mentored Obama in the summer of 1989, after his first year at Harvard Law School.[64] Howard Trienens hired Obama as an intern, even though it was rare for big law firms to hire first year law students.[65] It seems likely that either Thomas Ayers, a major client of Sidley and connected to Frank Marshall Davis, or Bernardine Dohrn, a former employee of Sidley and recently arrived from Obama's locale in New York City, recommended that Sidley hire Obama.

As we saw in the last chapter, it appears that Thomas Ayers helped Obama get into Harvard, which would make no sense unless they already knew each other. Ayers collaborated on business and philanthropic efforts with Black Panther Dr. Khalid al-Mansour, who Percy Sutton reported was soliciting funds and letters of recommendation to help Obama get into Harvard.[66] Coincidentally, the Weather Underground, according to a claim by Bernardine Dohrn, firebombed the home and car of a New York judge named Murtagh who was presiding over the "Black Panther 21" trial in the early 1970's.[67] Bill Ayers and Bernardine Dohrn knew al-Mansour when he was Donald Warden. At one point, Ayers, Dohrn, and Warden hid from the FBI together in San Francisco.[68]

Another associate of Tom Ayers, John L. McKnight, wrote a letter of recommendation to Harvard for Obama.[69] [70] McKnight, a Saul Alinsky admirer, was a Northwestern University professor when Tom Ayers was Chairman of the Board of Trustees for Northwestern University.

An eye witness reported that Obama was involved with the Ayers family shortly after he graduated from Columbia in the mid 1980's. According to Political Scientist Steve Diamond, a U.S. Postal worker claimed that Obama periodically visited the residence of Tom and Mary Ayers in Glen Ellyn, a suburb of Chicago. Allen Hulton, the mail carrier who serviced the Ayers residence for years, had numerous conversations with Mary Ayers. Such conversations would have been quite natural, because Hulton had graduated from the same high school as Tim Ayers, a son of Tom and Mary. In one of the conversations, Hulton claimed "Mrs. Ayers told me that her family had been helping out a brilliant young black man."[71]

Hulton claimed that he encountered Obama outside the Ayers residence one afternoon and that he chatted with him for a while. According to Hulton, Obama said he had come to thank the Ayers's for helping with his education.[72] Hulton also said he occasionally ran into Bernardine Dohrn, who was living with the Ayers's at the time.

Hulton claimed Mary Ayers said that she and Tom communicated in code with Bill Ayers and Bernardine Dohrn when they were fugitives. He also said that when he complained about senior management at the Post Office, Tom Ayers commented about "the struggle between the common man and those with means or power," which Hulton thought sounded Marxist.[73]

After graduating from Harvard as President of the *Harvard Law Review*, Obama could have gone to any legal firm in the country. He received advice from noted judges to pursue law clerkships that would culminate in a Supreme Court assignment. Instead, he chose to work for a small Chicago civil rights law firm with ties to the Ayers family. In 1991, Judson Miner of the Chicago law firm Davis Miner Barnhill & Galland offered Obama a job.[74] Miner was a law school classmate and fellow anti-war activist with Bernardine Dohrn at the University of Chicago.[75] Obama joined Miner's firm in 1993 after a brief stint working for ACORN's Project Vote.

Miner served as legal counsel to Chicago's mayor Harold Washington, from 1984 to 1987. Coincidentally, Valerie Jarrett, the long-time friend of Michelle and Barack Obama, also served as legal counsel for Harold Washington. Jarrett and Dohrn may both have been influential in arranging Obama's hire at Miner's law firm. As we shall see in the next chapter, the law firm of Davis Miner Barnhill & Galland connected Obama with Antoin Rezko and Allison Davis, both of whom later drew Obama into spurious real estate ventures.

Obama collaborated with organizations led by Bill and Tom Ayers that were focused on education reform in Chicago. The reform movement began in 1987 after a strike by the teachers' union. Bill Ayers was involved in the effort though the Alliance for Better Chicago Schools (ABC's), which he later chaired.[76] This alliance included the Developing Communities Project, which Barack Obama led at the time.[77] The alliance also included Chicago United, which Thomas Ayers led.[78]

These school reform efforts in Chicago got off to a rough start, so philanthropist Walter Annenberg stepped in to assist Thomas Ayers and other civic leaders. As part of a broader nationwide $500 million initiative headquartered at Brown University, Annenberg offered a $49.2 million grant for a five-year program called the Chicago Annenberg Challenge (CAC), which was intended to improve student achievement.[79] In 1994, Bill Ayers set up and chaired the Chicago School Reform Collaborative (CSRC) to develop a grant proposal for Annenberg. The CSRC was eventually awarded the money to launch the Chicago Annenberg Challenge.

Ayers and the CSRC hired Barack Obama in 1995 to be the Chairman of the newly formed CAC.[80] Ayers and the CSRC had been instructed by Brown University President Vartan Gregorian to "engage people who reflect the racial and ethnic diversity of Chicago" when staffing the CAC board.[81] Ken Rolling of the Woods fund, which had funded Obama's earlier stint as the head of the DCP, was recruited to be Executive Director.[82] Obama was chairman of the CAC until 1999 and a member of the board until 2001.[83]

It is unlikely that Ayers would have selected Obama out of millions of Chicagoans to lead this major project if they did not already know each other well. At the time, Obama was an unknown associate at a small law firm, and could hardly have been considered an expert on education reform. The board of the CAC featured several university presidents, including Stanley Ikenberry of the University of Illinois, who said, "It was unusual: here you had a person trained in the law chairing a board on school reform."[84] Clearly, Ayers must have had a significant relationship with Obama. It is hard to explain his preferential hire of Obama for the prestigious CAC position otherwise.

Ayers and Obama worked together for five years disbursing the original $49.2 million in seed money and raising perhaps as much as another $100 million from local philanthropies and businesses, often leveraging connections made by Thomas Ayers.[85] [86] The money was used to continue the radical school reform projects that Ayers, Obama, and others had started during the ABC's collaboration years earlier.

Ayers and Obama ran the CAC and related sub-projects out of third floor offices in a building at 115 S. Sangamon Street in Chicago, so it is reasonable to conclude that they got to know each other pretty well.[87] One of the projects funded by the CAC was the Small Schools Workshop (SSW), which was started by Bill Ayers in 1992. The CAC directed nearly one million dollars to this project.[88] [89] This was an amazingly clever and incestuous arrangement. Thomas Ayers and friends set up a philanthropic operation (the CAC), Bill Ayers ran the oversight committee (the CSRC), Obama was hired to run the CAC, and then Obama gave $1 million from the CAC to another Bill Ayers project (the SSW). That arrangement has "scam" written all over it. It also has all of the earmarks of a very personal relationship.

As Obama funneled money to Ayers for the Small Schools Workshop, Ayers hired Michael Klonsky, a former SDS member and founder of the Marxist-Leninist Communist Party, to help run it.[90] Mike's wife, Susan Klonsky, a former member of the SDS, was also recruited to help on the project.

During their CAC collaboration, Ayers and Obama funneled money to other organizations focused on radicalizing students, parents, and teachers. Reporter Stanley Kurtz wrote, "Instead of funding schools directly, it (the CAC) required schools to affiliate with 'external partners', which actually got the money. Proposals from groups focused on math/science achievement were turned down. Instead CAC disbursed money through various far-left community organizers, such as ACORN."[91]

The CAC's radical reform efforts in Chicago were similar to what Venezuelan dictator Hugo Chavez is doing with education in Venezuela. Coincidentally, Ayers is on the board of a Venezuelan think tank that is radicalizing education in Venezuela.[92] He made at least four visits to Caracas to assist Chavez's education reform efforts. During his 2006 visit, he told Chavez, "We share the belief that education is the motor-force of revolution….Teaching invites transformations, it urges revolutions small and large. La educacion es revolucion!"[93]

Ayers's adopted son, Chesa Boudin, is also assisting education reform in Venezuela. Boudin was awarded a Rhodes Scholarship in 2002 at the University of Chicago. Barack Obama wrote a personal letter of reference to Dennis Hutchinson, a fellow professor at the University of Chicago, in support of Boudin's scholarship application.[94] This implies that Obama not only knew Bill Ayers well, he knew his son Chesa well enough to be an effective personal reference.

Ayers and Obama collaborated to run the CAC and to coordinate the flow of its money to radical organizations. It is beyond incredible that Obama would later publicly claim that he barely knew Ayers. In addition to their CAC collaboration, they also appeared together on various academic panels. They appeared at the University of Illinois for a 2002 discussion called, "Intellectuals: Who Needs Them?"[95] They also appeared on a panel at the University of Chicago Medical Center for a 1997 discussion called, "Should a child ever be called a 'super predator?'" This panel discussion was coordinated by Michelle Obama.[96]

There is still no clear accounting of how Ayers and Obama disbursed the CAC money vacuumed up from Walter Annenberg, Thomas Ayers, and others. The CAC files, accumulated in 132 boxes, were prevented from being released to reporters until Ken Rolling, an Executive Director of the CAC, had an opportunity to "review" the files.[97]

The CAC did not accomplish anything significant, according to a University of Chicago team paid to assess the impact of their efforts. The conclusion of the team's 250 page report was that six years of CAC spending and activity had no impact. Schools that were assisted by the CAC did not have better test results than schools that didn't get CAC help. There was "no Annenberg effect," according to the report.[98] The audit stated: "There were no statistically significant differences in student achievement between Annenberg schools and demographically similar non-Annenberg schools."[99]

From 1999 to 2002, the two men who barely knew each other were fellow board members of the Woods Fund.[100] Barack had been a member since 1993, and Ayers joined him in 1999. The Woods Fund granted money to leftist organizations such as the Midwest Academy, the Tides Foundation, the Arab American Action Network, and ACORN.[101] Other notable recipients included Jeremiah Wright and the Northwestern University Law School Children and Family Justice Center, where former terrorist Bernardine Dohrn works.[102]

One of the recipients of Woods Fund largesse, the Midwest Academy (MA), was co-founded by Paul Booth, former National Secretary of the SDS and a trainee of Saul Alinsky's IAF.[103] The MA, which received $100,000 in grants from the Woods Fund, describes itself as "one of the nation's oldest and best known schools for community organizations, citizen organizations, and individuals committed to progressive social change."[104]

The Woods Fund was established by the Woods family, which owned the Sahara Coal Company, a major supplier to Commonwealth Edison, which was coincidentally headed by Thomas Ayers.[105] Coincidentally, the Woods Fund financed Obama's community organizer job at the Developing Communities Project in 1985. Coincidentally, the Woods Fund appointed Bill Ayers to its Board of Directors along with Obama. Coincidentally, the Woods Fund granted funds to Bernardine Dohrn's university department and to a law school classmate of Dohrn's. Since the Woods Fund board met quarterly, and since the membership of Ayers and Obama on the board overlapped three years, the two men would have been in at least twelve board meetings together. But, Bill Ayers was just another guy in Obama's neighborhood.

In 1995, Barack Obama ran for Illinois State Senator. The kick-off of his campaign was held in the home of Bill Ayers and Bernardine Dohrn.[106] The event was coordinated by Alice Palmer, the incumbent State Senator who was vacating the seat. She had handpicked Obama as the candidate to replace her. She arranged the meet-and-greet to introduce Obama to potential supporters. Palmer, a Marxist, probably recognized the affinity between her radical politics, the politics of the former SDS members who attended the party, and the radical inclinations of young Obama.[107]

Dr. Quentin Young, the family physician of Ayers and Dohrn and an SDS sympathizer who visited North Vietnam in 1972, attended the party. He said, "I can remember being one of a small group of people who came to Bill Ayers' house to learn that Alice Palmer was stepping down from the senate and running for Congress....It was a small group, half a dozen."[108] [109] Young subsequently contributed to Obama's campaign. Maria Warren, another attendee, wrote on her blog, "When I first met Barack Obama, he was giving a standard, innocuous little talk in the living room of those two legends-in-their-own-minds, Bill Ayers and Bernardine Dohrn. They were launching him—introducing him to the Hyde Park community as the best thing since sliced bread."[110]

Obama continued consorting with the Ayers family during his political career. He worked with Bill Ayers at the CAC while he was an Illinois State Senator. He also worked with Thomas Ayers and his son, John Ayers, on the Leadership Council of the Chicago Public Education Fund (CPEF).[111] Obama was on this council from 2001 to 2004, overlapping service with the two Ayers's. The CPEF was the organization that the CAC turned its assets over to when it expired.

Obama was a board member of the Joyce Foundation from 1994 to 2002. The Joyce Foundation funneled $600,000 to the CPEF, which Tom and John Ayers were involved in.[112] It also funneled hundreds of thousands of dollars to the Leadership for Quality Education, which was an umbrella group for another project that both John and Bill Ayers worked on.[113] In total, millions of dollars were funneled to projects involving the Ayers family from philanthropic foundations that Obama was a board member of.

When Obama ran for the U.S. Senate in 2004 and the Presidency in 2008, he used David Axelrod to help with his campaigns. Axelrod was a lobbyist for Commonwealth Edison, which Thomas Ayers led.[114][115] According to anti-terrorism officer Larry Johnson, Axelrod regularly coached Bill Ayers during Obama's campaigns on how to respond to questions about his relationship with Barack.[116]

In 1997, Ayers published a book titled *A Kind and Just Parent: The Children of the Juvenile Court.* It blamed American society for the behavior of criminals, and compared the American justice system to South Africa under apartheid. Obama endorsed the cover, describing the book as "A searing and timely account of the juvenile court system, and the courageous individuals who rescue hope from despair."[117]

When revelations about Ayers began to reflect badly on Obama's political career, the *Chicago Sun-Times* ran a story titled "Who is Bill Ayers?" The article suggested that the relationship between Ayers and Obama was benign, and that Ayers had reformed. The source in the article said, "What Bill Ayers…did forty years ago has nothing to do with" Obama's presidential run.[118] The source lauded Ayers's work in public education.

The source in the article was Marilyn Katz, an Obama supporter and former SDS member. Katz was in charge of SDS security during the 1968 Chicago riots. William Frapolly, an undercover police officer, testified that Katz trained rioters on how to use SDS weapons: "She had two types. One was a cluster of nails that were sharpened at both ends, and they were fastened in the center….She said these were good for throwing or putting underneath tires. She showed another set that was the same type of nails sharpened at both ends, but they were put through a Styrofoam cylinder."[119] Katz's arsenal also included bags of human excrement and cans of urine.[120]

Katz served on Obama's national finance committee and was listed as a "bundler" on his website committed to raising $100,000.[121] She hosted fundraisers for him in her home and personally donated thousands of dollars to his campaign. She also helped organize the now-famous October 2002 antiwar rally in Chicago where Barack Obama publicly opposed war in Iraq.[122] Katz once said she supported "sexual freedom and a democratic socialist paradise."[123]

What should we make of Katz's assertion that what Bill Ayers did 40 years ago meant nothing in the context of Barack Obama's political career? We should conclude that her statement is rubbish. Ayers and Dohrn *started* their bombing spree 40 years ago. They did not surrender to authorities until 1980, at which point Obama was already politically active and involved with an offshoot of the SDS. When Obama moved to New York City, the Weather Underground gang was all there, right in his neighborhood. Remnants of the gang were involved in anti-apartheid protests, just like Obama was.

What should we make of Katz's assertion that William Ayers is now a reformed citizen? Is it true that he has changed since his days as a terrorist, a Marxist, and an anti-American activist? Let's review the public record. Ayers was pictured trampling an American flag on a cover of the *Chicago Magazine*. The related 2001 article was titled "No Regrets."[124] In a 2001 *New York Times* interview, he said he was unrepentant for his violence: "I don't regret setting bombs….I feel we didn't do enough."[125] He also said that the notion of the United States as a decent place "makes me want to puke."[126]

In 2007, Ayers and Dohrn spoke at a reunion of SDS members. Ayers praised the rebelliousness of the SDS and quoted communist heroes.[127] Dohrn called the U.S. the "greatest purveyor of violence in the world" and said that she was living in "the belly of the beast" and "the heart of the monster."[128] According to Ayers's own blog, he was still carrying his SDS card in his wallet when he participated in a 2005 antiwar rally with Cindy Sheehan.[129]

In 2007, Dohrn said she wants to "remove capitalism, that evil thing that it is...he is…she is."[130] In a 2003 article for the Marxist periodical *Monthly Review*, she lauded domestic and foreign protests against American anti-terrorist security measures as a "resistance" to U.S. imperialism.[131] The Obama presidential campaign, unfazed by such anti-American rhetoric, defended Ayers and Dohrn in 2008 as "respectable fixtures of the mainstream in Chicago."[132]

Ayers and Dohrn released a new book in February 2009 titled *Race Course against White Supremacy*. They discretely waited until after the election and inauguration of Obama before releasing the book.

On January 20, 2009, Bill Ayers was "overflowing with happiness, relief, love" when he and Bernardine and thousands of Chicagoans celebrated Obama's inauguration in Grant Park.[133] Ayers and Dohrn spoke with an *NBC* reporter near the site of their 1969 "Days of Rage" riots. "I couldn't stop crying a couple of times. I found the exact spot where I was beaten 40 years ago," Ayers said.[134] They were perhaps celebrating the manifestation of a prophecy Dohrn made in 2006: "Stay vigilant. The light will come."[135] It is certainly illustrative that Ayers connected SDS riots in 1969 with Obama's inauguration in 2009. He connected two very big dots.

The Ayers's were celebrating two decades of purposeful nurturing of Obama's career. The Ayers family helped enable Obama's Harvard education, hired him into numerous jobs, worked with him on various boards, used their home to kick off his political career, and made connections for him in Illinois politics. Their nurturing built a foundation that helped a relatively unknown Chicago radical to suddenly become President. The 40-year-old vision of SDS radicals to take over America finally came to fruition with the election of Obama as President. This was an impressive accomplishment by Bill Ayers, who otherwise was "just a guy in the neighborhood."

One can imagine Ayers's vicarious thrill, in light of his youthful dreams to lead a revolution in America, seeing that his protégé was now in a position to do just that. Ironically, Obama's campaign logo, the blue oval with stripes on the ground, vaguely resembles the Weatherman logo with its semi-circle rainbow and lightning bolt.[136] [137] This logo is tattooed on Ayers's neck and also appeared on the dust jacket of his book *Fugitive Days*.[138] [139] The Weatherman logo resembles the lightning bolt in a circle logo of the British Union of Fascists and National Socialists (1935 to 1940).[140] [141]

What are we to think of this intimate 20-year relationship between the President of the United States and terrorists who declared war on "AmeriKKKa", bombed the Pentagon, and cheered when the Manson clan slaughtered Sharon Tate? What are we to make of the deeply intertwined lives and careers of Barack and Michelle Obama with a nefarious couple who continue to advocate Marxian destruction of private property and the middle class? And what are we to think of a President who blatantly lied about the extent of these relationships in order to deceive American voters, with the help of a complicit media?

Based on what we've seen in previous chapters, and what we will see in chapters to come, we should think the worst.

We've been had.

Chapter Seven

Meet Antoin Rezko

> *"Political language. . . is designed to make lies sound truthful and murder respectable, and to give an appearance of solidity to pure wind."*
>
> George Orwell

Politics in Illinois is often brutal and bare-knuckled. As we've learned from examining Barack Obama's career, lawyers are occasionally used to disqualify opponents from a ballot, and surrogates are sometimes used to publicize the divorce files of opponents to scandalize them into withdrawal. Politics in Illinois is sometimes done illegally, including the "pay-to-play" outrages involving Illinois Governor Rod Blagojevich and other political pariahs close to Obama. In one outrage, Blagojevich conspired to sell the U.S. Senate seat vacated by President-elect Obama. U.S. Attorney Patrick Fitzgerald called this conspiracy "sinister and appalling".[1] Four of the last nine Illinois governors were indicted on charges of corruption, and three were convicted. Such shameful abuse of political power, especially in Obama's base of Chicago, is disheartening to middle-class Americans who want to believe that democracy has a place for them.

Antoin Rezko was a central player in this corrupt Illinois political landscape. Rezko, a Syrian national, was recently convicted of 16 felonies, including fraud and bribery of public officials. He was Obama's largest campaign contributor and a major contributor to Blagojevich. He had ties to unscrupulous political and business agents in Illinois and in the Middle East.

This chapter explores Barack Obama's 17-year political and financial collaboration with Rezko and his shady cohorts. It will show that before Obama emerged as a media-created messiah in 2004, he was just another tainted Illinois politician wallowing in dubious deals and spurious relationships. It will show that his political world revolved around real estate scams, quid pro quos with wealthy patrons, and nepotism among a tight circle of self-serving opportunists.

Antoin (Tony) Rezko was born in 1955 in Syria and emigrated to the U.S. when he was 19. He settled in Chicago and earned degrees in civil engineering from the Illinois Institute of Technology. Early in his career, he designed nuclear power plants for an engineering firm and designed roads for the Illinois Transportation Department.

In the 1980's, Rezko began investing in real estate and fast food restaurants. His empire grew to include numerous low-income housing complexes, the first Subway restaurant in Chicago, a chain of Panda Express Chinese restaurants, and a chain of Papa John's pizzerias.

In 1984, Rezko joined Crucial Concessions, a company owned by Jabir Herbert Muhammad, the son of Nation of Islam leader Elijah Muhammad.[2] Rezko eventually became a senior manager there.[3] Crucial Concessions won a major food service contract for local beaches and parks shortly after Harold Washington was elected the first African-American mayor of Chicago in 1983.[4] In 1997, Crucial Concessions won a 10-year food services contract at O'Hare International Airport under the auspices of an affirmative action program.

In 1989, Rezko and partner Daniel Mahru formed a company called Rezmar and began rehabilitating tenements in Chicago, often with taxpayer money. Even though neither Rezko nor Mahru had any construction experience, Rezmar eventually received roughly $100 million in loans from various government agencies to renovate low-income public housing in Chicago.[5]

Despite the deluge of public funds, all 30 buildings Rezmar was involved in experienced financial difficulties. Many were foreclosed or abandoned.[6] The City of Chicago repeatedly sued Rezmar for failing to heat its properties.[7] Rezmar's architect said "every one of these properties has failed."[8] In other words, Rezko and Mahru were slumlords.

Rezko was a prolific political fundraiser and generous contributor to Illinois politicians. In return, politicians pulled strings to funnel piles of taxpayer money toward his real estate projects. Rezko and his companies contributed hundreds of thousands of dollars to various candidates. He helped raise $1.4 million for Rod Blagojevich's gubernatorial campaigns in 2002 and 2006.[9] He hosted Blagojevich's 2002 victory celebration at his mansion.[10]

Rezko and Blagojevich's wife, Patti, a real estate agent, collaborated on several property deals, earning her $38,000.[11] Rezko donated approximately $500,000 to various Blagojevich campaigns.[12] As a key adviser, he helped Blagojevich set up the state's first Democratic administration in two decades. With this intimate access to power, Rezko maneuvered to get his own cronies appointed to important offices, boards, and commissions.

Rezko ultimately abused his connections. In October 2006, he was indicted on multiple charges, including bribery and attempted extortion, during a federal investigation called "Operation Board Games."[13] The case broke when Joseph Cari, a major DNC fundraiser and the former Midwest field director for the 1988 Biden presidential campaign, confessed to his role in a kickback scandal.[14] The scheme was directed by Rezko and fellow conspirator Stuart Levine, who tried to extort millions of dollars from companies who wanted to do business with several Illinois state administration boards. Levine agreed to testify against Rezko and others involved in the scandal.

In June 2008, a jury found Rezko guilty of 16 of the 24 counts prosecuted by the government.[15] *CBS News* said the "high-profile federal trial provided an unusually detailed glimpse of the pay-to-play politics that has made Illinois infamous."[16] During the trial, prosecutors proved that Blagojevich advisor Rezko strong-armed businesses for millions in kickbacks.[17]

Obama was tangentially involved in the pay-to-play scandal that torpedoed Rezko. The Illinois Health Facilities Planning Act in 2003 helped enable the extortion plot of Rezko and Levine. Senate Bill 1332, the Senate version of the Act, was referred to Obama's Health and Human Services Committee when it was introduced. Obama's committee recommended passage of the bill to the full Senate, with the stipulation that the oversight committee established by the Act be reduced from 15 members to nine. It also recommended that these nine members should be appointed by the governor.[18]

These stipulations were critical, because they made it easier for Blagojevich, Rezko, and Levine to stack the committee with cronies. This enabled the kickbacks they successfully extorted in the pay-to-play scandal. The corrupt members of the rigged committee included three who contributed to Obama's campaigns. Some members of the committee also made large contributions to Blagojevich.

Prosecutor Patrick Fitzgerald omitted Obama's name from the Board Game trial records, along with other high-profile people. In the original indictment, Governor Blagojevich was referred to as "Public Official A." Obama was referred to as a "Political Candidate."[19] The rest of the indictment included major political contributors to Blagojevich, Obama, and Daley.

The Board Games trial was not the only misfortune for Rezko. While the jury was deliberating, an arrest warrant was issued for him in Las Vegas for passing bad checks related to $450,000 in gambling debts at Caesars Palace and Bally's. Another casino, the Bellagio, filed a similar civil complaint for $331,000.[20]

In 2005, Crucial Concessions lost its food service contract at O'Hare Airport. The affirmative action contract was disqualified because the nominal minority owner of Crucial Concessions, Jabir Herbert Muhammad, was merely a front for Rezko, who had been appointed trustee of Muhammad's affairs because of his failing health.[21] In March 2008, Muhammad sued Rezko, alleging that Rezko had swindled his assets from him.[22]

As Rezko's business ventures failed and his legal troubles mounted, he entered into several deals with Iraqi-born businessman Nadhmi Auchi. Rezko was imprisoned in Chicago's Metropolitan Correctional Center in 2008 when he violated his bail conditions by failing to disclose a $3.5 million loan from Auchi.[23] Judge Amy St. Eve was concerned that he was a flight risk, because he traveled frequently to the Middle East.[24]

Governor Blagojevich was the next kingpin to fall during the investigations into the Illinois political cesspool. In December 2008, federal prosecutors alleged that Blagojevich tried to trade his ability to appoint President-Elect Obama's successor in the U.S. Senate for either a position in Obama's administration or a position with a major labor organization. Blagojevich was impeached and removed from his office in January 2009.

According to a phone call secretly recorded by the FBI on the day after Obama's election, Blagojevich wanted Obama to "put something together...Something big" in return for agreeing to Obama's choice for the vacated seat.[25] Blagojevich said on tape, "I've got this thing and it's fucking golden, and, uh, uh, I'm just not giving it up for fuckin' nothing. I'm not gonna do it."[26] U.S. Attorney Patrick Fitzgerald later described it as conduct that "would make Lincoln roll over in his grave."[27]

Presidential advisor Valerie Jarrett was reportedly the candidate that Obama preferred to fill his Senate seat.[28] Blagojevich said on tape that he would not pick Obama's choice unless he was guaranteed a job paying up to $300,000 per year.[29] The person "negotiating" on behalf of Obama has not been identified. Some suspect that it was a high level member of SEIU. According to the *Wall Street Journal*, Andy Stern, the head of SEIU, has visited the White House at least 22 times as of October 2009.[30] It is likely that a number of go-betweens were used to minimize contamination of the White House staff.

Fitzgerald summarized the case against Blagojevich: "The breadth of corruption laid out in these charges is staggering. They allege that Blagojevich put a 'for sale' sign on the naming of a United States senator...."[31] When Fitzgerald had Blagojevich arrested, critics complained that the investigations were ended prematurely, perhaps preventing Obama from being dragged further into the scandal.

When questioned on December 9, 2008 about Blagojevich's arrest, Obama said, "I had no contact with the governor or his office" regarding the open senate seat.[32] However, the media reported on November 5, 2008 that Obama had met with the governor that day to discuss his replacement.[33] On November 23, 2008, David Axelrod told *Fox News Chicago* that Obama had "talked to the governor and there are a whole range of names, many of which have surfaced, and I think he has a fondness for a lot of them."[34]

Thus, Obama's denial of talks with Blagojevich is either a lie, or the other reports were lies. Axelrod later told the media he was "mistaken" when he said Obama had spoken with Blagojevich.[35] However, *Judicial Watch* claimed to have "obtained documents from the office of Illinois Governor Rod Blagojevich through the Freedom of Information Act related to Blagojevich's contacts with President-elect Obama and his transition team. The documents include a December 3, 2008, letter from Barack Obama following his December 2, 2008, meeting with Blagojevich...." The December 3, 2008 letter from Obama thanked Blagojevich for meeting with him and Joe Biden the day before.[36]

Obama had an active relationship with Blagojevich, so it would have been natural for them to discuss a topic as important as Obama's Senate replacement. Obama endorsed Blagojevich in 2002 and 2006. He was also a top advisor to the governor in his 2002 run for the governorship. Rahm Emanuel claimed that he and Obama were part of a small strategy group supporting Blagojevich's 2002 gubernatorial campaign. Emanuel said that they "participated in a small group that met weekly when Rod was running for governor. We basically laid out the general election, Barack and I and these two."[37]

Thus far, Obama has avoided being dragged by the legal system directly into the Blagojevich scandal. However, attorneys for Blagojevich have asked the courts to subpoena President Obama as a defense witness, arguing that he has personal knowledge of the allegedly illegal conversations that occurred and of the emissaries that were appointed as go-betweens. If Obama is forced to testify, it would be a highly charged and potentially damning event for him. Blagojevich's attorneys have asked the courts to make public Obama's two-hour interview with FBI agents regarding the case. Obama's commentary has thus far been redacted from case records. However, in June 2010, White House Chief of Staff Rahm Emanuel and Senior Advisor Valerie Jarrett were subpoenaed in the case.

Clearly, Obama and Rezko consorted with some sleazy sharks in the corrupt sea of Illinois politics. Rezko himself is crooked, unethical, manipulative, and surrounded by subversive characters. As we examine Barack Obama's 17-year relationship with this convicted criminal and his cohorts, let's consider an important question. Is it possible that a future President of the United States, who must rely on character judgment for major appointments and consequential decisions, could have been oblivious to Rezko's corrupt dealings for two decades, especially when some of those tainted dealings directly involved Obama?

After Obama graduated from Harvard in 1991, he turned down a job offer personally proffered by Rezko.[38] It is unclear what role Obama, the President of the *Harvard Law Review*, would have played at Rezmar, a shady real estate management firm that could fairly be called a slumlord organization. Chicago is a long way from Harvard, and Rezmar is a long way from clerking at the Supreme Court, which would have been Obama's most logical career path.

Rezko and Obama must have known each other prior to this, or else the asymmetrical job offer from Rezko was another of those bizarre "coincidences" that characterized Obama's career at every turn. One possible link between Rezko and Obama at that time was Thomas Ayers. Both Ayers and Rezko were financial donors to Chicago Mayors Washington and Daley. Thomas Ayers was also linked to Khalid al-Mansour, the Black Panther who helped arrange

Obama's Harvard education. Al-Mansour was an associate of radical professor Edward Said, who was an instructor of Obama at Columbia and an associate of Jabir Herbert Muhammad, who was Rezko's boss at Crucial Concessions.[39] Both Ayers and al-Mansour had already provided assistance to Obama, so it is not unreasonable to conjecture that one or both continued nurturing his career via their connections with Antoin Rezko.

Whether through Ayers or al-Mansour, Rezko became aware that Obama was somebody "special." A former Rezko employee remembered meeting Obama around that time: "Tony (Rezko) was taking him (Obama) around the office, introducing him and saying, 'He's going to do great things.'"[40]

Obama declined Rezko's job offer, however, choosing instead to work for the law firm Davis Miner Barnhill & Galland, after a brief stint working for ACORN's Project Vote. As we learned in the last chapter, name partner Judson Miner was a classmate and fellow antiwar activist with Bernardine Dohrn, wife of William Ayers. Coincidentally, Miner's law firm, which represented subsidized housing developers eager to tap into government funds, provided legal counsel for Rezmar. Thus, Obama ended up working for Rezko anyway, albeit indirectly. Obama's employer would eventually help Rezmar get millions of dollars in government funding for low-income housing developments.

Allison S. Davis, also a name partner in the law firm that hired Obama, later went into business with Rezko. Rezko eventually influenced Governor Blagojevich to appoint Davis to the Illinois State Board of Investment in 2003. As we shall see shortly, this gang was tightly connected and scratched each others' backs with disturbing regularity.

Over the course of a decade, Allison Davis, Antoin Rezko, and other partners received real estate parcels from Chicago City Hall covering several city blocks. They paid for some of the lots, but they got many for free. Davis and partners also received more than $100 million in taxpayer subsidies to build and rehabilitate housing, primarily for the poor.[41] Davis became a major player at City Hall, not only because of his involvement in quasi-public real estate development projects, but also for his political fundraising. He eventually contributed over $400,000 to politicians. His top beneficiaries included Mayor Daley, Governor Blagojevich, and Senator Obama, his former employee at his old law firm.[42]

Rezko was Obama's most prolific financial patron when Barack ventured into politics. In 1995, when Obama ran for the Illinois State Senate, Rezko's companies contributed $2,000, the first donation to Obama's first campaign.[43] Valerie Jarrett, Obama's campaign finance chairperson, worked with Antoin Rezko, Rita Rezko (his spouse), and Allison Davis to raise funds. Rezko raised more than $10,000 of the $100,000 Obama collected for his 1995 campaign.[44][45]

Rezko helped bankroll Obama in his 1996, 1998, 2000, 2002, and 2004 election campaigns. Rezko and his close friends contributed more than $250,000 to Obama's various campaigns, and they coordinated fundraising for hundreds of thousands of dollars more.[46] According to the Operation Board Games indictment against Rezko, a portion of his campaign contributions to Obama likely involved dirty money from the kickback scandal.[47]

Rezko was a member of Obama's campaign finance committee during Obama's 2004 U.S. Senate race, along with Jarrett and Davis.[48] The committee raised more than $14 million for Obama. The fund raising efforts included a lavish event that Rezko coordinated for Obama at his mansion.[49]

Rezko was connected to many shady Middle Easterners who contributed to Obama's campaigns, including Aiham Alsammarae. Alsammarae was the Iraqi Minister of Electricity from 2003 to 2005. He was imprisoned for defrauding Iraq of millions of dollars. Some of the fraud was related to an electric power plant project in Iraq that Rezko and Alsammarae were jointly developing. Obama was dragged into this deal by way of a company called Companion Security, which was set up in April 2006 by Rezko and others to train Iraqi security guards at a leased Illinois military facility. According to one of Rezko's partners, Rezko paid Alsammarae a $1.5 million bribe to win this contract.

Companion Security petitioned Obama's Senate staff for help in August 2006 to keep the deal alive after Alsammarae was imprisoned.[50] Rezko sent Companion Security partner Daniel Frawley to Obama's office to get him to write a letter to senior Iraqi officials.[51] At the time, Obama was a member of the Senate Foreign Relations committee. Obama's office interacted with representatives from Companion Security for six months, but abandoned the effort when Rezko was indicted on the Board Game charges.[52]

Alsammarae was extricated from prison in December 2006 in what he called "the Chicago way."[53] His escape was allegedly facilitated by Blackwater operatives who infiltrated Baghdad's Green Zone and spirited him out of Iraq on a forged Chinese passport. He ended up in Chicago and connected with Rezko, his old classmate from the Illinois Institute of Technology.[54] Alsammarae later posted his Oak Brook mansion, valued at $2.7 million, to help bail Rezko out of jail following his Operation Board Games indictment.[55]

Strangely, while Alsammarae was imprisoned in Iraq, his family requested help from Barack Obama. Obama's Senate office admitted seeking information from the U.S. State Department and the U.S. Consul in Iraq to assist Alsammarae in October 2006.[56] It is unclear why Obama had a compelling interest in an Iraqi criminal in Baghdad, particularly one who would later make remarks carried by Jordanian radio rooting for more insurgent attacks on U.S. troops. Alsammarae declared on the radio, "...I hope that the (insurgency) continues and avenges the Iraqi people...."[57] Coincidentally, Alsammarae contributed to Obama's presidential campaign, which Obama claimed he gave to charity.[58] A cursory connection of the dots leads to the suspicion that Rezko asked for Obama's assistance with Alsammarae, since Rezko and Alsammarae were working together on a massive development project, and Rezko and Obama were tightly connected politically.

There are many curiosities about Obama's relationship with Alsammarae. Why was Obama's office requested by Alsammarae's family to help get him out of prison in Baghdad? Why did Obama's office inquire into the matter through official channels? Who helped Alsammarae escape Iraq, right under the noses of American security forces? Why did Alsammarae, the former Minister of Electricity in Iraq, contribute to Obama's campaign? Why did Obama's office interact with Rezko's company regarding a business deal with Alsammarae? Why did Obama have anything to do with a high-powered Middle Easterner who publicly wished for more attacks on American troops?

Another shady Rezko associate who helped Obama was Joseph Aramanda, a former Chief Operating Officer of a Rezko company. Aramanda was mixed up in a $375,000 kickback scheme involving Glencoe Capital that was part of the Illinois pay-to-play conspiracy. Aramanda's son John was hired by Obama as an intern in his Washington Senate office in 2005, on the recommendation of Rezko. Aramanda donated $11,500 to Obama, likely from the proceeds of the illegal kickback scheme.[59] Aramanda also gave money to Obama's campaign for the U.S. House of Representatives in 2000. Obama denied knowing Aramanda, but that seems implausible, since Aramanda was a significant campaign contributor, he was a business partner of Rezko's, and his son worked for Obama.

But the most disturbing involvement Obama had with Rezko and cohorts was in the realm of real estate development. In 1999, journalist E.J. Dionne summarized Barack Obama's description of the mechanics of the Illinois real estate political patronage system: A politician awards contracts to the real estate developers, and in return the developers help finance the politician's reelection efforts. "They do well, and you get a $5M to $10M war chest," Obama told Dionne.[60]

That is exactly what transpired when Obama helped Rezko and friends in their real estate ventures over the course of a decade. Allison Davis, Obama's boss at Davis Miner Barnhill & Galland, left the firm in 1998 to invest with Antoin Rezko in a low-income housing project. The transaction was managed by Davis's old law firm. State Senator Obama played a role in the deal, despite the obvious conflicts of interest with Rezko, a steady campaign contributor, and Davis, his former boss. According to Jerome Corsi, "Obama wrote letters to city and state officials supporting his political patron Rezko's successful bid to get more than $14 million from taxpayers to build apartments for senior citizens."[61] This project, called Cottage View Terrace, was overseen by a Davis company called New Kenwood, LLC. Davis was on the Chicago Planning Commission when this deal was transacted. The city owned the parcel targeted for the project, which Davis and Rezko bought for $1. The project was outside of Obama's district, which makes his involvement even more inappropriate. The project included $855,000 in "development fees" for New Kenwood.[62]

Obama also helped Davis and Rezko get funding from charity in 2000 for their low income housing developments. When Obama served on the board of the Woods Fund with William Ayers, they invested $1 million in Neighborhood Rejuvenation Partners L.P., a company that Davis operated.[63] Coincidentally, Allison Davis contributed $5,000 to Obama's Hopefund PAC, and his family donated more than $25,000 to Obama's political campaigns.[64][65]

The chairman of the Woods Fund board at the time was Howard J. Stanback. Coincidentally, Stanback was a partner in Neighborhood Rejuvenation Partners, along with Davis.[66][67] He was also an employee of Davis at New Kenwood. Obama voted in favor of the Woods Fund investment in Neighborhood Rejuvenation Partners.[68] The conflicts of interest in these incestuous relationships were staggering. It is hard to imagine more suspicious quid pro quos, especially when Rezko, a central player in these deals, was eventually convicted of 16 counts of fraud and bribery. The funding from the Woods Fund and the letters from Obama's State Senate office soliciting on behalf of Rezko and Davis contradict Obama's presidential campaign disclaimer, "I've never done any favors for him (Rezko)".[69]

To make matters worse, the low-income projects managed by Rezko and Davis using taxpayer and charity money turned into operational nightmares. According to reporter Tim Novak, "Obama, who has worked as a lawyer and a legislator to improve living conditions for the poor, took campaign donations from Rezko even as Rezko's low-income housing empire was collapsing, leaving many African-American families in buildings riddled with problems – including squalid living conditions, vacant apartments, lack of heat, squatters and drug dealers."[70] At one of the complexes, a three year old boy was crushed to death by a rusted gate. Many of the buildings became uninhabitable. While Rezko seemingly could not find money to maintain his properties, he found hundreds of thousands of dollars to give to Obama's political campaigns.

Over nine years, Rezmar received almost $100 million in government assistance to renovate 30 Chicago buildings.[71] They pocketed development fees for these projects, but went delinquent on mortgage payments on many of them. Amazingly, they continued to get additional government loans for development projects while defaulting on earlier loans.

Other long-time Obama supporters were involved in government-subsidized housing projects that turned into disasters. Valerie Jarrett, a member of Obama's administration and his campaign finance committees, was the Executive VP of Habitat Company for more than a decade. Habitat Company managed a large subsidized housing complex called Grove Parc Plaza on behalf of the Chicago Housing Authority (CHA). The housing complex was eventually seized by the government due to chronic problems. Today, the Grove Parc units are facing demolition after being graded by federal inspectors as an 11 on a 100 point scale.[72] Grove Parc Plaza was in the district that Obama represented as a State Senator for eight years.[73]

Despite Jarrett's incompetence managing low income housing for the poor, Obama told the *Chicago Tribune*, "I trust her completely."[74] Jarrett, who was named in 2008 as one of the ten most corrupt politicians by *Judicial Watch*, has been tight with the Obama's for decades.[75] Michelle Obama shadowed Jarrett at various jobs throughout her career. Michelle was hired by Jarrett as a mayoral assistant in the Daley administration.[76] When Jarrett was assigned to run a new Department of Planning and Development, Michelle followed her as a "troubleshooter".[77] She also followed Jarrett to the University of Chicago Medical Center. Jarrett, Rezko, and Davis have been fixtures on various Obama campaign finance committees. Ironically, Obama appointed Jarrett as vice chair of the failed Chicago Olympics committee. The committee selected a site near Grove Parc as a proposed location for the 2016 Olympic Stadium.

Another Obama supporter, Cecil Butler, managed Lawndale Restoration, a subsidized housing complex that was seized by the government in 2006 after city inspectors found almost 2,000 code violations. Butler received a $51 million state loan for renovations.[78] Butler eventually defaulted on the loan and the complex was sold to the City of Chicago for $10 as part of the settlement. Lawndale residents protested against Obama in 2004, complaining that he ignored their plight while accepting $3,000 in campaign donations from Butler.[79] Coincidentally, Butler hired Valerie Jarrett's Habitat Company to help run Lawndale Restoration.

Obama used his political office to channel government funds to private developers to manage subsidized housing for the poor. Many of the recipients were his friends and contributors. More often than not, the apartments involved became cesspools. While Obama claimed political points for "assisting" poor renters, and while his friends and contributors were fed millions of public dollars, the poor people they were allegedly serving lost their homes and saw the surrounding neighborhoods deteriorate. Grove Parc tenant and Obama constituent Cynthia Ashley said, "No one should have to live like this, and no one did anything about it."[80]

Despite the failed projects and dissatisfied tenants, Obama thought everything was great. Shortly after becoming a State Senator, Obama told the *Chicago Daily Law Bulletin* that the partnership between the government and private developers in subsidized housing was working fine. "That's an example of a smart policy," he told the paper.[81] He sponsored bills in the State Senate that benefited developers of affordable housing. As President, he unveiled a plan in February 2009 to set up a $1 billion Housing Trust Fund "to rehabilitate housing in the nation's poorest neighborhoods."[82] Based on past precedents that Obama was intimately involved in, housing in poor neighborhoods will not actually be rehabilitated by this money. Instead, politically-connected power brokers in the real estate development industry will line their pockets with it.

The most egregious real estate interaction involving Rezko and Obama occurred when Rezko subsidized the purchase of a mansion for Barack and Michelle Obama in June 2005. The arrangement crossed the line of propriety in so many ways that Obama's alleged purity as a "new kind of politician" should never be mentioned again. We will explore the purchase of Obama's mansion in some detail, because the deal was a microcosm of the serpent-infested, pay-to-play culture of Illinois that Obama was immersed in.

Rezko steered Obama to the 6,400 square foot Georgian Revival mansion in Hyde Park. They toured the residence together before Obama made an offer.[83] The mansion had been renovated five years earlier by an employee of Rezko. It featured six bedrooms, six bathrooms, four fireplaces, a four car garage, a library, a solarium, and a wine cellar. It had antique Chinese washbasins, mahogany bookshelves, beveled glass doors, and a granite kitchen floor.[84] Obama paid $1.65 million for the house in June 2005, $300,000 below the list price.[85] This discount was unusual, because the sale occurred during the nationwide real estate boom. The $1.65 million was the same price the previous owners had paid five years earlier, even though median home prices in Chicago had increased roughly 50% since then.

Coincidentally, on the exact same day that Obama purchased the mansion, Rezko's wife Rita bought the empty 9,000 square foot lot adjoining the Obama residence for the full price of $625,000.[86] Both the residence and the lot were purchased from the same seller, Frederic Wondisford. It is important to note that the Obamas felt they could not afford to buy the house and the lot together, which was a requirement of Wondisford.[87]

It is also important to note that in May 2005, one month before the Obamas closed on the sale, the *Chicago Tribune* ran a profile of Rezko and the controversies he was involved in. The *Tribune* reported that Rezko "has been subpoenaed to supply any records he may have as part of a criminal investigation into allegations that the (Blagojevich) administration traded plum appointments for campaign cash."[88] Bear this in mind as we examine the particulars of this shady real estate transaction. Obama must have known at this point that he was executing a tainted deal with an unscrupulous operative.

The vacant lot that Rita Rezko purchased adjoined Obama's yard at the street corner. The two parcels together made for a very private and very attractive corner property. With a foot-tall concrete barrier and a wrought-iron fence surrounding the property, there was no access to the vacant lot, except through Obama's driveway. Thus, the vacant lot had no practical purpose for Rita. This invites speculation that Rezko's wife bought Obama a bigger lot in return for past or future considerations.

The transaction gets even more curious when the particulars are studied. The Cook County land records, where the deal was executed, show that Obama's mansion was sold by Wondisford to the Northern Trust Company land Trust #10209, which was presumably established by Obama for confidentiality.[89] The records also show that the vacant lot was sold by Wondisford to Rita Rezko. Strangely, the Cook County tax assessment records list William Miceli as the owner of Obama's address.[90] Miceli was Obama's supervisor for a period of time at the Chicago law firm Miner Barnhill & Galland. Miceli apparently signed the real estate documents on behalf of Obama's presumed land trust.

The plot thickens even more.   Kenneth J. Conner, who worked for the Mutual Bank of Harvey, the mortgage company that originated Rita Rezko's loan, filed a civil complaint in court alleging he was fired by Mutual Bank of Harvey because he objected to spurious land appraisals submitted on behalf of the Rezkos, with the complicity of the bank. "The entire deal amounted to a $125,000 payoff from Tony Rezko to Barack Obama," Conner said.[91]

Conner alleged that Mutual Bank obtained an appraisal from Adams Valuation Corp valuing the vacant lot at $625,000, on which the bank lent $500,000.[92] Conner claimed his analysis and another independent appraisal valued the parcel at $490,860. He alleged his appraisal was removed from the Mutual Bank file and he was fired for challenging the original questionable appraisals.[93]

To make the deal even messier, Rita Rezko sold one-sixth of her property, a 10-foot strip of the 60-foot wide lot, to Obama for $104,500 in January 2006, even though the unbuildable strip was valued by Obama's appraiser at only $40,500.[94] Rezko built a gated fence between the properties that allowed the Obamas continued access to the vacant lot. Obama paid for lawn maintenance for both properties.[95] What makes this sale of the 10 foot strip really peculiar is that the Cook County land records indicate that Rita Rezko deeded the *entire* vacant lot to the Obamas, even though they only paid for a portion of it.[96]

It is unclear how Rita Rezko qualified for her $500,000 loan or was able to make the $125,000 down payment on the vacant lot. Records presented during Rezko's Board Games trial by Rezko's attorney showed Rita had a salary of $37,000 and no significant assets, while Rezko himself was essentially penniless because of prior business failures and mounting legal troubles (although he was somehow able to afford 22 trips to the Middle East during a four-year period prior to his arrest).[97] This is where the tentacles of the transaction get even more bizarre. The *London Times* reported that Nadhmi Auchi, an Iraqi billionaire, loaned $3.5 million to Rezko three weeks before the Obamas purchased their mansion.[98] Auchi was allegedly a cousin of Saddam Hussein. He was an Oil Ministry Director before leaving Iraq in 1979.

The money was wired on May 23. 2005 from Auchi's General Mediterranean Holdings (GMH) company through a Panamanian company, Fintrade Services SA, and then finally into the Mutual Bank of Harvey, which is the bank that originated Rita's loan.[99] Fintrade's directors include Ibtisam Auchi, Mr. Auchi's wife.[100]

According to the *Associated Press*, "Rezko gave $700,000 of the money (from Auchi) to his wife and used the rest to pay legal bills and funnel cash to various supporters."[101] The implication is that Rezko's wife used her share of the Auchi loan to put a down payment on the property adjacent to the Obama mansion. Auchi later ended up with shares in a development project called Riverside Park that Rezko allotted to him by reducing his own shares, in exchange for forgiveness of the $3.5 million loan and other loans from Auchi that totaled $28 million.[102]

Obama claimed to have no connection to Auchi, but Barack and Michelle Obama attended an April 2004 dinner party at Rezko's home, where Auchi was the guest of honor, according to Board Games co-conspirator Stuart Levine.[103] According to the *Chicago Sun-Times*, Obama gave Auchi a big welcome and toasted him several times.[104] Also, Blagojevich, Obama, and Rezko met with Auchi at the Four Seasons Hotel in Chicago in the spring of 2004. Obama claimed that he was "coincidentally" at the same hotel as

Governor Blagojevich and Auchi, and joined the meeting as a casual, unplanned act.[105]

In 2004, Auchi was accused by the Pentagon of involvement in Saddam Hussein's Oil for Food scandal. Auchi's company, General Mediterranean Holdings, was the largest shareholder in the bank that siphoned hundreds of millions of Oil for Food money to U.N. officials and heads of state to influence support for Saddam Hussein and against the impending U.S. invasion of Iraq.[106] Auchi was also suspected of smuggling weapons to Saddam Hussein's regime. A Pentagon report said that Auchi had arranged for "significant theft from the U.N. Oil-for-Food Program to smuggle weapons and dual-use technology into Iraq."[107] Coincidentally, this scandalous activity was occurring at roughly the same time that Obama made his now-famous but then-unfashionable anti-Iraq war speech.

Auchi's U.S. visa was revoked in August 2004. According to prosecutors, Rezko worked with two unnamed Illinois officials to try to get the visa restored. One of them was alleged to be Obama.[108] The State Department refused to restore the visa, because Auchi was convicted in 2003 in France of receiving $100 million of illegal commissions in a scandal involving the oil company Elf Aquitaine.

Amrish Mahajan, the CEO of Mutual Bank of Harvey which originated Rita's loan, raised more than $500,000 during a six year period for disgraced Governor Blagojevich. He also loaned millions to Rezko and was a contributor to Obama.[109] Mahajan resigned in February 2009, perhaps because regulators said his bank had "unsafe and unsound banking practices and had violated laws or regulations."[110] Majahan's wife, Anita, was arrested for skimming millions from an Illinois state contract through her own business.[111]

Obama purchased the mansion with a discounted $1.3 million mortgage from Northern Trust.[112] The FEC reported in February 2009 that the Obamas received reduced loan rates that saved them $300 a month.[113] Northern Trust offered the favorable loan to the Obamas in anticipation of "long-term financial relationships" with them.[114] Northern Trust management includes John Rowe, who succeeded Tom Ayers as the CEO of Exelon (formerly Commonwealth Edison). "This was a business proposition for us," Northern Trust's president said.[115]

Kelly King Dibble, a coworker of Michelle Obama at the Chicago Planning Department, is now a Senior Vice President of Public Affairs at Northern Trust. Dibble formerly headed the Illinois

Summary

Housing Development Authority (IHDA) for Blagojevich. She had also worked for Rezko earlier in her career, and hosted a fundraiser for Obama.

To summarize this extraordinarily tainted transaction, Obama got a $300,000 discount on an already under-priced mansion in a hot real estate market. On the very same day, Rita Rezko purchased the adjoining yard for the full asking price, which was probably more than it was worth, and certainly more than it appears she could afford. The lot was useless to anyone but Obama, and may have since been deeded to Obama. The purchase of Rita's lot was financed by a bank that allegedly manipulated the appraisal and then fired the whistle blower. The down payment for the adjoining lot appears to have been funded by a loan from an accomplice of Saddam Hussein. Rezko sold a portion of the lot back to Obama at an inflated price when his legal troubles mounted, and built a gated fence for Obama that was only accessible from Obama's yard. Obama paid for lawn maintenance on a lot that was nominally not his. Obama received his loan at a below market rate from a bank that he had significant connections to.

Obama tried to insulate himself from Rezko's poisonous contamination during the presidential campaign by publicly declaring that he barely knew Rezko. He claimed that their relationship was limited to infrequent lunch meetings.[116] Not only did this ludicrous claim contradict their many interactions described in this chapter, John Thomas, an FBI mole, reported that he often saw Obama coming and going at Rezko's offices during 2004 and 2005.[117] Blagojevich was also observed frequently visiting Rezko. Three other sources claimed that Rezko and Obama spoke daily on the phone.[118] When confronted about this, Obama admitted that he and Rezko had known each other for 17 years and that Rezko was an active member of his campaigns. He also admitted that he relied upon Rezko to raise funds for him.[119]

Political campaigns run on money, and the convicted felon Rezko was Obama's key money man. This seedy connection drew Obama into other unsavory relationships, including criminals from the Middle East and high ranking officials of the disgraced Blagojevich administration. A number of these unsavory cohorts ended up in jail, including Rezko, Levine, and Alsammarae. Political campaigns also run on illusions. Obama's denial of deep involvement with Rezko and his cronies in the "Illinois Combine" obliterates the credibility of his lofty rhetoric like "change we can believe in."

When Rezko became a public-relations albatross, Obama identified more than $250,000 in campaign contributions that came from Rezko or close associates. He donated almost two-thirds of that amount to non-profit groups.[120] These donations, however, did not occur until after Rezko was arrested.[121] Even the dimwitted can identify a criminal when the handcuffs are clasped. But, it is disturbing that a man who was President of the *Harvard Law Review* and is now the President of the United States allegedly missed all of the obvious clues from Rezko during the 17 years leading up to the handcuffs.

For the middle class, it is important to realize that Obama's "new kind of politics" is really the old kind of "Chicago Way" politics, disguised with a smiley face. Obama is special only because his campaign managers were brazen enough to insist that he was, and the mainstream media were so partisan and complicit that they overlooked widespread evidence to the contrary. According to Chicago journalist Evelyn Pringle, "Without Rezko's fundraising, Obama would not have been elected to the Illinois Senate, or the U.S. Senate, and he would not have sold the books he wrote about himself, because like the Wizard of Oz, Obama is nobody special."[122] And just like the great and powerful Oz, who tried to bamboozle a naïve girl from Kansas, Obama tried to bamboozle middle-class America with the laughable illusion that he was immaculately conceived as a god-like politician that somehow stood above the mundane world. To the contrary, he was so deeply mired in the sordid ooze of Chicago politics that he was inseparable from it.

It is too strong and too early to suggest that Obama was a common criminal, but it is not too strong to suggest that of his friend Rezko, who was in fact convicted of 16 felonies. Obama swam in the filthy cesspool of graft and corruption known as Chicago politics with the reptilian Rezko for 17 years. He received a quarter of a million dollars in campaign contributions from Rezko during five election cycles, appointed Rezko to the finance committee of his senate campaign, collaborated with Rezko on a remarkably shady real estate deal, provided legal services to Rezko's firm, and helped funnel millions of dollars from charities and taxpayers to Rezko's failed real estate ventures that sometimes made life miserable for disadvantaged Chicagoans. Obama was dangerously tainted by Rezko's coterie of illicit friends and conspirators, including disgraced Governor Blagojevich.

Health care analyst David Catron wrote: "Barack Obama oozed from the same stinking Chicago swamp that produced Blagojevich, and a man whose formative years were spent wallowing in the muck with such creatures isn't likely to be long in the White House before the stench of pay-to-play politics begins to pervade the place."[123] Predictably, the same Chicago stench started to waft from the White House as taxpayer funds were used to bribe U.S. Senators to support health care legislation, sweetheart deals were arranged for staunch political patrons like ACORN and the UAW, and a Pennsylvania Senator was bribed with the offer of a government job in exchange for choosing not to run in a primary race.

So how did Obama explain his long, mutually beneficial relationship with the criminal Rezko to the *Chicago Tribune* in 2008? He said, "I assumed I would have seen a pattern (of corrupt behavior) over the past 15 years."[124] As with many of Obama's magically erudite sentences, one has to wonder what these words actually mean. Did he or did he not see the corrupt behavior of Rezko? If he didn't see it, what does that say about the ability of a man who holds the most powerful office in the free world to judge the character and motivation of other powerful players around him? If he did see it, that explains his attempt to hide behind an indecipherable sentence.

Reasonable people will conclude that Obama was fully aware of the corruption he was immersed in. Jay Stewart of the Better Government Association in Chicago told the *LA Times*: "Everybody in this town knew that Tony Rezko was headed for trouble. When he got indicted, there wasn't a single insider who was surprised. It was viewed as a long time coming…Why would have you be having anything to do with Tony Rezko, particularly if you're planning to run for president?"[125]

The only possible conclusion from this tale of Chicago politics is that Obama has a remarkable ability to deceive American voters.

George Orwell said, *"Political language. . . is designed to make lies sound truthful and murder respectable, and to give an appearance of solidity to pure wind."*

Pure wind indeed.

We've been had.

"There can be no liberty unless there is economic liberty."

Margaret Thatcher

Chapter Eight

Meet ACORN

> *"The only involvement I've had with ACORN was I*
> *represented them alongside the US Justice Department in*
> *making Illinois implement a motor voter law that helped*
> *people get registered at DMV's....It had nothing to do with*
> *us. We were not involved."*
>
> Barack Obama, in 10/15/08 debate with McCain

It is quite a challenge to select the most outrageous lie propagated by Barack Obama. His résumé of untruths is a frightful compilation that has somehow escaped the attention of the mainstream media. The untruth about ACORN that he fabricated during the 2008 presidential debates is certainly a candidate for the honor of most outrageous. To suggest that he was not involved with the renegade organization ACORN is like suggesting that a hen is not involved with laying eggs. Obama worked for ACORN, he was a trainer for ACORN, he was an attorney for ACORN on high-profile cases, he funded ACORN through philanthropic organizations, he paid ACORN to help with his political campaigns, and ACORN operatives actively supported his presidential candidacy. Obama *was* ACORN, in the sense that part of his career was spent as a community organizer, which is exactly what the Association of Community Organizations for Reform Now (ACORN) is a collection of.

This chapter examines the extensive relationship between ACORN and Barack Obama. ACORN and its shadowy satellite organizations are involved in many radical initiatives, including welfare proliferation, subprime mortgages, minority voter registration, and support for illegal immigration. According to their website: "ACORN is the nation's largest grassroots community organization of low- and moderate-income people with over 400,000 member families organized into more than 1,200 neighborhood chapters in 110 cities across the country."[1] It is the largest radical group in America. ACORN's "People's Platform" included the proto-fascistic declaration: "We will continue our fight until the American way is just one way, until we have shared the wealth...."[2] This motto is chanted like an article of religious faith at ACORN conventions. The "People's Platform" also made demands for gun control, unionization, higher taxes, and government-run healthcare.[3] ACORN is essentially a group committed to implementing socialism in America.

This chapter will show that ACORN is a clear and present danger to the integrity of U.S. financial, electoral, and civil institutions. The chapter begins with an examination of ACORN's history. We will study the key individuals who implemented Saul Alinsky's concept of using community "disorganizers" to overwhelm the infrastructure of America. They include Richard Cloward and Frances Fox Piven, the Bonnie and Clyde of radical agitators. They morphed Alinsky's concepts into a tactic of orchestrated chaos that became known as the Cloward-Piven Strategy. A key objective of the strategy was to induce systemic chaos in society to create momentum for a socialist revolution. According to Cloward, the underclass can only make progress when "the rest of society is afraid of them."[4] In that spirit, ACORN has been investigated for criminal activities in at least 14 states.

This chapter concludes with an examination of Barack Obama's career-long collaboration with ACORN. It will show that Obama was outrageously dishonest when he tried to deceive us about this skeleton in his political closet.

David Horowitz and Richard Poe provided an excellent account of the genesis of ACORN in their book, *The Shadow Party*. According to Horowitz and Poe, the story of ACORN began during the racial strife of the 1960's. In their words, "On 11 August 1965, the black district of Watts in Los Angeles erupted in violence after police used batons to subdue a man suspected of drunk driving. Riots raged for six days...leaving 34 dead. Democrats used the tragedy to promote an expansion of the welfare state, sponsoring new government programs to address the problem of the inner city poor."[5]

Two radical Columbia professors viewed such urban violence in the 1960's as an opportunity for revolution. Richard Andrew Cloward and Frances Fox Piven believed the growing violence meant that the underclass was finally ready to revolt against capitalism. However, they considered Johnson's Great Society programs to be impediments to the revolution, much like how the

Romans placated the rabble with free bread and circuses. In other words, the elites in America were using welfare to patronize the poor with a safety net, in order to prevent revolution.

After the Watts riots, Cloward and Piven proposed to catastrophically overload the Great Society welfare programs, in order to counter the government's efforts. Their strategy was formally published as an article titled "The Weight of the Poor: A Strategy to End Poverty," in the May 1966 edition of *The Nation* magazine.[6] Their plan was called the Cloward-Piven Strategy.[7]

Cloward and Piven observed that poor Americans were only taking advantage of half of the welfare benefits that they could. Their plan called for "cadres of aggressive organizers" to push more and more people onto the welfare rolls.[8] The purpose was not to make life better for the poor, but to overwhelm the welfare system with a tidal wave of additional obligations. Its subsequent collapse would undermine faith in the American system. Poor people would then revolt, and society would be compelled to replace capitalism with socialism. The Cloward-Piven Strategy was designed to lure poor people into becoming revolutionary foot soldiers on the march toward a Marxist state.[9]

Cloward and Piven observed that overwhelming the welfare system this way would not be just a one-time event, but a continuous drain on societal resources: "This kind of mass influence is cumulative because benefits are continuous. Once eligibility for basic food and rent grants is established, the drain on local resources persists indefinitely."[10] Their hypothesis has been confirmed by the multi-generational welfare dependency that has emerged in America's inner cities.

The Cloward-Piven Strategy epitomized the principles of the radical community organizer, Saul Alinsky, who advocated instigating change by forcing organizations to live up to their own well-intentioned rules. American society is instinctively generous, but it would inevitably fail, no matter how hard it tried, to keep up with the ever-increasing demands of the underclass. This failure would be portrayed as a shortcoming of capitalism, and it would be used to instigate widespread frustration and demands for "change". Of course, the "change" recommended by the radical community organizers would be socialism. Alinsky called this tactic "mass jujitsu", which meant using the strength of the enemy against itself. In this case, the strength being used against us was our own generosity and compassion.

Cloward and Piven first targeted their home city of New York, where millions of urban poor and free-spending politicians made it vulnerable to their strategy.[11] They enlisted radical black organizer George Wiley to execute their plan. Wiley was previously the chairman of a Congress for Racial Equality chapter. His wife, Wretha, was a member of the socialist Students for a Democratic Society.[12]

Wiley, a charismatic and respected organizer, began collaborating with Cloward and Piven in 1966.[13] In 1967, he founded the National Welfare Rights Organization (NWRO). Its mission was to implement the Cloward-Piven Strategy.[14] He hired agitators to storm welfare offices, bully social workers, and loudly demand benefits for welfare applicants. By 1969, NWRO had over 500 chapters nationwide.[15]

In New York City, the prime target of the NWRO, liberal mayor John Lindsay was an easy mark for the radicals. Protestors laid siege to City Hall, bearing signs saying "no money, no peace."[16] One case worker said, "People are beginning to act as if help from the government is a right instead of a privilege."[17] One welfare mother screamed at Mayor Lindsay, "It's my job to have kids, Mr. Mayor, and your job to take care of them."[18]

The *New York Times* outlined Wiley's tactics in 1970: "There have been sit-ins in legislative chambers, including a United States Senate committee hearing, mass demonstrations of several thousand welfare recipients, school boycotts, picket lines, mounted police, tear gas, arrests—and, on occasion, rock-throwing, smashed glass doors, overturned desks, scattered papers, and ripped out phones."[19]

Lindsay appeased the mob with increased welfare spending. He appointed Mitchell Ginsberg as welfare commissioner. Ginsberg was a Columbia colleague of Cloward and Piven, and equally radical.[20] When he made it easier to qualify for welfare, he was nicknamed "Come-and-Get-It" Ginsberg.[21]

The burden on New York City was staggering as welfare spending skyrocketed. According to Sol Stern of the Manhattan Institute, "By the early 1970's, one person was on the welfare rolls in NYC for every two working in the city's private economy."[22]

According to Horowitz and Poe, "Wiley's movement had been an economic disaster for American taxpayers and a social catastrophe for millions of poverty-stricken Americans who, thanks to Wiley's efforts, became locked in the cycle of welfare dependency....New York City-the financial capital of the world-effectively went bankrupt in 1975. The entire state of New York was nearly taken down with it."[23]

Rudy Giuliani, who became Mayor of New York in 1994, described the tragic results of Cloward and Piven's handiwork as "an effort at economic sabotage."[24] He cited Cloward and Piven for seeding the cultural transition to viewing welfare as a long-term entitlement rather than a short-term safety net.

The NWRO had similar "success" around the country. Sol Stern wrote in the *City Journal*: "From 1965 to 1974, the number of single-parent households on welfare soared from 4.3 million to 10.8 million, despite mostly flush economic times."[25]

The NWRO became a launching pad for ACORN. In June 1969, Wade Rathke, a member of the radical Students for a Democratic Society (SDS), was hired to help start an NWRO chapter in Massachusetts. George Wiley then sent him to Little Rock, Arkansas to lead an experimental new organization in June 1970.[26] The "Arkansas experiment" was an attempt to build a more inclusive community organizing network that would reach out to a broader spectrum of the underclass, and that would address social issues beyond just welfare. Arkansas was chosen because of its demographics and because significant "War on Poverty" money was flowing into the state.[27]

Rathke called his new group the Arkansas Community Organizations for Reform Now, or ACORN. He trained civil rights workers to be Alinsky-style community organizers. Later, when he opened chapters in other states, he changed the name to Association of Community Organizations for Reform Now.

Many of ACORN's leaders came from the NWRO and were disciples of Saul Alinsky and the Cloward-Piven Strategy.[28] According to Sol Stern, ACORN promoted "a 1960's-bred agenda of anti-capitalism, central planning, victimology, and government handouts to the poor." It pushed for "ever-more government control of the economy" and economic "redistributionism."[29]

Stern wrote, "Walk through just about any of the nation's inner cities, and you're likely to find an office of ACORN, bustling with young people working 12 hour days to 'organize the poor' and bring about 'social change'....It (ACORN) boasts two radio stations, a housing corporation, a law office, and affiliate relationships with a host of trade-union locals. Not only big, it is effective, with some remarkable successes in getting municipalities and state legislatures to enact its radical policy goals into law."[30]

ACORN's impact today is most visible in America's electoral process. This was an intentional strategy nurtured by Cloward and Piven for decades. They outlined their plan for this in a 1982 article titled "A Movement Strategy to Transform the Democratic Party."[31]

Cloward and Piven proposed to do to the voting system what they had done to the welfare system. They wanted to flood the polls with millions of new underclass voters to tilt the balance of political power leftward in America.[32] ACORN and splinter groups Project Vote and Human SERVE, both founded in 1982, were the main organizations that propagated this new vision.[33]

Cloward and Piven intended to use Alinsky's "mass jujitsu" to make the Democratic Party honor its ostensible mission as an advocate of the poor. According to David Horowitz and Richard Poe in their book *The Shadow Party*, "The expected conflict would also expose the hypocrisy of the Democratic Party, which would be 'disrupted and transformed,' the authors predicted. A new party would rise from the ashes of the old. Outwardly, it would preserve the forms and symbols of the old Democratic Party, but the new Democrats would be genuine partisans of the poor, dedicated to class struggle."[34]

Cloward and Piven embraced Alinsky's notion that "the resources of the Have-Nots are (1) no money and (2) lots of people....People can show their power by voting."[35] According to *Newsmax*, "By advocating massive no-holds-barred voter registration campaigns, they (Cloward and Piven) sought a Democratic administration in Washington D.C. that would redistribute the nation's wealth and lead to a totalitarian leftist state."[36]

ACORN's website reported: "Since 2004, ACORN has helped more than 1.7 million low-and moderate-income and minority citizens apply to register to vote."[37] ACORN's subsidiary, Project Vote, claims to have registered four million voters.[38]

A critical part of the strategy was to not only register millions of underclass voters, but also to disable the checks and balances in the electoral process itself. In order to loosen the standards for voter registration and to weaken the ability of officials to police the process, ACORN and its affiliate organizations, Project Vote and Human SERVE, pushed for the National Voter Registration Act (the "Motor-Voter" law). When Bill Clinton signed this legislation in 1993, Cloward and Piven stood behind him in places of honor.[39]

According to Horowitz and Poe, "The Motor-Voter bill eliminated many controls on voter fraud, making it easy to register but difficult to determine the validity of new registrations. Under the new law, states were required to provide opportunities for registration to any person who showed up at a government office to renew a driver's license or apply for welfare or unemployment benefits. 'Examiners were under orders not to ask anyone for identification or proof of citizenship,' notes *Wall Street Journal* columnist John Fund in his book *Stealing Elections*. 'States also had to permit mail-in voter registrations, which allowed anyone to register without personal contact with a registrar or election official. Finally, states were limited in pruning 'deadwood—people who had died, moved, or been convicted of crimes—from their rolls.'"[40]

The Motor-Voter Law made it easier for registrations to be submitted in the name of ineligible or non-existent people, like Mickey Mouse and Donald Duck. The law was cited as a breeding ground for voter fraud. According to the *Wall Street Journal*: "After 9/11, the Justice Department found that eight of the 19 hijackers were registered to vote...."[41] Richard Cloward, the intellectual inspiration for ACORN, told *CBS News* in 1996, "It's better to have a little fraud than to leave people off the rolls who belong there."[42]

"A little fraud" is an appallingly disingenuous way to describe the alleged criminal activity of ACORN. Here are some examples of how ACORN corrupted America's voter registration process:

- Hundreds of thousands of ACORN voter registrations have been determined to be fraudulent. The fraud includes phony names, false addresses, and duplicate registrations.[43]

- 5,000 voters registered by ACORN in St. Louis were sent letters by election officials asking for a reply. Fewer than 40 responded.[44]

- In Mississippi, Madison County has 123% more registered voters than *people* over the age of 18.

Mississippi's Secretary of State said, "It is terrible. Combined with the fact that we don't have voter ID in Mississippi, anybody can show up at any poll that happens to know the people who have left town or died—and go vote for them."[45]

- ACORN submitted over 237,000 voter registrations in Ohio, a key battleground state. Some counties in Ohio now have more registered voters than eligible voters. The *Wall Street Journal* noted: "In Ohio in 2004, a worker for one ACORN affiliate was given crack cocaine in exchange for fraudulent registrations that included underage voters, dead voters, and pillars of the community named Mary Poppins, Dick Tracy, and Jive Turkey."[46]

- In 2007, ACORN workers in Washington State submitted thousands of fraudulent registrations, including "voters" like "Frekkie Magoal" and "Fruto Boy Crispila". A prosecutor called it "an act of vandalism upon the voter rolls."[47] ACORN was fined $25,000 after their employees were convicted of voter registration fraud.

- ACORN registered the entire Dallas Cowboys starting line-up to vote — in Nevada.[48]

- In Detroit, with 600,000 residents 18 years or older, over 610,000 active voter registration cards are allegedly in circulation.[49] With national voter registration rates at around 65%, the number of real registered Detroit voters is likely about 420,000. That leaves almost 200,000 potentially phantom "voters" in a city where traditionally 95% vote Democratic.

- The registrar in Las Vegas said 48% of ACORN's registrations "are clearly fraudulent."[50] Nevada's Attorney General said that ACORN's training manuals "clearly detail, condone, and, indeed, require illegal acts."[51] A Clark County official saw "rampant fraud in the 2,000 to 3,000 registrations that ACORN turns in every week."[52] In May 2009, Nevada officials charged ACORN with 39 felonies for voter registration fraud.[53]

How did ACORN feel about the indictments? "We've had bad publicity before," said ACORN's head organizer in Nevada. "We're just community organizers, just like the president used to be."[54] In other words, ACORN's voter registration fraud is merely "bad publicity," rather than something fundamentally wrong.

George Soros has aligned his forces with ACORN. Soros and ACORN founder Wade Rathke are tightly connected. Rathke was not only the Chief Organizer of ACORN; he was on the boards of the Tides Foundation and its sister group, the Tides Center.[55] Maya Wiley, the daughter of George Wiley, is a board member of the Tides Center. She was formerly an advisor to Soros's Open Society Institute (OSI). Since 1999, Soros has contributed $17 million to the Tides Center.[56]

Soros and his OSI have also contributed heavily to ACORN. We will examine Soros's massive influence on the various organizations that orbit the Democratic Party in the next chapter, but it is important here to discuss one of his initiatives, the Secretary of State Project (SoSP). The SoSP is the icing on the cake for ACORN's electoral shenanigans.

The SoSP is funding Secretary of State candidates in key battleground states who are friendly to the ACORN vision. With sympathetic Secretaries of State in control of election protocol, it will be very difficult to prevent ACORN-orchestrated voter fraud. According to *Fox News*, the goal of the SoSP is to "target and capture the obscure, often overlooked office and implement election rule changes that give Democrats a better chance of winning a plurality. Among those changes that SoSP calls 'election protection,' are a loosening of voter registration requirements and a lessening of efforts to prevent fraudulent voting...."[57]

Democracy Alliance, a group created by billionaires George Soros and Peter Lewis, is funding the SoSP.[58] The SoSP was founded in July 2006 to specifically target Secretary of State Offices in states where Bush defeated Kerry by narrow margins. The project so far claims that it has installed 11 of their 13 backed Secretary of State candidates in key states, including West Virginia, Missouri, Oregon, New Mexico, Nevada, Iowa, and Ohio.[59] Jennifer Brunner, the Ohio Secretary of State who received $167,000 in funding from SoSP for her campaign, defied federal law in 2008 by refusing to verify 200,000 questionable new voter registrations.

The radicals are targeting Secretaries of State offices because recent history suggests that the office can influence close elections. In 2000, Florida's Secretary of State, Katherine Harris, played a role in sealing George W. Bush's presidential win. In 2004, Ohio's Secretary of State, Kenneth Blackwell, chose not to count some provisional ballots, which some believe ensured a close Republican win in Ohio that gave Bush a second term. In 2008, Minnesota's Secretary of State, Mark Richie, assisted the razor-thin win of their Senate seat by Al Franken, which gave a supermajority in the Senate to the Democrats. Richie had dismantled Minnesota's ballot reconciliation process, so that in 2008, when there were 17,000 more ballots cast than voters who voted, there was no way to sort out the mess. A watchdog group named the Minnesota Majority claims that Franken's 312 vote margin of victory can be attributed to 1,400 votes cast illegally by convicted felons.[60]

Such machinations fit hand-in-glove with ACORN's fraudulent voter registration efforts. With fraudulent voter registrations comes the very real risk of fraudulent absentee ballots and other abuses. The combined activities of ACORN and Soros's SoSP are likely to result in third-world style voting irregularities.

Another Soros machination that is consistent with ACORN efforts to create electoral system chaos is his support of a group called Progressive Campaigns, Inc (PCI). This group is deceptively circulating petitions to create bogus "TEA Party" groups on state ballots, in order to siphon off votes that might otherwise go to Republican candidates. The purpose is to divide conservative voters so that leftist candidates have a better chance to win. PCI is paying professional signature gatherers one dollar for every signature they collect on these ersatz petitions. No official TEA Party organization is behind these petitions.

Another way that ACORN harmed America involves home mortgages for high risk borrowers. There were many factors that caused the meltdown of the American financial system in 2008, but a critical one was the massive number of risky mortgages that had been underwritten for low income home buyers who had very little collateral. ACORN was deeply involved in this activity, which was yet another application of the Cloward-Piven Strategy of orchestrated chaos.

Let's review the events that led to the mortgage meltdown. The government's effort to socialize the risk of mortgages and make them available to marginal borrowers goes back to 1938, when FDR created the federal lending agency, Fannie Mae. A related organization called Freddie Mac was created in 1970. These Government Sponsored Enterprises (GSE's) did not have to adhere to the same rigid capitalization and oversight requirements that bound most financial institutions. Since these GSE's, which purchased many of the mortgages issued by private lenders, had essentially a guarantee of solvency by the Federal Government, private lenders reasonably assumed that any risky lending on their part would be insulated by the GSE's. Since banks knew that they could offload risky mortgages to the GSE's, they had little incentive to be careful about their lending.

The potential for risky mortgages dramatically increased in 1977 when Congress passed the Community Reinvestment Act (CRA), which was signed into law by Jimmy Carter. The Act was intended to mitigate presumed "redlining" discrimination against minority borrowers by requiring banks to offer credit throughout their marketing areas, regardless of borrower qualifications. The CRA encouraged lenders to write mortgages for previously unqualified borrowers, backed by the implied guarantees of Freddie and Fannie.

In 1995, President Clinton strengthened the CRA by mandating that lenders issue more mortgages to subprime borrowers. In effect, Clinton set quotas for banks to write mortgages for certain classifications of disadvantage borrowers. Failure to meet these quotas would exclude offending lending institutions from access to federal funds or backing from Fannie and Freddie. Clinton's executive order also permitted Fannie and Freddie to lend up to 40 times their capital in mortgages, whereas normal banks could only lend ten times their capital. The purpose of this was to increase the number of mortgages that could be underwritten, but the practical effect was to position the entire industry for catastrophic collapse if the real estate market went into a downward spiral. By 2008, Fannie and Freddie owned about half of the $12 trillion in outstanding mortgages, which was an unprecedented concentration of debt and risk.

In 2003, President Bush tried to modify Fannie Mae and Freddie Mac rules to minimize loans to people who would not qualify under standard lending protocol. In effect, he proposed rescinding the Clinton executive order that eased lending guidelines and increased the risk to the entire system. Senate Democrats used the threat of filibuster to kill the effort.

In 2005, Federal Reserve Chairman Alan Greenspan testified before Congress that Fannie and Freddie were houses of cards, because a recession would trigger a chain reaction of failed mortgages that would topple an over-leveraged financial empire. He said, "We are placing the total financial system of the future at a substantial risk."[61]

When the "Great Recession" started in 2007 and housing values plummeted, many of the risky mortgages went into default and foreclosure. The over-leveraged financial industry had insufficient assets and reserves to absorb the losses. The derivative investments based on the collateralized mortgages collapsed. The financial markets seized up, leading to the biggest panic since the Great Depression. While there were many contributing factors to this collapse, the CRA-mandated easing of lending guidelines was a major one, and it is relevant to the role that ACORN played in the mess.

ACORN used the CRA as a whip to encourage loans to low income home buyers. Economist Stan Leibowitz wrote, "In the 1980's, groups such as the activists at ACORN began pushing charges of redlining—claims that banks discriminated against minorities in mortgage lending."[62]

ACORN pushed the 1995 revisions signed by Clinton that sharpened the teeth of the CRA. ACORN then used the hammer of "racial equity" under the CRA to force subprime loans to low-income, high-risk borrowers. According to the *New York Post*: "A 1995 strengthening of the Community Reinvestment Act required banks to find ways to provide mortgages to their poorer communities. It also let community activists intervene at yearly bank reviews, shaking the banks down for large pots of money. Banks that got poor reviews were punished; some saw their merger plans frustrated; others faced direct legal challenges by the Justice Department."[63] Senator Phil Gramm called the CRA "a vast extortion scheme against the nation's banks."[64]

As this pressure from ACORN and others increased, flexible lending programs and subprime mortgages proliferated. It was not uncommon for ACORN to push loans with hooks like "100 percent financing...no credit scores...undocumented income...even if you don't report it on your tax returns."[65]

An April 1995 *Chicago Sun-Times* article described ACORN's tease for disadvantaged borrowers: "You've got only a couple thousand bucks in the bank. Your job pays you dog-food wages. Your credit history has been bent, stapled, and mutilated. You declared bankruptcy in 1989. Don't despair: You can still buy a house."[66] According to economist Stan Leibowitz, the current mortgage mess is "a direct result of an intentional loosening of underwriting standards—done in the name of ending discrimination, despite warnings that it could lead to wide-scale defaults."[67]

The dramatic expansion of risky mortgages culminated in the 2008 collapse of America's two largest mortgage providers, Fannie Mae and Freddie Mac, which then led to a $700 billion federal bailout of the financial industry. Fannie and Freddie's backing of the risky mortgages minimized the risk to lenders and investors that otherwise might have put a brake on such lending. As *Bloomberg* reported, "It is a classic case of socializing the risk while privatizing the profit."[68] At one point, almost half of the loans covered by Fannie and Freddie were classified as subprime.

Amazingly, ACORN leader Wade Rathke claimed that ACORN's use of the CRA as a hammer to proliferate subprime mortgages was their biggest achievement. He took credit on behalf of ACORN for 7 million marginal loans resulting from CRA legislation.[69] Middle class citizens who were financially devastated by the banking collapse probably considered ACORN's involvement a disaster, not an achievement.

Ironically, ACORN did an astounding public relations about-face in 2008. They spent decades pressuring lending institutions to authorize risky mortgages for poor borrowers. When the mortgage industry consequently collapsed, partially because the same poor borrowers went into foreclosure, ACORN accused the mortgage companies of predatory lending practices!

ACORN's advocacy of lending to risky borrowers was often conducted in an uncivilized manner. In the Alinsky tradition, ACORN pursued what Sol Stern described as "undisguised authoritarian socialism."[70] ACORN intimidated lenders by protesting at private businesses, harassing executives at their residences, and creating disturbances in bank lobbies to coerce loans for marginal borrowers.

Part of ACORN's revenue stream came from corporations that it intimidated into conciliatory settlements. ACORN essentially ran an extortion racket, which brought in more money than it received from foundations and churches combined.[71] They chose a corporate target, attacked it with relentless negative publicity or threats of lawsuits, reached a financial settlement, and then began again with another target. They called this model "Muscle for the Money".[72] Some ACORN insiders called it "protection", implying comparison to classic mafia tactics.[73] Shakedown targets included Sherwin-Williams, H&R Block, Jackson Hewitt, the Carlyle Group, and Money Mart.[74]

Another way that ACORN "muscled for the money" was to compel its organizers to go door-to-door in targeted (i.e., poor) neighborhoods to troll for membership dues. Their hard-sell approach followed an instruction booklet that coached them on "door knocking basics."[75] The manual essentially told them not to accept "no" for an answer. To get to "yes", they would promise to fight all of the "villains" that were oppressing the underclass, thus "rubbing raw the sores of discontent" in the fashion of Saul Alinsky. If the poor person being recruited complained that the dues were too expensive, then organizers were instructed to offer alternative payment plans until the recruit succumbed and joined ACORN.

ACORN's intimidation tactics included assisting evicted residents to break into their former homes and become squatters, despite having defaulted on their mortgages. ACORN and one client brazenly broke the foreclosure padlock off from a home in Baltimore and moved back in. "This is our house now," declared the ACORN representative.[76] This trespassing fell under the umbrella of an ACORN initiative called "Home Savers," which they planned at one point to expand to at least 22 cities.[77]

ACORN is turning its "orchestrated chaos" gun sights toward immigration "reform", which is another opportunity for the rogue organization to continue its effort to collapse America from within. ACORN is part of the Coalition for Comprehensive Immigration Reform, which includes Soros's Open Society Institute and the Service Employees International Union. The coalition's aim is to dramatically liberalize immigration policy.[78] Wade Rathke, the founder of ACORN, was invited to the White House for a strategy session on immigration reform.

Liberalized immigration will be the most explosive version of the Cloward-Piven Strategy. The stress of illegal immigration on many of our communities has been widely documented. The crime, overcrowding, and systemic strain place a heavy burden on society and government. Not only will liberalized immigration make these problems worse, if illegal immigrants are eventually granted citizenship, it will instantly create a huge pool of new voters eager to push for, and take advantage of, wealth-transfer programs and the politicians who support them. As Rush Limbaugh put it, amnesty for illegal immigrants is nothing more than the largest voter registration drive in history. It is a "Field of Dreams" for ACORN and their ilk. ACORN's activities should make the blood of every middle-class American boil. ACORN has a "decade-long history of voter fraud, embezzlement and misuse of taxpayer funds…," consumer Rights advocate James Terry testified to the House Judiciary Committee.[79]

ACORN's hypocrisy is appalling. They constantly troll for taxpayer funding, yet they have 200 liens for unpaid taxes totaling almost $4 million pending against them.[80] ACORN presses for living wage laws, yet they resisted paying such wages to their own workers.[81] ACORN is staunchly pro-union, yet when Dallas ACORN workers tried to unionize in 2003, the National Labor Relations Board charged ACORN with unfair labor practices and forced them to rehire three fired employees who were organizing the union drive. ACORN claims to be a defender of the underprivileged, to the point of instructing their activists to accuse critics of being racist, yet they throw low-paid minority employees to the wolves to insulate ACORN management from charges of fraud and illegalities.

In 2009, U.S. Representative Darrell Issa, the ranking Republican on the House Oversight and Government Reform Committee, released a report that declared: "The Association of Community Organizations for Reform Now (ACORN) has repeatedly and deliberately engaged in systemic fraud. Both structurally and operationally, ACORN hides behind a paper wall of nonprofit corporate protections to conceal a criminal conspiracy on the part of its directors, to launder federal money in order to pursue a partisan political agenda and to manipulate the American electorate. Emerging accounts of widespread deceit and corruption raise the need for a criminal investigation of ACORN."[82]

Here are highlights of this report:

- Dale Rathke, Wade Rathke's brother, embezzled $948,607 from ACORN's retirement and health care accounts. ACORN never reported the embezzlement to external authorities. The crime occurred in 1999, but was not uncovered until June 2008 because ACORN carried the theft as a "loan" on the books of a subsidiary organization. Drummond Pike, head of the Soros-funded

Tides Foundation, eventually paid off Dale Rathke's debt. The ACORN board finally removed both Dale and Wade Rathke in 2008.

- ACORN conspired to use taxpayer funds for partisan political activity.

- ACORN defrauded the IRS and violated the Fair Labor Standards Act.

Issa said, "It is outrageous that ACORN will be rewarded for its criminal acts by taxpayer money in the stimulus and is being asked to help with the U.S. census. This report shines a light on clear criminal conduct and it is abundantly clear that they cannot and should not be trusted with taxpayer dollars."[83]

It is unlikely that a Congress or White House controlled by Democrats will seriously address ACORN's malfeasances. In 2009, Congress considered hearings on ACORN's illegal activities, but Judiciary Chairman John Conyers told the *Washington Times* that an investigation would not happen because "the powers that be decided against it."[84] Congressman Steve King of Iowa said those powers procedurally could only be House Speaker Nancy Pelosi or President Obama.[85] As we shall see shortly, it is quite clear why Barack Obama would choose not to investigate his "friends".

If and when an investigation of ACORN occurs, it is likely to be quite challenging. In order to cover their tracks, ACORN operates hundreds of front groups.[86] Whenever there is an ethical problem or a legal violation involving one of these fronts, it is usually shut down and the offending members slither into another thicket of the ACORN forest.

Some ACORN employees, known as the "ACORN Eight," got fed up with the illegal activities and demanded an audit of ACORN books. One of them, Marcel Reid, said, "ACORN has been hijacked by a power-hungry clique that has its own political and personal agendas. We are fighting to take the group back."[87]

Anita MonCrief, a fired ACORN whistleblower, said that ACORN knew their organizers were submitting bogus voter registrations: "I have knowledge that they were striving for at one time a 40% accuracy rate."[88] MonCrief worked at Project Vote, an ACORN affiliate, in late 2007. She provided sworn testimony in a lawsuit filed by the Pennsylvania Republican Party that alleged:[89]

- ACORN was given lists of potential donors by several Democratic presidential campaigns, including Obama's. This likely violated ACORN's non-partisan tax status.

- ACORN's Project Vote development director Karyn Gillette was in contact with the Obama campaign while obtaining their donor list. MonCrief testified she was given a spreadsheet to use for convincing maxed-out Obama donors to contribute to ACORN's registration efforts.

- E-mail between ACORN and its subsidiaries Project Vote and CSI described working on "Obama campaign-related projects."[90]

- ACORN/Project Vote official Nathan Henderson-James warned ACORN to prepare for "conservatives…gearing up a major oppo research project on Obama."[91] Henderson-James obsequiously hedged his statement by writing, "Understand I'm not suggesting that we gear up to defend a candidate's campaign."[92]

In March 2009, attorney Heather Heidelbaugh testified to a House Judiciary subcommittee that concerns about ACORN had not been properly investigated and had been squelched by the media. Heidelbaugh, who was given information by Anita MonCrief, offered the following testimony:[93]

"…she (Ms. MonCrief) informed me that she had been a confidential informant for several months to the *New York Times* reporter, Stephanie Strom, who had been writing articles about ACORN based on the information that she had provided. The *New York Times* articles stopped when Ms. MonCrief, who is a Democrat and a supporter of the President, revealed that the Obama Presidential Campaign had sent its maxed out donor list to Karyn Gillette of the Washington, D.C. ACORN office and asked Gillette and Ms. MonCrief to reach out to the maxed out donors and solicit donations from them for Get Out the Vote efforts to be run by ACORN. Upon learning this information and receiving the list of donors from the Obama Campaign, Ms. Strom reported to Ms. MonCrief that her editors at the *New York Times* wanted her to kill the story because, and I quote, 'it was a game changer.' That's when Ms. MonCrief telephoned me on October 21, 2008. Ms. Strom never wrote another article about ACORN for the *New York Times* for the remainder of the period before Election Day, i.e. November 4, 2008."

The *New York Times* published six ACORN articles written by Strom between July and October of 2008. However, when Strom discovered that the Obama campaign had given its maxed out donors list to ACORN so that they could exploit the same contributors for "get out the vote" funding, the *Times* killed the project, just two weeks before the election. This was likely due to concerns that the interaction between ACORN and the Obama campaign was illegal. Strom told Anita MonCrief, "I have just been asked by my bosses to stand down. They want me to hold off on coming to Washington. Sorry, I take my orders from higher up sometimes. Anyway, I'm sorry about this, and we'll still be in touch...."[94]

ACORN is a rogue agent in America society. It is the incarnation of Saul Alinsky's radical vision. It is the practical expression of its radical intellectual founders, Cloward and Piven. It is an enemy of the middle class, because its constituents will use any means, legal or illegal, to transfer power and wealth to the underclass. It is brandishing its weapon of orchestrated chaos to attack elements of our society that are very dear to us, including the electoral process, the mortgage financing system, and immigration law. The rest of this chapter will examine Barack Obama's considerable involvement with this rogue organization.

Barack Obama probably became exposed to the Cloward-Piven Strategy when he was an undergraduate student at Columbia University in New York City. The strategy had certainly gained notoriety by then, particularly in New York City, which had recently been bankrupted by it. Richard Cloward was still a Sociology professor at Columbia when Obama was enrolled. Since Obama was majoring in Political Science, and since he had a penchant for associating with radical professors and students, it would have been very natural for him to study under Cloward or to associate with him. It is impossible to verify this, because Obama refuses to release his

Columbia records. The Cloward connection may be one of the reasons why.

Obama's first job after getting his law degree was with Project Vote, which *Time* magazine called a "nonpartisan arm" of ACORN.[95] He was hired to be the Chicago-based director of Project Vote in 1992. It is possible that he was steered in this direction by Cloward, or perhaps by Bill Ayers, who was a fellow SDS member with Wade Rathke, the founder of ACORN.

Obama's Project Vote team registered 150,000 minority Chicagoans.[96] The T-shirts that Obama's volunteers wore proclaimed, "It's a power thing!" which is consistent with Obama's training by Alinsky acolytes earlier in his career.[97]

After Obama finished his Project Vote assignment, he helped train ACORN organizers and staff in the methods of Saul Alinsky. He conducted leadership training sessions for ACORN intermittently between 1993 and 2003.[98] He was recruited for this role by Madeline Talbott, the director of the Chicago ACORN.[99] The *LA Times* reported, "At the time, Talbot worked at the social action group ACORN and initially considered Obama a competitor. But, she became so impressed with his work that she invited him to help train her staff."[100] According to Stanley Kurtz, senior fellow at the Ethics and Policy Center, Obama ran workshops to teach traditional Alinsky "direct action." Kurtz described "direct action" as heavy-handed tactics to intimidate lenders into giving "Ninja" loans—no income, no job, and no assets—to unqualified borrowers. Talbott, recognizing Obama's efforts, said, "Barack has proven himself among our members…we accept and respect him as a kindred spirit, a fellow organizer."[101]

Obama represented ACORN in 1995 as their attorney in a lawsuit involving Illinois's implementation of the Motor Voter Law.[102] The law, which allowed voter registration by postcard, had been resisted by Republican Governor Jim Edgars, who foresaw the potential for election fraud that was inherent in such a lax environment. The law said government officials were "under orders not to ask anyone for identification or proof of citizenship."[103]

In September 2005, U.S. Senator Obama sponsored a resolution expressing the "sense of Congress that any effort to impose photo identification requirements for voting should be rejected."[104] This resolution complemented ACORN's massive voter registration fraud. If photo ID is not required, ill-intentioned voters can vote multiple times under phony names. The potential for fraud is compounded if absentee ballots are used.

Obama also represented ACORN as an attorney in its 1995 efforts to force the expansion of Community Reinvestment Act (CRA) authority under Clinton. *Investor's Business Daily* confirmed Obama's involvement: "The revisions also allowed for the first time the securitization of CRA-regulated loans containing subprime mortgages. The changes came as radical 'housing rights' groups led by ACORN lobbied for such loans. ACORN at the time was represented by a young public-interest lawyer in Chicago by the name of Barack Obama."[105]

In a related 1994 case known as Buycks-Roberson v. Citibank, Obama and other attorneys successfully litigated charges that Citibank was making too few loans to minority applicants.[106] Obama argued that Citibank should be forced to make more subprime loans to borrowers who were poor credit risks.

Obama helped funnel philanthropic money to ACORN. When he sat on the board of the Woods Fund, they made annual grants of approximately $70,000 to ACORN from 2001 to 2005, for a total of $355,000.[107] As director of the Chicago Annenberg Challenge, Obama also granted money to Madeline Talbott of Chicago ACORN.[108]

When Obama ran for Illinois State Senator in 1995, he developed a collaborative relationship with the socialist New Party. Frances Fox Piven, coauthor of the Cloward-Piven Strategy, was a New Party member and a board member of the Democratic Socialists of America. She became a member of Progressives for Obama when his political career broadened nationally.

Obama's involvement with ACORN's subprime mortgage litigation connected him with key players in the lending industry. In his few years as a U.S. Senator, Obama received campaign contributions of $126,349 from Fannie Mae and Freddie Mac. This was more than any other legislator in America, except for the $165,400 received by veteran Senator Chris Dodd.[109] Fannie and Freddie clearly felt that they had a Congressional friend in Obama.

Obama's presidential campaign staff included executives who were culprits in the financial system meltdown in 2008, including former Fannie Mae CEO Jim Johnson and the CEO of the failed Superior Bank of Chicago, Penny Pritzker.

Jim Johnson was forced to resign as the chair of Obama's vice presidential search committee after a government oversight agency revealed that he had cooked Fannie Mae's books during his tenure as CEO in order to exaggerate profits.[110] The exaggerated profits resulted in unwarranted bonuses for Johnson and other executives. Additionally, Johnson improperly received more than $7 million in real estate loans at reduced rates from Countrywide Financial Corporation.[111]

Penny Pritzker was the Finance Chairperson of Obama's presidential campaign. The Superior Bank of Chicago failed when she was CEO, wiping out millions in uninsured savings of customers. She was named in a RICO class action law suit and was described as the "Michael Milken of the subprime mortgage crisis" for packaging bad loans with good ones at Superior. [112] [113]

In February 2009, Obama committed to bail out homeowners who irresponsibly signed mortgages they could not honor, using $275 billion of taxpayer money. With grand socialist aplomb, he stated, "If we move forward with purpose and resolve—with a deepened appreciation for how fundamental the American dream is and how fragile it can be when we fail in our collective responsibilities—then I am confident we will...secure that dream for ourselves and for generations to come."[114] It's not clear what he meant by failed collective responsibilities. Perhaps he was referring to his and ACORN's involvement in the financial meltdown, or perhaps the involvement of his cohorts Johnson and Pritzker.

ACORN assisted Obama during several election campaigns. According to the *Wall Street Journal*, "In 1996, Mr. Obama filled out a questionnaire listing key supporters for his campaign for the Illinois Senate. He put ACORN first (it was not an alphabetical list)."[115] According to Chicago ACORN leader Toni Foulkes, "We have invited Obama to our leadership training sessions to run the session on power every year, and, as a result, many of our newly developing leaders got to know him before he ever ran for office. Thus, it was natural for many of us to be active volunteers in his first campaign for state senate and then his failed bid for U.S. Congress. By the time he ran for U.S. Senate, we were old friends."[116] ACORN executive Maude Hurd said that Obama was the candidate who "best understands and can affect change on the issues ACORN cares about".[117]

In 2007, Obama expressed mutual feelings to a gathering of ACORN members: "I've been fighting alongside ACORN on issues you care about my entire career."[118] ACORN's PAC endorsed

Obama for the presidency in February 2008, when Hillary Clinton was still the prohibitive favorite in the Democratic primaries.[119]

The collaboration between ACORN and Obama was not always on the proper side of the law. In August 2008, Michelle Malkin reported that "there's much more to the story of Obama's amended campaign finance reports than what Obama and the Obamedia will tell you….What we have here, essentially, is Obama using a non-profit group called Citizens Services, Incorporated (CSI) as a front to funnel payments to ACORN for campaign advance work."[120]

Before the Ohio primary in 2008, Obama became the first national politician to hire ACORN for get-out-the-vote services. Obama's campaign paid $832,598 to CSI.[121] CSI has the same 1024 Elysian Fields, New Orleans address as ACORN's national headquarters.[122] The Obama campaign initially told the FEC that it had hired CSI to do "polling, advance work, and staging major events," rather than the voter recruitment services they actually performed.[123] The Obama campaign later amended its filing with the FEC.[124]

ACORN is partially funded with federal tax money, so Obama's use of an ACORN surrogate for partisan politics was at best a conflict of interest and at worst illegal. Jim Terry, chief public advocate for the Consumer Rights League, said: "ACORN has a long and sordid history of employing convoluted Enron-style accounting to illegally use taxpayer funds for their own political gain. Now it looks like ACORN is using the same type of convoluted accounting scheme for Obama's political gain."[125]

These shady practices appear to have been intentional. Chicago ACORN leader Toni Foulkes declared, "ACORN is active in experimenting with methods of increasing voter participation in our low and moderate income communities in virtually every election. But in some elections we get to have our cake and eat it too: work on non-partisan voter registration and GOTV (get out the vote), which also turns out to benefit the candidate we hold dear."[126] In other words, the voters that they target to register are also the voters most likely to vote for their favored candidates.

In *The Audacity of Hope*, Obama expressed a clear understanding of how politicians manipulate election outcomes: "A congressional district is drawn by the ruling party with computer-driven precision to ensure that a clear majority of Democrats or Republicans reside within its borders. Indeed, it's not a stretch to say that most voters no longer choose their representatives; instead, representatives choose their voters."[127]   Obama's incestuous relationship with ACORN demonstrated that some politicians not only choose their voters, they pick the organizations that *register* their chosen voters.   As Joseph Stalin put it, "The people who cast the votes decide nothing.   The people who count the votes decide everything."[128]

ACORN uses taxpayer money to conduct this Stalinist charade. According to Michelle Malkin, "This left-wing group takes in 40% of its revenues from American taxpayers…and has leveraged nearly four decades of government subsidies to fund affiliates that promote the welfare state and undermine capitalism and self-reliance, some of which have been implicated in perpetuating illegal immigration and encouraging voter fraud."[129]   This is a form of suicide for middle-class taxpayers, because they are funding an organization committed to *destroying* the middle class.

This middle-class suicide pact is just in its infancy. Now that Obama is President and the Democrats control Congress, federal funding for ACORN appears to be increasing. This is difficult to prove, given the labyrinthine organization structure of ACORN and the vast network of federally funded community grants. However, an additional $5 billion was included in the federal budget for Community Development Block Grant programs and for Housing and Urban Development programs. These are funding avenues that the affiliate groups under the ACORN umbrella have traditionally usurped.[130]

The Obama administration selected ACORN in March 2009 to help the U.S. Census Bureau with the count in 2010.[131]   Minnesota Representative Michele Bachmann expressed concern during an interview that information from the 2010 census will be abused. She said the questions have become "very intricate, very personal," which is a particular concern if a lawless organization like ACORN participates in the census.[132]   "I know for my family the only question we will be answering is how many people are in our home," she said. "We won't be answering any information beyond that, because the Constitution doesn't require any information beyond that."[133]

Let's summarize. When describing his relationship with ACORN in a debate with McCain, Obama told us, "It (ACORN) had nothing to do with us. We were not involved." Nothing could be further from the truth. As a trainer for ACORN, as a leader of

ACORN's Project Vote, as an attorney representing ACORN's successful efforts to water down voter registration rules, as ACORN's lawyer pushing risky mortgages, as a beneficiary of ACORN's campaign assistance, as a philanthropic supporter of ACORN, and as President of the U.S. giving ACORN additional funding and broadened missions in our society, Barack Obama's entire career has been intertwined with the radical group.

Obama promised ACORN that it would have power in his administration. "Before I even get inaugurated, during the transition, we're going to be calling all of you in to help us shape the agenda," he told the Heartland Democratic Presidential Forum, a gathering of community organizers that included ACORN.[134] "We're going to be having meetings all across the country with community organizations so that you have input into the agenda for the next presidency of the United States of America."[135] He assured them that they would be actively involved in the first 100 days of his administration.

As usual, Obama spoke with forked tongue about his relationship with ACORN. On the one hand, he assured us he "was not involved" in their activities. On the other hand, here is what he told ACORN members in February 2008: "I come out of a grass-roots organizing background. That's what I did for three and half years before I went to law school. That's the reason I moved to Chicago was to organize. So this is something that I know personally, the work you do, the importance of it. I've been fighting alongside ACORN on issues you care about my entire career. Even before I was an elected official, when I ran Project Vote voter registration drive in Illinois, ACORN was smack dab in the middle of it, and we appreciate your work."[136]

How is it possible that Obama's deception about ACORN escaped the attention of middle-class voters? Negligence by the mainstream media is the primary reason. Without the mass media's shameless complicity and suppression of Obama's radical background, he would still be an obscure Chicago community organizer or a petty Illinois politician.

Obama and the mass media continued to ignore ACORN's abominations even after damning videos surfaced in the summer of 2009 that highlighted ACORN's willingness to help a posing pimp and prostitute cheat the IRS, set up a prostitution ring, facilitate underage sex, and bring illegal aliens across the border. The videos by James O'Keefe and Hannah Giles triggered criminal investigations by Attorneys General in several states, but not by Congress or the White House.

When *Fox News* aired these videos, the fallout was brutal to ACORN. Its brand became so tarnished that it feared contributors and partners would abandon them to avoid guilt by association. "That 20-minute video ruined 40 years of good work," said Sonja Merchant-Jones, former co-chairwoman of ACORN's recently closed Maryland chapter. "But if the organization had confronted its own internal problems, it might not have been taken down so easily."[137]

When cornered by a massive public outcry, both the U.S. House of Representatives and the U.S. Senate voted to de-fund ACORN in September 2009.[138] This was mere posturing, however, because these temporary stays of funding were scheduled to expire just a few months later. Indeed, in December 2009, the House Appropriations Committee reversed its funding stay.

ACORN sued the Federal Government over its September 2009 funding "ban". In December 2009, U.S. District Court Judge Nina Gershon issued a federal injunction against the ban, on the pretext that ACORN was "singled out by Congress for punishment that directly and immediately affects their ability to continue to obtain federal funding, in the absence of a judicial, or even administrative, process adjudicating guilt."[139] This was a bizarre ruling that suggested organizations have an inherent right to federal funding, and that Congress no longer has the right to determine how to spend taxpayer funds. In a March 2010 memo, Peter Orszag, Obama's director of the Office of Management and Budget, authorized government agencies to resume funding of ACORN as a result of Gershon's ruling.[140]

While the federal funding question was being debated, ACORN began changing its identity in order to distance itself from damning publicity. ACORN International officially changed its name to "Community Organizations International".[141] Then, state and local chapters began splitting off from the national group and changing their names. A senior official close to the group declared, "ACORN has dissolved as a national structure of state organizations. Consistent with what the internal recommendations have been, each of the states is developing plans for reconstitution, independence, and self-sufficiency."[142] As examples, the New York chapter of ACORN changed its identity to "New York Communities for Change." The California Chapter of ACORN changed its name to "Alliance of Californians for Community Empowerment."[143]

In March 2010, the ACORN board met and essentially dissolved its national structure. According to spokesperson Kevin Whelan, ACORN was to close its remaining field offices in April 2010, and settle all outstanding obligations.[144] It appears that the national organization, including its website, was effectively idled on April 1, 2010. It remains to be seen, however, what identity this chameleon-like group will assume next. It is likely that a replacement organization will emerge to tap the flow of money from the federal government, leftist groups, and dues-paying members.

Obama's extensive, concealed relationship with ACORN is another compelling reason why the middle class ought to be deeply skeptical of him. ACORN, like Obama, is hell-bent on driving major changes in our society that will ultimately decimate the middle class. ACORN's support for a larger welfare state, illegal immigration, voter fraud, subprime mortgages, and government-run health care are targeted directly at grabbing wealth and power from the middle class in America.

Long ago, Ronald Reagan chastised welfare rights activists for the way that Big Government institutionalized poverty and perpetuated it as a way of life across generations. As more and more of the underclass fall into this trap, more and more workers from the middle class will have to sacrifice their standard of living to support them. As ACORN's former leader Wade Rathke told Megyn Kelly of *Fox News*, "We do believe in equitable distribution of any benefits and rights people have".[145] This comes dangerously close to the Marxist credo, "From each according to his ability, to each according to his need."

In that same interview, Rathke confessed, "I am a dangerous guy."[146] In his new book, *Citizen Wealth: Winning the Campaign to Save Working Families*, he challenged community organizers to continue overwhelming all federal aid programs. One of the chapters, "The 'Maximum Eligible Participation' Solution," describes a modern version of the Cloward-Piven Strategy based on widespread internet access to applications for government aid.[147] This is an ominous foreshadowing that ACORN, in whatever guise it eventually assumes when it reconstitutes itself, will continue its mission to siphon wealth from middle-class taxpayers.

This attack on the middle class has been ongoing ever since the Cloward-Piven Strategy was published in 1966. ACORN's radical initiatives have pushed us closer toward the orchestrated chaos that Cloward and Piven hoped for. With the advent of the Obama administration, we are seeing an explosion of new government intrusions that are diminishing our Constitutionally-guaranteed rights and undermining the limited-government concepts in our Constitution. The radicals in Washington are not uniters; they are incurable champions of class warfare in the classic mold of ACORN and Saul Alinsky. As Cloward and Piven made clear, the intent of the Orchestrated Chaos Strategy is not to provide sinecures for the poor, but to duplicitously enlist the poor in a proletarian offensive to establish socialism in America.

Obama sold a piece of his soul to the devil with his unholy, symbiotic association with the criminal organization ACORN. He also sold pieces of his soul to many other devils, including the Ayers family, socialist organizations, Black Nationalists, Antoin Rezko, Jeremiah Wright, and, as we shall see in the next chapter, George Soros.

None of these devils are friendly to the middle class. Rather, they are all expressly at *war* with the middle class. And these devils collectively own Barack Obama's soul. He owes everything to them, and nothing to us.

We've been had.

"Freedom is never more than one generation away from extinction. We didn't pass it to our children in the bloodstream. It must be fought for, protected, and handed on for them to do the same."

Ronald Reagan

Chapter Nine

Meet George Soros

"Now it's our Party: We bought it, we own it...."

Eli Pariser, head of MoveOn PAC

In the first eight chapters, we reviewed Barack Obama's biography, relationships, and influences. These say a great deal about his character and how he will govern as President of the United States. But they don't tell us *how* he got elected President. We saw in the last chapter that ACORN savaged the integrity of the electoral process to aid and abet their chosen radical candidates. But ACORN is just a small cog in the machine that enthroned Obama. ACORN's unethical activities alone do not explain how an obscure politician from Illinois, with almost no national or international experience, suddenly rose to the pinnacle of American politics.

This chapter explains Obama's sudden rise by introducing George Soros and his powerful network. We have already learned that Obama is firmly committed to transferring wealth to the underclass because of his socialist pedigree. But, understanding *how* Obama got elected will lead us to a very different world that he also owes his political allegiance to. This is an elitist world of exclusive universities like Harvard and Columbia, oligarchic financial institutions like Goldman Sachs and Citigroup, billionaire financiers like George Soros and Peter Lewis, and international non-governmental organizations like the Ford Foundation and the Trilateral Commission.

Middle-class citizens should do some simple reckoning during this chapter. If Obama's socialist pedigree will drive him to transfer wealth to the underclass, and if his behind-the-scenes political allegiances will drive him to transfer wealth to the elitists (insert your own cynical anecdote here about government bail-outs of Goldman Sachs, AIG, Big Education, Big Labor, the International Monetary Fund, Fannie Mae, or other well-heeled power brokers), where does that leave the middle class?

The simple answer is that it leaves the middle class stuck between subsidizing the underclass and subsidizing the wealthy elites. There's an old saying that if you can't figure out who the sucker is in a con, it's you. Guess what? If you're in the middle class, you're the sucker in this con, no matter what political party you voted for. Trillions will go to the poor. Trillions will go to the Wall Street bankers and the government-sinecure elitists. The middle class will eventually pay for it all when the bills come due.

George Soros is a rogue Hungarian-born billionaire and a one-man international wrecking crew. He has the ability and the propensity to undermine the political and financial structures of entire countries. He made a fortune speculating in currency markets, often by plotting to weaken currencies to profit from the wreckage. He once said, "If truth be known, I carried some rather potent messianic fantasies with me from childhood....It is a sort of disease when you consider yourself some kind of God, the creator of everything, but I feel comfortable about it now since I began to live it out."[1]

Soros broke the Bank of England to enrich himself and supported regime changes in Eastern Europe to amuse himself. His latest target is the United States of America. He publicly declared that removing George W. Bush from office was a "matter of life and death,"[2] and that if someone could guarantee it, he would surrender his entire fortune to assist in that regime change.[3]

Soros is the de facto puppet master of the Democratic Party. He is its largest contributor, and he supports more than 30 leftist organizations that are now the real party machinery of the DNC. Eli Pariser, a director of the Soros-funded MoveOn PAC, said of the Democratic Party: "Now it's our party: we bought it, we own it...."[4]

Soros abhors Western principles and wants to establish a borderless "Open Society" that rejects the U.S. Constitution. He is one of the most powerful men on earth. He is reportedly worth $14 billion. His shenanigans in financial markets cause currencies to go up or down. As he reaps billions from these gyrations, others correspondingly lose billions. Sometimes whole nations suffer.

This chapter examines George Soros's biography and his profound influence on the Democratic Party. It also discusses how his coercive sway over America's electoral machinery elevated Barack Obama to the Presidency.

George Soros is the son of Jewish writer Tivadar Soros. He was born as Gyorgy Schwartz on August 12, 1930 in Budapest, Hungary. In 1936, the family changed its name to the more ethnically Hungarian Soros, in response to growing anti-Semitism. In 1944, Nazi Adolf Eichmann arrived in Hungary to oversee the "processing" of Hungarian Jews. Tivadar Soros arranged fake identity papers for his children, who were shipped out to various Christian families to protect them. George ended up with a Ministry of Agriculture agent whose job was to issue deportation orders to Jews and confiscate their property.

The Soros family moved to England in 1947 after Hungary fell under Soviet control. For a brief period, the Communists afforded young Soros an alternative view of the world. He told his father in 1946, "I'd like to go to Moscow to find out about communism. I mean that's where the power is. I'd like to know more about it."[5] This yen for proximity to power foreshadowed Soros's future as one of the world's most prolific power brokers.

George graduated from the London School of Economics in 1952 and began work at a merchant bank. In 1956, he moved to New York City with $5,000 in his pocket. While working as an arbitrage trader, he developed a theory he called "reflexivity". He postulated that the reaction of traders to market trends affects the valuation of markets in a pro-cyclical "virtuous or vicious" manner. In other words, markets react not only to real economic information, but also to how market participants themselves are reacting. This causes markets to gyrate as they overshoot or undershoot their equilibriums.

Soros realized that he could not exploit his concept of reflexivity until began investing on his own. He quit his job in 1973 to form an investment company that became the Quantum Fund, which is how he earned most of his fortune. This fund is headquartered in Curacao, beyond U.S. Government oversight. During a three-year span, the Quantum Fund quadrupled in value. As a result, *Institutional Investor* magazine named Soros "the world's greatest money manager" in 1981.[6] [7] In 1994, *Financial World* declared that his 1993 profits "exceeded the gross domestic product of at least 42 member nations of the United Nations."[8]

Many financiers rake in extraordinary wealth. What distinguishes Soros is his ruthless disregard for sovereign nations and the institutions that enabled his wealth accumulation. He blackened his soul while attacking the financial structures of whole countries for enormous personal gain.

For example, Soros gambled $10 billion in 1992 that the British pound would lose value compared to the German mark. He bought Deutschmarks and dumped pounds, while the Bank of England did the reverse. Other investors joined with Soros on the attack. After weeks of maneuvering, the British were forced to devalue the pound by 20%. Soros's profit was nearly $2 billion. He was consequently dubbed "the man who broke the Bank of England."[9]

Soros's financial machinations were not always legal. In 1988, he bought shares in the French bank Societe Generale to illicitly benefit from advance knowledge of a takeover attempt. A French court ruled in 2002 that it was insider trading and Soros was fined $2.3 million.[10]

The *New York Times* said, "When Soros speaks, world markets listen."[11] In 1993, Soros informed the *Times of London,* "I expect the mark to fall against major currencies."[12] His mere words caused the Deutschmark to plummet in value in world markets. In 1998 he said that Russia ought to devalue the ruble.[13] Consequently, during the Russia-gate scandal, the ruble plummeted in value and Russia sank into a depression and defaulted on its IMF loans.[14] The head of the U.S. House Banking Committee called the induced collapse "one of the greatest social robberies in human history."[15]

Soros's assaults on countries were sometimes for political rather than financial gain. His involvement in Georgia's Rose Revolution was considered crucial to the 2003 uprising that toppled President Eduard Shevardnadze. The *LA Times* quoted Soros: "I'm delighted by what happened in Georgia, and I take great pride in having contributed to it."[16] He reportedly spent $42 million supporting revolution leader Mikhail Saakashvili. Many believe he was instrumental in several other coups in Eastern Europe, including the 1989 Velvet Revolution in the Czech Republic. At one point, Soros bragged that "the former Soviet Empire is now called the Soros Empire."[17] Keep this "regime change" hobby in mind when we discuss his impact on America later in the chapter.

Many governments have either banned Soros from activity in their nations or are prosecuting him for illegalities. Turkmenistan and Russia banned Soros-sponsored initiatives. Soros's foundation in Belarus was fined $3 million for tax and currency violations. Kazakhstan prosecuted the Soros Foundation for tax evasion. When Soros short-sold the Malaysian currency, thereby trashing Malaysia's economy, Malaysian Prime Minister Mohamad called Soros "a villain and a moron"[18] and said "the poor people in these countries will suffer, and they are the people that have to be protected from George Soros, who has so much money and power but is totally thoughtless."[19]

Soros's speculation against Thailand's currency caused it to plummet in value. He is now considered an "economic war criminal" in Thailand.[20]   Thai activist Weng Tojirakarn said, "We regard George Soros as a kind of Dracula. He sucks the blood from the people."[21]   Taiwan threatened criminal charges against "any person cooperating with Soros funds."[22]

Before we examine Soros's rogue influence on American affairs, it is important to understand his philosophical bearings. According to David Horowitz and Richard Poe in their book *The Shadow Party*, "all of his (Soros's) political and philanthropic activities are directed towards one goal—fostering what he calls the 'open society.' The term was coined in 1932 by the French philosopher Henri Louis Bergson. Bergson defined as 'closed' those societies whose moral code is tribal and chiefly concerns the good of the tribe itself. Those societies which base their morality upon 'universal' principles, which seek the good of all mankind, Bergson defined as 'open.'"[23]

Philosopher Karl Popper expanded on Bergson's concepts. According to Horowitz and Poe, "Popper argued that even Christianity is insufficiently 'open' because it excludes people who do not embrace its beliefs. To be truly 'open,' a society must accord equal respect to all beliefs, showing no favoritism toward any particular one. A truly open person never assumes that his beliefs are superior to someone else's….One who claims possession of 'ultimate truth' is an 'enemy' of the open society."[24]

As Horowitz and Poe observed, even the American political system can't live up to Popper's ideal. Americans regard rights such as liberty as absolute and inalienable. Popper, on the other hand, believed that absolute truth cannot be found, even in the U.S. Constitution. As we shall see later, this is one reason why Soros ignores the Constitution.[25]

Popper documented his philosophy in *The Open Society and Its Enemies*, a book published in 1945.[26] Soros studied under Popper in London and considered him his spiritual mentor.[27] Soros's Open Society Institute (OSI) got its name and inspiration from Popper's concepts.[28]

Since 1979, Soros's Open Society foundations have contributed $5 billion to left-wing causes.[29] Soros has been described as the "Godfather of World Socialism."[30] He described himself as a "stateless statesman."[31] His Open Society foundations operate in more than 50 countries.[32] In 1993, Soros established the U.S. branch of the OSI to support his socialist initiatives in America.

According to Richard Poe and David Horowitz on their website discoverthenetworks.org, Soros's OSI agenda looks remarkably like that of Barack Obama and the radical wing of the Democratic Party. The OSI agenda as summarized by Poe and Horowitz is presented below, with slight abridgment:[33]

- Promoting the view that America is institutionally oppressive

- Promoting the election of leftist political candidates

- Depicting American militarism as unjust, unwarranted, and immoral

- Promoting open borders, mass immigration, and neutering of current immigration laws

- Promoting expanded social welfare programs funded by higher taxes

- Promoting social welfare benefits and amnesty for illegal aliens

- Advocating unilateral disarmament and a steep reduction in military spending

- Promoting government-run healthcare

- Promoting radical environmentalism as a wealth-transferring mechanism

- Bringing American foreign policy under the control of the United Nations

- Promoting racial and ethnic preferences in academia and the business world

- Promoting taxpayer-funded abortion-on-demand

- Advocating stricter gun-control measures

Despite being a tycoon and a cutthroat financier, Soros despises capitalism and Western principles. "The richest 1% of the world's population receives as much as the poorest 57%," Soros said in *George Soros on Globalization*.[34] To resolve this imbalance, he proposed curbing "global capitalism."[35][36] He could solve some of the imbalance by giving his own money to the poor, but as we shall see shortly, he is using a big chunk of it to facilitate regime change in America instead.

Soros considers America an enemy of his philosophy. Our heritage and culture of individual liberty protected by a Constitution compels most of us to reject his vision of a borderless international welfare state. In Soros's globalist worldview, not only is individual sovereignty irrelevant, so is the sovereignty of the United States.

Aryeh Neier has been the President of Soros's Open Society Institute since 1993. Earlier in his career, he was a leader of the Socialist League for Industrial Democracy, which eventually morphed into the Students for a Democratic Society (SDS).

Coincidentally, some of Neier's brethren in the SDS directly supported Obama's career, including Bill Ayers, Carl Davidson, Bernardine Dohrn, and Wade Rathke, the founder of ACORN. Neier's SDS connection is perhaps one of the ways that Soros became aware of Obama as a young radical politician. This cadre of SDS radicals has been percolating through our culture for four decades.

Groups funded by the OSI are a "who's who" of the radical left and socialism in America, including ACORN, MoveOn.org, the ACLU, the Malcolm X Grassroots Movement, NARAL, the NAACP, and the National Council of La Raza.

Soros used the OSI to infiltrate American politics, culminating in the creation of what David Horowitz and Richard Poe dubbed the Shadow Party, which is a subterranean faction that controls the Democratic Party. The Shadow Party is the mechanism that Soros used to push radicals into power and to elevate Obama to the Presidency.

According to Poe and Horowitz in their book *The Shadow Party*:

"The Shadow Party is the real power driving the Democrat machine. It is a network of radicals dedicated to transforming our constitutional republic into a socialist hive. The leader of these radicals is...George Soros. He has essentially privatized the Democratic Party, bringing it under his personal control. The Shadow Party is the instrument through which he exerts that control....It works by siphoning off hundreds of millions of dollars in campaign contributions that would have gone to the Democratic Party in normal times, and putting those contributions at the personal disposal of Mr. Soros. He then uses that money to buy influence and loyalty where he sees fit....The Shadow Party derives its power from its ability to raise huge sums of money. By controlling the Democrat purse strings, the Shadow Party can make or break any Democrat candidate by deciding whether or not to fund him."[37]

According to Poe and Horowitz, the Shadow Party was born in July 2003 when a team of strategists and donors met at Soros's estate on Long Island.[38] The attendees included Morton Halperin of the OSI, former Clinton staffer John Podesta, labor leader Steve Rosenthal, and Democratic fundraiser Peter Lewis, among others.[39] Soros sketched out a strategy for deposing Bush in the 2004 election. One participant reported, "By morning, the outlines of a new organization began to emerge, and Mr. Soros pledged $10 million to get it started."[40] That organization was America Coming Together (ACT), an activist group assigned to harness the manpower of unions, environmentalists, and civil rights organizations.[41]

By early 2004, the Shadow Party infrastructure included seven non-profit groups, including MoveOn.org, Center for American Progress, America Votes, America Coming Together, The Media Fund, Joint Victory Campaign 2004, and the Thunder Road Group LLC.[42]

This umbrella coalition was allied with other left-wing groups such as ACORN, AFL-CIO, AFSCME, the American Federation of Teachers, the Association of Trial Lawyers of America, Environment 2004, the National Education Association, and the Service Employees International Union (SEIU).[43]

Soros personally contributed to numerous left-wing politicians, including Charles Rangel, Al Franken, John Kerry, Wesley Clark, Howard Dean, Hillary Clinton, Tom Daschle, Charles Schumer, Joseph Biden, Al Gore, Barbara Boxer, and Barack Obama.[44] Soros was described by Bill Clinton's Deputy Secretary of State Strobe Talbott as a "national treasure."[45] He is essentially the treasurer of the radical faction of the Democratic Party.

Soros has essentially taken over the Democratic Party with the various organizations that he funds. In 2004, the Shadow Party contributed $300 million to the Democrats.[46] Republican National Committee spokeswoman Christine Iverson said, "George Soros has purchased the Democratic Party, and he who pays the piper calls the tune."[47]

But how did Soros "buy" the Democratic Party? The answer lies in the McCain-Feingold Bipartisan Campaign Reform Act of 2002, which Soros pushed for years.

Republican Senator John McCain and Democrat Senator Russ Feingold co-sponsored legislation to reform how federal election campaigns were funded. McCain-Feingold banned large donations to the Democrat and Republican National Committees, but it did not restrict donations to "527" organizations. A "527" group is named after a provision in the U.S. tax code. Such groups, though not directly affiliated with political parties, influence the nomination and election of favored candidates for public office. They do not have to report their finances to the FEC.

Donors can contribute unlimited amounts to a 527 group. This creates the opportunity for distorted influence in the political process. In the case of the Democrat Party, the Soros-sponsored 527's can reel in huge contributions, while the DNC itself is hamstrung by McCain-Feingold. This opens the door for rogues like Soros to assert political control through financial leverage.

McCain-Feingold went into effect in November 2002. According to Horowitz and Poe, Soros immediately began taking advantage of it. Allusions to a shadow party began creeping into the press. The *Washington Post* wrote about "shadow organizations" springing up to circumvent McCain-Feingold.[48] In September 2003, Lorraine Woellert of *Business Week* applied the term Shadow Party specifically to the network of 527 groups that Soros was assembling.[49]

Soros's team of wealthy donors now contributes far more than prior campaign finance laws would have permitted them to donate directly to the Democrat Party. As a result, Democrats are now dependent on Soros and his cronies for money.[50] In politics, money is often synonymous with power. Soros has a lot of both.

Thus far, we have examined the influence of George Soros on the Democratic Party. Now, let's examine the role that he played in abetting Obama's career and ascension to the White House.

Soros has overtly supported Obama since Barack's run for the U.S. Senate in 2004, donating $60,000 to his campaign. Four members of the Soros family also donated to Obama's 2004 campaign, making Obama one of only a handful of candidates, including Hillary Clinton, Tom Daschle and Barbara Boxer, to receive such support.[51]

Why did Soros single Obama out at this point, when he was still an obscure Illinois politician? There are thousands of state-government legislators around the country. Why did Soros include this unknown Chicago politician in equal favor with established national luminaries such as Hillary Clinton? We have already surmised that OSI President and SDS founder Aryeh Neier might have alerted Soros to the articulate radical in Chicago who was bonding with Neier's old SDS allies, Bill Ayers and Bernardine Dohrn. But, to fully understand the evolution of the Soros/Obama connection, we have to begin with the career of Ann Dunham, Obama's mother.

Ann moved to Indonesia from Hawaii after marrying Lolo Soetoro. She taught English at the American embassy in Jakarta. She also set up a village credit program for the United States Agency for International Development (USAID), and worked for the Ford Foundation formulating loan programs for poor Indonesian entrepreneurs. She traveled widely to countries such as Thailand, Nepal, India, Bangladesh, Pakistan, and China. During her career, she came in contact with some influential people.

One of those influential people was Peter Geithner, who oversaw the Ford Foundation's microfinance operation in Indonesia when Ann Dunham worked there. He later became the director of the Asian program at the Ford Foundation, working out of New York.[52] Thus, Peter and Ann knew each other and collaborated on microcredit projects. Ironically, their respective offspring, Timothy Geithner and Barack Obama, ended up working closely together a generation later. Tim Geithner, whose career led him to become the President of the Federal Reserve Bank of New York, joined Obama's administration as Treasury Secretary.

Another influential person was Zbigniew Brzezinski, formerly a key member of Carter's administration and the first head of David Rockefeller's Trilateral Commission, a cabal of international power brokers. In the 1980's, Brzezinski led the Institute for Communist Affairs at Columbia University in New York, specializing in Russian affairs. During that time, Obama majored in political science at Columbia and studied Sovietology under Brzezinski.[53] Coincidently, both Brzezinski and Obama were in Pakistan at the same time in 1981, shortly before Obama enrolled at Columbia.[54] Their visits occurred when Pakistan was under martial law and the U.S. State Department was discouraging travel there. Obama's 1981 trip overseas also included a visit to his mother Ann.

Prior to transferring to Columbia in New York, Barack Obama, by his own admission, was dabbling in drugs and the counter-culture at Occidental College in Los Angeles. Ann had already tried to correct his chronic lack of ambition in high school, which he noted in *Dreams from My Father*. He wrote that he felt like "letting her know that her experiment with me had failed."[55]

Here's the hypothesis. It is based on circumstantial information, which is all that is available, since Obama refuses to elaborate on this period of his life or to release any documentation related to it. Ann Dunham asked Peter Geithner for assistance in Barack's erstwhile career, since she was living on the other side of the world and needed help setting Barack on a more productive path. Peter would have been her only influential connection in America. Geithner, who was well connected in New York, enlisted the help of Brzezinski. If the Ford Foundation was indeed a CIA front as reported by numerous sources, Geithner may have intersected previously with Brzezinski, who was reportedly also involved with the CIA. To conclude the hypothesis, Brzezinski recruited Obama to Columbia College, New York's premiere university, to study under him and get serious about his academic career.

This hypothesis implies that Obama later picked Tim Geithner as Treasury Secretary out of obligation. It explains why Obama clung tenaciously to him despite a horrendously damning tax evasion scandal (Geithner, who now oversees the IRS in his cabinet position, cheated on his tax returns for many years, failing to pay over $34,000 in Social Security taxes when he worked for the IMF, despite signing forms acknowledging the requirement to do so).[56] Obama clung to Geithner even though *The Nation* magazine called his selection "Obama's biggest mistake."[57]

This hypothesis explains why Obama suddenly left Occidental College in California, where he had Hawaii-like warm weather, a full scholarship, and many friends, to go to Columbia in New York, where he was a stranger in a strange land, except for this hypothetical Geithner/Brzezinski protectorate instigated by his mother. According to a 2007 *LA Times* article, Obama helped lead the Occidental College Junior Varsity basketball team to an undefeated season, which makes it even more unusual that he would suddenly leave for Columbia.[58]

Soros, who was a member of the Trilateral Commission, probably knew Trilateral Commission cofounder and fellow New Yorker Brzezinski.[59][60] Perhaps Brzezinski introduced Obama to Soros. Soros was a contributor to the Ford Foundation, and his OSI was a contributor to most of the organizations that subsequently orbited around Obama, including the DCP, ACORN, the Woods Fund, the CAC, and the Joyce Foundation.

Aryeh Neier, who is President of Soros's OSI and a compatriot of SDS radicals Ayers and Dohrn, may also have alerted Soros to Obama, a charismatic young politician in Chicago who was close to the Ayers family. Soros surely would have been intrigued by a rising star who shared his anti-capitalist and internationalist world view, especially one educated by fellow Trilateral Commissioner Brzezinski.

To summarize the hypothesis, what began as a favor from Peter Geithner to Ann Dunham to help young Barack divert himself from the lifestyle of an alienated drifter in California, grew into a career-abetting juggernaut that included college mentoring by Brzezinski and then major foundational support and political leveraging by George Soros. Along the way, Timothy Geithner became involved with the New York financial oligarchy that would later become a golden goose for Obama's national political career. Brzezinski eventually became a key foreign policy advisor on Obama's presidential campaign staff and took credit for the arguments in Obama's now-famous 2002 antiwar speech.[61][62]

Coincidentally, Brzezinski's daughter Mika, who is the sidekick for Joe Scarborough on *MSNBC*'s *Morning Joe* program, led the partisan support for Obama on that show during the presidential election, which caused insiders to dub the network "Obamavision."[63][64]

Even though the preceding hypothesis is circumstantial, it is clear that Soros and Obama connected along the way. Soros eventually became known as Obama's "money man."[65] In February 2004, Soros met Obama for breakfast at the Four Seasons Hotel in Chicago. Soros came away from that discussion "very impressed."[66] In June 2004, he hosted a fundraiser at his home in New York for Obama's U.S. Senate campaign.[67] According to Soros spokesperson Michael Vachon, Obama was the only political candidate that Soros met with personally in the 2004 election cycle.[68] This is a curious distinction, because at the time, Obama was just one among thousands of state-level legislators.

Ever since Obama excelled during his "audition" as the keynote speaker at the Democratic convention in Boston in 2004, he was financed by Soros and other billionaires. They essentially created a national politician out of nothing more than Obama's hyperbolic oratory and a lot of money from New York.[69] Prior to this, Obama had no national or international achievements, no discernable record, no experience as an executive, and no national brand recognition. The honor of being keynote speaker at the convention was a clear signal that powerful forces were aiding the otherwise obscure Chicago politician. In *The Audacity of Hope*, Obama wrote, "the process by which I was selected as the keynote speaker remains something of a mystery to me."[70] He also wrote "by that time I had become accustomed to outlandish things happening in my campaign."[71]

Obama won his 2004 U.S. Senate race, despite accomplishing almost nothing in his first six years in the Illinois State Senate. He got 26 bills passed his final year there, but that was because Emil Jones, who became President of the Illinois Senate in 2003 when Democrats took the majority, became his "godfather." Jones designated Obama as the author of many bills that were actually written and championed by other state legislators with more seniority.[72] It is unclear what motivated Jones to artificially abet Obama's rise to stardom.

It is clear, though, that Jones's "assistance" jump-started Obama's march to national prominence. Prior to 2004, Obama was a relatively obscure politician, even in Illinois. Fewer than 20% of *Illinois* voters knew who he was. Obama directly sought out Jones to assist him in his quest for notoriety. According to a *New York Times* account, Obama told Jones, "You have the power to make a U.S. Senator." Jones asked, "If I've got that kind of power, do you know of anyone that I can make a United States Senator?" Obama replied, "Me."[73]

Rickey Hendon, one of the Illinois State Senators that Emil Jones swiped legislation from to give to Obama, told the *Houston Press*, "No one wants to carry the ball 99 yards all the way to the one-yard line, and then give it to the halfback who gets all the credit and the stats in the record book."[74] He also suggested that Obama would run for the "king of the world" if the position was available.[75]

It didn't take long for Obama to become dissatisfied being a mere U.S. Senator and not "king of the world." Despite his vacuous background and brief tenure in the U. S. Senate, Obama brashly contemplated a run for the Presidency. Such audacity, not of hope but of political hubris, was likely fueled by the knowledge that powerful forces could help catapult him over thousands of other more deserving and experienced politicians. It was also an audacity of hypocrisy, because Obama declared in November 2004, "I can unequivocally say I will not be running for national office in four years."[76] Even as he was making that fallacious statement, some of his Senate campaign workers were already visiting Iowa to establish relationships with the caucus machinery there.

On December 4, 2006, Obama met George Soros in Manhattan to discuss his presidential aspirations. Afterward, Soros introduced Obama to wealthy prospective supporters, including UBS U.S. head Robert Wolf. A week later, Wolf met with Obama to map out campaign strategy. He eventually raised $500,000 for Obama's campaign.[77][78]

With money and connections assured, Obama, whose Senate accomplishments were limited to passing two minor bills (one of which was to name a post office), announced the creation of a presidential exploratory committee on January 16, 2007.[79] A few days later, the *New York Daily News* reported that Soros would back Obama in the Democratic primary over Hillary Clinton, his previous gleam in the eye.[80] This was a remarkable turn of events, since Clinton was a clear frontrunner and Obama an obscure long-shot at best. Soros announced, "I have very high regard for Hillary Clinton, but I think Obama has the charisma and the vision to radically reorient America in the world."[81]

Steven Gluckstern, formerly the Chairman of Soros's Democracy Alliance, hosted a fundraising party for Obama at his home in New York. A photo of the event, published in *New York* magazine April 2007, shows George Soros seated obsequiously behind Obama, with puppet-master haughtiness.[82] In May 2007,

Soros hosted a party for Obama at the mansion of Paul Tudor Jones, who runs Tudor Investment Corporation.[83]

Thus, Obama's meteoric rise from obscurity was fueled by money from Soros and his network of financiers. The public mythology is that Obama's campaign emerged from a grassroots movement and was financed by millions of small donations. The truth is that the seed money for his campaign came from a small cabal of extraordinarily wealthy power brokers. His campaign was born of his audacity and that of these wealthy brokers. While the eventual small donations from average citizens became useful to Obama, his candidacy would have been non-existent without the billionaire seed money.

This should cause average citizens who think they have some influence over the Democratic Party to think again. Remember, this cabal of billionaires cast its lot behind a candidate who barely registered on the presidential radar screen. At the time, Hillary Clinton was the frontrunner in what seemed like a coronation rather than a primary race. The implication is that no gambit is a long shot if the game is rigged.

Seven of Obama's top 14 donors were officers and employees of major Wall Street firms, including Goldman Sachs, UBS, Lehman Brothers, JP Morgan Chase, Citigroup, Morgan Stanley, and Credit Suisse.[84] These companies had financially supported Hillary Clinton, until Soros broke ranks and supported Obama. The influence of these Wall Street power brokers continued right into Obama's presidency. Obama's White House has seen a steady stream of Wall Street executives and financiers. The visitor registry includes Citigroup's Vikram Pandit, Goldman Sachs CEO Lloyd Blanfein, JP Morgan Chase's Jamie Dimon, and Morgan Stanley's John Mack.[85]

According to Don Fredrick in *The Obama Timeline*, Senator Obama received as a U.S. Senator "about $300,000 in contributions each year from Goldman Sachs, Lehman Brothers, Bear Stearns, Fannie Mae, Freddie Mac, AIG, Countrywide Financial, and Washington Mutual."[86] According to Michelle Malkin, hedge funds and private equity firms donated $2,992,456 to Obama in 2008.[87] At least 100 Obama campaign bundlers were investment CEO's and brokers.[88]

In a remarkable show of hypocrisy, Obama lambasted credit card companies in June 2008, declaring, "We need a President who will look out for the interests of the hardworking families, not just their big campaign donors and corporate allies."[89] Immediately after the speech, he attended a fundraiser at Credit Suisse, one of his major backers from the financial industry.[90] As Obama's campaign progressed, the billionaire cabal supporting him grew to include Rupert Murdoch, owner of the *Fox News Channel*, and Warren Buffet, the founder of the fabulously successful Berkshire Hathaway fund.

In another show of hypocrisy, Obama promised that he would collaborate with Senator McCain to use only public funds for the fall campaign in 2008. This policy was a mainstay of his early campaigning for the presidency. However, when Midas-like cash began pouring in, he flip-flopped and chose instead to forego public campaign financing.

But it was more than just billionaire money that abetted Obama's campaign. Soros's Shadow Party operatives grabbed the ball from the financial oligarchs and ran with it. One ball-carrier was the Soros-backed Media Matters for America. This organization monitors the "inaccuracies" of conservative journalists and media personalities. It characterizes conservative assertions as "lies", "smears", "slander", or "falsehoods."[91] Media Matters pays listeners and watchers to monitor conservative broadcasts for controversial sound bites and mistakes. The mistaken or inflammatory bites are then relentlessly hammered by liberal-leaning mainstream media outlets. One of their projects was to pressure the Federal Government to ban Rush Limbaugh from American Forces Radio and Television Service.[92] [93] The Obama campaign was a clear beneficiary of the "hate Bush" and "distrust Republicans" media frenzy that was inflamed by Media Matters.

Another agent of the Shadow Party is the 1.4 million-member MoveOn.org.[94] Soros jump-started this radical organization by supporting founder Wes Boyd, who had launched the website during the Clinton impeachment trial in 1998. Early on, Soros donated $1 to MoveOn.org for every $2 Boyd raised from his members.[95] Soros and friends contributed $6.2 million at its inception.[96] Soros's son Jonathan is involved with MoveOn.org's activities.[97]

MoveOn.org attacked General Petraeus with the famous September 2007 "General Betray Us" full page ad in the *New York Times*.[98] This was part of the Shadow Party push to demonize the war in Iraq and the Republican Party along with it. Strangely, MoveOn.org has chosen not to demonize the Obama administration for continuing the overseas conflicts that began during the Bush administration.[99]

Soros is adept at using the media to influence political trends. Every year, he gives tens of millions of dollars to media operations that support candidates who share his agenda. These media groups use the money to coordinate sympathetic publications, press releases, and activities.

Soros's media tinkering began in 1996 when he launched the Soros Documentary Fund to "spur awareness, action and social change."[100] This fund helped finance several hundred documentaries. In 2001, the fund was absorbed into the Sundance Institute. Its mission evolved to "support the production of documentaries on social justice, human rights, civil liberties, and freedom of expression issues around the world."[101]

Journalist Rondi Adamson wrote that most of the documentaries produced by these organizations "are highly critical of some aspect of American life, capitalism, or Western culture."[102] Their themes convey "that America is a troubling if not sinister influence in the world, that the War on Terror is a fraud and terrorists are misunderstood freedom fighters, and that markets are fundamentally unjust."[103]

According to Adamson, filmmaking was part of Soros's strategy to influence American culture. Soros said, "Documentary films raise awareness and inspire action. The Open Society Institute gave vital support to filmmakers working to expose human rights abuses and helped the films find the widest possible audience."[104]

Soros has significant connections in the broadcast media. PBS broadcaster Bill Moyers is a trustee of Soros' Open Society Institute.[105] David Halperin, the founding director of the Soros-funded American Constitution Society, is the brother of Mark Halperin. Mark Halperin was the political director of *ABC News* until 2007, and is now a political analyst for *Time*. Mark issued a memo during the 2004 campaign instructing his reporters to be less critical of John Kerry than George Bush.[106] Halperin confessed to media analysts at a November 2008 conference on the presidential election that the mainstream media engaged in "extreme bias, extreme pro-Obama coverage." He also said, "It's the most disgusting failure of people in our business since the Iraq War."[107]

Flash forward to June 24, 2009, when the media and government became one. *ABC* became a giant megaphone for President Obama to propagandize the American people to support government-run health care. *ABC News* anchor Charlie Gibson hosted *World News* directly from the White House. The network moderated a forum called "Prescription for America" during prime time in the East Room. *ABC* excluded any opposing viewpoints on the broadcast, despite a request from angry Republicans to get equal air time, and despite offers from conservative organizations to pay for opposing ads.[108] The mainstream media has essentially become a fourth branch of the government under the Obama administration, much like Pravda in the Soviet Union.

Anita Dunn, Obama's White House Communications Director, revealed the media advantage that the Obama camp had during the election. At a January 2009 event discussing the media tactics of the Obama campaign, she said, "Very rarely did we communicate through the press anything that we didn't absolutely control….One of the reasons we did so many of the David Plouffe (an Obama campaign manager) videos was not just for our supporters, but also because it was a way for us to get our message out without having to actually talk to reporters; we just put that out there and make them write what Plouffe had said as opposed to Plouffe doing an interview with a reporter. So it was very much we controlled it as opposed to the press controlled it."[109]

Coincidentally, Anita Dunn orchestrated an effort by the Obama White House to marginalize dissenting media voices, including *Fox News* and Rush Limbaugh. Specifically, Dunn challenged the Pravda collection of media outlets like *ABC* and *NBC* to exclude *Fox News* from news-gathering efforts, because *Fox News* "is not a legitimate news organization."[110] This is the same Anita Dunn who expressed admiration for Chairman Mao of Communist China, who probably used similar tactics during his regime.[111]

This leftist media bias is apparent in the way they cover politicized events. When Cindy Sheehan was protesting the war outside Bush's Crawford Ranch, there were more reporters than actual protestors. Four years later, when Sheehan held a protest *against* Obama on Martha's Vineyard, reporters were conspicuously absent. When *hundreds of thousands* of concerned citizens gathered in Washington on September 12, 2009 to express their discontent with the Obama administration, the media was almost invisible. For many media outlets, events aren't considered "news" until a left-leaning reporter with a microphone or a camera decides they are.

A disturbing example of this was the unremitting coverage of the Iraq war by the mainstream media, which spewed out a steady stream of negative "news" from the war zone in order to tarnish the Republicans. However, in December 2008, *ABC*, *CBS*, and *NBC* stopped sending full-time correspondents to Iraq even though it was still an active war zone.[112] After Obama's election, the war in Iraq was no longer news, because the left-leaning media decided it wasn't.

The Soros network of foundations funds a variety of radical media operations, including the Center for Media Education, the Independent Media Institute, the Proteus Fund, the Youth Media Council, the Media & Democracy Coalition, the Media Action Grassroots Network, Public Radio International, and the Free Press Foundation.[113]

Let's take a peek at the Free Press Foundation, which has received at least $1 million from Soros's Open Society Institute. In the socialist *Monthly Review*, Free Press Foundation cofounder Robert McChesney declared, "Our job is to make media reform part of our broader struggle for democracy, social justice, and, dare we say it, socialism."[114] McChesney wrote an article for *Monthly Review* titled "A New Deal Under Obama?," in which he declared, "In the end, there is no real answer but to remove brick by brick the capitalist system itself, rebuilding the entire society on socialist principles."[115] He also wrote, "We need to do whatever we can to limit capitalist propaganda, regulate it, minimalize it, and perhaps even eliminate it."[116]

Obama won the 2008 election because everything that the electorate knew about him was pre-packaged and carefully meted out by media sycophants. He was carried aloft by a tidal wave of orgiastic support and messianic acclaim from the media and popular culture.

With less than a year of experience as a U.S. Senator, he was on the cover of *Newsweek*. In April 2005, just months after he was sworn in as a neophyte Senator, *Time* magazine called him one of "the World's Most Influential People."[117] His memoir was on the *New York Times* best seller list for 54 weeks. The audio book version of *Dreams from My Father* won a Grammy in the "best spoken word album" category. In October 2005, the British journal *New Statesman* named him one of the "10 People Who Could Change the World."[118] In January 2008, author Deepak Chopra called his candidacy a "quantum leap in American consciousness."[119] In December 2007, Oprah Winfrey said Obama's "tongue (is) dipped in the unvarnished truth."[120] In February 2008, *MSNBC* anchor Chris Matthews gushed,

"He (Obama) seems to have the answers. This is the New Testament."[121]

Remember, less than four years prior to all of this manufactured media acclaim and financial support from Soros, Obama was an obscure and unaccomplished state politician, and only 20% of the people in his *home state* of Illinois even knew who he was.

The media and cultural adulation continued unabated after Obama was elected President. In December 2008, *Time* magazine named him its "Person of the Year." *Newsweek* editor Evan Thomas declared, "…in a way, Obama's standing above the country—above the world, he's sort of God."[122] Incredibly, the Nobel Committee awarded him its 2009 Peace Prize, for which he was nominated after having been President for *just 11 days*. A painting titled "The Truth" depicted Obama as a crucified messiah with a crown of thorns.[123]

Clearly, Obama had a media and cultural support network that was exceptionally unusual, especially since he had not really earned any of the caricatured hero worship that became eerily akin to the outlandish "Dear Leader" demagoguery usually found only in totalitarian regimes.

By June 3, 2008, Barack Obama had leveraged this manufactured adulation to win more committed delegates in the concluded Democratic primaries than Hillary Clinton. However, she had not yet conceded defeat. Clinton and her supporters were still working to swing the "super delegates" her way before the convention. Three days later, a bizarre incident occurred that perhaps illustrated the influence of the forces supporting Obama and raised questions about who really is controlling the political process in America. The following account of this incident is adapted from Don Fredrick's version in his book *The Obama Timeline*.

On June 6, 2008, reporters traveling with Obama boarded his campaign plane near Washington, D.C. to head for Chicago. However, Obama never boarded, opting for an unannounced meeting instead. One reporter challenged Obama spokesman Robert Gibbs: "Why were we not told about this meeting until we were on the plane, the doors were shut, and the plane was about to taxi off?" Gibbs answered, "Senator Obama had a desire to do some meetings, others had a desire to meet with him tonight in a private way, and that is what we are doing."[124] When the plane landed in Chicago, Gibbs admitted that Obama was meeting with Hillary Clinton at an undisclosed location.

The meeting may have been at the Westfields Marriott in Chantilly, Virginia, which was about three miles from where Obama's plane departed without him. At the Marriott, Henry Kissinger, David Rockefeller, and other elites were attending the annual conference of the Bilderberg Group, which is an organization analogous to the Trilateral Commission and the Council on Foreign Relations. Conspiracy theorists believe that these secretive groups are the puppeteers of a grand scheme to establish a powerful New World Order that is superior to the political governments of individual nations. Other attendees included Ben Bernanke, Chairman of the Federal Reserve Board; Tim Geithner, President of the New York Federal Reserve; Don Graham, CEO of the *Washington Post*; Eric Schmidt, CEO of Google; and various bankers, politicians, and media magnates.[125]

Suspiciously, the Marriott's fire alarm went off, and the hotel staff cleared out reporters covering the Bilderberg Group. Reporters at the hotel claimed it was swarming with security. Convoys with armed Secret Service escorts arrived at the hotel with unidentified occupants. Of course, the mystery surrounding Obama's meeting with Clinton and the suspicious events at the Bilderberg event invite speculation that Obama and Clinton met there.[126]

On June 7, the day after the suspected Bilderberg Group rendezvous with Obama, Hillary Clinton conceded the Democratic primary race to Obama.[127] Perhaps it was an uncanny coincidence, but it sure smells like Obama's powerful "protectorate" finalized the primary in a secret meeting.

In addition to media support and Wall Street money, Soros-funded groups provided cadres of campaign workers for Obama. America Coming Together (ACT) was given $18 million by Soros to coordinate "get-out-the-vote" activities.[128] ACT deployed 5,000 organizers supported by 80,000 volunteers to troll for left-leaning voter registrations in battleground states. Patrick Gaspard, the national field director of ACT, was appointed Obama's national political director right after the election. Under Gaspard's tenure at ACT, the organization was fined $775,000 for illegally redirecting money set aside for generic voter registrations to specific Democratic candidates instead.[129] This was the 3rd largest civil penalty ever levied by the FEC.

Another "get-out-the-vote" organization that received OSI and Soros funding was ACORN. This group fielded thousands of activists to support leftist candidates, sometimes in ways that savaged our electoral process. As we saw in the last chapter, ACORN was charged with voter registration fraud in at least 14 states. Citizens Services, Inc., an ACORN subsidiary, likely broke federal election laws and IRS regulations by overtly supporting the Obama campaign. Anti-capitalist groups like ACORN are being consolidated into a large umbrella operation called the Apollo Alliance. Van Jones, a leader of Apollo, was forced to resign as Obama's Green Jobs czar when his deep involvement in communist and other extremist activities was exposed. The Apollo Alliance is sponsored by the Tides Foundation, which is heavily funded by Soros. The Apollo Alliance is an attempt to unify three key activist arms of the radical left—labor unions, environmentalists, and the social justice movement. Apollo believes that government is the solution to most social and economic problems.[130]

The labor wing of this alliance includes the SEIU, the AFL-CIO, and the United Steelworkers. The SEIU PAC alone contributed $27 million to Obama in 2008.[131] The SEIU claims on its website to have knocked on 1.87 million doors, made 4.4 million phone calls, and mailed more than 2.5 million fliers in support of Obama.[132] The SEIU, the fastest growing union in America, is a perfect ally for Obama, because they aim to "kill capitalism" and "turn America back over to its rightful owners: our hard working union employees."[133] Andrew Stern, the head of SEIU, visited the White House at least 20 times in the first nine months of Obama's presidency, according to the White House visitor's log.[134] Politico.com declared, "Andrew Stern practically lives at the White House."[135]

Van Jones described the Apollo Alliance as a "grand unified field theory for progressive left causes."[136] He is an archetypal leader for a radical organization like Apollo. Jones described how he converted to communism after being imprisoned for his involvement in the 1992 L.A. riots: "I met all these young radical people of color—I mean, really radical Communists and anarchists. And it was like: this is what I need to be part of. I spent the next 10 years of my life working with a lot of those people I met in jail, trying to be a revolutionary."[137]

Van Jones is also the founder of Standing Together to Organize a Revolutionary Movement (STORM), a Maoist organization that he was involved with for ten years.[138] STORM was a radical organization that advocated a Marxist revolution in America and the destruction of capitalism. Jeff Jones, another radical member of the Apollo Alliance board, helped found the terrorist Weather

Underground, along with Bill Ayers. [139] He was also a member of the socialist SDS, just like Aryeh Neier, the head of Soros's OSI, and Wade Rathke, the founder of ACORN.

The Apollo Alliance is helping draft legislation for the Obama administration. They are emulating the example set four years earlier by the Soros/OSI-sponsored Progressive Legislative Action Network (PLAN). According to David Horowitz, PLAN's mission was to seed state legislatures with "model" legislation to support their radical goals. [140] PLAN is now called the Progressive States Network (PSN).

Have you ever wondered who writes the complex 1,000 page congressional bills that seem to magically appear from out of nowhere? PSN and the Apollo Alliance have ghost written recent bills sponsored by Democrats. The $800 billion Stimulus Bill of 2009, which basically rewarded patrons of the radical left, was drafted by the Apollo Alliance. [141] Senate Majority Leader Harry Reid thanked them for helping to write it. [142] Phil Kerpen of Americans for Prosperity said the Apollo Alliance "put out a draft stimulus bill (the Apollo Economic Recovery Act) in 2008...that included almost everything that ended up being in the final stimulus bill." [143]

Soros sponsoring radical organizations to ghost-write legislation is audacious enough, but nothing compares to the sheer audacity of his conspiracy to instigate regime change in America.

Soros told the *Washington Post* in November 2003 that ousting the Republicans from the White House "is the central focus of my life…a matter of life and death." [144] He also said, "America under Bush is a danger to the world, and I'm willing to put my money where my mouth is." [145]

Soros had earlier supported regime changes in Eastern Europe, so it was not uncharacteristic for him to conspire to do the same in America. "I do not accept the rules imposed by others," he wrote in *Soros on Soros*. "I am a law-abiding citizen, but I recognize that there are regimes that need to be opposed rather than accepted. And in periods of regime change, the normal rules don't apply." [146] Soros said in January 2007 that "America needs to...go through a certain de-Nazification process." [147]

Soros created the Shadow Party described earlier in this chapter to end the Bush regime, although his ambition extended beyond just defeating Bush. In a *Newsweek* story, "Can a Billionaire Beat Bush?", writer Marcus Mabry explained that even if Bush wins in 2004, Soros "will set about assembling the infrastructure" of a "new left."[148]

Soros failed in his mission to dethrone Bush in 2004, but his Shadow Party did succeed in helping the Democrats retake Congress in 2006. More significantly, the momentum and infrastructure created by this regime change effort culminated in Barack Obama's election as President in November 2008.

Now that Obama is President, what is his agenda? Perhaps we should ask Soros. According to the White House registry of visitors, Soros visited the White House four times in the first six months after Obama took office.[149] Their discussions were private, but it is uncanny how accurate Soros's "prediction" was about Obama's agenda, according to a November 2008 interview with Soros:

> "I think we need a large stimulus package which will provide funds for state and local government to maintain their budgets — because they are not allowed by the constitution to run a deficit. For such a program to be successful, the federal government would need to provide hundreds of billions of dollars. In addition, another infrastructure program is necessary. In total, the cost would be in the 300 to 600 billion dollar range....I think this is a great opportunity to finally deal with global warming and energy dependence. The U.S. needs a cap and trade system with auctioning of licenses for emissions rights. I would use the revenues from these auctions to launch a new, environmentally friendly energy policy."[150]

> The interviewer interjected: "Your proposal would be dismissed on Wall Street as 'big government.' Republicans might call it European-style 'socialism.'"[151] Soros replied:

> "That is exactly what we need now. I am against market fundamentalism. I think this propaganda that government involvement is always bad has been very successful — but also very harmful to our society....At times of recession, running a budget deficit is highly desirable....In 2010, the Bush tax cuts will expire and we should not extend them. But we will also need additional revenues."[152]

There is also curious similarity between Soros's international objectives and those of Obama's administration. One example is the initiative to reduce global poverty through the United Nations Millennium Project. The U.S. contribution to this international effort was sponsored by Barack Obama when he was a U.S. Senator, in form of legislation called the Global Poverty Act (GPA).

According to David Horowitz and Richard Poe in their book, *The Shadow Party*, Obama's GPA legislation and the related U.N. Millennium Project are programs to siphon wealth from advanced nations to third world nations, primarily in Africa and Islamic regions. Rich nations are expected to contribute 0.7% of their GNP each year until 2015. This equates to $235 billion per year, of which the U.S. is expected to contribute $140 billion. The U.S. contribution will be funded by Obama's proposed Global Poverty Act, if it is eventually enacted by Congress.[153]

Coincidentally, the man assigned to manage this international bonanza for the U.N. was Jeffrey Sachs, a former Harvard economist and long time Soros associate. Sachs had earlier worked with Soros to implement "shock therapy" programs in Eastern Europe and Russia.[154] U.N. Secretary-General Kofi Annan appointed Sachs as the Director of the U.N. Millennium Project, which the *Canada Free Press* called, "The largest global wealth redistribution program ever conceived."[155] Soros was so committed to the Millennium Project that he pledged $50 million of his own money in September 2006.[156]

The April 2009 G20 conference that Obama participated in planted the seeds for another Soros international initiative called Special Drawing Rights (SDR's). Soros has been pushing this concept for a long time. In 2001, just days after 9/11, Soros said, "It is not enough to fight terrorism, we must also address the social conditions that provide a fertile ground from which volunteers who are willing to sacrifice their lives can be recruited. And, here, I think I do have something to contribute to the debate....I propose issuing Special Drawing Rights, or SDR's, that the rich countries would pledge for the purpose of providing international assistance. This is an initiative that could make a substantial amount of money available almost immediately....If the scheme is successfully tested, it should be followed by an annual issue of SDR's and the amounts could be scaled up so that they could have a meaningful impact on many of our most pressing social issues."[157]

The April 2009 "London Summit, Leaders' Statement" summarized the proceedings of the G20 conference and was therefore implicitly supported by participant Obama. The statement began with boilerplate socialist pabulum: "We start from the belief that prosperity is indivisible; that growth, to be sustained, has to be shared; and that our global plan for recovery must have at its heart the needs and jobs of hard-working families, not just in developed countries but in emerging markets and the poorest countries of the world too; and must reflect the interests, not just of today's population, but of future generations too."[158] The statement also declared, "We have agreed to support a general SDR allocation which will inject $250B into the world economy and increase global liquidity...."[159] In effect, this authorized the International Monetary Fund (IMF) to print a de facto world currency out of thin air.

Soros told *CNBC*'s Maria Bartiromo that the G20 conference was a "success", probably because the G20 leaders' statement mirrored his own global vision.[160]

The London G20 Summit also endorsed a new global warming treaty and the creation of a global Financial Stability Board (FSB). The FSB would "...extend regulation and oversight to all systemically important financial institutions, instruments, and markets." It also urged nations to "...endorse and implement...tough new principles on pay and compensation and to support sustainable compensation schemes and the corporate social responsibility of all firms."[161] In other words, the FSB established protocol for worldwide regulation of private businesses, including American ones.

Coincidentally, these G20 initiatives mirror the principles of the Socialist International.[162] The American affiliate of the Socialist International is the Democratic Socialists of America, which endorsed Obama during his presidential run. Carol Browner, Obama's Director of White House Energy and Climate Change Policy, was formerly a member of the Socialist International's Commission for a Sustainable World Society.[163]

The G20 initiatives require Congressional approval, but that's hardly a reassuring firewall for American taxpayers, especially when Congress has already supported extravagant domestic initiatives like TARP, the Stimulus Bill, and government-run health care.

Soros's fingerprints are all over these international initiatives to undermine U.S. sovereignty and to transfer American wealth to foreign countries. It is tempting to speculate that Soros tried to directly sabotage the United States during a critical juncture of the

2008 presidential election. On September 6, 2008, McCain lead Obama in a Gallup poll by five points and appeared to have momentum in the presidential race.[164] Shortly thereafter, a financial "crisis" erupted that reversed this momentum and helped determine the outcome of the election.

According to U.S. Representative Paul Kanjorski, Chairman of the House Capital Markets subcommittee, here is what Treasury Secretary Paulson and Federal Reserve Chairman Bernanke told Congress in a September 2008 closed-door session: "On Thursday, 9/15, at roughly 11:00 a.m., the Federal Reserve noticed a tremendous draw down of money market accounts in the USA to the tune of $550 billion dollars in a matter of an hour or two. Money was being removed electronically. The Treasury tried to help, opened their window and pumped in $150 billion but quickly realized they could not stem the tide. We were having an electronic run on the banks. So, they decided to close down the accounts. Had they not closed down the accounts, they estimated that by 2:00 that afternoon, within three hours, $5.5 trillion would have been withdrawn and the entire economy of the United States would have collapsed, and within 24 hours the world economy would have collapsed….It would have been the end of our economic and political system."[165]

An intriguing question is what role did Soros play in this run on banks? No official determination of who triggered it has been announced. Soros certainly had the publicly-declared motive (to destroy the Republicans), he had a demonstrated history of attacking the currencies of particular countries (recall his moniker as the Man Who Broke the Bank of England), and he was allied with a billionaire cabal that had sufficient resources to trigger such an event. Most importantly, the political candidate he had been backing since 2007 had suddenly fallen behind near the end of the presidential race in 2008.

In typical fashion, Soros profited from the 2008 economic collapse, which adds to suspicion about his role in it. He made $1.1 billion during the financial chaos. He said in March 2009, "I'm having a very good crisis."[166] He told *The Australian* newspaper that everything was coming together, "the American election, the financial crisis…."[167] He also said, "I have to admit that I actually flourish, I'm more stimulated by bust. On the one hand, there's the tremendous human suffering, which is very distressing. On the other hand, to be able to handle the situation is exhilarating."[168] In 2007, when the financial tsunami was beginning to sweep across the world, Soros earned an astounding $2.9 billion.[169]

Profit aside, the economic collapse prompted growth in government stimulus spending and economic intervention worldwide, which had to please the socialist Soros. In fact, he said of the world financial crisis to *The Australian* newspaper: "It is, in a way, the culminating point of my life's work."[170]

If there is still doubt that Soros is one of the puppet masters manipulating Obama's strings, consider Obama's stunningly hypocritical loan to Brazil to develop oil resources off its coast. The loan was made even though the Obama administration is fundamentally opposed to oil exploration off the U.S. coast. Obama also supports an enormously expensive cap-and-trade program to *limit* fossil fuel consumption in America.

The United States Government committed to lend two billion dollars from its Export-Import Bank to Brazil's state-owned oil company, Petrobras, for off-shore oil exploration in the Tupi oil field near Rio de Janeiro.[171] There are at least two counts of staggering hypocrisy by Obama in this action. First, Obama has consistently castigated U.S. oil companies for taking taxpayer subsidies, yet he opened up the (empty) U.S. Treasury to help a Brazilian oil company. Second, Obama and his Congressional allies have blocked new exploration of American oil fields off both shores in an effort to impede our oil addiction and reduce greenhouse gases, yet he helped Brazil do just the opposite.

What compelled Obama to loan our money to a Brazilian oil company, an act that is not only contrary to American taxpayer interests, but also contrary to Obama's own deeply ingrained energy philosophy? Here is a possible explanation: George Soros repositioned himself to get dividends in Petrobras just a few days before Obama made the commitment to support Petrobras's offshore drilling in a potentially lucrative oil field.[172] Welcome to Obama's "new kind of politics." Soros has been determined to install a puppet in the White House. It looks like he finally has one.

The Hungarian-born Soros does not like America. In his words, "The main obstacle to a stable and just world order is the United States."[173] In *The Bubble of American Supremacy*, he said "the Declaration of Independence is also open to different interpretations"[174] and that its principles "are not self-evident truths but arrangements necessitated by our inherently imperfect understanding."[175][176]

According to David Horowitz and Richard Poe, Soros hired an army of radical mercenaries to wage war against America. With his vast fortune, he constructed a Shadow Party that is not accountable to the American people or subject to their will. It is simultaneously the party of rebels *and* the party of rulers.[177] It has unified the underclass and the elitist class in a war against the middle class. That is why Soros was dubbed the "Lenin of the 21st Century" by *Ripon Forum* magazine.[178]

"My goal is to become the conscience of the world," Soros narcissistically confessed to biographer Michael Kaufman.[179] What stunning self-importance! Soros believes he is the arbiter of regime change and the puppeteer of compliant marionettes. He's a rogue agent with incredible influence over America's fortunes.

Obama spent his adult life learning from middle class haters and socialists, including Frank Marshall Davis, the radical activist Saul Alinsky, the Black Liberation theologians James Cone and Jeremiah Wright, the SDS terrorists William Ayers and Bernadine Dohrn, the community disorganizers at ACORN, and assorted other radicals and Marxist college professors who worshipped at the altar of wealth redistribution.

There is not a single free-market capitalist in Obama's entire political and philosophical lineage. As we will see in the next chapter, his policies will delay economic recovery, lead to chronic joblessness, discourage energy production and increase its cost, discourage investment, ration healthcare, expropriate private businesses in favor of government and union ownership, create unprecedented government debt, increase our borrowing from foreign countries, deflate the U.S. Dollar, and expand the size and scope of government.

Milton Friedman told us: "The two chief enemies of the free society or free enterprise are intellectuals on the one hand and businessmen on the other, for opposite reasons. Every intellectual believes in freedom for himself, but he's opposed to freedom for others….He thinks there ought to be a central planning board that will establish social priorities….The businessmen are just the opposite— every businessman is in favor of freedom for everybody else, but when it comes to himself, that's a different question. He's always the special case. He ought to get special privileges from the government…."[180] Obama is the ultimate Columbia/Harvard intellectual who believes his judgment is superior to ours. Soros is the ultimate businessman who believes that the world is his playground, which means that all of the rules should be bent in his favor.

Obama is not only an advocate for the underclass, he is the puppet of billionaire oligarchs who lack conscience and who will economically rape America. He will lead the middle class to a new period of austerity and perpetual economic malaise. At the same time, he will siphon wealth to the Wall Street benefactors that empowered him and to the victimized underclass that he is the champion of.

Middle class citizens, including those who voted for Obama, should pause to consider how much control they actually have over where he and his powerful supporters are leading this country. What appeared to be a Camelot-like ascendance by Obama was really the culmination of decades-old radical movements funded and coordinated by billionaire money. Obama hinted at this political facade when he said, "I think that oftentimes ordinary citizens are taught that decisions are made based on the public interest or grand principles, when, in fact, what really moves things is money and votes and power."[181] Behind this façade is an underclass/elitist alliance that will annihilate the middle class on the way to Big Government and diminished individual rights and wealth.

It is possible that Soros's and Obama's vision for the future of the world harkens back to the earliest days of the SDS, the group that helped spawn the socialist revolution unfolding in America today. Soros's right-hand man, Aryeh Neier, co-founded the SDS. Obama was immersed among SDS veterans his entire life. To understand how we arrived at today's political predicament, let's reflect back on the Weatherman war council meeting in Michigan in 1969. Let's ponder the words of Ted Gold, the leader of the Mad Dog faction of the Weatherman who would eventually blow himself into eternity a few months later making bombs in a Greenwich Village townhouse.

Gold said that the Weatherman was an "agency of the people of the world" that would run America after the defeat of U.S. imperialism.[182] Perhaps that agency has arrived in the form of billionaire jackals like Soros and United Nations initiatives like the Millennium Project and Special Drawing Rights. Perhaps that agency has arrived in the form of an ascending Big Government that will transfer our wealth to the underclass here and abroad, reallocate our resources to fight global warming, and weaken our Constitution to usher in the borderless open society that Soros and his ilk fought for decades to achieve.

Here was Gold's punch line at the Weatherman war council meeting 40 years ago: "If it will take fascism, we'll have to have fascism."[183]

Fascism? Is that the ominous storm brewing on our horizon? In the February 1997 edition of *Atlantic Monthly*, Soros declared: "The main enemy of the open society, I believe, is no longer the communist but the capitalist threat."[184] He also said, "I contend that an open society may also be threatened from…excessive individualism."[185] Journalist Matthew Vadum wrote about Soros: "The liberal billionaire-turned-philanthropist has been buying up media properties for years in order to drive home his message to the American public that they are too materialistic, too wasteful, too selfish, and too stupid to decide for themselves how to run their own lives."[186] In other words, the state must intercede in our lives to make our decisions for us. That is essentially the meaning of fascism, and that is essentially Obama's and Soros's view. We are on the verge of subsuming ourselves into the beckoning womb of government, in exchange for allowing the state to become our parent, our provider, and our moral compass. Other societies have made this mistake. It always ends badly.

Obama hinted at this vision during a nationally televised propagandizing of the $800 billion Stimulus Bill in February 2009. He told America that "only government" can end the recession.[187] He said the "private sector is so weakened by this recession, the federal government is the only entity left with the resources to jolt our economy back to life."[188] According to Don Fredrick, Obama's statement echoed Mussolini, who wrote in the *Doctrine of Fascism*, "State intervention in economic production arises only when private initiative is lacking or insufficient, or when the political interests of the State are involved. This intervention may take the form of control (auto companies, perhaps?), assistance (banks, perhaps?), or direct management (health care, perhaps?)."[189] [190]

Obama's advisor and Columbia mentor Zbigniew Brzezinski wrote a book in 1970 called *Between Two Ages: America's Role in the Technetronic Era*, which described his vision of the future: "The technetronic era involves the gradual appearance of a more controlled society. Such a society would be dominated by an elite, unrestrained by traditional values. Soon it will be possible to assert almost continuous surveillance over every citizen and maintain up-to-date complete files containing even the most personal information about the citizen. These files will be subject to instantaneous retrieval by authorities."[191]

Ominously, Obama's Department of Homeland Security (DHS) issued a memo in April 2009 warning about rising "rightwing extremist activity" as the TEA Party movement was starting.[192] The memo, called "Rightwing Extremism: Current Economic and Political Climate Fueling Resurgence in Radicalization and Recruitment," was sent to law enforcement agencies around the country. It warned against citizens who reject "federal authority in favor of state or local authority."[193] Allegedly, the FBI issued an internal memo to all 56 field offices to perform surveillance of the April 2009 tax protests and to keep track of the organizers.

The DHS "right wing extremism" memo also warned that returning veterans could be dangerous: "The possible passage of new restrictions on firearms and the return of military veterans facing significant challenges reintegrating into their communities could lead to the potential emergency of terrorist groups or lone wolf extremists capable of carrying out violent attacks."[194] The American Legion veterans group sent DHS head Janet Napolitano a letter objecting to the Rightwing Extremism report that said, "I think it is important for all of us to remember that Americans are not the enemy. The terrorists are."[195]

Don't be so sure that the terrorists are the enemy, in the eyes of Obama's embryonic socialist administration. As Obama hands over trillions of dollars to the banking oligarchy of Soros and his billionaire cohorts, and as he hands over trillions more to the underclass, recall the folk adage about cons. If you can't figure out who the sucker is, it's you. Sadly, the middle class of America has been conned into redistributing its wealth not only to the poor, but also to the rich. Worse yet, the elitists executing this scam seemingly believe that they know better than us how to run our own lives.

In 2007, Bill Ayers described America as an "incipient fascist country".[196] He may be right.

We've been had.

Chapter Ten

Meet Your Future

> *"The American people will never knowingly adopt socialism, but under the name of liberalism they will adopt every fragment of the socialist program until one day America will be a socialist nation without ever knowing how it happened."*[1]
>
> Norman Thomas, American Socialist

When a storm gathers, the sky darkens as massive purple clouds of potential fury tower over nearby treetops. Ominous crackles of lightning and rolling volleys of thunder intensify. The dank smell of approaching rain heralds a visceral drop in temperature. Dogs bark in primal alarm. Birds take flight as trees bend against onrushing winds. As branches pelt the house, you call the kids indoors and nervously watch the horizon. This one looks bad. You sense it deep down in your chest, that place where a tightly wound ball of fear jangles your nerve endings with electricity. You suddenly feel a cold wave of anxiety, a gut-wrenching sense of dread and impending calamity.

There is a violent storm gathering in America. It is not a storm of pounding hail and howling wind, but rather a storm of political conflict and financial peril. For two centuries, Americans embraced core values of individual liberty, limited government, and free-market capitalism. But in recent decades, our Constitutional Republic has been buffeted by the chilling winds of collectivism. Rushing in are the creeds of subservience, Big Government, and socialism. Michelle Obama heralded the full fury of this storm when she announced with Ivy League elitism, "we are going to have to make sacrifices; we are going to have to change our conversation; we're going to have to change our traditions, our history; we're going to have to move to a different place as a nation."[2]

Barack Obama characterized this storm during a victory speech with a remark drenched in unintentional irony: "This was the moment…when we came together to remake this great nation…"[3] By "remake" he means transitioning to socialism. By "remake" he means transferring our wealth to the underclass and empowering elites to run our lives from a massive bureaucracy in Washington. The word "remake" echoes his constant campaign call for "change." It is the change he learned from Saul Alinsky. It is the revolution that the Students for a Democratic Society hoped for. It is the Open Society that George Soros has been cultivating. Obama's "change" mantra is a remarkable con with dreadful consequences for the middle class.

Shortly before the election in 2008, Barack Obama said, "We are five days away from fundamentally transforming the United States of America."[4] This chapter examines the transformative policies of the Obama administration. It projects their impact on America in the coming years. In other words, this chapter previews your future in a socialist America.

Obama is "remaking" America with reckless abandon. He is dispensing great gobs of imaginary Monopoly money measured in trillions. He is committing us to enormous future liabilities, the cost of which will not weigh upon us until after the 2012 elections. His administration is teeming with radicals and academics that are insentient to the impact of their policies on the American economy.

He deceitfully ran as a centrist during the 2008 general election, but now he is executing policies as extremist as his radical pedigree presaged. Even after the election, Obama continued deceiving America. In February 2010, he pontificated, "We simply cannot continue to spend as if deficits don't have consequences, as if waste doesn't matter, as if the hard-earned tax dollars of the American people can be treated like Monopoly money; as if we can ignore this challenge for another generation."[5] To make such an outlandishly disingenuous statement in 2010 after the obscene spending of his administration in 2009 is the height of hypocrisy and a sign of arrogant disdain for the intelligence of voters.

Even leaders from other countries can read the handwriting on our walls. Obama is being warned by former socialist countries not to follow the destructive path that they've already learned brutal lessons from. Czech Prime Minister Mirek Topolanek slammed Obama's economic plans as a "road to hell."[6] Russian Prime Minister Vladimir Putin declared, "Excessive intervention in economic activity and blind faith in the state's omnipotence is another possible mistake….Instead of streamlining market mechanisms, some are tempted to expand state economic intervention to the greatest possible extent....In the 20th Century, the Soviet Union made the state's role absolute. In the long run, this made the Soviet economy totally uncompetitive. This lesson cost us dearly. I am sure nobody wants to see it repeated."[7] Embarrassingly, even Communist China warned the U.S. against reckless government spending.

Obama is ignoring their admonitions. He is smitten by the siren song of Saul Alinsky and his other socialist mentors. He is rushing headlong toward Big Government. He is abandoning the limited government and free market principles that have been our touchstone for centuries. His administration is bailing out failing companies and irresponsible individuals. They are squandering resources on radical constituencies, and burdening us with suffocating debt. Every initiative of the Obama administration is geared toward transferring wealth, rather than creating it. They are ignoring Thomas Jefferson's observation: "My reading of history convinces me that most bad government results from too much government."[8] Obama is like Opposite George in a *Seinfeld* episode – every instinct of Obama is wrong for America, and we would be better off in almost every measure if he did the opposite of what he wanted.

Ron Bloom, Obama's manufacturing czar, summarized the administration's anti-capitalist perspective: "Generally speaking we get the joke. We know that the free market is nonsense....We kind of agree with Mao that political power comes largely from the barrel of a gun."[9] Obama misinterpreted his 53% - 47% victory over McCain as a mandate to discard capitalism and embrace socialism. Ironically, four years earlier he suggested that Bush should have seen his "51-48 victory as a call to humility and compromise rather than an irrefutable mandate."[10] Apparently, three more margin points means that a socialist revolution is in order, rather than humility and compromise.

Obama's presumed mandate to transition to socialism means that the middle class is going to be devastated by the transfer of its wealth to the underclass. Ironically, the middle class will also be devastated by the transfer of wealth and power to the elites of the education establishment, the banking and investment oligarchy, and the various healthcare and energy industries that will be nationalized into government bureaucracies and run by public service unions. In short, Obama will bail out the poor, and enrich the elites. That leaves the middle class crushed in a brutal fiscal vice.

During the 2008 election, Obama conned us into believing that he was an advocate for the middle class. Nothing could be further from the truth. His largest campaign contributors were investment and banking companies like Goldman Sachs, UBS, JPMorgan Chase, Citigroup, Lehman Brothers, and Morgan Stanley.[11] These companies are being fed trillions of our dollars in bailouts and stimulus funds. The rich will not pay for Obama's spending spree, because they do not collectively make enough money. Many of the rich are *recipients* of Obama's spending spree, including the bankers, the government bureaucrats who administer the infrastructure of the welfare system and the consultants and academic elites who thrive on government grants.

Even if the administration tries to confiscate the wealth of the rich who *don't* feed at the government trough, we will simply see a mass exodus of assets and skill, just like the brain drain that devastated England when they tried to soak their rich. As Soros put it, "the people who require a social safety net cannot leave the country, but the capital the welfare state used to tax can."[12] In other words, rich people can freely move their assets around the world to avoid higher taxes, if they so choose. No matter how this plays out, the middle class will be left holding the bag for Obama's scam.

Obama foisted this con on the middle class by invoking the specter of "crisis" during the election. His policies are a great political bait-and-switch ploy. His stimulus programs are not really designed to jumpstart the moribund economy, but rather to implement his radical agenda. His cap-and-trade proposal will not save the environment, but it will nationalize the energy industry and create another lucrative source of taxation to feed his socialist ambitions. His government takeover of health care will not make health care better or more affordable, but it will absorb nearly 20% of the economy into the sphere of government and take control over intimate parts of our personal lives. His housing and mortgage proposals will not fix the toxic debt problem, but they will transfer wealth to the underclass and effect control over the financial industry.

Obama foreshadowed this con in his book *The Audacity of Hope*. First, he wrote that he is in favor of capitalism, but only as long as it is socialism: "I am optimistic about the long-term prospects for the U.S. economy and the ability of U.S. workers to compete in a free trade environment—but only if we distribute the costs and benefits of globalization more fairly across the population."[13] Then, he wrote that it is a politician's job to foist such cons: "Today's politician…may not lie, but he understands that there is no great reward in store for those who speak the truth, particularly when the truth may be complicated."[14]

The Obama administration *is* blatantly honest about taking advantage of crises to justify the implementation of its agenda. Rahm Emanuel, Obama's Chief of Staff, said, "Never let a serious crisis to go to waste. What I mean by that is it's an opportunity to do things you couldn't do before."[15] Hillary Clinton, Obama's Secretary of State, reiterated Emanuel's "never waste a good crisis" mantra when speaking to the European Parliament.[16] President Obama declared there is "great opportunity in the midst of great crisis."[17] They have duped many into accepting the false dichotomy that the mere existence of a crisis justifies an unprecedented government grab for power. If a private business gouged consumers during a crisis, it would be called an outrage. When the government gouges us, the radicals tell us it is for our own good.

With Obama in the White House allied with a complicit Congress, the radicals are going for broke. To them, every problem is a crisis, and every solution includes more government, higher spending, and intrusions on our liberty. They are force-feeding us socialism with the ridiculous syllogism that something must be done, socialism is something, therefore we must move toward socialism. A simple reading of history illustrates the folly of this. When Japan had an economic crisis, their government launched massive stimulus packages, propped up failing companies, lowered interest rates to zero, and nationalized the banks. As a result, they lost an entire generation to economic stagnation and became mired in unprecedented debt.

Our government has gone on a spending spree that dwarfs all others. Obama's $3.7 trillion 2010 budget increases non-defense spending to 20% of American GDP, the highest level in U.S. history. This budget does not account for the impending explosion in Social Security and Medicare outlays nor the government-run health care and cap-and-trade programs. His administration said that "the new budget is a means to altering the very architecture of American life, with government playing a much larger role than before."[18]

In April 2010, Douglas Elmendorf, the head of the Congressional Budget Office, said: "U.S. fiscal policy is unsustainable, and unsustainable to an extent that it can't be solved through minor changes. It's a matter of arithmetic."[19] Federal Reserve Chairman Ben Bernanke warned Congress that "given the significant costs and risks associated with a rapidly rising federal debt, our nation should soon put in place a credible plan for reducing deficits to sustainable levels...."[20] It's not clear why Bernanke waited until after the Obama administration had already squandered our future before he sounded the alarm.

Ironically, Obama conned us into believing that he *opposed* rampant deficit spending when he chastised the Bush administration in *The Audacity of Hope*: "We say we value the legacy we leave the next generation and then saddle that generation with mountains of debt."[21] Then, he wrote that the only solution is to cut government spending: "If we're serious about avoiding such a future, then we'll have to start digging ourselves out of this hole. On paper, at least, we know what to do. We can cut and consolidate nonessential programs. We can rein in spending on health-care costs."[22] What a magnificent con! Right after taking the oath of office, he ignored his own admonitions and launched a deficit spending rampage unlike any other, and later signed into law a massive new health care entitlement program.

Let's examine Obama's staggering profligacy. Every taxpayer should be appalled by the $800 billion price tag of his American Recovery and Reinvestment Act (the Stimulus Bill). The bill included $750 million for community development block grants that eventually go to groups like ACORN, which was investigated for voter registration fraud in many states. It included $6 billion for mass transit, even though most urban transit systems are so inefficient they already require taxpayers to subsidize 50% of their costs. It included $252 billion in Medicaid, unemployment benefits, and tax "rebates" to people who didn't pay income taxes, essentially moving a pile of money from productive to unproductive people. It included 9,000 pork barrel earmarks for special interests, such as $200,000 for gang member tattoo removal.

The $800 billion Stimulus Bill added 32 new government programs, many of which will continue indefinitely. As Ronald Reagan once observed, a government program is the closest thing we have to eternal life. Unfortunately, this perpetual government intrusion into our lives is exactly what the Obama administration intended. The bill was essentially a political patronage bonanza that funded pet projects the radicals have sought for 40 years. The Congressional Budget Office reported that Obama's economic recovery package will actually hurt the economy more in the long run than if the government had simply done nothing, because it will crowd out more productive activity.[23] The bill, which was intended to jump-start the economy and reduce unemployment, failed miserably. Unemployment went up and stayed up after it was implemented.

Obama's $3.7 trillion 2010 budget does not include the next gargantuan government spending spree, which will be for nationalized health care. Early estimates of the health care reform bill suggest a price tag of $1 trillion over ten years. Using Orwellian illogic, Joe Biden told an AARP gathering that the only way for the government to avoid bankruptcy was to spend another trillion dollars on health care.[24] Absurdly, Obama echoed this illogic during an *ABC News* interview.[25]

The Obama administration is also proposing massive increases in education spending. He declared, "I'm going to put billions of dollars into early childhood education that makes sure that our African-American youth, Latino youth, poor youth of every race, are getting the kind of help that they need...."[26] Unfortunately, the problems with our education system have nothing to do with how much money we spend. The U.S. spends more per pupil than every other country, yet our achievement test scores rank below many other industrialized nations. Our kids will not be any smarter for Obama's spending proposals, but our wallets will be emptier.

Obama's spending orgy will graciously include the rest of the world, because he supports the Global Poverty Act. If this bill is enacted, it will execute the mandate imposed by the United Nations to spend 0.7% of our GDP, or $843 billion over 13 years, to ameliorate poverty overseas. This bill is just another transfer of wealth to poor people, government bureaucrats, and perhaps even brutal dictators and their regimes. It is essentially an international tax on Americans by the United Nations.

Incredibly, Obama also intends to transfer wealth from the middle class to resolve the problems of *history,* in the form of indirect reparations for slavery. Obama declared, "I consistently believe that when it comes to...reparations, the most important thing for the U.S. Government to do is not just offer words, but offer deeds."[27] He later clarified that he's not advocating direct payments to descendents of slaves, but rather government programs that will "close the gap" between races.[28] He believes that the government should enact "major redistributive change" through assistance programs that are nominally available to all people who qualify, knowing that African-Americans will disproportionately benefit from them.[29]

It's easy to spend trillions upon trillions of dollars. Just ask any socialist. But the real gut check is deciding where to get the mountains of "mad money" from. Government money can only come from three sources. Governments can tax money from citizens, they can print it out of thin air, or they can borrow it. All three have terrible consequences, if done in excess. Sadly, because of Obama's outlandish spending spree, our government will have to do all three excessively. This is the real crime against the middle class, which will bear the brunt of all three excesses.

Let's discuss the excessive borrowing first. Obama's spending during his first four years in office will more than double the national debt. Clearly, the U.S. government can't afford its lifestyle. The government is borrowing from the Social Security trust fund, foreign nations, American bondholders, our children, and people who aren't even born yet. It is unsustainable, and it will end badly for everyone.

In 2009 alone, Federal Government debt *increased* by roughly $20,000 for each family of four. So, despite the spending restraints of your family, you and your children fell $20,000 further in debt because of the government. And your family will fall another $20,000 further in debt this year, and the year after that, and also the year after that, ad infinitum. We haven't directly felt the impact yet, because the payments for this debt are not due until some point in the future. But we will feel the impact eventually. The government can con middle class voters, but it can't con reality.

There is a massive present cost of this debt that can't be ignored or postponed. In 2009, the federal government spent $200 billion on interest for its debt. The more the government spends on interest, the less the rest of us can spend on items that are personally important to us. More than half of the $9 trillion in debt that the federal government will incur in the next decade will be because of *interest* expenses.[30] In other words, we are borrowing just to pay interest on earlier borrowing.

Let's put this fiduciary calamity in perspective. If you spent $2 million dollars every day of every year, from the birth of Christ until today, you will not have spent as much as Obama *borrowed* to cover just his 2009 spending. In four years of his administration, Obama's budget deficits will be greater than the *combined* deficits of all of the other presidents over the course of 233 years. Obama's deficit in just 2009 was greater than the last five Bush deficits *combined*. Ironically, the mainstream media called Bush's biggest deficit a "deficit disaster," but described Obama's deficits as "breathtakingly bold." [31] His deficits are not bold, they are obscene. He is borrowing almost $5 billion *per day.*

The government's total debt exceeded $12 trillion by January 2010. This is equal to $40,000 of debt for every man, woman, and child in our country.

Deficit spending is not inherently bad, in the proper context. Many families do it, particularly to make important investments like housing and education. But, such borrowing only makes sense when the likelihood of future income and wealth is sufficient to cover the interest and repay the debt. On the other hand, if government debt grows faster than GDP over the long term, disaster awaits. It is waiting for us now.

When public debt grows faster than GDP, interest expenses crowd out real investment. When investment drops, GDP suffers due to missed opportunities for efficiency gains. Then, while the interest expense of government debt rises, the ability to pay for it declines. Worse yet, when lenders sense that a country has lost control of its finances, they begin demanding risk premiums on top of normal interest rates. This further drives up interest expenses, and further reduces the ability of a country to grow and prosper. This is how some countries have gone into death spirals (Greece is a poignant example today). It is one of the possible modes of collapse that we must begin to fear in America.

We should fear not just the current national debt, but also future debt that we are already obligated to. The true deficit of the Federal Government, including future unfunded obligations like Social Security and Medicare benefits, is $60 trillion, which is four times the U.S. annual GDP and exceeds the annual GDP of the entire world.

Even though we have promised citizens trillions of dollars in future Social Security and Medicare benefits, there is not a single penny set aside for them. All of the cash receipts from the past decades for these programs have either been paid out to beneficiaries or have been diverted to the general budget of the Federal Government.

When the government reports that the Social Security trust fund has a surplus, they are really reporting that the trust fund holds an enormous pile of worthless IOU's stored in a government filing cabinet in West Virginia. The general fund of the Federal Government wrote these IOU's when they borrowed money from

Social Security to maintain the illusion that we could afford our massive spending programs. There is *nothing* in the Social Security trust fund. Sure, the trust fund will eventually cash in the IOU's when retiree benefits exceed payroll taxes currently going into the trust fund, but the other arm of the government that is obligated to repay the IOU's doesn't have any money either. It's a situation akin to when a sailor takes a loan against his 401(k) account, spends it all in a drunken reverie, and then wakes up the next morning to realize he now owes himself the very money that he thought he had saved his whole life. He is not only penniless, he is indebted to himself.

According to economist John Williams, author of the website Shadow Government Statistics, "Put simply, there is no way the government can possibly pay for the level of social welfare benefits the federal government has promised unless the government simply prints cash and debases the currency, which the government will increasingly be doing….The public has a right to know just how bad off the federal government budget deficit situation really is, especially since the situation is rapidly spinning out of control. The federal government is bankrupt. In a post-Enron world, if the federal government was a corporation such as General Motors, the president and senior Treasury officers would be in federal penitentiary."[32]

Social Security is a time bomb about to go off. For decades, we had far more workers than retirees, which allowed us to accumulate a "surplus" in the trust fund that was in turn "loaned" to the Federal Government, which in turn squandered it all. Unfortunately, the day of reckoning has arrived, partly because the Baby Boomers are starting to retire, and partly because the dramatic rise in unemployment during the current recession cut Social Security contributions from workers and employers. Social Security revenue will barely exceed benefits paid to retirees in 2010, according the Congressional Budget Office.

Social Security taxes will either have to be raised, or retirement benefits cut. Starting in 2010, the Federal Government will not be able to borrow "surpluses" from the Social Security trust fund any more, and it will eventually have to begin paying back the mountain of IOU's held by the trust fund in order to keep benefits flowing to seniors. This will have a staggering impact on the Federal deficit. The Social Security trust fund holds essentially zero cash and $2.4 trillion of IOU's payable by the general fund of the government. This really means $2.4 trillion payable by taxpayers, most of who incorrectly believe that they have already funded Social Security.

Many state and local governments also have their own underfunded pension plans, including a $62 billion shortfall in California and a $59 billion shortfall in New York City. These plans are underfunded because our civic leaders have been recklessly over-generous in making future commitments to civil service workers, and because the recent economic collapse has devastated the net worth of pension funds. This means that we must either raise taxes or cut pension payments to support civil service retirees. Reality will not allow any other option.

There are only two options for paying the principal and interest on our debt. One option is to dramatically increase taxes. The other option is to devalue our currency by printing money.

Let's discuss taxation first. Since the rich don't collectively make enough money to fund Obama's socialist initiatives, the tax collectors will eventually come after the vast middle class. The Obama administration is already mentally preparing us for this. Obama told us we are selfish if we want to keep our income instead of giving it to the government.[33] He also told us, "I do think at a certain point you've made enough money."[34] Biden told wealthy Americans it was their patriotic duty to pay more taxes.[35] These pariahs ignore the reality that the tax burden on a middle class wage earner, including income taxes, property taxes, sales taxes, Social Security taxes, Medicare taxes, and user fees, has already exceeded that of a feudal serf, who only had to contribute one third of his labor to his baron.

Middle-class voters should be angry that Obama lied about the coming tax increases in order to get elected. During the election, he claimed that he would not raise taxes on 95% of Americans.[36] He also claimed that only those making $250,000 per year would see increased taxes.[37]

These absurd promises will be impossible to keep. The *Wall Street Journal* reported that if we instituted a 100% tax rate on everyone earning $250,000 or more, the revenue would still not eliminate Obama's deficits. If the government confiscated 100% of the income of everyone making $75,000 or more, it would barely have enough to cover planned expenditures for 2010. Since tax rates of 100% are unspeakable, simple math tells us that people making less than $75,000 are going to pay more taxes sometime during the Obama administration.

Many of the coming tax increases on the middle class will be hidden or deceptive. For example, Obama intends to allow some or all of the Bush tax cuts to expire after 2010. This means that income, dividend, and capital gains tax rates will all increase dramatically. Obama will tell you that expiring tax cuts aren't technically a tax increase, but there will be no confusion about this when your paycheck is lighter. In June 2007, Obama said about the Bush tax cuts, "…people didn't need them, and they weren't even asking for them, and that's why they need to be less, so that we can pay for universal health care and other initiatives."[38] If Obama allows all of the Bush tax cuts to expire, taxes will go up by an estimated $3 trillion over ten years, which would be the largest peacetime tax hike in American history. Taxes would increase by $2,600 annually for the average household. The biggest percentage increases would hit the *lowest* income brackets.

Another deceptive tax increase is likely to be a Value Added Tax (VAT). The Obama administration established a Deficit Commission in 2010 which has begun evaluating the implementation of a VAT. The VAT would be a tax on producers at each level of the manufacturing supply chain. Thus, this stealth tax would be buried in the cost (and the price) of nearly every product made in America. Every consumer would pay this hidden tax, regardless of income level. Coincidentally, the Deficit Commission will not make its formal recommendations until shortly after the mid-term elections in November 2010.

The 2009 Stimulus Bill also deceptively planted the seeds for future tax increases. Almost $60 billion was earmarked for states to permanently expand assistance programs for poor people. However, the stimulus funding is only available for a few years. When that money runs out, the states will have to continue supporting the higher level of benefits set by the stimulus mandates. This will strain local budgets and increase pressure for state and local tax increases.

Another deceptive tax hit to the middle class is likely to come from increased taxes on businesses, which will pass them on to their customers. Obama has discussed taxing income that U.S. multinationals earn overseas, even if the profits are not returned to the U.S. America has the second highest corporate tax in the world. Since the high U.S. tax currently applies only when money is mailed home, firms can compete overseas by keeping their income overseas. If Obama changes this, the middle class will pay higher prices for goods and services when businesses pass their higher taxes through.

The threat of higher corporate taxes has already motivated U.S. companies to move offshore, including Tyco International,

Ingersoll-Rand, and Accenture. An Accenture board member said, "What shareholder would ever vote to incorporate in a country that taxes your worldwide income?"[39]

Middle class Social Security and Medicare taxes will also have to increase. As the Baby Boomers retire and fewer workers support them, the annual cap on Social Security payroll taxes for anyone making over $106,000 per year will have to go up. This will also result in a tax increase on employers, because the 12.4% Social Security tax is equally split between employers and workers.

The Obama administration is considering other subtle tax increases on the middle class. These include potentially eliminating the tax break for 401(k) contributions, eliminating the deduction for charitable contributions, reducing the Child Tax Credit, and taxing dividends as ordinary income rather than at the 15% rate.

A brutal stealth tax increase on the middle class will happen when the Alternative Minimum Tax (AMT) impacts more and more tax filers. The Congressional Budget Office estimated that 28 million middle income filers will automatically get hit by the AMT, unless Congress takes steps to prevent this. When the AMT comes into play, it almost always increases tax liability as compared to normal income tax calculations.

Another brutal stealth tax increase on the middle class will come in the form of higher energy costs as energy providers pass through impending cap-and-trade taxes to their consumers. The purpose of cap-and-trade is to limit manmade greenhouse gases to combat global warming, even though the most abundant greenhouse gas (by far) is water vapor. Cap-and-trade will indirectly increase taxes on everyone who consumes energy. According to Senator Jim Inhofe of Oklahoma, the estimated $300 billion tax increase from cap-and-trade is equivalent to $1,000 each year for every American.

Obama's Environmental Protection Agency (EPA) isn't even waiting for cap-and-trade legislation. It has already declared carbon dioxide to be a pollutant and it has begun regulating this greenhouse gas because of the "danger" it poses to people.[40] Such alarmism ignores the fact that every living creature exudes greenhouse gases, either through breathing or flatulence. Cows exude more greenhouse gas than all of the SUV's in the world. Such senseless EPA regulations will accomplish nothing but higher costs for businesses and higher prices for consumers.

In contradiction to the EPA's concern about carbon dioxide and global warming, a comprehensive report prepared by scientist and public policy expert Christopher Monckton in March 2009 for the U.S. House Committee on Energy and Commerce declared: "...the Committee should consider again, and carefully, the question whether the anthropogenic effect on global mean surface temperature has - albeit inadvertently - been considerably exaggerated. Upon this question all else depends. If climate sensitivity is as low as theory and the satellite data are agreed in showing it to be, then that is the end of the 'climate crisis,' and it would be foolish to spend trillions on addressing a non-problem when there are so many real problems that need to be addressed."[41]

More bluntly, anthropogenic global warming is a scam. It is a Trojan horse being used by socialists to siphon money from taxpayers to the government. More than 31,000 U.S. scientists, including 9,000 Ph.D.'s in atmospheric science, climatology, Earth science, and environment, signed a petition rejecting the notion that the human production of greenhouse gases is damaging Earth's climate. The petition declares: "There is no convincing scientific evidence that human release of carbon dioxide, methane, or other greenhouse gases is causing or will, in the foreseeable future, cause catastrophic heating of the Earth's atmosphere and disruption of the Earth's climate. Moreover, there is substantial scientific evidence that increases in atmospheric carbon dioxide produce many beneficial effects upon the natural plant and animal environments of the Earth."[42]

According to Fred Singer, Professor Emeritus of Environmental Science at the University of Virginia, global warming is caused by the Sun, not by human activity. "The evidence we have shows an extremely strong correlation with solar activity. The (Earth's) temperature follows the solar activity and the correlation is very strong."[43] Remarkably, as solar activity has ebbed in the last decade, so have global temperatures.

Obama reportedly cranked up the thermostat in the Oval Office on his first day. According to David Axelrod, "He likes it warm. You could grow orchids in there."[44] Contrast that with Obama's words during the 2008 campaign: "We can't drive our SUV's and eat as much as we want and keep our homes on 72 degrees at all times....That's not leadership. That's not going to happen."[45] Translation: *"You're* not going to be able to set your thermostat to 72 degrees...but I will!"

The global warming scam is the perfect ruse for advocates of Big Government. Saul Alinsky, the original "change" master, advocated using environmental issues to push the radical agenda: "Once you organize people around something as commonly agreed upon as pollution, then an organized people is on the move."[46] Almost daily, environmental alarmists publish predictions that global warming will cause disasters around the globe, including rising seas, mass starvation, and extinction of species. Not surprisingly, all of the countermeasures needed to slay the unseen monster require higher taxes, more bureaucrats, and increased regulation of businesses and individuals.

Global warming is the perfect ruse because there can be no objective way to know if the expensive countermeasures will help. We will, however, be objectively poorer and less free. The real agenda of the radicals was hinted at during the December 2009 Global Warming Summit in Copenhagen. The biggest standing ovation came when Marxist Hugo Chavez said, "...let's not change the climate, let's change the system....Capitalism is a destructive model that is eradicating life, that threatens to put a definitive end to the human species."[47]

The recently enacted government takeover of health care is another misleading boondoggle that will result in higher taxes. This intrusion by the Federal Government into 17% of our national economy will limit our medical options, lead to rationing, and cost an additional $1 trillion dollars to cover currently uninsured citizens. Ironically, one of the ways the government is considering to pay for its takeover of health care is to tax employee health benefits, which is precisely the same proposal made by McCain that Obama derided during the campaign as "the largest middle-class tax in history."[48] Apparently, Obama thinks the largest middle-class tax in history is now a good idea.

Estate taxes, otherwise known as death taxes, are likely to increase from zero to 55%. This will devastate small business and farm owners as they try to pass their assets to their children. Many of their assets will have to be liquidated to pay the government rather than be bequeathed to their descendents.

There is one whimsical option for solving our debt problem that was suggested by Jay Leno amid a flurry of tax-cheating Obama nominations. He said, "I think Barack Obama is a genius....Do you ever notice when Barack Obama nominates someone, the first thing they do is pay their taxes? He's found a way to pay off the deficit. Nominate every single person in the country one at a time, until they pay off the deficit."[49] There was one special day in Congress that was drenched in delicious irony when *tax cheat* Timothy Geithner testified in front of *tax cheat* Charlie Rangel's House Ways and Means Committee on how to *reduce tax cheating* by ordinary citizens.[50][51]

One of the falsehoods propagated by radicals is that the rich do not pay their fair share of taxes. To the contrary, our tax system is progressive at the top end, and the subsidies provided to citizens on the bottom end are generous. The top 1% of income earners pays 32% of all Federal income taxes. The top 2% pay as much income tax as the bottom 95% combined. The bottom 40% pay zero Federal income taxes, and in many cases are actually subsidized by the Federal tax code through programs such as Earned Income Credit. The radicals will tell us that we should soak the rich even more to pay for their Big Government ambitions, but as mentioned earlier, even if we took *everything* from the rich, it still wouldn't be enough. All indicators point to the middle class as the eventual victims of the government's spending spree.

The middle class should be offended by the arrogance of our gluttonous government officials, who spend and spend while the rest of us feel the terrible burden of the Great Recession. Taxpayers are facing pay cuts, shortened hours, layoffs, reduced benefits, and delayed gratification as they choose not to buy things. In the meantime, government bureaucrats are spending like drunken sailors and taking on record levels of debt. Government is one of the very few sectors of the economy adding workers. There are now 380,000 Federal Government employees who make over $100,000 per year. Eighteen months ago, that number was only 260,000. There are now 66,000 who make more than $150,000. Eighteen months ago, there were only 30,000.[52]

In October 2008, 100 distinguished economists, including five Nobel Prize winners, signed a statement explaining why Barack Obama's misguided tax hikes would harm our economy. They concluded that "Barack Obama's economic proposals are wrong for the American economy….(They) defy both economic reason and economic experience."[53]

According to these economists, "Barack Obama argues that his proposals to raise tax rates and halt international trade agreements would benefit the American economy. They would do nothing of the sort. Economic analysis and historical experience show that they would do the opposite. They would reduce economic growth and decrease the number of jobs in America. Moreover, with the credit crunch, the housing slump, and high energy prices weakening the U.S. economy, his proposals run a high risk of throwing the economy into a deep recession. It was exactly such misguided tax hikes and protectionism, enacted when the U.S. economy was weak in the 1930's, that greatly increased the severity of the Great Depression."[54]

Senator Judd Gregg of New Hampshire warned, "The practical implication of this is bankruptcy for the United States. There's no other way around it. If we maintain the proposals that are in this budget over the ten-year period that this budget covers, this country will go bankrupt. People will not buy our debt, our dollar will become devalued. It is a very severe situation."[55]

Obama's spending and taxation policies are blatantly antagonistic toward innovation, productivity, and growth. They directly punish success and reward failure. They declare war on small businesses, which typically generate the bulk of new jobs and innovations that drive economic growth. They declare war on wealth, which is the very fount of investment and capital that entire societies are built upon.

When Obama tries to soak the rich, they will likely find some other place to live or to stash their wealth. This has already happened in Maryland. When Maryland had trouble balancing its budget, it raised taxes on millionaires. In 2007, Maryland had roughly 3,000 million-dollar income tax returns. In 2008, after the tax was implemented, there were mysteriously only 2,000 such returns. Instead of a revenue bonanza, the state experienced a $100 million *drop* in collections from millionaires.[56] A likely explanation is that many of them simply moved away to avoid the tax. Middle class taxpayers in Maryland will now have to shoulder a bigger share of the tax burden than ever before.

The Tax Foundation estimated how high Federal income tax rates would have to go in order to fund Obama's spending without additional borrowing. For example, for couples filing joint returns, the tax rates for the $17,151 - $69,600 income bracket would have to rise from 15% to 28.1%. The tax rates for the $69,601 - $140,500 income bracket would have to rise from 25% to 46.8%. The tax rates for the $140,501 - $214,100 bracket would have to rise from 28% to 52.4%.[57] This is not to suggest that the Obama administration has announced their intention to do this (yet). It is, however, to suggest that reality will *require* this to happen at some point. When the government is borrowing almost half of the annual spending in its budget, it is unavoidable that *taxes will have to nearly double at some point.*

There are alternatives to these frightening tax increases, but they are equally as ugly. We've already discussed one alternative, which is to keep borrowing money and hope our children forgive us when their lifestyles are diminished in order to pay our debts. Another alternative is to induce inflation by printing money. Politicians that fear getting "fired" by angry taxpayers for directly raising taxes will likely resort to this insidious form of stealth taxation. Governments benefit from inflation because they use the money they print to fund their spending sprees. Unfortunately, when money is printed, citizens become poorer as their investments and savings lose buying power due to the devalued dollar. Printing money does not create wealth, it silently steals it. It is essentially a tax on wealth, including middle-class wealth.

We will have a period of deflation during the current recession as excess capacity and sluggish velocity of money drive down prices worldwide. But, in the long run, the government has little choice but to print money and create inflation. Taxpayers will become angrier and angrier as more and more tax increases are enacted. And as the national debt mounts, it will become harder to find lenders to loan us enough money, especially with interest rates near zero in order to drive economic expansion.

We are heavily dependent on foreign countries lending us money by investing in our Treasury bills. However, foreign countries are becoming more reluctant to do so, because they are frightened of reckless U.S. spending. It is irrational for them to hold U.S. debt when their investments lose value as the dollar loses value. Treasury bond auctions have already started to sputter. The Federal Government printed a trillion dollars in 2009 alone to essentially buy its own debt from itself, because there were not enough willing lenders at such low interest rates and at such high risk.

Foreigners hold about 55% of outstanding U.S. debt. China holds nearly a trillion dollars, and Japan holds nearly $600 billion. These countries can hinder our ability to finance our debt by simply refusing to buy more Treasury bills. One reason they might refuse is fear that our government will default on its debt. Prices have risen on credit default insurance on U.S. Government bonds. For a brief period, it cost more to insure U.S. Government debt than to insure debt issued by McDonald's.[58] In other words, a hamburger joint was considered a safer investment than the U.S. Government.

As lenders resist investing in America, our government has four options. First, it can raise interest rates to entice lenders to overcome their fears. This is not a likely option, because raising interest rates will depress economic activity and lead to another recession. Second, it can raise taxes instead of borrowing money. This will happen to some degree, but as voters edge closer to a tax revolt, this option will become tenuous. Third, it can dramatically cut spending to reduce the need to borrow. This is not a likely option, because it would derail the socialist programs the radicals are pushing. Fourth, it can print money to cover its own debt. This is the option that will be relied upon the most, because it is the most politically expedient.

Unfortunately for the middle class, there will be considerable collateral damage when the government prints money. First, inflation will make the money in our savings accounts worth less in the future as the buying power of the dollar diminishes. Second, inflation will increase the cost of government interest payments. Under inflation, interest rates must rise to compensate lenders for the declining value of money over time. Currently, our interest expenses are about $200 billion per year. If interest rates rise to just 10% (which is not as high as rates rose under Carter), the government's annual interest expenses will climb to $1 trillion, which is more than current Federal spending for education, energy, and defense—combined. Third, inflation will retard long-term economic activity. Under inflation, it is better to borrow than to save, because dollars are worth less in the future than today. When people borrow more and save less, there is less social capital available for investment, which ultimately leads to economic decline.

Government printing presses won't be the only contributor to inflation. Upward pressure on energy prices will also occur when Obama's policies increase the cost of fossil fuel sources. For example, in January 2008, Obama said this about coal-generated electricity: "So, if somebody wants to build a coal-powered plant, they can; it's just that it will bankrupt them because they're going to be charged a huge sum for all that greenhouse gas that's being emitted."[59] He also said, "When I was asked earlier about the issue of coal, you know, under my plan of a cap and trade system, electricity rates would necessarily skyrocket....That will cost money. They will pass that money on to consumers."[60]

A related inflation risk is Obama's strategy to impede exploration for domestic oil and natural gas. The Omnibus Public

Land Management Act of 2009 added two million acres to the 107 million acres of federally-owned wilderness area.[61] That area is bigger than Montana and Wyoming combined. This legislation made eight trillion cubic feet of natural gas and 300 million barrels of oil off-limits to American consumers. As a Senator, Obama voted against drilling for oil and natural gas in the Arctic National Wildlife Refuge (ANWR). "We cannot drill our way out of the problem," he said. "Instead of subsidizing the oil industry, we should end every single tax break the industry currently receives and demand that 1% of the revenues from oil companies with over $1 billion in quarterly profits go toward financing alternative energy research and the necessary infrastructure."[62]

Ethanol is one of Obama's preferred sources of alternative energy. In *The Audacity of Hope*, he wrote: "The bottom line is that fuel-efficient cars and alternative fuels like E85, a fuel formulated with 85 percent ethanol, represent the future of the auto industry."[63] Unfortunately, by 2008 ethanol proved itself an unmitigated disaster. It consumed more energy to produce than it yielded as a final product. It was causing record-high food prices in the U.S. as farmland was diverted to producing fuel. Thus, not only were Obama's energy policies driving the cost of energy up, they were inflating the cost of food. Higher prices caused by the ethanol scam were just another form of indirect taxation on the middle class.

Inflation, whether caused by printed money or by rising costs of key resources like energy and food, will have terrible long term consequences for America. One of the consequences is that the U.S. dollar will be worth less. It may even cease to be the international reserve currency. Reckless spending and borrowing by the U.S. Government has spooked foreign countries that have historically used the U.S. dollar as the benchmark for world economic activity. They are frightened that the declining worth of the dollar will devastate the value of their dollar-denominated holdings and drive up the cost of dollar-denominated resources like oil.

China in particular is agitating for change. They have long relied on the dollar as the international currency for denominating commodity prices and as a safe place to invest its significant reserves earned through trade with the U.S. The Chinese would like to remove the threat of a weakened dollar to their wealth by establishing an international currency, which they made clear at the April 2009 G20 summit in London.

In March 2009, Chinese Premier Wen Jiabao declared: "Of course we are concerned about the safety of our assets….I would like to call on the United States to honor its words, stay a credible nation and ensure the safety of Chinese assets."[64]   Nobu Su, head of Taiwan's TMT group, said that "China has woken up. The West is a black hole with all this money being printed."[65]

The Chinese are working to convince other countries to abandon the dollar as the reserve currency by 2018.   As the U.S. continues down the path of fiscal insanity, more and more countries will jump onto this bandwagon.   Once this ball starts rolling downhill and the dollar loses its status as the international reserve currency, its value will drop even further as countries divest themselves. According to Nobel Prize winning economist Dr. Paul Samuelson, "…we must accept that at some future date there will be a run on the dollar.   Probably the kind of disorderly run that precipitates a global financial crisis."[66]

The radicals in Washington are so eager to transition to socialism that they are willing to spend our children's wealth, induce inflation by printing oodles of money, and allow the U.S. dollar to decline.   But, financial devastation alone is not sufficient for them. Socialism not only involves transferring (and destroying) wealth, it involves controlling, regulating, and even nationalizing industries.

The Obama administration is increasing government control over the banking, finance, automotive, energy, and health care industries.   The grand scope of their ambition is breathtaking, given the importance of those industries to our economy and our lives. Venezuelan President Hugo Chavez, a Marxist, joked, "Hey, Obama has just nationalized nothing more and nothing less than General Motors.   Comrade Obama! Fidel (Castro), careful or we are going to end up to his right."[67]   When Chavez and Castro worry that they might be more conservative than Obama, we have reason for grave concern here in America.

The government now has partial ownership of two icons of American industry, General Motors and Chrysler.   The property rights of investors were ignored during the government-managed bankruptcies of these two companies.   Secured creditors received zero compensation during the liquidations, while the UAW, an unsecured creditor but a patron of the Obama administration, was given ownership stakes in the restructured companies.   GM Chairman Rick Wagoner was forced to resign during the bankruptcy proceedings, but UAW President Ron Gettelfinger was not.

The government has also taken equity positions in banks, investment firms, and insurance conglomerates, after stuffing these financial institutions with $700 billion of our money via the Troubled Asset Relief Program (TARP). Kenneth Feinberg, the U.S. Treasury Department special paymaster, ordered five companies that received government bailouts to slash 2010 compensation for executives.[68] Some companies who were uncomfortable with government intervention in their businesses tried to return the money, but were told that they could not. According to the *Wall Street Journal*, one bank was threatened with "adverse consequences" if it persisted in trying to return TARP money.[69]

Is such meddling proper for a government nominally responsible for protecting individual rights and private property? According to Ayn Rand, "The right to property is the right of use and disposal. Under fascism, men retain the semblance or pretense of private property, but the government holds total power over its use and disposal."[70] Is fascism too strong of a description for the direction that Obama's policies are headed in? Consider this: The Obama administration asked Congress to give Treasury Secretary Geithner unprecedented authority to seize companies whose collapse would damage the economy. Senator Bob Corker called this "truly breathtaking" and something that "should send a chill through all Americans who believe in free enterprise."[71]

Obama declared that only the government had sufficient resources to resuscitate the economy, which absurdly ignores centuries of America history.[72] It is a pronouncement that only a socialist or a fascist could make. The government is not going to save our economy, it is going to take our middle-class wealth and transfer it to someone else who is either poor or very rich. For example, the government proposed establishing a "bank" that will buy the bad debt of other banks, in order to save them from collapse. In return, taxpayers will get stuck with an artificial bank that owns nothing but bad loans. Nobel Prize-winning economist Joseph Stiglitz said, "The Geithner plan is very badly flawed....Quite frankly, this amounts to robbery of the American people."[73] Such control of private business by the state is part of the definition of fascism.

The government is also moving toward nationalizing the energy industry by controlling what land can be used for exploration, how much carbon can be emitted into the atmosphere, what fees have to be paid in order to produce energy, what alternative energy technologies will be subsidized with our tax dollars, what kinds of appliances we can have in our homes, and what vehicles will be allowed in the marketplace.

The government is even going to coerce our churches to muddle in energy affairs. Obama's Advisory Council on Faith-Based and Neighborhood Partnerships recommended to the EPA that they provide financial assistance to churches that agreed to preach the environmental religion. The Council said, "Regional (EPA) staff would work to engage local faith-and community-based groups to help meet the Obama administration targets for greening buildings and promoting environmental quality."[74]

Is government meddling in energy a good thing or a bad thing? Consider this: The U.S. Department of Energy was created to make us less dependent on imported foreign oil. This department now has a $24 billion budget and 16,000 government employees. And yet, after 32 years of this expensive bureaucracy, we are far more dependent on foreign oil than we were back in 1977. Such failure is a harbinger of the ineptitude we can expect when the government takes even greater control of the energy industry.

The government is also taking over the health care industry. The Obama administration signed health care legislation that will eventually result in higher taxes, reduced services, lower quality, and greater government intervention in our private decisions about health care. We are heading down the path of government-controlled health care that European countries, who have already tried it, are starting to retreat from because of poor quality and long waits. Remarkably, we may become more socialistic than the European countries we mocked for decades.

If you are in the middle class, you will get less health care at a higher cost. You will stand in line behind people who don't pay for health care, perhaps including illegal immigrants who may get amnesty, and therefore coverage. If you are elderly, you will eventually be told that a government efficiency formula has determined that expensive drugs and surgeries are not appropriate for you, since you have too few years left for society to benefit from the "investment."

As government takes greater control of industry after industry, its size and power will expand. Likewise, public sector labor unions that parasitically feed off the government monopoly over taxpayers will also grow in size and power. The effect of this will be extortion of wealth from hard-working middle-class taxpayers to highly-compensated government bureaucrats whose job is to impede our lives somehow. It will be a transfer of wealth from citizens who produce to citizens who live off those who produce.

Obama has always collaborated with unions. Here's how he described his relationship with unions that supported his campaigns: "I owe those unions. When their leaders call, I do my best to call them back right away. I don't consider this corrupting in any way; I don't mind feeling obligated...."[75] Here's how he described his relationship with the giant service sector union SEIU: "I've spent my entire adult life working with SEIU. I'm not a newcomer to this. I didn't suddenly discover SEIU on the campaign trail."[76] Andy Stern, President of the SEIU, visited the White House 22 times in the first eight months after Obama's inauguration.[77]

Stern pointed out the symbiosis between labor unions and Obama's vision for America. He said that he wants the economy judged on "whether we have shared prosperity, not just growth...the government has a role in distributing wealth and social benefits. We are at a historic crossroads...we are witnessing the first new American economic plan led by the government, not necessarily by the private sector."[78]

Obama promised unions that he would pass the Employee Free Choice Act (EFCA). He pledged to "make it the law of the land when I am president of the United States."[79] EFCA would effectively eliminate secret-ballot elections during union drives. This would allow union organizers to strong-arm workers until they agree to support a union drive. This truly Orwellian legislation would empower unions to not only extort businesses, but to extort workers to extort businesses. And when government workers are involved, unions will be empowered to extort workers to extort government agencies to extort taxpayers. The rest of us will be the chumps at the bottom rung of this extortion food chain.

Public sector unions will always support left-leaning politicians, because they know these politicians will advocate bigger government, which means more unionized government workers, which means more union dues, which means more money to support leftist politicians. Everybody does well in this vicious cycle, except taxpayers and private businesses. In January 2010, the Department of Labor announced that there are now more unionized government workers than unionized private sector workers. They also announced that Washington, D.C. had the lowest unemployment rate of any city in the nation. Six of the wealthiest counties in the country are on the outskirts of Washington, D.C. The public sector is currently the only part of the U.S. economy that is growing, and public sector unions are the only unions increasing their membership. The implication is that the only "business" booming in America is government and their unionized employees.

The Obama administration is pushing unionization in order to multiply the army of voters eager to move us toward socialism. Another army that might abet the leftward drift of our government is illegal immigrants. The Obama administration is building momentum for immigration reform legislation. This will portend badly for middle-class taxpayers.

In July 2007, Obama spoke to the National Council of La Raza (NCLR). NCLR is an advocate for open borders and amnesty for illegal immigrants. He told them, "I will never walk away from the 12 million undocumented immigrants who live, work, and contribute to our country every single day."[80] In July 2008, he told them, "The system isn't working when 12 million people live in hiding, and hundreds of thousands cross our borders illegally each year; when companies hire undocumented immigrants instead of legal citizens to avoid paying overtime or to avoid a union; when communities are terrorized by ICE immigration raids....We'll make the system work again for everyone....And together, we won't just win an election; we will transform this nation."[81]

By "transforming this nation," it is likely that Obama means giving amnesty to illegal aliens. He can't evict them from the country, because that would violate his promise not to turn his back on them. If he doesn't give them amnesty, it would violate his commitment to "transform the nation."

Amnesty will be another burden on middle-class America. It will enable a new segment of the underclass to lay claim to taxpayer wealth via government services. It will also create another massive voter block that will support Democrats out of gratitude, which will accelerate the drift toward socialism. The ten million Latino voters in the 2008 presidential election leaned decidedly toward Obama.

Obama made clear his support for illegal aliens in May 2010 when he vociferously criticized a new Arizona statute that empowered local law enforcement professionals to enforce existing Federal laws regarding identification requirements for aliens. Obama condemned the Arizona bill without even reading it, despite the fact that the bill was simply authorizing local enforcement of the policies of his Federal bureaucracy. He even collaborated with a foreign leader, Mexican President Felipe Calderon, in a public denouncement and criticism of the legislation of an American state. In other words, he sided with the foreign leader responsible for the invasion of aliens across our Southern border, and sided against his own citizens in Arizona who were simply trying to protect their border from that foreign leader.

Obama is weakening America in the face of external threats in other ways. Unlike many "responsibilities" that Obama has invented for our government, defending our nation against terrorists and foreign invaders is constitutionally required of him as Commander-in-Chief. Despite this obligation, national defense is one of few areas of the budget that he is seeking to *shrink*.

Obama is anxious to cut military spending, because he wants to reallocate our financial resources to his socialist agenda. His Secretary of Defense, Robert Gates, proposed cuts in defense spending that will reduce acquisition of ships, planes, high-tech military hardware, and equipment to protect and rescue soldiers.[82]

Obama used the power of his office to diminish America's standing abroad. His apology tours in Germany, England, Egypt, the Middle East, and Asia portrayed America as an arrogant imperialist nation, rather than as an honorable and generous nation that has frequently rallied to the defense and aid of the entire world. He does not see American soldiers as defenders of freedom, but as reckless agents who are "just air-raiding villages and killing civilians."[83]

Obama criticized our allies and kowtowed to our enemies. He bowed to King Abdullah of Saudi Arabia, which the *Washington Times* called "a shocking display of fealty to a foreign potentate" and an "extraordinary protocol violation."[84] He bowed to Emperor Akihito and Empress Michiko of Japan, but not to Queen Elizabeth of England.[85] During a July 2007 debate, he said that he would meet without preconditions some of the world's most villainous dictators, including Mahmoud Ahmadinejad and Kim Jong Il.[86] In a botched attempt to appease Russia, he terminated a new missile defense system in Eastern Europe, the day after the rogue nation North Korea launched a missile capable of reaching Poland. Russia snubbed Obama's appeasement by announcing a program to help Iran's nuclear program. Some of our gravest enemies, including Muammar Qaddafi, Fidel Castro, and Kim Jong-Il, *endorsed* Obama for President.[87]

Obama's groveling and apologies appear to have earned nothing but international disdain. President Nicolas Sarkozy of France reportedly described Obama's position on Iran as "utterly immature."[88]   Allegedly, a report from France's Directorate-General for External Security quoted Sarkozy describing Obama as a "mad lunatic."[89]

According to Mortimer Zuckerman, Editor-in-Chief of *U.S. News & World Report*, a renowned Asian leader remarked, "We are convinced that he (Obama) is not strong enough to confront his enemy. We are concerned that he is not strong enough to support his friends."[90]   Nobel laureate Lech Walesa said in February 2010: "They (the United States) don't lead morally and politically any more. The world has no leadership. The United States was always the last resort and hope for all other nations. There was the hope, whenever something was going wrong, one could count on the United States. Today, we lost that hope."[91]

Obama's policy of treating terrorism as a criminal rather than a military matter is another threat to our security.   As political analysts Dick Morris and Eileen McGann explained, "Obama urged us to go back to the era of criminal-justice prosecution of terror suspects, citing the successful efforts to imprison those who bombed the World Trade Center in 1993....That prosecution, and the ground rules for it, had more to do with our inability to avert 9/11 than any other single factor.   Because we treated the 1993 WTC bombing as simply a crime, our investigation was slow, sluggish and constrained by the need to acquire admissible evidence to convict the terrorists. As a result, we didn't know that Osama bin Laden and al-Qaeda were responsible for the attack until 1997—too late for us to grab Osama when Sudan offered to send him to us in 1996."[92]   In an unprecedented move, Obama's administration decided to put 9/11 mastermind Khalid Sheikh Mohammed on criminal trial in New York City, the primary scene of the slaughter of Americans.[93]

Obama emasculated our most effective defenses against terrorism, our intelligence agencies.   He promoted disclosure of sensitive and compromising information under the Freedom of Information Act.   He vilified and threatened to prosecute agents who successfully used aggressive (and effective) interrogation techniques to prevent terrorist attacks.   He ordered the Guantanamo Bay detention facility to be closed and the captured enemy combatants housed there to be relocated inside America.   He turned the blind eye of political correctness to the terrorist massacre at Fort Hood.   He released information on U.S. intelligence methods, ignoring the counsel of four former CIA Directors.   He required our soldiers to read Miranda rights to captured enemy combatants in the heat of battle.

Obama's policies project weakness to rogue nations and international terrorists who will interpret his passivity as an invitation for further mischief. Just as Clinton's passivity led to the attacks of 9/11, Obama's treatment of terrorists as "man-caused disasters" is the kind of namby-pamby political correctness that will embolden the cutthroats who despise and wish to kill us. He added troops to the war in Afghanistan, while announcing to our enemies an exact timetable for them to leave. He did this during a speech in which he never made reference to victory, because he doesn't like the word.[94] Afghanistan is called the graveyard for empires. Politically compromised battle plans and public disclosure of tactics will certainly endanger American soldiers and lead to failure there.

The Obama administration is also weakening the foundation of our society. The bedrock of our political system, the U.S. Constitution, is slowly being eroded as the guarantor of limited government and sovereign individual rights. This must necessarily happen under Obama's administration, because his lust for socialism is the antithesis of limited government and individual rights. The U.S. Constitution and the aspirations of the Obama administration cannot co-exist in any meaningful way.

As Obama pursues his agenda to take wealth and liberty from the middle class, he will appoint activist judges who are sympathetic to an end-run around the Constitution. Sonia Sotomayor, his first pick for the Supreme Court, is an "empathetic" justice who will legislate from the bench and establish "policy", based on remarks she made before her nomination.[95] [96] His second pick, Elena Kagan, wrote her senior thesis at Princeton on the topic of socialism in New York City. Near the end of her thesis, she wistfully wrote, "In our own times, a coherent socialist movement is nowhere to be found in the United States. Americans are more likely to speak of a golden past than of a golden future, of capitalism's glories rather than of socialism's greatness."[97] The Obama administration will rely on justices like Sotomayor and Kagan to "authenticate" unconstitutional transfers of wealth and power to the elites and to the underclass.

In *The Audacity of Hope*, Obama wrote: "...just as I recognize the comfort offered by the strict constructionist, so I see a certain appeal to this shattering of myth, to the temptation to believe that the constitutional text doesn't constrain us much at all, so that we are free to assert our own values unencumbered by fidelity to the stodgy traditions of a distant past. It's the freedom of the relativist, the rule breaker, the teenager who has discovered his parents are imperfect and has learned to play one off of the other—the freedom of the apostate."[98] He also wrote: "…I have to side with Justice Breyer's view of the Constitution—that it is not a static but rather a living document, and must be read in the context of an ever-changing world."[99]

That is exactly what a constitution is *not*. Our Constitution is a firm commitment to the basic moral and philosophical principles of our society. It is not an infinitely malleable tool to help facilitate "change", especially the socialistic change that Obama is peddling. While it is possible and sometimes desirable to change the Constitution as our society evolves, the prescribed process for doing so is extremely burdensome, by design. As John Locke noted, the foundations of a society should not be changed for light and transient reasons. They should certainly not be changed at the behest of one leader or nine justices.

One of the first casualties in an Obama world of a "living" Constitution will be dissent by opposing voices. The radicals are intent on implementing some version of a strategy previously called the "Fairness Doctrine". The goal of this doctrine was to minimize the influence of conservative and Christian talk radio. Obama's FCC is preparing to use regulatory constraints like "diversity", "localism", and the "public interest" to steer broadcast content more toward the left end of the political spectrum.[100] Obama's acting FCC Chairman, Michael Copps, said he believes the government should enforce media "diversity" and make sure radio programming is "more reflective" of "public interest."[101] He said, "If markets cannot produce what society really cares about, like a media that reflects the true diversity and spirit of our country, then government has a legitimate role to play."[102] The market dominance of conservatives and Christians on the radio is fueling the desire of the radicals to find non-market ways to marginalize the voices that oppose Obama's "change."

Democratic Senator Benjamin Cardin proposed a "Newspaper Revitalization Act" that would give the increasingly obsolete newspaper industry Federal subsidies in exchange for influence over their editorial decisions.[103] This would essentially make newspapers mouthpieces of the government, which is clearly antagonistic to the First Amendment. Here is Obama's perspective: "I am concerned that if the direction of the news is all blogosphere, all opinions, with no serious fact-checking, no serious attempts to put stories in context, that what you will end up getting is people shouting at each other across the void but not a lot of mutual understanding."[104] His self-serving implication is that if newspapers become extensions of his government, the news that they report will be inherently unimpeachable. Nothing could be further from the truth. The unique purpose of the independent news industry in our society is to shine a bright spotlight on those in power in order to enforce transparency and accountability. Once a newspaper becomes beholden to political leaders for its survival and its content, it may as well change its name to *Government Times*, just as GM is now laughingly called Government Motors.

Another First Amendment battleground will be the internet. Cass Sunstein, one of Obama's many czars, has argued that the internet is inherently anti-democratic because of the way users can select information of their own choosing.[105] He said, "A system of limitless individual choices, with respect to communications, is not necessarily in the interest of citizenship and self-government."[106] Not only is this perspective self-contradictory and nonsensical, it is another indication of the administration's interest in increasing control over the flow of information. Expect to hear more discussion about how to regulate the activity of bloggers on the internet. Obama's second Supreme Court nominee, Elena Kagan, wrote in 1996, "If there is an 'overabundance' of an idea in the absence of direct governmental action—which there well might be when compared with some ideal state of public debate—then action disfavoring that idea might 'un-skew,' rather than skew, public discourse."[107] In other words, if the internet or any other medium becomes skewed toward the conservative end of the political spectrum, then government intervention to "un-skew" it is desirable.

The government's yearning to control dissent includes a growing focus on controlling how our children think. Public schools are run by administrators and unionized teachers who are paid by the government, so they are inherently reluctant to dissent against the collectivist masters that feed them. As Upton Sinclair put it, "It is difficult to get a man to understand something, when his salary depends upon his not understanding it."[108] From the age of five onward, our children are exposed to far more indoctrination at school than they get at home. Most of that indoctrination leans to the left.

Obama was involved for years in radicalizing the Chicago public school system with his accomplice, William Ayers. He tiptoed back into that arena in September 2009 when he addressed school students nationwide, encouraging them to work hard and to participate in community service. Before his speech, teachers were coached to read books about Obama and ask students why it is important that they listen to him and other elected officials. During the speech, teachers were instructed to challenge the kids to write down key points about what Obama was challenging them to think about and do.

Obama's budget includes $10 billion for "Zero to Five" education, which will give government-funded educators access to the minds of our children for the only five years that they are currently free from indoctrination.[109] Obama also signed into law the Edward M. Kennedy Serve America Act (formerly called the Generations Invigorating Volunteerism and Education Act). This $6 billion legislation created 175,000 new "service opportunities" for young adults under AmeriCorps.[110] [111] It established additional organizations to focus on issues dear to the radicals, including Clean Energy Corps, Education Corps, Healthy Futures Corps, Global Energy Corps, and Green Jobs Corp.

The bill's opponents said it was a tool for proselytizing young "volunteers." Ominously, the original version of the bill proposed to create a "Congressional Commission on Civic Service." If the original version of the bill had passed, this commission would have explored "whether a workable, fair, and reasonable mandatory service requirement for able young people could be developed and how such a requirement could be implemented in a manner that would strengthen the social fabric of the nation."[112] This provision was stricken from the bill due to negative publicity.

In his book, *The Plan: Big Ideas for America*, Chief of Staff Rahm Emanuel wrote, "We propose universal civilian service for every young American. Under this plan, all Americans between the ages of eighteen and twenty-five will be asked to serve their country by going through three months of basic training, civil defense preparation and community service."[113]

Obama was a founding board member of a youth service group called Public Allies in 1992. Michelle Obama was the Executive Director for Public Allies Chicago for several years. Obama plans to use this group as the model for his national service corps.[114] Public Allies deploys 2,200 community organizers to agitate for "justice" and "equality" in major U.S. cities. "I get to practice being an activist and get paid for it," declared a Public Allies participant.[115]

Public Allies, which gets half of its funding from the U.S. Government, is a training ground for future Obamas. It brags that 80% of its graduates go on to work in nonprofit or government jobs. It's training the "next generation of nonprofit leaders."[116] This is consistent with Barack and Michelle's general disdain for the private sector. Michelle said, "We left corporate America, which is a lot of what we're asking young people to do. Don't go into corporate America. Become teachers. Work for the community. Be social workers."[117] Barack told graduating students at Wesleyan University, "Individual salvation depends on collective salvation."[118] If our kids are not all good socialists yet, it's not from lack of trying by the Obamas and their fellow radicals.

Many in the education establishment are eager to radicalize American youth along the lines of Obama's vision. At a school in Massillon, Ohio, students in a government class passed out internship applications for the Organizing for America group, which uses the web address barackobama.com.[119] This organization is recruiting students to "build on the movement that elected President Obama by empowering students across the country to help us bring about our agenda."[120] The recommended reading list for recruits includes Saul Alinsky's *Rules for Radicals* and chapters from Obama's *Dreams from My Father*.[121]

Julian Huxley wrote in his 1947 book, *UNESCO: It's Purpose and Its Philosophy*: "The task before UNESCO (the United Nations Educational, Scientific, and Cultural Organization)…is to help the emergence of a single world culture…at the moment, two opposing philosophies of life confront each other…individualism versus collectivism…capitalism versus communism…Christianity versus Marxism. Can these opposites be reconciled, this antithesis be resolved in a higher synthesis?….if we are to achieve progress, we must learn to un-crystallize our dogmas."[122] In essence, he said we need to embrace the dialectic materialism of Marx and Hegel, the theoretical mechanism that would facilitate the evolution from capitalism to communism.

Such "synthesis", such philosophical compromise between diametrically opposed world views, is not meant to find peace in the world, but rather to weaken the foundation of one world view so that it can be supplanted by another. Efforts like the Serve America Act and Public Allies are designed to change our culture from one of capitalism, individual rights, and individual responsibility; to one of socialism, collective rights, and collective responsibility. This cultural change is being driven through our children. Initiatives like Public Allies and the Serve America Act are designed to "uncrystallize" young minds from the current cultural paradigm, fill them with a passion for service and collectivism, "refreeze" them with the new ideology, and thereby establish a generational foundation for socialism in America.

Aldous Huxley wrote in his 1946 edition of *Brave New World*: "A really efficient totalitarian state would be one in which the all-powerful executive of political bosses and their army of managers control a population of slaves who do not have to be coerced, because they love their servitude. To make them love it is the task assigned…to ministries of propaganda, newspaper editors, and schoolteachers."[123]

Youth indoctrination models are common in collectivist states. The Soviets called their version Praxis. Praxis was a program in which students learned practical collectivism, a mind-changing process that was the centerpiece of "service learning" in their schools and communities.[124] The primary goal behind group service learning was not compassion, but subservience to the collective. If there were in fact any good results from group service, they were of secondary importance to the inculcation of communal purpose and activity. Socialism by definition requires individuals to subsume themselves into the great collective. That is what Hegel meant with his proto-socialist concept of the "Species Being."

The Soviet praxis model was similar to National Socialist programs in Nazi Germany. Young Germans from ages 10 to 19 had to serve in the Hitler Youth Program.[125] Youth service was a source of cheap labor, and it was a way for the Nazis to propagandize an entire generation. Hitler told a crowd in 1933: "When an opponent says, 'I will not come over to your side,' I calmly say, 'Your child belongs to us already….What are you? You will pass on. Your descendents, however, now stand in the new camp. In a short time, they will know nothing else but this new community.'"[126] Hitler also said, "The Youth of today is ever the people of tomorrow. For this reason we have set before ourselves the task of inoculating our youth with the spirit of this community at a very early age, at an age when human beings are still unperverted and therefore unspoiled."[127]

We are being force-fed a "new community" by the radicals. A monumental change is taking place in the relationship between the state and the individual in America. America is rapidly descending from a representative Constitutional Republic of free and independent citizens to a collectivist socialist state that is larger and more intrusive than the autocratic British monarchy we revolted against two centuries ago. This "change" will not bode well for the middle class.

We are at a dangerous tipping point in our democracy. Mob rule is about to overwhelm our Constitutional protections. Roughly 55% of eligible voters pay Federal income taxes, and the remaining 45% don't. Once that ratio becomes unfavorable for the taxpayers, they will be exposed to an electoral majority that could simply choose to vote their wealth away. The radicals with the "share the wealth" mantra who invaded Washington after the 2008 election are eager to push America over that tipping point.

When we are told that the Constitution is a flexible "living document," we are really being told that the rule of law is flexible, our rights are flexible, and the limits on government are flexible. If that is the case, then our rights and the Constitution mean nothing—they can be subsumed by the whims and fancies of the moment. Such "flexibility" leaves us essentially defenseless against the marauding mob of socialist wannabes that has gained political control.

This mob, operating with the "end justifies the means" morality of Saul Alinsky, has declared war on the middle class and on the concept of constitutionally-protected individual rights. The prize for the mob in this conflict is parasitic socialism. The cost to us is everything we hold dear. Like a plague of locusts that consumes everything in its path, the radicals are flooding the voting booths with armies of "victims" and "dependents" who will vote for the radicals in hope of leeching onto American taxpayers to get all of their needs and wishes fulfilled. Thomas Paine postulated two centuries ago that the world consists of taxpayers and those who live upon the taxpayers. He predicted that those who live upon the taxpayers will work tirelessly to expand their role as parasites. Today, the parasites are on the verge of winning. They will devour the middle class, which is the heart and soul of our country, leaving behind the skeletal remains of a once-vibrant society.

In *The Audacity of Hope*, Obama clearly stated that he doesn't embrace the American system of free enterprise. He described capitalism as "chaotic and unforgiving," and said that he wants to roll back the "ownership society."[128] [129] This is to be expected, since socialist mentors have guided his entire life, including Barack Obama Sr., Frank Marshall Davis, disciples of Saul Alinsky, Richard Cloward, Frances Piven, William Ayers, Malcolm X, Alice Palmer, Carl Davidson, Jeremiah Wright, George Soros, ad nauseum.

Obama's antipathy to capitalism ignores the warnings of conservative author Dr. Adrian Rogers: "You cannot legislate the poor into freedom by legislating the wealthy out of freedom. What one person receives without working for, another person must work for without receiving. The government cannot give to anybody anything that the government does not first take from someone else. When half of the people get the idea that they do not have to work because the other half is going to take care of them, and when the other half gets the idea that it does no good to work because somebody else is going to get what they worked for, that my dear friend, is about the end of any nation. You cannot multiply wealth by dividing it."[130]

P.J. O'Rourke put it more bluntly: "Freedom is not empowerment. Empowerment is what the Serbs have in Bosnia. Anybody can grab a gun and be empowered. It's not entitlement. An entitlement is what people on welfare get, and how free are they? It's not an endlessly expanding list of rights – the 'right' to education, the 'right' to health care, the 'right' to food and housing. That's not freedom, that's dependency. Those aren't rights; those are the rations of slavery – hay and a barn for human cattle. There is only one basic human right, the right to do as you damn well please. And with it comes the only basic human duty, the duty to take the consequences."[131]

Unfortunately, these perspectives are falling on more and more deaf ears in today's culture. A great "change" is taking place in America, a change that is transforming the individual from a sovereign entity protected by the Constitution into submissive chattel of the state. America is devolving into a collectivist gang-state controlled by elites whose mission is to corral the rest of us into a great uniform proletarian herd. This "change" is being embraced without understanding its true nature. Norman Thomas, an American socialist, predicted this: "The American people will never knowingly adopt socialism, but under the name of liberalism they will adopt every fragment of the socialist program until one day America will be a socialist nation without ever knowing how it happened." Karl Marx said, "Democracy is the road to socialism."[132]

It is foolish to believe that compromise is possible between our capitalist foundations and the socialistic ambitions of the radicals. Lenin, an iconic Marxist, said: "As long as capitalism and socialism exist, we cannot live in peace: in the end, one or the other will triumph."[133] In other words, no long-term compromise is possible between socialism and capitalism. The premises, worldviews, and practical applications of each are diametrically opposed. A society that tries to accommodate both will never achieve lasting tranquility.

Pope Benedict XVI, describing the fall of the Soviet Union, offered a powerful perspective on this in *Truth and Tolerance*: "...where the Marxist ideology of liberation had been consistently applied, a total lack of freedom had developed, whose horrors are now laid bare before the eyes of the entire world. Wherever politics tries to be redemptive, it is promising too much. Where it wishes to do the work of God, it becomes not divine, but demonic."[134]

Marxism can only end in demonic results. The Marxists in Russia murdered 40 million of their own. The Marxists in China eliminated 70 million. The Marxists in Vietnam and Cambodia each slaughtered two million. These "testimonials" lay bare the dictum of Lenin that no peace is possible until all enemies of socialism are destroyed, from without and from within.

Obama declared during a Colorado campaign stop: "We cannot continue to rely on our military in order to achieve the national security objectives that we've set. We've got to have a civilian national security force that's just as powerful, just as strong, just as well funded. People of all ages, stations, and skills will be asked to serve."[135] Why do we need a strong civilian national security force? We already have the most powerful defense capabilities in the world. Perhaps it is because socialism always hides its totalitarian aims under the banner of coercive community service or "civilian national security."

Obama wrote in *The Audacity of Hope*: "In 1941, FDR said he looked forward to a world founded upon four essential freedoms: freedom of speech, freedom of worship, freedom from want, and freedom from fear. Our own experience tells us that those last two freedoms—freedom from want and freedom from fear—are prerequisites for all others."[136] This is the entrée into collectivism for Obama. The vain hope to be absolved from want and fear is the nose of the socialist camel under the capitalist tent. The temptation of being freed from self-responsibility by the state is the great tease for the middle class, the great proffering of poisoned gingerbread. If we succumb to the temptation, we will find ourselves serving the state, in order for the state to serve us. If we succumb to the temptation, we will find ourselves trapped by totalitarian logic in which the "rights" of some become "liens" on others. In the Orwellian paradigm of the socialists, freedom is not possible without chains.

Michelle Obama told us that Barack will require us to "volunteer" our time. He will "recommend" that we meet "obligatory volunteer goals."[137] Barack said, "I will ask for your service and your active citizenship when I am President of the United States…this will be a cause of my presidency."[138] This is where the words of Pope Benedict XVI come crashing home: "Wherever politics tries to be redemptive, it is promising too much. Where it wishes to do the work of God, it becomes not divine, but demonic." There is a vital difference between community activism and socialism. It is one thing for individuals to express their faith by doing God's work on Earth with acts of charity. It is another thing altogether to leverage the financial, military, and police apparatus of the government to forcibly compel individuals to do the work of a god they call the state. Altruism enforced by the power of the state can never be God-like; it can only be destructive of individual rights and liberty. Transfer of wealth compelled by the state is not charity; it is theft on the grandest of scales.

The beauty of our Constitution is that it is designed to allow the free exercise of altruism without the evil of state compulsion and confiscation. Our Constitution creates the opportunity for individuals to pursue moral redemption in a way that is appropriate for each of them. Socialism obliterates moral redemption with guns and tax collectors. As Ayn Rand put it, "Morality ends where a gun begins."[139]

Obama has appointed an army of czars to administer his illusory policies of redemption, the profane work of his own statist god. He has created new government positions through executive order that require no senate approval. These czars are therefore beholden, not to the American people, but to Obama himself. In effect, he is creating a two-tiered government, one tier consisting of its public face, in the form of Cabinet Secretaries who are subject to public approval and scrutiny, and another tier consisting of shadowy czars of questionable background and intent who are subject only to Obama's approval.[140]

What are these furtive, unaccountable forces doing with our trillions of dollars? How much more of our wealth must be siphoned to Goldman Sachs, General Motors, and the rest of the elite robber barons who howl at the moon of calamity and beg for more and more corporate welfare? How much more of our liberty must be sacrificed on the altar of collective enslavement to our lowest common denominators? Why must we tolerate an Information and Regulatory Czar who wanted to outlaw hunting and who supported giving animals the legal right to file lawsuits?[141] Why must we countenance a Science Czar who advocated compulsory sterilization and who believed that we should have fewer people, a global police force, and a Planetary Government?[142]

The statist beast is insatiable, as it always has been, absent a powerful Constitution compelling limited government. We have already accumulated more debt than any country in history. And yet our leaders pursue even more debt, as they construct the foundation of socialism with the building blocks of government-run health care and government-controlled energy. There will be no end to it, because their envy of our wealth is boundless, and their hatred of our freedom is absolute. Through it all, we will be beguiled with temptresses named "Hope" and "Change", which were the campaign leitmotifs of National Socialism too.[143] [144] One of Hitler's slogans was "Alles muss anders sein!," or "Everything must be different!"[145]

The middle class will not only bear the brunt of this "change", the middle class will evaporate. Socialism is not a productive politico-economic system. It is a parasite, and a mindless parasite at that, because it is too foolish to know when to stop bleeding its host. When the host dies, when responsibility, initiative, investment, and ambition fade into oblivion in America, there will be nothing left but to stand in line for scarce goods and rue the passing of our greatness. This will be of little concern to the elites who orchestrated the disaster, because they will still have sufficient power and guns to siphon the meager resources left in our society for their own use. This has been true in all collectivist dictatorships. The party leaders live like kings, while the worker bees are scolded that they must sacrifice and live barren lifestyles marked only by slavish commitment to the sacrosanct state. The demise of America's greatness will also be of little concern to the helplessly dependent lemmings of the underclass. They will be groveling along with us for scraps, but with conspiratorial gleams in their eyes from the knowledge that they helped collapse us into collective poverty in a fit of envy and sloth emblematic of Cloward and Piven's Orchestrated Chaos.

This is no longer a contest between Republicans and Democrats. It is a fight against socialism. It is a fight for the survival of the middle class. It is a fight for our Constitutional Republic. It is a fight for our unalienable rights to life, liberty, and the pursuit of happiness. If socialism wins out, we will all be poorer and we will all have fewer rights than before. Socialism is a system with a proven track record of abuse, failure, and destruction.

Even now, certain constituencies of Obama that have been his strongest supporters are experiencing dreadful results wrought by failed collectivism. After just one and a half years of Obama's administration, African-Americans are being devastated by unemployment approaching 35%, which is close to what the general population experienced during the Great Depression. The 19-28 year old age group is being crushed by unemployment approaching 25%. The next decade of their lives is already being called lost. In the decades after that, their generation will get stuck with the bill for today's spending. This is because no politician is suicidal enough to raise taxes to match our current level of spending, and the current administration has no intention of reducing the spending. The city of Detroit, which has been managed by leftist radicals for decades, epitomizes the moral hazard of socialism and the abject failure of collectivism. To get a sneak preview of the socialist America of tomorrow, look at Detroit today.

This administration is perhaps the most divisive in history. As the government takes a larger and larger role in our lives, the classic fault lines in our society are widening. As we all compete for our "share" of the diminishing socialist loot, races will be pitted against each other, generations will vie for position against each other, and economic classes will reach for metaphorical torches and pitchforks to assault each other.

At what point will the middle class of America revolt against this insanity? At the close of Obama's first year in office, general U.S. unemployment was at 17% under the broad "U6" gauge. Trillions of dollars of equity evaporated from retirement accounts and real estate. Over 300,000 properties were foreclosed in just October 2009. More Americans lost their homes in 2009 than during the entire Great Depression. Seven million more homes are on the precipice of foreclosure. In December 2009, the government increased the cap on taxpayer "insurance" of mortgage insurers Fannie Mae and Freddie Mac from $200 billion to infinity. This means they are fearful of a massive collapse of the real estate market.

If that collapse happens, the financial losses will become a gargantuan obligation of every taxpayer. Analysts believe that nearly half of the mortgages that Fannie and Freddie insure, which total in the trillions, are toxic.

Of course, much of this has been blamed on Bush by the radicals. There are two problems with this diversionary tactic, however. First, the Democrats have controlled Congress since January 2007. Congress controls the purse-strings of our government. Second, the Bush administration was also a tragic disappointment to champions of limited government, as it too flirted with collectivism in a misguided effort to assuage moderates. Remember, this battle is no longer a struggle between Democrats and Republicans. It is a struggle by the middle class against collectivism spawned by politicians of all persuasions.

This storm has been brewing for decades. It is only now that we feel its ferocity as the shutters and shingles of our tidy suburban homes are blown off. The ends have been played against the middle. The last half-century has been a giant pincer movement against the middle class, with the underclass clamoring for more and more transfers of wealth, and the elites clamoring for more and more corporate welfare and control of our lives.

Obama is just the denouement of a long play, the smiling and waving engineer of a train that left the station of collectivism decades ago. That train is now a runaway juggernaut as both major political parties jockey to gain the support of the political center, ironically by promising to promiscuously spend the wealth of the political center. The reality that the middle class has yet to fully comprehend is that both major political parties are not really jockeying for the center, they are in a bidding war for the right to *attack and devour* the center. We've been had by both parties, and it's imperative that we come to grips with that realization.

Advocates of limited government and individual rights need to stand up now and confront this socialist threat to our country. If Obama, Reid, and Pelosi are still running this country three years from now, the American way of life will be irretrievably lost. The programs that they are implementing day after day in Washington will soon be irreversible. Once government-run health care is fully implemented, there will be no undoing it. There will only be waiting lists for procedures that the government will ration for the middle class, but will give away for free to the underclass. Once illegal immigrants are given amnesty, free education, health care, and other social benefits, there will be no undoing it. There will only be a reduced standard of living, class warfare, and bi-lingual signs everywhere.

Forget your retirement plans. With Social Security funds already spent, the nation trillions of dollars in debt, massive new entitlement programs being created, taxes soon to rise everywhere, and energy costs increasing due to ascetic environmental programs, retirement will be beyond your reach. You will have to work your entire life with your nose to the grindstone. As you do so, think deeply about those people in the underclass who have become generationally dependent upon your support, and those elites whose lives have been enriched by your bail-outs and sacrifices. You will be a slave to them.

The middle class will be the victim in Obama's grand march toward socialism. He supports the underclass with wealth transfers and myriad government programs. He supports the elites with corporate bailouts and millions of bureaucratic jobs. His staff is a gilded roster of Washington and Wall Street insiders. His biggest campaign supporters were bankers and insurance moguls. David Rockefeller is a family friend. Soros is his puppeteer. Where does the middle class fit in this picture? If you can't figure out who the mark is in a con, it's you.

One thing is certain. If Obama and the radicals are allowed to finish their mission, there will be no middle class in America, just as there is no middle class in any collectivist regime anywhere in the world. Money doesn't grow on trees. Prosperity doesn't come from government printing presses. Obama's "Hope" and "Change" are far more likely to yield dependency and disappointment than freedom and prosperity.

When Toto pulled back the curtain to reveal what was behind the smoke and mechanical artifices in Oz, the myth of the all-powerful Wizard imploded. Instead of an imposing, otherworldly, godlike force, the Wizard was just a shriveled old sideshow con man. Likewise, when the media-abetted deification of Obama is finally pierced by the arrow of harsh reality, we will see instead a professional community agitator accomplished in hypocrisy, deceit, misinformation, and not much else. We will see a conniving alchemist yearning to transform government spending into real wealth, in a modernized version of the age-old urge to turn lead into gold.

Obama is just a huckstering smiley face concealing a con of great consequence. He will flash his charming grin at the cameras and recite rhetoric with grandiose pomposity from a teleprompter. He will tell us that he is pursuing some nonsense called The Third Way, a philosophy that is part capitalism and part socialism. Unfortunately, the half of his philosophy that exalts the state and empowers it to intrude in our lives will inevitably overwhelm the other half. It has always been that way, because the state has the implied force of guns and the very real power to confiscate wealth. It is not possible to be half free, at least not for long.

The Democrats have become the party of Big Government, wealth transfers, and corporate bail-outs, with a nominal bias toward civil libertarianism. The Republicans are becoming the party of Big Government, wealth transfers, and corporate bail-outs, with a nominal bias toward free market capitalism. The center point between these two still leaves Big Government, wealth transfers, and corporate bail-outs firmly entrenched. The debate around this center point is really just lip service regarding civil liberties and free markets, to whatever extent that Big Government graciously allows them to play out. In a sense, it's like two wolves and a sheep voting on what's for dinner. One wolf is the wealthy elites. The other wolf is the underclass. The rest of us are the sheep. We all know how the vote will come out.

An alternative center point in our polity is a return to our core principle of limited government, wherein us middle class sheep have unalienable Constitutional rights that protect us from political carnivores. From a civil liberty perspective, this means less government intrusion in our individual lives and behaviors. From an economic perspective, this means less government intrusion in the free market. Colloquially, this means that the government should keep its hands off our families and our wallets.

This will have to be the center point that the middle class eventually forces political parties to gravitate toward, if it is to survive. This is the revolution that must happen in America, and it must happen quickly. The good news is that the middle class has sufficient numbers to execute this revolution politically. The bad news is that few in the middle class truly understand the con that has been foisted upon them by their leaders.

This alternative center point is firmly rooted in individual rights and freedom. Freedom means that our economic activity should be voluntary, and the government should stay out of our personal affairs. Freedom means that the government should stay out of our wallets, out of our privacy, out of educating our kids, out of influencing our moral conduct, and out of our businesses. The government should protect our rights, not control our lives.

The political platform of a movement focused on this alternative center point would be built upon the pillars of limited government, individual rights, individual responsibility, and the U.S. Constitution. Such a platform would:

- **Embrace fiscal responsibility**, which means advocating a dramatic *downsizing* in government spending, commitments, and involvement. It means recognizing that individuals are responsible for their lives, not society.

- **Embrace a strong national and civil defense**, but only for the purpose of protecting, with extreme prejudice, our citizens, our property, and our interests from attack by rogue nations, terrorists, and criminals. Limited government is inconsistent with nation-building and occupying foreign lands.

- **Embrace immigrants coming to America**, as is our tradition, but only if they do so lawfully and can carry their own weight. Limited government is inconsistent with taking on waves of illegal immigrants dependent on state handouts.

- **Insist on a judiciary that adheres to the Constitution**, rather than one that seeks to unilaterally change the Constitution. The role of the judiciary is to ensure our rights to life and property are protected from the majority, not dissolved by the majority.

- **Embrace a limited-government perspective on social issues.** This may run counter to the intuition of certain conservatives, but it is incongruous to demand less government in most things, while insisting that government stick its nose in moral, ethical, or religious affairs. In the context of limited government, civil libertarianism will not threaten social values held dear by conservatives or liberals. If civil liberty is properly honored, *all* people should be free to live their lives as they choose, according to the values that are dear to them, as long as they respect the similar rights of others.

- **Embrace economic growth**. A growing prosperity is the only way that our society will be able to support an improved standard of living for the next generations while supporting the commitments that we have already made to the current generations for programs such as Social Security. Our society should allow free markets to allocate capital and labor, to price assets and resources, and to choose winners and losers. Strong economic growth is the only "change" that benefits everyone. It offers the potential for all people to come out ahead, not just certain groups. It promotes trade, which is the amicable and voluntary tie that binds not only citizens in America, but also countries around the world. Prosperity is the true fount of "hope". This kind of hope is the ultimate defense against civil unrest and the rise of totalitarianism.

Today's problems are political and philosophical. The central issue of the debate is individual liberty versus socialism. Democracy can only save itself from itself when enough people realize that we need a return to limited government, not surrender to Big Government. Our society will be saved from communal suicide only when enough people realize that capitalism is the sole internally consistent philosophy that will achieve our goals of efficiency, privacy, fairness, and security.

This battle needs to be won before there are so many people dependent on the government that socialism is simply the default mechanism of survival for the majority, because the next step in that cause and effect sequence will be the destruction of America. A frightening harbinger of this societal Armageddon occurred after an October 2008 campaign stop by Obama in Florida. An Obama supporter told a reporter, "I won't have to worry about putting gas in my car. I won't have to worry about paying my mortgage. You know, if I help him, he's gonna help me."[146] The Obama supporter probably did not ponder what would happen to America if *nobody* worried about these things.

It is up to the middle class to save America. Reagan told us: "We are a nation that has a government, not the other way around."[147] Lincoln told us: "We the people are the rightful masters of both Congress and the courts, not to overthrow the Constitution, but to overthrow the men who pervert the Constitution."[148] Common sense tells us that this is a situation of our own making, and therefore a situation that we can correct. We elected the politicians who legislated and executed this mess, so therefore we can vote them out of office.

Simple math lays before us the scope of our challenge. There are 100 Senators, 435 Congressmen, and one President. These 536 quislings spend the trillions, set the tax rates, burden us with the debt, print the bogus money, create the regulations, kowtow to the lobbyists and the bankers, bribe the underclass with entitlement programs, appoint the czars, select the judges, hire the millions of bureaucrats, grant themselves pork barrel sugarplums, and collaborate with the media, cultural, and education elites to con the middle class into a self-destructive conspiracy of the lemmings.

Reagan also told us: "No arsenal or no weapon in the arsenals of the world is as formidable as the will and moral courage of free men and women."[149] Free men and women, it is time to exercise our will and moral courage, before we slip completely into the abyss of totalitarianism. We essentially have three options.

One option is to quietly accept this catastrophe and melt silently into the darkness as the "change" that Obama and the radicals are implementing becomes absolute, leaving us and our children to wallow in debt and lost "hope." However, this option is morally and spiritually repugnant to those who cherish liberty and understand the dangers of Big Government.

A second option is non-violent revolution, perhaps in the form of succession from the union. Many states have introduced sovereignty resolutions that underscore their right to separate from the union, if necessary. The Montana resolution ends with: "That if any act of Congress becomes law or if an Executive Order or Judicial Order is put into force related to the reservations expressed in this resolution, Montana's 'Compact With the United States' is breached and all powers previously delegated to the United States by the federal Constitution and Bill of Rights revert to the states individually."[150]

But it is not yet time for widespread civil disobedience or succession. Our institutions are too grand, our history too elegant, our communities too sacred, and our lives too precious to engage in acts that could precipitate another civil war.

The third and most appropriate option is to vote every scoundrel out of office who believes that our lives are chattel to be bargained away in a grand socialist experiment that has no possible outcome other than abject failure and enslavement to the Leviathan. The dire situation we face was created through politics, and we must exhaust every effort to resolve it through politics. The war between the advocates of limited government and the advocates of collectivism must first be fought at the ballot box, just like Saul Alinsky concluded many decades ago. He knew that he had to win the heart and soul of the middle class in order to achieve socialism by popular vote. The warning to the middle class today is that socialism has no place in it for you, other than for you to serve as the oxen that wear the yokes.

The first step in fixing the situation is to recognize the problem. The problem is that we in the middle class have unwittingly been used as pawns by the elites and by the underclass. Consequently, we are being devoured by both. We have been conned by a giant political pincer movement. Quite simply, *we've been had*. It's time for us to get mad as hell, or disappear.

It is no longer sufficient to just show up at the polls every few years and vote. My wife and I had an epiphany on Election Day in November 2008. When the results of the election came in, we shed some tears, sank into a depression, and mourned the incipient dissolution of our great country. Later that evening, it dawned on us that we had not earned the right to be angry and despondent. Sure, we had done our civic duty and voted. But, voting on Election Day is like going to church on Sunday. Just as being a true Christian requires participation every day, not just on Sunday, being a true citizen requires participation every day, not just on the first Tuesday in November.

Being a true citizen requires becoming an active warrior in the political battle against socialism. Being a true citizen requires convincing fellow Americans that morality is on the side of limited government. Being a true citizen requires working tirelessly to mobilize fellow patriots to rally to the defense of our Constitution. Being a true citizen requires speaking out against every encroachment on our liberty and holding our leaders accountable for every wayward decision. Being a true citizen requires a refusal to leave the world to our children in the mess that is now. Our fathers and forefathers left our generation a priceless jewel of a country. It is on the verge of being destroyed. It is up to every one of us to save it.

The epiphany that my wife and I experienced launched this book project and inspired us to join the TEA Party movement. Millions of others have joined too. Over one million Americans attended TEA Parties on Tax Day in 2009, and then again on Tax Day in 2010. Middle class revolts are erupting around the country, including Virginia, New Jersey, and Massachusetts, where senatorial candidate Scott Brown immortalized himself by correctly identifying Ted Kennedy's vacant seat as "the people's seat."[151] The TEA Party movement has learned the lesson that Alinsky taught the radicals: Either sit at home and feel sorry for your selves, or organize, build power, and take control during the next elections.

In his first Inaugural Address, Lincoln said, "This country...belongs to the people who inhabit it. Whenever they shall grow weary of the existing government, they can exercise their constitutional right of amending it, or their revolutionary right to dismember or overthrow it."[152]

Martin Luther King, Jr. said, "The hottest place in hell is reserved for those who remain neutral in times of great moral conflict."[153]

Edmund Burke told us, "The only thing necessary for the triumph of evil is for good men to do nothing."[154]

Millions of good men and women in America are choosing to do something about our dire predicament.

Will you?

Refuse to be had any longer!

"Let us be sure that those who come after will say of us in our time, that in our time we did everything that could be done. We finished the race; we kept them free; we kept the faith."

Ronald Reagan

I

128, 129, 130, 131, 132,
133, 134, 136, 137, 138
Israel, 113, 114, 115, 119,
120, 122, 123, 130, 134,
135, 136
Issa, Darrell, 195

J

Jackson, Jesse, 50, 119
Jacobs, John, 143
Jakarta, 35, 36, 116, 117, 218
Japan, 129, 245, 258, 266
Jarrett, Valerie, 150, 152, 165,
166, 168, 171, 172
Jarrett, Vernon, 150
Jefferson, Thomas, 22, 59, 87,
138, 243
Jesse James Gang, 143
jihad, 114, 128, 135, 136
Johnson, Jim, 201
Johnson, Lyndon, 77, 79, 91,
109, 183
Jones, Emil, 221, 222
Jones, Jeff, 149, 231
Jones, Paul Tudor, 223
Jones, Van, 230
Jong Il, Kim, 266
Joyce Foundation, 49, 157,
220
JP Morgan Chase, 223, 244
Judicial Watch, 51, 165, 172

K

Kagan, Elena, 268, 270
Kanjorski, Paul, 235
Katz, Marilyn, 157, 158
Kazakhstan, 212

Kellman, Gerald, 40, 41, 42,
67, 79, 83
Kelly, Megyn, 206
Kennedy, John F., 109, 112,
126
Kennedy, Robert, 77, 78, 79
Kennedy, Robert F., 144
Kennedy, Ted, 19, 287
Kenya, 18, 33, 35, 36, 92, 93,
116, 130, 131, 132, 138
Kerry, John, 58, 189, 217, 225
Keyes, Alan, 53, 54
Khalidi, Rashid, 122, 130
Kibaki, Mwai, 131, 132
Kind and Just Parent, (Ayers),
157
King Abdullah, 120, 135, 266
King, Martin Luther Junior,
59, 77, 112, 126, 287
King, Steve, 196
Kissinger, Henry, 144, 229
Klonsky, Mike, 101, 154
Klonsky, Susan, 154
Kruglik, Mike, 79, 83
Kwanzaa, 124
Kyoto, 103

L

labor union, 23, 64, 66, 70,
100, 230, 263, 264
Laubach Literacy Institute
(LLI), 116
Lawndale Restoration, 172
Leadership for Quality
Education, 157
League for Industrial
Democracy, 90, 104, 215
Leary, Timothy, 144
Lebanon, 114

M

Chapter One

[1] Fernando Suarez, "Clinton Says She and McCain Offer Experience, Obama Offers Speeches", CBS News, March 1, 2008; available online at: http://www.cbsnews.com/blogs/2008/03/01/politics/fromtheroad/entry3896372.s html [accessed December 23, 2009].

[2] J.R. Dunn, "Obama as Liberal Messiah", American Thinker, January 14, 2008; available online at: http://www.americanthinker.com/2008/01/obama_as_liberal_messiah.html [accessed December 23, 2009].

[3] Jerome R. Corsi, "Is Obama the Messiah?", World Net Daily, February 23, 2008; available online at: http://www.wnd.com/index.php?fa=PAGE.view&pageId=57090 [accessed December 23, 2009].

[4] "Obama Warns SC Voters of 'Hoodwinking'", ABC News, January 3, 2008; available online at: http://blogs.abcnews.com/politicalradar/2008/01/obama-warns-sc.html#top [accessed December 28, 2009].

[5] "Malcolm X Quotes", Black Voices, February 2, 2006; available online at: http://www.blackvoices.com/black_news/mlk/canvas/_a/malcolm-x-quotes/20060218134409990001 [accessed December 28, 2009].

[6] "Interview with Saul Alinsky, Part Two", The Progress Report, 2003; available online at: http://www.progress.org/2003/alinsky3.htm [accessed December 28, 2009].

[7] "Remarks of Senator Barack Obama: Super Tuesday", Organizing for America, February 5, 2008; available online at: http://www.barackobama.com/2008/02/05/remarks_of_senator_barack_obam_46.php [accessed December 28, 2009].

[8] "Quotes by Margaret Thatcher", Goodreads, copyright 2010; available online at: http://www.goodreads.com/author/quotes/198468.Margaret_Thatcher [accessed December 28, 2009].

Chapter Two

[1] Barack Obama, *Dreams from My Father: A Story of Race and Inheritance*, (New York: Three Rivers Press, 2004), p. 438.

[2] Maureen Dowd, "The 46-Year-Old Virgin", The New York Times, September 5, 2007; available online at: http://select.nytimes.com/2007/09/05/opinion/05dowd.html?_r=1 [accessed December 28, 2009].

[3] Spengler, "Obama's Women Reveal His Secret", Asia Times Online, February 26, 2008; available online at: http://www.atimes.com/atimes/Front_Page/JB26Aa01.html [accessed December 28, 2009].

[4] Virginia Prostrel, "Teddy, JFK, and Obama", Forbes.com, August 27, 2009; available online at: http://www.forbes.com/2009/08/27/edward-kennedy-rfk-jfk-

glamour-obama-politics-opinions-contributors-virginia-postrel.html [accessed December 28, 2009].

[5] Tony Blankley, "Obama's Blank Screen Deception", Real Clear Politics, January 28, 2009; available online at: http://www.realclearpolitics.com/articles/2009/01/obamas_collectivist_nationalis.html [accessed December 28, 2009].

[6] Ross Mackenzie, "Et Al Ad Nauseam: 2008 and all that", Townhall.com, January 1, 2009; available online at: http://townhall.com/columnists/RossMackenzie/2009/01/01/et_al_ad_nauseam_2008_and_all_that [accessed December 28, 2009].

[7] Aaron Klein, "Michelle Contradicts Obama Nativity Story", World Net Daily, October 27, 2009; available online at: http://www.wnd.com/index.php?pageId=114259 [accessed December 28, 2009].

[8] Jerome R. Corsi, *The Obama Nation: Leftist Politics and the Cult of Personality*, (New York: Threshold Editions, 2008), p. 44.

[9] Jerome R. Corsi, "Did Obama's Grandmother Say He was Born in Kenya?", World Net Daily, August 24, 2009; available online at: http://www.wnd.com/index.php?pageId=107524 [accessed January 3, 2010].

[10] "Certificate of Live Birth (COLB)", The Obama File, copyright 2010; available online at: http://theobamafile.com/ObamaCOLB.htm [accessed June 17, 2010].

[11] Obama, *Dreams from My Father*, p. 125-126.

[12] Pamela Geller, "CNN Tells, Sells More Lies about Palin – it's Time to Expose the Truth about Obama", Atlas Shrugs, August 1, 2009; available online at: http://atlasshrugs2000.typepad.com/atlas_shrugs/2009/08/cnn-tells-sells-more-lies-about-palin-its-time-to-expose-the-truth-about-obama.html [accessed January 3, 2010].

[13] Pamela Geller, "How Could Stanley Ann Dunham have Delivered Barack Hussein Obama Jr. in August of 1961 in Honolulu, when Official University of Washington Records Show Her 2,680 Miles Away in Seattle Attending Classes that Same Month.", Atlas Shrugs, October 24, 2008; available online at: http://atlasshrugs2000.typepad.com/atlas_shrugs/2008/10/how-could-stanl.html [accessed January 3, 2010].

[14] "Obama Lied to Kids", Catholic Femina, September 10, 2009; available online at: http://www.catholicfemina.com/2009/09/obama-lied-to-kids.html [accessed January 4, 2010].

[15] David Maraniss, "Obama in Hawaii: Father was Ambitious, Proud", Honolulu Advertiser, August 29, 2008; available online at: http://www.honoluluadvertiser.com/article/20080829/NEWS05/808290416/Obama-in-Hawai%5C-i--Father-was-ambitious—proud [accessed January 4, 2010].

[16] Nick Pisa, "Barack Obama's 'Lost' Brother Found in Kenya", Telegraph.co.uk, August 20, 2008; available online at: http://www.telegraph.co.uk/news/worldnews/northamerica/usa/barackobama/2590614/Barack-Obamas-lost-brother-found-in-Kenya.html [accessed January 4, 2010].

[17] Barack Obama, *The Audacity of Hope: Thoughts on Reclaiming the American Dream,* (New York: Vintage Books, A Division of Random House, 2006), p. 323.

[18] Julian Dunraven, J.D., M.P.A., "Could Obama be Disqualified from the Election? The Federal Courts will Decide", Slapstick Politics, October 24, 2008; available on line at: http://slapstickpolitics.blogspot.com/2008/10/could-obama-be-disqualified-from.html [accessed January 5, 2010].

[19] "Obama's Childhood Records Vindicate Corsi Book", World Net Daily, August 17, 2008; available online at: http://www.wnd.com/index.php?fa=PAGE.view&pageId=72667 [accessed January 5, 2010].

[20] James Taranto, "From the WSJ Opinion Archives", Wall Street Journal, December 3, 2007; available online at: http://www.opinionjournal.com/best/?id=110010940 [accessed January 5, 2010].

[21] Corsi, *The Obama Nation*, p. 40.

[22] Ibid., p. 48-49.

[23] Obama, *Dreams from My Father,* p.77.

[24] Jerome R. Corsi, "Marxist 'Mentor' Sold Drugs with Obama", World Net Daily, October 30, 2008; available online at: http://www.wnd.com/index.php?fa=PAGE.view&pageId=79467 [accessed January 6, 2010].

[25] Obama, *Dreams from My Father*, p. 97.

[26] Ibid., p. 91.

[27] "Obama's Perverted Communist Friend Frank Marshall Davis", Right Truth, August 26, 2008; available online at: http://righttruth.typepad.com/right_truth/2008/08/obamas-peverted-communist-friend-frank.html [accessed April 27, 2010].

[28] Cliff Kincaid, "Obama's Red Mentor Praised Red Army", Accuracy in Media, April 30, 2008; available online at: http://www.aim.org/aim-report/obamas-red-mentor-praised-red-army/%20%20accessed [accessed January 10, 2010].

[29] Obama, *The Audacity of Hope,* p. 38.

[30] Obama, *Dreams from My Father*, p. 93.

[31] Johnny Brannon, "Hawai'i's Imperfect Melting Pot a Big Influence on Young Obama", Honolulu Advertiser.com, February 10, 2007; available online at: http://the.honoluluadvertiser.com/article/2007/Feb/10/ln/FP702100346.html [accessed January 11, 2010].

[32] Hans Nichols, "Angry Obama the Pothead is not how They Remember Him in Hawaii", Telegraph.co.uk, March 25, 2007; available online: http://www.telegraph.co.uk/news/worldnews/1546645/Angry-Obama-the-pothead-is-not-how-they-remember-him-in-Hawaii.html [accessed January 11, 2010].

[33] Terry K., "Obama Record Found in Concrete", Obama Records, November 4, 2009; available online at: http://obamarecords.com/?p=143 [accessed January 11, 2010].

[34] Don Fredrick, *The Obama Timeline: From His Birth in 1961 through His First 100 Days in Office,* (New York, Bloomington: iUniverse, Inc., 2009), p. 29-30.

[35] Obama, *Dreams from My Father*, p. 98.

[36] Robert Henderson, "Barack in His Own Words (Part I of III)", DiscovertheNetworks.org, March 27, 2009; available online at: http://www.discoverthenetworks.org/Articles/Barack%20Obama%20in%20His%20Own%20Words%20Part%20I.html [accessed April 12, 2010].

[37] Obama, *Dreams from My Father*, p. 105.

[38] Ibid., p. 115.

[39] Ibid., p. 139-140.

[40] Janny Scott, "Obama's Account of New York Years Often Differs from what Others Say", The New York Times, October 30, 2007; available online at: http://www.nytimes.com/2007/10/30/us/politics/30obama.html [accessed January 12, 2010].

[41] Fredrick, *The Obama Timeline*, p. 44.

[42] Obama, *Dreams from My Father*, p. 133.

[43] Corsi, *The Obama Nation*, p. 129.

[44] Obama, *Dreams from My Father*, p. 155.

[45] Serge Kovaleski, "Obama's Organizing Years, Guiding Others and Finding Himself", The New York Times, July 7, 2008; available online at: http://www.nytimes.com/2008/07/07/us/politics/07community.html [accessed May 18, 2010].

[46] Byron York, "What did Obama do as a Community Organizer?", National Review Online, September 8, 2008; available online at: http://article.nationalreview.com/print/?q=OWMxNGUxZWJjYzg1NjA0MTlmZDZmMjUwZGU3ZjAwNmU [accessed January 13, 2010].

[47] Fredrick, *The Obama Timeline*, p. 47.

[48] Obama, *Dreams from My Father*, p. 200-201.

[49] Obama, *The Audacity of Hope*, p. 240-241.

[50] Corsi, *The Obama Nation*, p. 185.

[51] "New Republic: Reverend Wright was a Muslim Turned Christian", Israelinsider.com, April 14, 2008; available online at: http://web.israelinsider.com/Articles/Politics/12784.htm [accessed March 25, 2010].

[52] Obama, *The Audacity of Hope*, p. 246.

[53] Ibid., p. 245.

[54] Obama, *Dreams from My Father*, p. 280-286.

[55] Ibid., p. 283.

[56] "Talking Points", Trinity United Church of Christ, copyright 2008; available online at: http://www.tucc.org/index.php?option=com_content&task=view&id=19 [accessed March 25, 2010].

[57] Lee Cary, "Obama's Mentor's Mentor", American Thinker, February 22, 2008; available online at: http://www.americanthinker.com/2008/02/obamas_mentors_mentor.html [accessed March 25, 2010].

[58] Corsi, *The Obama Nation*, p. 177.

[59] "The Black Value System", Trinity United Church of Christ, copyright 2008; available online at: http://www.trinitychicago.org/index.php?option=com_content&task=view&id=1 14 [accessed March 25, 2010].

[60] John Perazzo, "Why does Obama's Pastor Matter?", FrontPageMag.com, February 4, 2008; available online at: http://97.74.65.51/readArticle.aspx?ARTID=29768 [accessed March 25, 2010].

[61] Stanley Kurtz, "Jeremiah Wright's 'Trumpet'", Ethics and Public Policy Center, May 15, 2008; available online at: http://www.eppc.org/publications/pubid.3394/pub_detail.asp [accessed March 25, 2010].

[62] Brit Hume, "Obama's Pastor says Black People should not Sing 'God Bless America'", FoxNews.com, March 13, 2008; available online at: http://www.foxnews.com/story/0,2933,337748,00.html [accessed March 27, 2010].

[63] Obama, *Dreams from My Father*, p. 293.

[64] Ryan Lizza, "Barack Obama's Unlikely Political Education", DiscovertheNetworks.org, March 9, 2007; available online at: http://www.discoverthenetworks.org/Articles/bobamasunlikelypoliticaledu.html [accessed March 27, 2010].

[65] Steve Gilbert, "Obama's Racist, America-Hating Church", Sweetness &Light, January 25, 2007; available online at: http://sweetness-light.com/archive/barack-obamas-church-ultra-left-and-afrocentric [accessed March 27, 2010].

[66] Kim Chipman, "Obama's Chicago Pastor no Longer Serving on Campaign (Update 3)", Bloomberg.com, March 15, 2008; available online at: http://www.bloomberg.com/apps/news?pid=20601070&sid=aktQHpFJxzsM&ref er=home [accessed March 27, 2010].

[67] "Obama's Minister: U.S. 'No. 1 Killer in the Word'", World Net Daily, March 14, 2008; available online at: http://www.wnd.com/?pageId=58928 [accessed May 18, 2010].

[68] "Obamacide - Obama's Church Reprinted Hamas Manifesto", Creeping Sharia, March 18, 2008; available online at: http://creepingsharia.wordpress.com/2008/03/18/obamacide-obamas-church-reprinted-hamas-manifesto/ [accessed March 27, 2010].

[69] Aaron Klein, "Obama, Farrakhan Share Cover of Wright's Monthly", World Net Daily, May 14, 2008; available online at: http://www.wnd.com/index.php?fa=PAGE.view&pageId=64260 [accessed March 27, 2010].

[70] Kyle-Anne Shiver, "What Would MLK Do?", National Review Online, August 22, 2008; available online at: http://article.nationalreview.com/366908/what-would-mlk-do/kyle-anne-shiver [accessed March 27, 2010].

[71] Alexander LaBrecque, "Obama's Religious Ruse: His 'Conversion'", American Thinker, October 15, 2008; available online at: http://www.americanthinker.com/2008/10/obamas_religious_ruse_his_conv_1.ht ml [accessed March 27, 2010].

[72] Obama, *The Audacity of Hope*, p. 255.

[73] Michelle Malkin, "Obama's 'Big Press Conference' on Wright", Michelle Malkin, April 29, 2008; available online at: http://michellemalkin.com/2008/04/29/obamas-big-press-conference/ [accessed March 27, 2010].

[74] Nedra Pickler, "Obama's Church Enters Spotlight", Black Voices, March 23, 2007; available online at: http://www.blackvoices.com/black_news/headlines_features/canvas_news_articles/_a/obamas-church-enters-spotlight/20070323094009990001 [accessed March 27, 2010].

[75] Jodi Kantor, "Disinvitation by Obama is Criticized", The New York Times, March 6, 2007; available online at: http://www.nytimes.com/2007/03/06/us/politics/06obama.html [accessed March 27, 2010].

[76] "Transcript of Obama's Speech", CNNPolitics.com, March 18, 2008; available online at: http://www.cnn.com/2008/POLITICS/03/18/obama.transcript/ [accessed January 14, 2010].

[77] Byron York, "For Obama, the Danger from Wright isn't over", National Review Online, April 30, 2008; available online at: http://article.nationalreview.com/356045/for-obama-the-danger-from-wright-isnt-over/byron-york [accessed March 27, 2010].

[78] Jason Horowitz, "Obama Divorces Wright", The New York Observer, April 29, 2008; available online at: http://www.observer.com/2008/obama-divorces-wright [accessed March 27, 2010].

[79] David Freddoso, The Case Against Barack Obama: The Unlikely Rise and Unexamined Agenda of the Media's Favorite Candidate, (Washington D.C.: Regnery, 2008), p. 168.

[80] Ibid.

[81] "Rev. Wright Says 'Them Jews' Won't Let Obama Talk to Him", FoxNews.com, June 10, 2009; available online at: http://www.foxnews.com/politics/2009/06/10/rev-wright-says-jews-wont-let-obama-talk/ [accessed March 27, 2010].

[82] Obama, Dreams from My Father, p. 276.

[83] Fredrick, The Obama Timeline, p. 52.

[84] Alex45, "Something about Obama", The Next Right, August 30, 2008; available online at: http://www.thenextright.com/alex45/something-about-obama [accessed April 27, 2010].

[85] Jack Cashill, "Why Obama is Mum about Harvard", www.cashill.com, September 11, 2008; available online at: http://www.cashill.com/natl_general/why_obama_is_mum.htm [accessed January 14, 2010].

[86] Ibid.

[87] Fredrick, The Obama Timeline, p. 60.

[88] Ibid., p. 61.

[89] Pamela Geller, 'Obama's Mythical Intelligence', Atlas Shrugs, May 31, 2008; available online at:

http://atlasshrugs2000.typepad.com/atlas_shrugs/2008/05/obama-mythical.html [accessed January 14, 2010].

[90] Dave Pierre, "LA Times' Glowing Coverage of Obama in Full Throttle", NewsBusters, January 28, 2007; available online at: http://www.newsbusters.org/node/10464 [accessed April 27, 2010].

[91] Corsi, *The Obama Nation*, p. 134.

[92] "Barack Obama Early Life and Career", Egypt.com News, November 15, 2008; available online at: http://news.egypt.com/en/news/us-presidential-election/barak-obama-early-life-and-career.html [accessed January 14, 2010].

[93] Corsi, *The Obama Nation*, p. 135.

[94] "The Kennedy School Saguaro Seminar", Saguaro, copyright 2007; available online at: http://www.hks.harvard.edu/saguaro/participants/obama.htm [accessed May 19, 2010].

[95] "Tony Rezko", Wikipedia, modified December 28, 2009; available online: http://en.wikipedia.org/wiki/Tony_Rezko [accessed January 14, 2010].

[96] Fredrick, *The Obama Timeline*, p. 62.

[97] Ibid., p. 69.

[98] John, "Crossing Paths Daily: Obama and Ayers Shared an Office (Update: For Three Years)", Verum Serum, October 16, 2008; available online at: http://www.verumserum.com/?p=2907 [accessed January 14, 2010].

[99] Corsi, *The Obama Nation*, p. 137.

[100] Ibid.

[101] Freddoso, *The Case Against Barack Obama*, p. 2.

[102] "CNN Report Accusing Obama of 'Getting a Little Dirty' in Challenging Political Opponents Ignored Facts Undermining Allegations", Media Matters, June 2, 2008; available online at: http://mediamatters.org/research/200806020007 [accessed May 19, 2010].

[103] Freddoso, *The Case Against Barack Obama*, p. 3.

[104] David Jackson, "Barack Obama: I Trusted Rezko", Chicago Tribune, March 15, 2008; available online at: http://www.chicagotribune.com/news/politics/obama/chi-obama-rezkomar15-archive,0,1215722.story [accessed January 25, 2010].

[105] Associated Press, "Obama: Rezko Raised up to $250,000 for Him", MSNBC, March 14, 2008; available online at: http://www.msnbc.msn.com/id/23641581 [accessed January 25, 2010].

[106] Tim Novak, "Obama's Letters for Rezko", Chicago Sun-Times, June 13, 2007; available online at: http://www.suntimes.com/news/politics/425305,CST-NWS-obama13.article [accessed January 25, 2010].

[107] David Schaper, "Examining Obama's 'Present' Vote in Illinois", NPR, January 23, 2008; available online at: http://www.npr.org/templates/story/story.php?storyId=18348437 [accessed January 29, 2010].

[108] "Chicago Politics", The Obama File, copyright 2010; available online at: http://www.theobamafile.com/ObamaIllinois.htm [accessed May 19, 2010].

[109] "Illinois State Archives Letter Raises Questions about Obama's Records Claim", Judicial Watch, March 27, 2008; available online at:

http://www.judicialwatch.org/illinois-state-archives-letter-raises-questions-about-obama-s-records-claim [accessed January 29, 2010].

[110] Andrew C. McCarthy, "Acorn's White Horse", National Review Online, October 20, 2008; available online at: http://article.nationalreview.com/375719/acorns-white-horse/andrew-c-mccarthy?page=1 [accessed February 1, 2010].

[111] Deroy Murdock, "Obama Squirrels Away His Links to ACORN", National Review Online, October 16, 2008; available online at: http://article.nationalreview.com/375167/obama-squirrels-away-his-links-to-acorn/deroy-murdock [accessed February 1, 2010].

[112] Christopher Wills, "Obama Learned from Failed Congress Run", USA Today, October 24, 2007; available online at: http://www.usatoday.com/news/politics/2007-10-24-3157940059_x.htm [accessed February 1, 2010].

[113] Obama, *The Audacity of Hope,* p. 128.

[114] Suarez, "Clinton Says She and McCain Offer Experience, Obama Offers Speeches", op. cit.

[115] Obama, *The Audacity of Hope,* p. 23.

[116] Freddoso, *The Case Against Barack Obama,* p. 47-48.

[117] Ibid., p. 48.

[118] Jill Stanek, "Threepeat: LA Times/Chicago Tribune again Help Obama make the Close", Jill Stanek, October 31, 2008; available online at: http://www.jillstanek.com/archives/2008/10/the_hypocrisy_o.html [accessed February 2, 2010].

[119] William Voegeli, "The Rise and Fall of Blair Hull", The Claremont Institute, March 19, 2004; available online at: http://www.claremont.org/publications/pubid.339/pub_detail.asp [accessed February 2, 2010].

[120] Webster Griffin Tarpley, *Obama: The Postmodern Coup*, (Joshua Tree: Progressive Press, 2008), p. 148.

[121] Shrinkermd, "Does Anyone Remember Jack Ryan and Obama's Senate Run Four Years Ago?", Free Republic, August 23, 2008; available online at: http://www.freerepublic.com/focus/news/2066926/posts [accessed May 20, 2010].

[122] Ibid.

[123] Obama, *The Audacity of Hope*, p. 249-250.

[124] Ibid., p. 247.

[125] Mark Murray, "Is Obama the Most Liberal Senator?", MSNBC, January 31, 2008; available online at: http://firstread.msnbc.msn.com/archive/2008/01/31/625886.aspx [accessed February 2, 2010].

[126] "Michelle Obama Strikes Again: Ignorant, Racist, 'That's America'", The Rush Limbaugh Show, March 27, 2008; available online at: http://www.rushlimbaugh.com/home/daily/site_032708/content/01125108.guest.html [accessed February 2, 2010].

[127] Bill O'Reilly, "Does Michelle Obama Dislike America?", FoxNews.com, February 20, 2008; available online at: http://www.foxnews.com/story/0,2933,331428,00.html [accessed February 2, 2010].

[128] Noel Shepard, "Michelle Obama: America is 'Just Downright Mean'", NewsBusters, March 5, 2008; available online at: http://newsbusters.org/blogs/noel-sheppard/2008/03/05/michelle-obama-america-just-downright-mean [accessed February 2, 2010].

[129] Fredrick, *The Obama Timeline*, p. 114.

[130] Freddoso, *The Case Against Barack Obama*, p. 117.

[131] Michelle Malkin, *Culture of Corruption: Obama and His Team of Tax Cheats, Crooks, and Cronies,* (Washington, D.C.: Regnery Publishing, Inc., 2009), p. 69.

[132] Ibid., p. 53.

[133] Jim Geraghty, "One of Obama's Earmark Requests was for the Hospital that Employs Michelle Obama", National Review Online, March 13, 2008; available online at: http://campaignspot.nationalreview.com/post/?q=OGRiMWFhNWY4MTgzMjI3NjEzNGQwMWFiMTlhYmRhN2Y [accessed February 2, 2010].

[134] Fredrick, *The Obama Timeline*, p. 91.

[135] Michelle Malkin, "Sunday Meditation: Obama and the Punishment of Unborn Life", Michelle Malkin, March 30, 2008; available online at: http://michellemalkin.com/2008/03/30/sunday-meditation-obama-and-the-punishment-of-unborn-life [accessed February 4, 2010].

[136] Ed Morrissey, "There are a lot of Things above Obama's 'Pay Grade'", Hot Air, August 17, 2008; available online at: http://hotair.com/archives/2008/08/17/there-are-a-lot-of-things-above-obamas-pay-grade/ [accessed February 4, 2010].

[137] Deacon Keith A. Fournier, "Obama's Promise to Sign Freedom of Choice Act the Subject of New TV Commercial", Catholic Online, October 15, 2008; available online at: http://www.catholic.org/politics/story.php?id=30049 [accessed February 4, 2010].

[138] Freddoso, *The Case Against Barack Obama*, p. 204.

[139] Corsi, *The Obama Nation*, p. 215.

[140] Chris Matthews", DiscovertheNetworks.org, n.d.; available online at: http://www.discoverthenetworks.org/printindividualProfile.asp?indid=1759 [accessed April 12, 2010].

[141] Ibid.

[142] Dana Milbank, "President Obama Continues Hectic Victory Tour", The Washington Post, July 30, 2008; available online: http://www.washingtonpost.com/wp-dyn/content/article/2008/07/29/AR2008072902068.html [accessed March 27, 2010].

[143] Patrick Casey, "Obama on Rejecting Public Finance System: Slicker than Bill Clinton ever Dreamed of Being", The Next Right, June 19, 2008; available online at: http://www.thenextright.com/patrick13/obama-on-rejecting-public-finance-system-slicker-than-bill-clinton-ever-dreamed-of-being [accessed May 21, 2010].

[144] Chelsea Schilling, "Dig this: Media Actually Probed other Candidates", World Net Daily, August 10, 2009; available online at: http://www.wnd.com/?pageId=106051 [accessed May 21, 2010].

[145] "Obama: 'This is Your Victory'", CNNPolitics.com, November 5, 2008; available online at: http://edition.cnn.com/2008/POLITICS/11/04/election.president/index.html [accessed February 6, 2010].

[146] Obama, *Dreams from My Father*, p. 437.

[147] "Ronald Reagan", Wikiquote, modified February 6, 2010; available online at: http://en.wikiquote.org/wiki/Ronald_Reagan [accessed February 6, 2010].

Chapter Three

[1] Saul D. Alinsky, *Rules for Radicals: A Pragmatic Primer for Realistic Radicals*, (New York: Vintage Books, A Division of Random House, 1971), Forward.

[2] "Saul Alinsky", DiscovertheNetworks.org, copyright 2003-2009; available online at: http://www.discoverthenetworks.org/individualProfile.asp?indid=2314 [accessed May 24, 2010].

[3] "Interview with Saul Alinsky, Part 5", The Progress Report, 2003; available online at: http://www.progress.org/2003/alinsky6.htm [accessed February 15, 2010].

[4] David Horowitz and Richard Poe, *The Shadow Party: How George Soros, Hillary Clinton, and Sixties Radicals Seized Control of the Democratic Party*, (Nashville: Thomas Nelson, Inc., 2006), p. 58.

[5] Matthew Vadum, "Left-Wing Radicalism in the Church: CCHD and ACORN", Human Events, October 26, 2009; available online at: http://www.humanevents.com/article.php?id=34070 [accessed February 15, 2010].

[6] Horowitz and Poe, *The Shadow Party*, p. 58-59.

[7] Kovaleski, "Obama's Organizing Years, Guiding Others and Finding Himself", op. cit.

[8] Ibid.

[9] Alinsky, *Rules for Radicals*, p. 3.

[10] "Interview with Saul Alinsky, Part Ten", The Progress Report, 2003; available online at: http://www.progress.org/2003/alinsky11.htm [accessed February 15, 2010].

[11] "Everyone's Favorite Radical", On the Media from NPR, August 7, 2009; available online at: http://www.onthemedia.org/transcripts/2009/08/07/01 [accessed February 15, 2010].

[12] David Horowitz, *Barack Obama's Rules for Revolution: The Alinsky Model*, (Sherman Oaks: David Oaks Freedom Center, 2009), p. 9-10.

[13] Obama, *Dreams from My Father*, p. 155.

[14] Mred, "Obama to Republicans: 'You Lost' Obama to GOP 'I Won'", Invincible Armor, January 23, 2009; available online at:

http://invinciblearmor.blogspot.com/2009/01/obama-to-republicans-you-lost.html [accessed May 21, 2010].

[15] Diane Alden, "Saul Alinsky in South Dakota", Newsmax.com, January 7, 2003; available online at: http://archive.newsmax.com/archives/articles/2003/1/7/21053.shtml [accessed February 16, 2010].

[16] David Horowitz, "To Have and Have Not: Alinsky, Beck, Satan, and Me, Part IV", FrontPageMag.com, August 19, 2009; available online at: http://97.74.65.51/readBlog.aspx?BLOGID=1051 [accessed May 21, 2010].

[17] Edward Sisson, "My 'Best Education'", World, October 10, 2008; available online at: http://www.worldmag.com/webextra/14535 [accessed February 16, 2010].

[18] Alinsky, *Rules for Radicals*, p.113.

[19] Ibid., p. 194-195.

[20] Ryan Lizza, "The Agitator", The New Republic, March 19, 2007; available online at: http://www.tnr.com/article/the-agitator [accessed February 16, 2010].

[21] Ibid.

[22] Alinsky, *Rules for Radicals*, p. 61.

[23] Corsi, *The Obama Nation*, p. 130-131.

[24] Ibid., p. 131.

[25] Ibid.

[26] "Interview with Saul Alinsky, Part 8", The Progress Report, 2003; available online at: http://www.progress.org/2003/alinsky9.htm [accessed February 15, 2010].

[27] Ibid.

[28] UrbanAdder22, "Saul Alinsky, the 'Community Organizer' Who Taught Obama that the 'Power for Change' is with the Middle Class", Islamic Danger to Americans, September 30, 2008; available online at: http://islamicdanger4u.blogspot.com/2008/09/saul-alinsky-community-organizer-who.html [accessed April 12, 2010].

[29] "Quotes and Excerpts from Rules for Radicals", Kjos Ministries, n.d.; available online at: http://www.crossroad.to/Quotes/communism/alinsky.htm [accessed February 17, 2010].

[30] James Lewis, "Obama, Alinsky, and Scapegoats", American Thinker, April 24, 2009; available online at: http://www.americanthinker.com/2009/04/obama_alinsky_and_scapegoats.html [accessed February 18, 2010].

[31] Chelsea Schilling, "NEA Raves to Teachers about Alinsky 'Guidebook'", World Net Daily, November 3, 2009; available online at: http://www.wnd.com/index.php?pageId=114881 [accessed February 18, 2010].

[32] "Interview with Saul Alinsky, Part Two", The Progress Report, op. cit.

[33] Alinsky, *Rules for Radicals*, p. 184.

[34] Ibid., p. 185.

[35] Ibid., p. 189.

[36] "Interview with Saul Alinsky, Part Two", The Progress Report, op. cit.

[37] Ibid.

[38] Alinsky, *Rules for Radicals*, p. 188-190.

[39] Laura Ingle, "Are People Bitter in Pennsylvania?", FoxNews.com, April 12, 2008; available online at: http://onthescene.blogs.foxnews.com/tag/allentown/ [accessed February 21, 2010].

[40] Alinsky, *Rules for Radicals*, p. 127.

[41] Ibid.

[42] Ibid., p. 128.

[43] Ibid., p. 130.

[44] Ibid., p. 128.

[45] Ibid., p. 152.

[46] Ibid., p. 150.

[47] Ibid., p. 24.

[48] "Interview with Saul Alinsky, Part Ten", The Progress Report, op. cit.

[49] Alinsky, *Rules for Radicals*, p. 10-11.

[50] Ibid., p. 25.

[51] Ibid., p. 26.

[52] Mark Silva, "Michelle Obama: World 'As is…won't do'", The Swamp, August 25, 2008; available online at: http://www.swamppolitics.com/news/politics/blog/2008/08/michelle_obama_wor ld_as_is_jus.html [accessed May 31, 2010].

[53] "Interview with Saul Alinsky, Part Four", The Progress Report, 2003; available online at: http://www.progress.org/2003/alinsky5.htm [accessed February 22, 2010].

[54] "Interview with Saul Alinsky, Part Seven", The Progress Report, 2003; available online at: http://www.progress.org/2003/alinsky8.htm [accessed February 22, 2010].

[55] Alinsky, *Rules for Radicals*, p. 29.

[56] Ibid., p. 12-13.

[57] Ibid., p. 129-130.

[58] "Interview with Saul Alinsky, Part Seven", The Progress Report, op. cit.

[59] Alinsky, *Rules for Radicals*, p. xxi.

[60] Ibid., p. 44.

[61] Ibid., p. 25.

[62] Schilling, "NEA Raves to Teachers about Alinsky 'Guidebook'", op. cit.

[63] Robert Owens, "A Fine Tribute", American Chronicle, June 29, 2009; available online at: http://www.americanchronicle.com/articles/view/107994 [accessed February 22, 2010].

[64] "Interview with Saul Alinsky, Part Ten", The Progress Report, op. cit.

[65] Horowitz and Poe, *The Shadow Party*, p. 56.

[66] "Hillary Clinton's Wellesley College Thesis – The Rosetta Stone", The Cassandra Page, June 26, 2005; available online at: http://cassandra2004.blogspot.com/2005/06/hillary-clintons-wellesley-college.html [accessed February 22, 2010].

[67] Horowitz and Poe, *The Shadow Party*, p. 56.

[68] Andrew Walden, "Hillary's Choice: Political Power and Alinsky", The American Thinker, January 17, 2008; available online at:

http://www.americanthinker.com/2008/01/hillarys_choice_political_powe.html
[accessed February 22, 2010].

[69] Andrew Walden, "There is only the Fight", FrontPageMag.com, August 21, 2007; available online at: http://97.74.65.51/readArticle.aspx?ARTID=27822 [accessed May 21, 2010].

[70] Richard Poe, "Hillary, Obama and the Cult of Alinsky", Rense.com, January 13, 2008; available online at: http://www.rense.com/general80/fon.htm [accessed May 21, 2010].

[71] Horowitz, *Barack Obama's Rules for Revolution*, p. 11-12.

[72] Horowitz and Poe, *The Shadow Party*, p. 59-60.

[73] Ibid., p. 60.

[74] George J. Marlin, "ACORN's Problems – and the Church", The Catholic Thing, September 23, 2009; available online at: http://www.thecatholicthing.org/content/view/2231/26/ [accessed March 28, 2010].

[75] Ibid.

[76] Ibid.

[77] Ibid.

[78] "Stunk vs. US Department of Commerce Bureau of Census et al. DCD 09-cv-1295 w Exhibits 091609", p. 16, Scribd., September 16, 2009; available online at: http://www.scribd.com/doc/21924600/Strunk-Response-to-MPSJ-MTD-09-Cv-1295-w-Exhibits-091609 [accessed February 23, 2010].

[79] Marlin, "ACORN's Problems – and the Church", op. cit.

[80] Alinsky, *Rules for Radicals*, p.13.

[81] "Essay: Radical Saul Alinsky: Prophet of Power to the People", Time Magazine, March 2, 1970; available online at: http://www.time.com/time/magazine/article/0,9171,904228-1,00.html [accessed February 24, 2010].

[82] Robert Ringer, "Saul, Barack and Me, Part 2", World Net Daily, December 18, 2009; available online at: http://www.wnd.com/index.php?fa=PAGE.view&pageId=119310 [accessed April 28, 2010].

[83] "Interview with Saul Alinsky", The Progress Report, 2003; available online at: http://www.progress.org/2003/alinsky2.htm [accessed May 22, 2010].

[84] Horowitz, *Barack Obama's Rules for Revolution*, p. 12.

[85] "Saul Alinsky", DiscovertheNetworks.org, op. cit.

[86] "Barack Obama and the Gamaliel Foundation", RomanticPoet's Weblog, October 12, 2009; available online at: http://romanticpoet.wordpress.com/2009/10/12/barack-obama-and-the-gamaliel-foundation-community-action-utilizing-faith-and-saul-alinsky-training/ [accessed May 22, 2010].

[87] Vadum, "Left-Wing Radicalism in the Church: CCHD and ACORN", op. cit.

[88] Katherine Thomas, "Stealth Marxism through Gamaliel Foundation. Obama 'Proudly' Connected. It is Time to Enforce Separation of Church and State!", The RomanticPoet's Weblog, November 23, 2009; available online at: http://romanticpoet.wordpress.com/2009/11/23/stealth-marxism-through-

gamaliel-foundation-obama-proudly-connected-it-is-time-to-enforce-separation-of-church-and-state/ [accessed March 7, 2010].

[89] Fredrick, *The Obama Timeline*, p. 48.

[90] David Moberg, "Obama's Third Way", NHI, Spring 2007; available online at: http://www.nhi.org/online/issues/149/obama.html [accessed March 7, 2010].

[91] Pamela Geller, "Obama and Gamaliel's Freak Show: Faith Hijacking Strategy", Atlas Shrugs, August 20, 2009; available online at: http://atlasshrugs2000.typepad.com/atlas_shrugs/2009/08/obama-and-gamaliels-freak-show-faith-hijacking-strategy.html [accessed March 28, 2010].

[92] Corsi, *The Obama Nation*, p. 133.

[93] Horowitz, *Barack Obama's Rules for Revolution*, p. 12-13.

[94] "Why Organize?", Illinois Issues, September 2008; available online at: http://illinoisissues.uis.edu/archives/2008/09/whyorg.html [accessed March 8, 2010].

[95] Jerry Kane, "Cry Wolf: A Clarion Call to Separation of Church and State", American Daughter, October 1, 2009; available online at: http://frontpage.americandaughter.com/?tag=reverend-jeremiah-wright [accessed March 28, 2010].

[96] "Why Organize?", Illinois Issues, op. cit.

[97] Biochemky, "Is Barack Hussein Obama II a Marxist Maoist, Leninist, Stalinist, or Just a Run of the Mill Communist? (He's not a Capitalist!)", Townhall.com, February 19, 2010; available online at: http://obamashiddenagenda.blogtownhall.com/2010/02/19/is_barack_hussein_obama_ii_a_marxist_maoist,_leninist,_stalinist,_or_just_a_run_of_the_mill_communist_he%E2%80%99s_not_a_capitalist!.thtml [accessed March 8, 2010].

[98] Fredrick, *The Obama Timeline*, p. 61.

[99] "Guess Who Recommended Obama to Enter Harvard", World Net Daily, September 24, 2008; available online at: http://www.wnd.com/index.php?fa=PAGE.view&pageId=76170 [accessed March 8, 2010].

[100] Ibid.

[101] Ibid.

[102] Alinsky, *Rules for Radicals*, p. 128.

[103] Stanley Kurtz, "Senator Stealth", National Review Online, November 1, 2008; available online at: http://article.nationalreview.com/377241/senator-stealth/stanley-kurtz [accessed May 22, 2010].

[104] Marc Ambinder, "The Rise of the Alinsky Explanation", The Atlantic, August 12, 2009; available online at: http://www.theatlantic.com/politics/archive/2009/08/the-rise-of-the-alinsky-explanantion/23168/ [accessed March 8, 2010].

[105] Bud Meyers, "Obama's Early Years in New York Finally Revealed?", Buds Blog, September 22, 2009; available online at: http://tobuds.com/blogs/blog6.php/2009/09/22/obama-ayers-and-dohrn-the-early-years-in [accessed May 22, 2010].

[106] Fredrick, *The Obama Timeline*, p. 69.

[107] Freddoso, *The Case Against Barack Obama*, p. 148-149.

[108] "Woods Fund of Chicago", DiscovertheNetworks.org, copyright 2003-2009; available online at: http://www.discoverthenetworks.org/funderprofile.asp?fndid=5340&category=79 [accessed March 8, 2010].

[109] "Obama's Radical Roots and Rules", Investors.com, August 14, 2008; available online at: http://www.investors.com/NewsAndAnalysis/Article.aspx?id=495281 [accessed March 8, 2010].

[110] Judi McLeod, "Saul Alinsky's Son: 'Obama Learned His Lesson Well'", Canada Free Press, September 2, 2008; available online at: http://www.canadafreepress.com/index.php/article/4784 [accessed March 8, 2010].

Chapter Four

[1] The King is Coming, "How did Jefferson Know????", Daily Paul, July 7, 2009; available online at: http://www.dailypaul.com/node/98692 [accessed March 10, 2010].

[2] Jon Meacham and Evan Thomas, "We are All Socialists now", Newsweek, February 16, 2009; available online at: http://www.newsweek.com/id/183663 [accessed March 10, 2010].

[3] Jodie T. Allen and Richard Auxier, "Socialism, American-Style", Pew Research Center Publications, March 12, 2009; available online at: http://pewresearch.org/pubs/1149/america-socialism-free-market-tension [accessed April 13, 2010].

[4] "Karl Marx Quotes", Brainy Quote, copyright 2010; available online at: http://www.brainyquote.com/quotes/quotes/k/karlmarx136396.html [accessed April 28, 2010].

[5] Nathan Richter, "FDR-Obama's Illustrious Predecessor?", The Globalist, November 5, 2008; available online at: http://www.theglobalist.com/StoryId.aspx?StoryId=6872 [accessed March 10, 2010].

[6] "Socialism in America", United States History, copyright 2001-2010; available online at: http://www.u-s-history.com/pages/h1669.html [accessed March 10, 2010].

[7] "League for Industrial Democracy", Wikipedia, modified March 6, 2010; available online at: http://en.wikipedia.org/wiki/League_for_Industrial_Democracy [accessed March 10, 2010].

[8] "Obama's Hidden Agenda and Covert Cadre of Marxists, Communists, Progressives, Radicals, Socialists", Pronk Palisades, August 25, 2009: available online at: http://raymondpronk.wordpress.com/2009/08/25/obamas-hidden-agenda-and-cadre-of-marxists-communists-progressives-radicals-socialists-destroying-capitalism-and-the-american-republic/ [accessed May 24, 2010].

[9] "Students for a Democratic Society (SDS, founded 1959)", DiscovertheNetworks.org, copyright 2003-2009; available online at: http://www.discoverthenetworks.org/groupProfile.asp?grpid=6723 [accessed March 10, 2010].

[10] Ibid.

[11] David Horowitz, *Unholy Alliance: Radical Islam and the American Left*, (Washington D.C.: Regnery Publishing, 2004), p. 57.

[12] James Pethokoukis, "Did Barack 'Spread the Wealth' Obama Just Blow the Election?", U.S. News and World Report, October 16, 2008; available online at: http://www.usnews.com/money/blogs/capital-commerce/2008/10/16/did-barack-spread-the-wealth-obama-just-blow-the-election.html [accessed March 10, 2010].

[13] Ben Smith & Jeffrey Ressner, "Long-Lost Article by Obama's Dad Surfaces", Politico, April 15, 2008; available online at: http://www.politico.com/news/stories/0408/9610.html [accessed March 10, 2010].

[14] Corsi, *The Obama Nation*, p. 111.

[15] "Like Father, Like Son", Investors.com, August 19, 2008; available online at: http://www.investors.com/NewsAndAnalysis/Article.aspx?id=454957 [accessed March 10, 2010].

[16] Corsi, *The Obama Nation*, p. 111-112.

[17] Fredrick, *The Obama Timeline*, p. 6.

[18] Andrew Walden, "What Barack Obama Learned from the Communist Party", American Thinker, July 8, 2008; available online at: http://www.americanthinker.com/2008/07/what_barack_obama_learned_from.html [accessed March 11, 2010].

[19] Larry Liddell, "What do We Really Know about Obama?", The Obama Report, May 26, 2008; available online at: http://obamareport.blogspot.com/2008/05/what-do-we-really-know-about-obama.html [accessed March 11, 2010].

[20] Walden, "What Barack Obama Learned from the Communist Party", op. cit.

[21] Tim Jones, "Barack Obama: Mother not Just a Girl from Kansas", Chicago Tribune, March 27, 2007; available online at: http://www.chicagotribune.com/news/politics/obama/chi-0703270151mar27-archive,0,2623808.story [accessed March 11, 2010].

[22] Andrew Walden, "The Unitarian Church and Obama's Religious Upbringing", American Thinker, December 27, 2008; available online at: http://www.americanthinker.com/2008/12/obama_from_unitarian_to_libera_1.html [accessed March 11, 2010].

[23] "Frank Marshall Davis", Conservapedia, modified January 24, 2010; available online at: http://www.conservapedia.com/Frank_Marshall_Davis [accessed March 11, 2010].

[24] Kincaid, "Obama's Red Mentor Praised Red Army", op. cit.

[25] "Frank Marshall Davis", Wikipedia, modified March 9, 2010; available online at: http://en.wikipedia.org/wiki/Frank_Marshall_Davis [accessed March 11, 2010].

[26] Paul Kengor, "Dreams from Frank Marshall Davis", American Thinker, October 30, 2008; available online at: http://www.americanthinker.com/2008/10/dreams_from_frank_marshall_dav.htm l [accessed March 11, 2010].

[27] Walden, "What Barack Obama Learned from the Communist Party", op. cit.

[28] "Frank Marshall Davis", DiscovertheNetworks.org, copyright 2003-2009; available online at: http://www.discoverthenetworks.org/individualProfile.asp?indid=2323 [accessed March 11, 2010].

[29] Trevor Loudon, "Obama File 37 Obama's Mentor, Frank Marshall Davis – was He Still a Communist?", New Zeal, October 16, 2008; available online at: http://newzeal.blogspot.com/2008/10/obama-file-37-overlap-obamas-mentor.html [accessed March 11, 2010].

[30] "Frank Marshall Davis", DiscovertheNetworks.org, op. cit.

[31] Obama, *Audacity of Hope*, p. 38.

[32] Perry Hicks, "The Long March: Obama's Victories has come as Surprise to Even the Most Ardent Political Observers. However, He didn't Just Happen. He was made over a Span of 44 Years", Part 2, GulfCoastNews.com, May 3, 2009; available online at: http://www.gulfcoastnews.com/GCNanalysisLongMarchPart2050309.htm [accessed May 22, 2010].

[33] Scott Baker and Liz Stephans, "B-Cast Interviews Dr. John C. Drew on Obama's Early Marxist Years", Conservative Blog Watch, February 13, 2010; available online at: http://www.conservativeblogwatch.com/2010/02/13/b-cast-interviews-dr-john-c-drew-on-obamas-early-marxist-years/ [accessed March 29, 2010].

[34] Trevor Loudon, "America's First Red President?", Encyclopedia Britannica, January 2009; available online at: http://www.britannica.com/bps/additionalcontent/18/36156697/Americas-FIRST-RED-President [accessed March 12, 2010].

[35] "History that must be Told, Part 16", Newswatch Magazine, October 2008; available online at: http://www.newswatchmagazine.org/oct08/index2.shtml [accessed May 22, 2010].

[36] Obama, *Dreams from My Father,* p. 123.

[37] James H. Cone, *A Black Theology of Liberation*, (New York: Orbis Books, 1990), p. 8.

[38] "Typical Race Hustling", Red Planet Cartoons, March 24, 2008; available online at: http://www.redplanetcartoons.com/index.php/2008/03/ [accessed March 15, 2010].

[39] "Jeremiah A. Wright, Jr.", DiscovertheNetworks.org, n.d.; available online at: http://www.discoverthenetworks.org/printindividualProfile.asp?indid=2307 [accessed March 29, 2010].

[40] Stanley Kurtz, "Audacity vs. Capitalism", National Review Online, April 21, 2008; available online at: http://corner.nationalreview.com/post/?q=NjFhMGZjOWE3YzYyYmM0ZmU3 MDdkZmU5MDQ0MDQzYjI [accessed March 29, 2010].

[41] Robert W. McChesney, "Journalism, Democracy,... and Class Struggle", Volume 52, Number 6, Monthly Review, copyright 2000; available online at: http://www.monthlyreview.org/1100rwm.htm [accessed March 29, 2010].

[42] "The Chicago Network: Wright, in Recent Speech, Hailed 'No-Nonsense' Marxism", WorldTribune.com, November 2, 2009; available online at: http://www.worldtribune.com/worldtribune/WTARC/2009/ss_politics0855_11_0 2.asp [accessed March 29, 2010].

[43] Andrew C. McCarthy, "Why won't Obama Talk about Columbia?", National Review Online, October 7, 2008; available online at: http://article.nationalreview.com/374119/why-wont-obama-talk-about-columbia/andrew-c-mccarthy [accessed March 15, 2010].

[44] Fredrick, *The Obama Timeline*, p. 63.

[45] Corsi, *The Obama Nation*, p. 137.

[46] Ibid.

[47] Fredrick, *The Obama Timeline*, p. 73.

[48] Cliff Kincaid, "Communism in Chicago and the Obama Connection", p. 2-3, DiscovertheNetworks.org, n.d.; available online at: http://www.discoverthenetworks.org/Articles/chicago-obama%5B1%5D.pdf [accessed March 15, 2010].

[49] "Alice Palmer", DiscovertheNetworks.org, copyright 2003-2009; available online at: http://www.discoverthenetworks.org/individualProfile.asp?indid=2325 [accessed March 15, 2010].

[50] P.J. Gladnick, "Will MSM Report on Obama Membership in Socialist New Party?", NewsBusters, October 8, 2008; available online at: http://newsbusters.org/blogs/p-j-gladnick/2008/10/08/will-msm-report-obama-membership-socialist-new-party [accessed March 15, 2010].

[51] Judi McLeod, "The United Socialist States of America: A Messiah Manufactured by Marxism", Canada Free Press, October 16, 2008; available online at: http://www.canadafreepress.com/index.php/article/5600 [accessed March 15, 2010].

[52] Fredrick, *The Obama Timeline*, p. 72.

[53] McLeod, "The United Socialist States of America: A Messiah Manufactured by Marxism", op. cit.

[54] Fredrick, *The Obama Timeline*, p. 72.

[55] Erick Erickson, "Obama and the New Party", Human Events, June 10, 2008; available online at: http://www.humanevents.com/article.php?id=26913 [accessed March 15, 2010].

[56] Ibid.

[57] Jim Simpson, "The Cloward-Piven Strategy, Part III: Conspiracy of the Lemmings", American Daughter, October 27, 2008; available online at: http://frontpage.americandaughter.com/?p=2114 [accessed March 15, 2010].

[58] Ibid.

[59] Dee Gerrish, "Barack Obama's Connections to Socialism, Communism and Racial Divisiveness", Obama Watch Blog, December 18, 2009; available online at: http://www.obamawatchblog.com/2009/12/barack-obamas-connections-to-socialism-communism-and-racial-divisiveness/ [accessed May 23, 2010].

[60] Ibid.

[61] Ibid.

[62] Aaron Klein, "Another Weatherman Terrorist a Player in the Obama Campaign", World Net Daily, September 26, 2008; available online at: http://www.wnd.com/index.php?fa=PAGE.view&pageId=76234 [accessed June 4, 2010].

[63] "Tom Hayden", DiscovertheNetworks.org, copyright 2003-2009; available online at: http://www.discoverthenetworks.org/individualProfile.asp?indid=1334 [accessed March 15, 2010].

[64] Klein, "Another Weatherman Terrorist a Player in the Obama Campaign", op. cit.

[65] Ibid.

[66] "Old American Red Groups", The Red Encyclopedia, modified July 11, 2002; available online at: http://reds.linefeed.org/past.html [accessed March 15, 2010].

[67] "Communist Party (Marxist-Leninist) (USA)", Wikipedia, modified March 15, 2010; available online at: http://en.wikipedia.org/wiki/Communist_Party_(Marxist%E2%80%93Leninist)_(USA) [accessed March 15, 2010].

[68] Andrew McCarthy, "Another Communist in Obama's Orb", National Review Online, October 22, 2008; available online at: http://article.nationalreview.com/376079/another-communist-in-obamas-orb/andrew-c-mccarthy?page=1 [accessed March 31, 2010].

[69] Fredrick, The Obama Timeline, p. 163.

[70] Susan Freis Falknor, "Is Barack Obama a 'Red Diaper Baby'?", Blue Ridge Forum, October 8, 2008; available online: http://blueridgeforum.com/?p=196 [accessed March 15, 2010].

[71] "Who is David Axelrod – Obama's Political Advisor", The Traditional Values Coalition, March 5, 2008; available online at: http://www.traditionalvalues.org/read/3275/who-is-david-axelrod--obamas-political-advisor/ [accessed March 15, 2010].

[72] Ibid.

[73] "The Organization", Democratic Socialists of America, n.d.; available online at: http://www.dsausa.org/about/index.html [accessed March 15, 2010].

[74] Ibid.

[75] Democrats Socialists of America, n.d.; available online at: http://www.dsausa.org/dsa.html [accessed March 15, 2010].

[76] Aaron Klein, "Newspaper Shows Obama Belonged to Socialist Party", World Net Daily, October 24, 2008; available online at: http://www.wnd.com/index.php?fa=PAGE.view&pageId=78945 [accessed March 15, 2010].

[77] Steve Gilbert, "Democratic Socialists of US Back Obama", Sweetness and Light, October 9, 2008; available online at: http://sweetness-light.com/archive/democratic-socialists-of-us-endorse-obama [accessed March 15, 2010].

[78] "Where We Stand", Democratic Socialists of America, n.d.; available online at: http://www.dsausa.org/about/where.html [accessed March 15, 2010].

[79] "Democratic Socialists of America (DSA)", DiscovertheNetworks.org, copyright 2003-2009; available online at: http://www.discoverthenetworks.org/groupProfile.asp?grpid=6428 [accessed March 15, 2010].

[80] Jim Simpson, "Conspiracy of the Lemmings: Barack Obama and the Conspiracy of the Manufactured Crisis; Part II", Stop the ACLU, October 31, 2008; available online at: http://www.stoptheaclu.com/2008/10/31/conspiracy-of-the-lemmings-barack-obama-and-the-strategy-of-manufactured-crisis-part-ii/ [accessed March 15, 2010].

[81] El Marco, "America's Tea Party Movement", Looking at the Left, February 2010; available online at: http://www.lookingattheleft.com/2010/02/americas-teaparty-movement/ [accessed March 15, 2010].

[82] "Is Barack Obama a Marxist Mole?", USA Survival News, n.d.; available online at: http://www.usasurvival.org/ck2.22.08.html [accessed April 28, 2010].

[83] Simpson, "The Cloward-Piven Strategy, Part III: Conspiracy of the Lemmings", op. cit.

[84] "Cornel West", DiscovertheNetworks.org, copyright 2003-2009; available online at: http://www.discoverthenetworks.org/individualProfile.asp?indid=813 [accessed March 16, 2010].

[85] Ibid.

[86] "The Candidates Allies, Associates, and Influences", Global News Daily, copyright 2008-2010; available online at: http://www.globalnewsdaily.com/ [accessed March 16, 2010].

[87] Ibid.

[88] Ibid.

[89] "Raw Data: Transcript of Obama's Notre Dame Address", FoxNews.com, May 17, 2009; available online at: http://www.foxnews.com/politics/2009/05/17/raw-data-transcript-obamas-notre-dame-address/ [accessed March 16, 2010].

[90] Mark Steyn, "Live Free or Die", Imprimis, April 2009; available online at: http://www.hillsdale.edu/news/imprimis/archive/issue.asp?year=2009&month=04 [accessed March 16, 2010].

[91] Barack Obama, "Barack Obama: My Spiritual Journey", Time, October 16, 2006; available online at: http://www.time.com/time/magazine/article/0,9171,1546579,00.html [accessed April 1, 2010].

[92] "Vladimir Lenin Quotes", Brainy Quotes, copyright 2010; available online at: http://www.brainyquote.com/quotes/quotes/v/vladimirle125951.html [accessed March 16, 2010].

[93] Perry Hicks, "The Long March: It has been a 106 Year Struggle to Socialize America. If Action isn't Taken Now, that Dream may soon be a Reality", GulfCoastNews.com, April 1, 2009; available online at: http://www.gulfcoastnews.com/GCNanalysisLongMarch040109.htm [accessed April 28, 2010].

[94] David Horowitz, *Unholy Alliance*, p. 55.

[95] Sam Webb, "Off and Running: Opportunity of a Lifetime", PoliticalAffairs.net, speech delivered at People's Weekly World Event in Cleveland Ohio January 31,

2009; available online at: http://www.politicalaffairs.net/article/articleview/8085/ [accessed March 16, 2010].
[96] Fredreka Schouten, "Clinton Fundraisers Ready to Aid Obama, Party", USA Today, June 13, 2008; available online at: http://www.usatoday.com/news/politics/election2008/2008-06-12-fundraisers_N.htm [accessed March 16, 2010].
[97] "Questions over Obama's Off-the-Cuff Remark", FoxNews.com, October 15, 2008; available online at: http://www.foxnews.com/story/0,2933,438302,00.html [accessed June 9, 2010].

Chapter Five

[1] "Obama Has Never Been a Muslim, and is a Committed Christian", Organizing for America, November 12, 2007; available online at: http://www.barackobama.com/factcheck/2007/11/12/obama_has_never_been_a_muslim_1.php [accessed March 16, 2010].
[2] Geller, "How could Stanley Ann Dunham have Delivered Barack Hussein Obama Jr. in August of 1961 in Honolulu, when Official University of Washington Records Show Her 2680 Miles Away in Seattle Attending Classes that Same Month?", op. cit.
[3] "Black Nationalist", Answers.com, copyright 2010; available online at: http://www.answers.com/topic/black-nationalism [accessed April 28, 2010].
[4] Ibid.
[5] Ibid.
[6] Ibid.
[7] Fredrick, The Obama Timeline, p. 29.
[8] Ibid.
[9] "Malcolm X", Answers.com, copyright 2010; available online at: http://www.answers.com/topic/malcolm-x [accessed April 28, 2010].
[10] "Malcolm X - The Real Reason why He Exit the Nation of Islam - He knew that they gonna Kill Him", Encyclopedia.com, copyright 2010; available online at: http://www.encyclopedia.com/video/IcFUqObRDkc-malcolm-x-real-reason-why.aspx [accessed March 16, 2010].
[11] Eric Pement, "Louis Farrakhan and the Nation of Islam, Part I", Cornerstonemag.com, copyright 1999; available online at: http://www.cornerstonemag.com/features/iss111/islam1.htm [accessed March 16, 2010].
[12] "Black Panther", Answers.com, copyright 2010; available online at: http://www.answers.com/topic/black-panther [accessed April 28, 2010].
[13] Ibid.
[14] David Horowitz, Unholy Alliance, p. 134.
[15] Ibid.
[16] Ibid.
[17] Ibid., p134-135.
[18] Ibid., p. 136.

[19] "6 Days War: Crucial Quotes", SixDayWar.co.uk, copyright 2007; available online at: http://www.sixdaywar.co.uk/crucial_quotes.htm [accessed March 16, 2010].

[20] Horowitz, *Unholy Alliance*, p. 135.

[21] Robert, "On Tariq Ramadan and the Muslim Brotherhood", Jihad Watch, November 17, 2008; available online at: http://www.jihadwatch.org/2008/11/on-tariq-ramadan-and-the-muslim-brotherhood.html [accessed April 28, 2010].

[22] David Horowitz, *Unholy Alliance*, p. 123.

[23] Ibid., p. 124.

[24] Ibid., p. 126.

[25] Ibid., p. 125-126.

[26] "Radical Islam's Alliance with the Socialist Left", DiscovertheNetworks.org, copyright 2003-2009; available online at: http://www.discoverthenetworks.org/viewSubCategory.asp?id=291 [accessed March 17, 2010].

[27] David Horowitz, *Unholy Alliance*, p. 126-127.

[28] Ibid., p. 125.

[29] Ibid., p. 139-140.

[30] Ibid., p. 140.

[31] Ibid., p. 143.

[32] Bernard Lewis, "A War of Resolve", Wall Street Journal, April 26, 2002; available online at: http://www.opinionjournal.com/editorial/feature.html?id=105001985 [accessed March 17, 2010].

[33] "The Muslim Students Association and the Jihad Network", FrontPageMag.com, May 8, 2008; available online at: http://97.74.65.51/readArticle.aspx?ARTID=30339 [accessed April 28, 2010].

[34] Osama bin Laden, "Declaration of Jihad against the Americans Occupying the Land of the Two Holiest Sites", Wikisource, modified August 14, 2008; http://en.wikisource.org/wiki/Osama_bin_Laden's_Declaration_of_War [accessed March 31, 2010].

[35] "Osama bin Laden's Jihad", Mid East Web, n.d.; available online at: http://www.mideastweb.org/osamabinladen1.htm [accessed May 31, 2010].

[36] David Horowitz, *Unholy Alliance*, p. 141.

[37] Ibid.

[38] Ibid., p. 144-145.

[39] Debbie Schlussel, "Barack Hussein Obama: Once a Muslim, Always a Muslim", Debbie Schlussel, December 18, 2006; available online at: http://www.debbieschlussel.com/2750/barack-hussein-obama-once-a-muslim-always-a-muslim/ [accessed March 17, 2010].

[40] Fredrick, *The Obama Timeline*, p. 3-4.

[41] "Is Barack Obama a Muslim Wolf in Christian Wool?", Israel Insider, March 27, 2008; available online at: http://web.israelinsider.com/Articles/Politics/12745.htm [accessed March 18, 2010].

[42] Thomas Lifson, "The 'Obama is a Muslim' Smear Continues", American Thinker, September 8, 2008; available online at: http://www.americanthinker.com/blog/2008/09/the_obama_is_a_muslim_smear_co.html [accessed March 17, 2010].

[43] Naseem Jamali, "Obama's 'Muslim Identity': An Asset for Iraq Exit Strategy", alJazeera.com, April 7, 2008; available online at: http://aljazeera.com/news/newsfull.php?newid=136482 [accessed March 17, 2010].

[44] Corsi, *The Obama Nation*, p. 22.

[45] Gellar, "How Could Stanley Ann Dunham have Delivered Barack Hussein Obama Jr. in August of 1961 in Honolulu, when Official University of Washington Records Show Her 2680 Miles Away in Seattle Attending Classes that Same Month?", op. cit.

[46] Ibid.

[47] "AP Photo of School Register Reveals 'Barry Soetoro' as Muslim Indonesian", Israel Insider, August 14, 2008; available online at: http://web.israelinsider.com/Articles/Politics/13056.htm [accessed March 17, 2010].

[48] Aaron Klein, "Obama was 'Quite Religious in Islam'", World Net Daily, April 3, 2008; available online at: http://www.wnd.com/index.php?pageId=60559 [accessed March 17, 2010].

[49] "AP Photo of School Register Reveals 'Barry Soetoro' as Muslim Indonesian", Israel Insider, op. cit.

[50] Jodi Kantor, "A Candidate, His Minister and the Search for Faith", The New York Times, April 30, 2007; available online at: http://www.nytimes.com/2007/04/30/us/politics/30obama.html [accessed March 17, 2010].

[51] "Who Exactly is Barack H. Obama?", Ortzion, copyright September 2008-2009; available online at: http://www.ortzion.org/news59-Obama-special_4.html [accessed March 31, 2010].

[52] Klein, "Obama was 'Quite Religious in Islam'", op. cit.

[53] Ibid.

[54] Ibid.

[55] "Education", The Obama File, copyright 2008; available online at: http://theobamafile.com/ObamaEducation.htm [accessed March 31, 2010].

[56] Ibid.

[57] Ibid.

[58] Corsi, *The Obama Nation*, p. 60.

[59] Ibid.

[60] Kyle, "'My Muslim Faith' For Dummies", Right Wing Watch, September 9, 2008; available online at: http://www.rightwingwatch.org/content/%E2%80%9Cmy-muslim-faith%E2%80%9D-dummies [accessed March 18, 2010].

[61] Ibid.

[62] Obama, *Audacity of Hope*, p. 258.

[63] Corsi, *The Obama Nation*, p. 70.

[64] Obama, *Dreams from My Father*, p. 100.

[65] "Quotable Quote, Franz Fanon", Good Reads, copyright 2010; available online at: http://www.goodreads.com/quotes/show/113708 [accessed March 18, 2010].

[66] Obama, *Dreams from My Father*, p. 86.

[67] Ibid., p. 97.

[68] "List of Barack Obama's Friends and Associates", Metapedia, modified June 8, 2009; available online at: http://en.metapedia.org/wiki/List_of_Barack_Obama's_friends_and_associates [accessed March 18, 2010].

[69] "Education", The Obama File, op. cit.

[70] Ibid.

[71] Ibid.

[72] Adam Goldman and Robert Tanner, "Old Friends Recall Obama's Years in LA, NY", The Seattle Times, May 15, 2008; available online at: http://seattletimes.nwsource.com/html/localnews/2004417706_apyoungobama2n dldwritethru.html [accessed March 18, 2010].

[73] Obama, *Dreams from My Father*, p. 139.

[74] McCarthy, "Why won't Obama Talk about Columbia?", op. cit.

[75] Edward Alexander, "Professor of Terror", Commentary, August 1989; available online at: http://www.commentarymagazine.com/viewarticle.cfm/professor-of-terror-7594 [accessed March 18, 2010].

[76] Gil Ronen, "Arab-American Activist Says Obama Hiding Anti-Israel Stance", IsraelNationalNews.com, March 23, 2008; available online at: http://www.israelnationalnews.com/News/News.aspx/125656[accessed March 18, 2010].

[77] Ted Belman, "Obama's 'Change' comes through Agitating a Community, not Uniting All Communities", Global Politician, April 4, 2008; available online at: http://www.globalpolitician.com/24421-obama-elections [accessed February 16, 2010].

[78] Ross Goldberg, "Obama's Years at Columbia Are a Mystery", The New York Sun, September 2, 2008; available online at: http://www.nysun.com/new-york/obamas-years-at-columbia-are-a-mystery/85015/ [accessed March 19, 2010].

[79] Scott, "Obama's Account of New York Years Often Differs from what Others Say", op. cit.

[80] John Dietrich, "Obama's Burden of Brightness", American Thinker, May 7, 2010; available online at: http://www.americanthinker.com/2010/05/obamas_burden_of_brightness.html [accessed May 27, 2010].

[81] Amanda Carpenter, "Another Radical Obama Association?", SRNNews.com, August 26, 2008; available online at: http://srnnews.townhall.com/news/politics-elections/2008/08/26/another_radical_obama_association [accessed March 19, 2010].

[82] Fredrick, *The Obama Timeline*, p. 52.

[83] Ibid.

[84] Jerome R. Corsi, "Did Radical Muslims Help Send Obama to Harvard?", World Net Daily, July 21, 2009; available online at: http://www.wnd.com/index.php?pageId=104684 [accessed March 31, 2010].

[85] Pamela Geller, "Obama's Benefactor: Dr. Khalid al Mansour, I Presume…", Atlas Shrugs, August 27, 2008; available online at: http://atlasshrugs2000.typepad.com/atlas_shrugs/2008/08/obamas-benefact.html [accessed March 20, 2010].

[86] Ken Timmerman, "Obama Had Close Ties to Top Saudi Adviser at Early Age", Newsmax.com, September 3, 2008; available online at: http://newsmax.com/KenTimmerman/obama-sutton-saudi/2008/09/03/id/339914 [accessed March 20, 2010].

[87] "Factbox-Saudi Billionaire Prince Alwaleed", Reuters, November 12, 2007; available online at: http://www.reuters.com/article/idUSL1266773620071112 [accessed March 20, 2010].

[88] Timmerman, "Obama Had Close Ties to Top Saudi Adviser at Early Age", op. cit.

[89] Kenneth R. Timmerman, "Obama's Harvard Years: Questions Swirl", Newsmax.com, September 23, 2008; available online at: http://newsmax.com/KenTimmerman/obama-harvard-/2009/12/14/id/342454 [accessed March 20, 2010].

[90] Raymond, "The Obama-Mansour Connection", Jihad Watch, September 6, 2008; available online at: http://www.jihadwatch.org/2008/09/the-obama-mansour-connection.html [accessed March 20, 2010].

[91] Timmerman, "Obama Had Close Ties to Top Saudi Adviser at Early Age", op. cit.

[92] Ibid.

[93] Timmerman, "Obama's Harvard Years: Questions Swirl", op. cit.

[94] "Weatherman", DiscovertheNetworks.org, copyright 2003-2009; available online at: http://www.discoverthenetworks.org/groupProfile.asp?grpid=6808 [accessed April 28, 2010].

[95] "Weather Underground (Organization)", Wikipedia, modified April 28, 2010; available online at: http://en.wikipedia.org/wiki/Weather_Underground_(organization) [accessed April 28, 2010].

[96] Aaron Klein, "Obama's Website Yanks 'Black Panthers' Plug", World Net Daily, March 19, 2008; available online at: http://www.wnd.com/index.php?pageId=59398 [accessed March 21, 2010].

[97] Charles A. Radin, "Saudi Donates $20M to Harvard", Boston Globe, December 13, 2005; available online at: http://www.boston.com/news/local/articles/2005/12/13/saudi_donates_20m_to_harvard/ [accessed April 29, 2010].

[98] Corsi, *The Obama Nation*, p. 193.

[99] Ibid.

[100] Ibid.

[101] "Obama and Islam – The Early Years", The Obama File, copyright 2009; available online at: http://theobamafile.com/_Islam/ObamaIslamEarlyYears.htm [accessed May 27, 2010].

[102] Ibid.

[103] "Ali Abunimah", DiscovertheNetworks.org, copyright 2003-2009; available online at: http://www.discoverthenetworks.org/individualProfile.asp?indid=1426 [accessed March 22, 2010].

[104] Ibid.

[105] Ibid.

[106] Ibid.

[107] Aaron Klein, "Obama 'Friend': End of Israel 'Within Reach'", World Net Daily, January 30, 2009; available online at: http://www.wnd.com/index.php?pageId=87454 [accessed March 22, 2010].

[108] Ibid.

[109] Obama, *Dreams from My Father,* p. 282.

[110] Manya A. Brachear, "Rev. Jeremiah A. Wright, Jr.: Pastor Inspires Obama's 'Audacity'", Chicago Tribune, January 21, 2007; available online at: http://www.chicagotribune.com/news/politics/chi-070121-obama-pastor,0,1574186.story [accessed March 22, 2010].

[111] "Rev. Dr. Jeremiah A. Wright, Jr. and United Church of Christ Talking Points", Minnesota Conference - United Church of Christ, n.d.; available online at: http://www.uccmn.org/ministrygroups/emmaus/Sacred%20Conversations%20on%20Race/Talking%20Points%20on%20Jeremiah%20Wright.pdf [accessed April 1, 2010].

[112] Thomas Lifson, "Barack Obama Running on His Religion", American Thinker, February 5, 2008; available online at: http://www.americanthinker.com/2008/02/barack_obama_running_on_his_re.html [accessed March 22, 2010].

[113] Jason Byassee, "Africentric Church", The Christian Century, May 29, 2007; available online at: http://www.christiancentury.org/article.lasso?id=3392 [accessed April 1, 2010].

[114] Stanley Kurtz, "Wright 101", National Review Online, October 14, 2008; available online at: http://article.nationalreview.com/374927/wright-101/stanley-kurtz [accessed April 1, 2010].

[115] Freddoso, *The Case Against Barack Obama*", p. 158-159.

[116] Ibid., p. 159.

[117] Ibid., p. 160.

[118] "Obama Pastor's Theology: Destroy 'The White Enemy'", World Net Daily, March 17, 2008; available online at: http://www.wnd.com/?pageId=59230 [accessed March 22, 2010].

[119] "Video Transcripts: Seven Reasons why Barack Obama is not a Christian", Christian Anti-Defamation Commission, January 5, 2009; available online at: http://www.christianadc.org/news-and-articles/227-video-transcripts-seven-reasons-why-barack-obama-is-not-a-christian [accessed May 27, 2010].

[120] "James Cone", DiscovertheNetworks.org, copyright 2003-2009; available online at: http://www.discoverthenetworks.org/individualProfile.asp?indid=2315 [accessed April 1, 2010].

[121] Ibid.

[122] "Video Transcripts: Seven Reasons why Barack Obama is not a Christian", Christian Anti-Defamation Commission, op. cit.

[123] "The Black Value System", Trinity United Church of Christ, op. cit.

[124] "Our History", Trinity United Church of Christ, copyright 2008; available online at: http://www.trinitychicago.org/index.php?option=com_content&task=view&id=1 2&Itemid=27 [accessed April 1, 2010].

[125] Aaron Klein, "Obama Church Published Hamas Terror Manifesto", World Net Daily, March 20, 2008; available online at: http://www.wnd.com/index.php?pageId=59456 [accessed March 22, 2010].

[126] Byassee, "Africentric Church", op. cit.

[127] Richard Cohen, "Obama's Farrakhan Test", The Washington Post, January 15, 2008; available online at: http://www.washingtonpost.com/wp-dyn/content/article/2008/01/14/AR2008011402083.html [accessed April 1, 2010].

[128] Ibid.

[129] Bud White, "The Birth of Whitey: Black Liberation Theology and the Nation of Islam", No Quarters, June 20, 2008; available online at: http://www.noquarterusa.net/blog/2008/06/20/the-birth-of-whitey-black-liberation-theology-and-the-nation-of-islam/ [accessed April1, 2010].

[130] Steve Gilbert, "What was Cut out of Wrights 'Audacity'", Sweetness & Light, October 1, 2008; available online at: http://sweetness-light.com/archive/what-was-cut-out-of-wrights-audacity-sermon [accessed May 28, 2010].

[131] Jim Geraghty, "Obama's Pastor's other Comments on 9/11", National Review Online, March 13, 2008; available online at: http://campaignspot.nationalreview.com/post/?q=YTI5YWIxOGZhN2Q3YmEw YTVjNDk2ZWY3OGYyMmU1MWQ [accessed April 1, 2010].

[132] Brian Ross and Rehab El-Buri, "Obama's Pastor: God Damn America, U.S. to Blame for 9/11", ABC News, March 13, 2008; available online at: http://abcnews.go.com/Blotter/DemocraticDebate/story?id=4443788&page=1 [accessed March 27, 2010].

[133] "Barack Obama, Nation of Islam, and Black Liberation Theology", Intelligent Conservatism, March 20, 2008; available online at: http://www.intelligentconservatism.com/?p=32 [accessed April 4, 2010].

[134] Ibid.

[135] Corsi, The Obama Nation, p. 181.

[136] Malcolm X, "Malcolm X", Wikiquote, available online at: http://en.wikiquote.org/wiki/Malcolm_X [accessed May 30, 2010].

[137] Peter Ferrara, "The Supreme Court in the Balance", The American Spectator, September 10, 2008; available online at: http://spectator.org/archives/2008/09/10/the-supreme-court-in-the-balan [accessed April 4, 2010].

[138] "Barack Obama, Nation of Islam, and Black Liberation Theology", Intelligent Conservatism, op. cit.

[139] Dr. Jeremiah A. Wright Jr., "The African-American Religious Experience", Swan's Commentary, May 5, 2008; available online at: http://www.swans.com/library/art14/zig096.html [accessed April 1, 2010].

[140] John Perazzo, "The Closing Argument", DiscovertheNetworks.org, November 3, 2008; available online at: http://www.discoverthenetworks.org/individualProfile.asp?indid=2336 [accessed May 28, 2010].

[141] Ibid.

[142] Bob McCarthy, "Obama Organized Farrakhan's 'Million Man March'", Now Public, April 2, 2008; available online at: http://www.nowpublic.com/world/obama-organized-farrakhan-s-million-man-march [accessed March 22, 2010].

[143] Perazzo, "Why Does Obama's Pastor Matter?", op. cit.

[144] Ken Timmerman, "Obama-Farrakhan Ties Are Close, Ex-Aide Says", Newsmax.com, November 3, 2008; available online at: http://newsmax.com/InsideCover/farrakhan-obama-islam/2008/11/03/id/326298 [accessed March 22, 2010].

[145] "Louis Farrakhan Quotes", Brainy Quote, copyright 2010; available online at: http://www.brainyquote.com/quotes/quotes/l/louisfarra206793.html [accessed April 29, 2010].

[146] Derek Brown, "Quotes from Louis Farrakhan", Guardian.co.uk, July 31, 2001; available online at: http://www.guardian.co.uk/uk/2001/jul/31/race.world1 [accessed April 29, 2010].

[147] Christopher Hitchens, "Are We Getting Two for One?", Slate, May 5, 2008; available online at: http://www.slate.com/id/2190589/?from=rss [accessed March 22, 2010].

[148] "Louis Farrakhan", DiscovertheNetworks.org, copyright 2003-2009; available online at: http://www.discoverthenetworks.org/individualProfile.asp?indid=1325 [accessed March 22, 2010].

[149] Geller, "How Could Stanley Ann Dunham have Delivered Barack Hussein Obama Jr. in August of 1961 in Honolulu, when Official University of Washington Records Show Her 2680 Miles Away in Seattle Attending Classes that Same Month?", op. cit.

[150] Ibid.

[151] Ibid.

[152] Ibid.

[153] Guarino, "Obama Nation 7", Guarino, September 6, 2008; available online at: http://guarino.typepad.com/guarino/2008/09/obama-nation-7-8.html [accessed March 22, 2010].

[154] Dr. Don Boys, "Senator Obama: Repudiate Black Muslim Bigot Farrakhan and Black Preacher Wright!", Canada Free Press, January 18, 2008; available online at: http://www.canadafreepress.com/index.php/article/1440 [accessed March 22, 2010].

[155] "Louis Farrakhan", DiscovertheNetworks.org, op. cit.

[156] Ibid.

[157] Ibid.

[158] Ibid.

[159] Askia Muhammad, "Farrakhan Addresses World at Saviors' Day 2008", The Final Call, May 5, 2008; available online at: http://www.finalcall.com/artman/publish/National_News_2/Farrakhan_addresses_world_at_Saviours_Day_2008_4427.shtml [accessed April 1, 2010].

[160] "Exclusive Interview with Minister Louis Farrakhan", The Final Call, January 9, 2008; available online at: http://www.finalcall.com/artman/publish/article_4256.shtml [accessed March 23, 2010].

[161] David Huntwork, "The 99 Most Memorable, Interesting and Outrageous Political Quotes of 2008", January 8, 2009; available online at: http://www.globalpolitician.com/25367--political-quotes [accessed April 9, 2010].

[162] "Barack Hussein Obama", DiscovertheNetworks.org, copyright 2003-2009; available online at: http://www.discoverthenetworks.org/individualProfile.asp?indid=1511 [accessed April 30, 2010].

[163] Jim Davis, "Obama's Church: Cauldron of Division", Newsmax.com, August 9, 2007; http://archive.newsmax.com/archives/articles/2007/8/8/194812.shtml [accessed April 4, 2010].

[164] Freddoso, The Case Against Barack Obama, p. 149.

[165] Gerrish, "Barack Obama's Connections to Socialism, Communism and Racial Divisiveness", op. cit.

[166] Rachel Neuwirth, "Barack Obama's Anti-Israel Alliances", Family Security Matters, October 24, 2008; available online at: http://www.familysecuritymatters.org/publications/id.1566/pub_detail.asp [accessed March 23, 2010].

[167] Ibid.

[168] Andrew C. McCarthy, "The L.A. Times Suppresses Obama's Khalidi Bash Tape", National Review Online, October 27, 2008; available online at: http://article.nationalreview.com/376504/the-ila-timesi-suppresses-obamas-khalidi-bash-tape/andrew-c-mccarthy [accessed March 23, 2010].

[169] Ibid.

[170] Ibid.

[171] Ibid.

[172] Corsi, The Obama Nation, p. 142.

[173] Ibid., p. 93.

[174] Ibid., p. 101.

[175] Ibid., p. 93.

[176] Ibid., p. 107.

[177] Fredrick, The Obama Timeline, p. 119-120.

[178] Pamela Geller, "Kenya: Obama's Violent Islamist Ally, Odinga, Goes to Iran", Atlas Shrugs, May 31, 2009; available online at:

http://atlasshrugs2000.typepad.com/atlas_shrugs/2009/05/kenya-obamas-violent-islamist-ally-odinga-goes-to-iran.html [accessed March 23, 2010].

[179] Fredrick, *The Obama Timeline*, p. 119.

[180] Corsi, *The Obama Nation*, p. 96.

[181] Mike Flannery, "Obama's Criticism Irks Kenyan Government", CBS 2 Chicago, August 28, 2006; available online at: http://cbs2chicago.com/topstories/Barack.Obama.Kenya.2.331658.html [accessed March 23, 2010].

[182] Corsi, *The Obama Nation*, p. 96.

[183] Fredrick, *The Obama Timeline*, p. 119.

[184] Pamela Geller, "Odinga and Obama both Luo: 'We are Taliban'", Atlas Shrugs, June 17, 2008; available online: http://atlasshrugs2000.typepad.com/atlas_shrugs/2008/06/odinga-and-obam.html [accessed March 23, 2010].

[185] Pamela Geller, "Manchurian Candidate", Atlas Shrugs, January 9, 2008; available online at: http://atlasshrugs2000.typepad.com/atlas_shrugs/2008/01/manchurian-cand.html [accessed March 23, 2010].

[186] Corsi, *The Obama Nation*, p. 104-105.

[187] Kerry Picket, "When will MSM Report Obama's Support for Kenyan Tyrant Odinga?", NewsBusters, October 12, 2008; available online at: http://newsbusters.org/blogs/kerry-picket/2008/10/12/when-will-msm-report-obamas-support-kenyan-tyrant-raila-odinga [accessed March 23, 2010].

[188] Corsi, *The Obama Nation*, p. 97.

[189] Paula Abeles, "Obama and Odinga: The True Story", Canada Free Press, August 8, 2008; available online at: http://www.canadafreepress.com/index.php/article/4353 [accessed March 23, 2010].

[190] "Kenyan Leader Demands President Resign", USA Today, February 10, 2008; available online at: http://www.usatoday.com/news/world/2008-02-10-kenya-politics_N.htm [accessed March 23, 2010].

[191] Mark Hyman, "Hyman: Obama's Kenya Ghosts", WashingtonTimes.com, October 12, 2008; available online at: http://www.washingtontimes.com/news/2008/oct/12/obamas-kenya-ghosts/ [accessed March 23, 2010].

[192] Fredrick, *The Obama Timeline*, p. 119.

[193] Jerome R. Corsi, "Obama Raised $1 Million for Foreign Thug's Election", World Net Daily, October 14, 2008; available online at: http://www.wnd.com/index.php?pageId=78035 [accessed March 23, 2010].

[194] Corsi, *The Obama Nation*, p. 112-113.

[195] Fredrick, *The Obama Timeline*, p. 132.

[196] Tom Baldwin, "Barack Obama Sacks Adviser over Talks with Hamas", Times Online, May 10, 2008; available online at: http://www.timesonline.co.uk/tol/news/world/us_and_americas/us_elections/article3897414.ece [accessed March 24, 2010].

[197] Michael Goldfarb, "They Need More White People", WeeklyStandard.com, April 8, 2008; available online at: http://www.weeklystandard.com/weblogs/TWSFP/2008/04/they_need_more_whi te_people.asp [accessed March 24, 2010].

[198] Ibid.

[199] "Obama's Muslim Adviser Resigns", Human Events, August 6, 2008; available online at: http://www.humanevents.com/article.php?id=27932 [accessed March 24, 2010].

[200] Raymond, "New Obama 'Muslim Outreach Advisor' Met with Islamic Organizations Associated with Hamas and Muslim Brotherhood", Jihad Watch, October 10, 2008; available online at: http://www.jihadwatch.org/2008/10/new-obama-muslim-outreach-advisor-met-with-islamic-organizations-associated-with-hamas-and-muslim-br.html [accessed March 24, 2010].

[201] "Why Does Fox News Promote Terror-Tied, FBI-Shunned Group?", World Net Daily, January 11, 2010; available online at: http://www.wnd.com/index.php?fa=PAGE.view&pageId=121694 [accessed March 24, 2010].

[202] "Cornel West", DiscovertheNetworks.org, op. cit.

[203] Joe Kaufman, "Radical Muslims for Obama", FrontPageMag.com, February 5, 2008; available online at: http://97.74.65.51/readArticle.aspx?ARTID=29724 [accessed March 24, 2010].

[204] "Supporters", The Obama File, copyright 2008; available online at: http://theobamafile.com/Obamasupporters.htm [accessed March 24, 2010].

[205] Ken Timmerman, "Secret, Foreign Money Floods into Obama Campaign", Newsmax.com, September 28, 2009; available online at: http://newsmax.com/Politics/Obama-fundraising-illegal/2008/09/29/id/325630 [accessed April 1, 2010].

[206] Ibid.

[207] "Wash. Times' McCaslin Misrepresented FEC Spokesman, Advisory Opinions, to Raise Questions about Clinton's Elton John Concert", Media Matters, March 27, 2008; available online at: http://mediamatters.org/print/research/200803270011 [accessed April 1, 2010].

[208] Pamela Geller, "Obama's Foreign Donors: The Media Averts It's Eyes", American Thinker, August 14, 2008; available online at: http://www.americanthinker.com/2008/08/obamas_donor_contributions_sil.html [accessed March 24, 2010].

[209] Ibid.

[210] Pamela Gellar, "Obama's Donation Obamanation: Saputra, Anton, Indonesia", Atlas Shrugs, August 10, 2008; available online at: http://atlasshrugs2000.typepad.com/atlas_shrugs/2008/08/obamas-donation.html [accessed March 24, 2010].

[211] Aaron Klein, "Mideast Leader: Obama a Muslim who Studied in Islamic Schools", World Net Daily, October 17, 2008; available online at: http://www.wnd.com/index.php?pageId=78309 [accessed March 24, 2010].

[212] Rick Moran, "Are Foreign Donations Powering the Obama Campaign?", American Thinker, October 2, 2008; available online at:

http://www.americanthinker.com/blog/2008/10/are_foreign_donations_powering.
html [accessed March 24, 2010].

[213] Pamela Geller, "Call for an Audit of Obama's Campaign Finances", Big
Government, January 25, 2010; available online at:
http://biggovernment.com/pgeller/2010/01/25/call-for-an-audit-of-obamas-
campaign-finances/ [accessed April 1, 2010].

[214] "Gaza Youth Support Obama's Presidential Bid", ynetnews.com, August 31,
2008; available online at: http://www.ynetnews.com/articles/0,7340,L-
3590065,00.html [accessed March 25, 2010].

[215] "Obama and Islam", The Obama File, copyright 2010; available online at:
http://theobamafile.com/_Islam/ObamaIslamCandidate.htm [accessed May 29,
2010].

[216] Allahpundit, "Good News: U.S. to Pledge $900 Million to Rebuild Gaza", Hot
Air, February 23, 2009; available online at:
http://hotair.com/archives/2009/02/23/good-news-us-to-pledge-900-million-to-
rebuild-gaza/ [accessed March 25, 2010].

[217] "Obama Issues Executive Order to Resettle Gazan Arabs into U.S.A.", Live
Leak, n.d.; available online at: http://www.liveleak.com/view?i=f29_1233931813
[accessed March 26, 2010].

[218] Matthew Kalman, "Clinton Announces Million-Dollar Scholarship Program
for Palestinian Students", The Chronicle, March 9, 2009; available online at:
http://chronicle.com/article/Clinton-Announces/42530 [accessed March 26,
2010].

[219] Breitbart, "US Gives 50,000 Dlrs for Quake-Hit Italy", Breitbart.com, April 6,
2009; available online at:
http://www.breitbart.com/article.php?id=CNG.15148f36e80f2222604c174cd120f
a19.381&show_article=1 [accessed June 5, 2010].

[220] Tom Baldwin, "President Obama's First Call 'Was to President Abbas'",
Times Online, January 22, 2009; available online at:
http://www.timesonline.co.uk/tol/news/world/us_and_americas/us_elections/artic
le5563280.ece [accessed June 5, 2010].

[221] Jake Tapper, "President Obama Does First Formal TV Interview as President
with Al-Arabiya", ABC News, January 26˙2009; available online at:
http://blogs.abcnews.com/politicalpunch/2009/01/president-ob-10.html [accessed
June 5, 2010].

[222] Amir Taheri, "Pathetic 'Message'", New York Post, January 29, 2009;
available online at:
http://www.nypost.com/p/news/opinion/opedcolumnists/item_Q5w4YGEiSfIGL
hiAsM73SJ;jsessionid=35F96CF77295F7D8038BB1FDEF3AC5FA [accessed
June 5, 2010].

[223] Michael D. Shear and Glenn Kessler, "Obama Voices Hope for Mideast Peace
in Talk with Al-Arabiya TV", The Washington Post, January 27, 2009; available
online at: http://www.washingtonpost.com/wp-
dyn/content/article/2009/01/26/AR2009012602035.html [accessed March 26,
2010].

[224] Jake Tapper, "Military Commission Charges Dropped against Terrorist Suspect Al-Nashiri", ABC News, February 5, 2009; available online at: http://blogs.abcnews.com/politicalpunch/2009/02/president-oba-2.html [accessed June 5, 2010].

[225] "French Leader Sarkozy Slams Obama, Warns He Might be Insane", The European Union Times, April 9, 2010; available online at: http://www.eutimes.net/2010/04/french-leader-sarkozy-slams-obama-warns-he-might-be-insane/ [accessed May 2, 2010].

[226] Andrew Walden, "Obama's War", American Thinker, June 10, 2008; available online at: http://www.americanthinker.com/2008/06/obamas_war.html [accessed March 26, 2010].

[227] Ronald Kessler, "'Man-Caused Disasters' New Term for Terrorism", Newsmax.com, March 23, 2009; available online at: http://newsmax.com/RonaldKessler/napolitano-terrorism/2009/03/23/id/328984 [accessed March 26, 2010].

[228] Pat Boone, "Essay: The President without a Country", NewsBusters, September 3, 2009; available online at: http://newsbusters.org/blogs/pat-boone/2009/09/03/essay-president-without-country [accessed March 26, 2010].

[229] John Hawkins, "Obama: We do not Consider Ourselves a Christian Nation", Right Wing News, April 7, 2009; available online at: http://rightwingnews.com/mt331/2009/04/obama_we_do_not_consider_ourse.php [accessed March 26, 2010].

[230] "Obama: U.S. not at War with Islam", FoxNews.com, April 6, 2009; available online at: http://www.foxnews.com/politics/2009/04/06/obama-war-islam/ [accessed March 26, 2010].

[231] Ibid.

[232] Fredrick, The Obama Timeline, p. 512.

[233] Ibid.

[234] Ibid., p. 560.

[235] Ibid., p. 560-561.

[236] "Obama: Israel is 'a Constant Sore'", Little Green Footballs, May 12, 2008; available online at: http://littlegreenfootballs.com/article/29921_Obama-Israel_is_A_Constant_Sore [accessed June 5, 2010].

[237] Domenico Montanaro, "Obama Asked about Connection to Islam", MSNBC, December 22, 2007; available online at: http://firstread.msnbc.msn.com/archive/2007/12/22/531492.aspx [accessed April 29, 2010].

Chapter Six

[1] Rich Noyes, "Barack Obama and Bill Ayers: Stanley Kurtz Makes the Connection", NewsBusters, September 23, 2008; available online at: http://newsbusters.org/blogs/rich-noyes/2008/09/23/barack-obama-bill-ayers-stanley-kurtz-makes-connection [accessed March 26, 2010].

[2] Kim, "Thomas G. Ayers, 1915-2007", Cinnamon Swirl, June 18, 2007; available online at: http://kimallen.sheepdogdesign.net/cinnamon/2007/06/thomas-g-ayers-1915-2007.html [accessed March 26, 2010].

[3] Lucinda Franks and Thomas Powers, "Bitter Ann Arbor Experiences Radicalized Diana", Eugene Register-Guard, September 22, 1970; available online at: http://news.google.com/newspapers?nid=1310&dat=19700922&id=AsoTAAAAIBAJ&sjid=VOEDAAAAIBAJ&pg=6935,4478898 [accessed March 26, 2010].

[4] Chuck Ayoub, "Bob Dylan Lyrics", Bob Dylan Lyrics, n.d.; available online at: http://www.bobdylanlyrics.net/ [accessed April 29, 2010].

[5] "Weatherman", DiscovertheNetworks.org, op. cit.

[6] Bud Meyers, "Bill Ayers and Bernardine Dohrn: Cold Case Files", Bud's Blog, September 22, 2009; available online at: http://tobuds.com/blogs/blog6.php [accessed April 29, 2010].

[7] "Bill Ayers", DiscovertheNetworks.org, copyright 2003-2009; available online at: http://www.discoverthenetworks.org/individualProfile.asp?indid=2169 [accessed March 26, 2010].

[8] "We are Against Everything that is Decent and Good", CACC Newsletter, February 1, 1970; available online at: http://www.schwarzreport.org/Newsletters/1970/february1,70.htm [accessed April 2, 2010].

[9] "Ayers' Group Foresaw Genocide of Capitalists", World Net Daily, October 23, 2008; available online at: http://www.wnd.com/index.php?pageId=78929 [accessed March 26, 2010].

[10] "Bill Ayers", DiscovertheNetworks.org, op. cit.

[11] "Bill Ayers", Wikipedia, modified March 26, 2010; available online at: http://en.wikipedia.org/wiki/Bill_Ayers [accessed March 26, 2010].

[12] David Horowitz, "The Sick Mind of Noam Chomsky", FrontPageMag.com, September 26, 2001; available online at: http://97.74.65.51/readArticle.aspx?ARTID=24447 [accessed May 29, 2010].

[13] Cliff Kincaid, "Tribune Covers for Obama's Terrorist Friends", Accuracy in Media, May 7, 2008; available online at: http://www.aim.org/aim-column/tribune-covers-for-obamas-terrorist-friends/ [accessed March 26, 2010].

[14] Christopher C. Harmon, "Fire, Seen through Frosted Glass", Claremont Institute, January 14, 2004; available online at: http://www.claremont.org/publications/pubid.321/pub_detail.asp [accessed March 26, 2010].

[15] Ibid.

[16] Kincaid, "Tribune Covers for Obama's Terrorist Friends", op. cit.

[17] "Weatherman", DiscovertheNetworks.org, op. cit.

[18] Linda Harvey, "Bill Ayers' 'Gay' Agenda for Your Kids", World Net Daily, October 13, 2008; available online at: http://www.wnd.com/index.php?pageId=77640 [accessed March 26, 2010].

[19] "Exclusive: 'H&C' Uncovers Bill Ayers Dedications", FoxNews.com, October 31, 2008; available online at:

http://www.foxnews.com/story/0,2933,445556,00.html [accessed April 29, 2009].

[20] "William Ayers' Forgotten Communist Manifesto: Prairie Fire", Zombietime, October 22, 2008; available online at: http://zombietime.com/prairie_fire/ [accessed April 29, 2010].

[21] Joseph Farah, "Meet Mr. and Mrs. William Ayers", World Net Daily, April 25, 2008; available online at: http://www.wnd.com/index.php?pageId=62481 [accessed April 29, 2010].

[22] "Bill Ayers", DiscovertheNetworks.org, op. cit.

[23] "One-Degree of Separation: Obama's Weathermen Ayers and Dohrn (5 Updates)", Rezko Watch, April 24, 2008; available online at: http://rezkowatch.blogspot.com/2008/04/one-degree-of-separation-obamas_24.html [accessed March 26, 2010].

[24] Thomas Ryan, "RNC Forecast: Severe 'Weather' Watch", FrontPageMag.com, August 30, 2004; available online at: http://97.74.65.51/readArticle.aspx?ARTID=11605 [accessed April 29, 2010].

[25] Jesse Rigsby, "NLG: The Legal Fifth Column", FrontPageMag.com, April 25, 2003; available online at: http://97.74.65.51/readArticle.aspx?ARTID=18513 [accessed March 26, 2010].

[26] Brenda J. Elliot, "'Clandestine Agents of the Cuban Government'-Ayers, Dohrn, Myers (Updated 2x)", RBO, June 7, 2009; available online at: http://therealbarackobama.wordpress.com/2009/06/07/clandestine-agents-of-the-cuban-government-ayers-dohrn-myers/ [accessed March 26, 2010].

[27] "Radical from '60s Stoked by Barack", World Net Daily, April 29, 2008; available online at: http://www.wnd.com/index.php?pageId=62917 [accessed March 26, 2010].

[28] Scott Swett and Roger Canfield, "Obama's Foul Weather Friends", American Thinker, September 16, 2010; available online at: http://www.americanthinker.com/2008/09/obamas_foul_weather_friends.html [accessed March 26, 2010].

[29] Ibid.

[30] "Bernardine Dohrn", DiscovertheNetworks.org, copyright 2003-2009; available online at: http://www.discoverthenetworks.org/individualProfile.asp?indid=2190 [accessed March 26, 2010].

[31] Cliff Kincaid, "Terrorists on Tour", Canada Free Press, April 24, 2009; available online at: http://www.canadafreepress.com/index.php/article/10519 [accessed March 26, 2010].

[32] Daniel Burton-Rose, "Guerrillas in our Midst", LiP Magazine, February 15, 1999; available online at: http://www.lipmagazine.org/articles/featrose_9_p2.htm [accessed March 26, 2010].

[33] "Bernardine Dohrn", DiscoverTheNetworks.org, op. cit.

[34] "We are Against Everything that is Decent and Good", CACC Newsletter, op. cit.

[35] "The Pacifica Radio/UC Berkeley Social Activism Sound Recording Project", Berkeley Library, radio address June 1970; available online at:

http://www.lib.berkeley.edu/MRC/pacificaviet.html#1970 [accessed March 26, 2010].

[36] Deroy Murdock, "Obama's Weathermen Pals should Worry You", National Review Online, October 13, 2008; available online at: http://article.nationalreview.com/374666/obamas-weathermen-pals-should-worry-you/deroy-murdock [accessed March 26, 2010].

[37] Cliff Kincaid, "FBI Informant Implicates Obama Associate in Murder", Accuracy in Media, November 2, 2008; available online at: http://www.aim.org/aim-column/fbi-informant-implicates-obama-associate-in-murder/ [accessed April 2, 2010].

[38] Sharon Cohen, "Former '60s Radical Weathers Post-Sept. 11 Critical Storm", Los Angeles Times, September 30, 2001; available online at: http://articles.latimes.com/2001/sep/30/news/mn-51464 [accessed March 27, 2010].

[39] Ben Smith, "Obama Once Visited '60s Radicals", Politico, February 22, 2008; available online at: http://www.politico.com/news/stories/0208/8630.html [accessed March 27, 2010].

[40] Murdock, "Obama's Weathermen Pals Should Worry You", op. cit.

[41] Zee Towner, "Obama and Dohrn and Ayers", American Thinker, October 21, 2008; available online at: http://www.americanthinker.com/2008/10/obama_and_dohrn_and_ayers.html [accessed March 11, 2010].

[42] Cliff Kincaid, "Bernadette (sic) Dohrn, Bill Ayers and the Bomb that Killed a Cop", WorldTribune.com, March 3, 2009; available online at: http://www.worldtribune.com/worldtribune/WTARC/2009/ss_terror0180_03_03.asp [accessed March 27, 2010].

[43] Fredrick, The Obama Timeline, p. 70-71.

[44] "Bill Ayers", DiscovertheNetworks.org, op. cit.

[45] Indepundant, "A Short List of Obama's Friends and Associates", Barack Obama File, October 20, 2008; available online at: http://www.barackobamafile.com/about/a-list-of-obamas-friends-and-associates/ [accessed April 29, 2010].

[46] "Bernardine Dohrn", DiscovertheNetworks.org, op. cit.

[47] Cliff Kincaid and Wes Vernon, "Blood on the Hands of Obama's Terror Associate", Canada Free Press, July 24, 2008; available online at: http://www.canadafreepress.com/index.php/article/4095 [accessed June 1, 2010].

[48] Ibid.

[49] James Lewis, "On Bill Ayers and Small 'c' Communists", American Thinker, October 15, 2008; available online at: http://www.americanthinker.com/2008/10/on_bill_ayers_and_small_c_comm.html [accessed April 29, 2010].

[50] "William Ayers' Forgotten Communist Manifesto: Prairie Fire", Zombietime, op. cit.

[51] Swett and Canfield, "Obama's Foul Weather Friends", op. cit.

[52] Towner, "Obama and Dohrn and Ayers", op. cit.

[53] Meyers, "Obama's Early Years in New York Finally Revealed?", op. cit.

[54] "Barack Obama's Close Encounter with the Weather Underground", Zombietime, October 27, 2008; available online at: http://zombietime.com/obama_and_the_weather_underground/ [accessed April 2, 2010].

[55] Trevor Loudon, "Obama File 84 why was Obama's 'Brain' Valerie Jarrett so Happy to Hire Communist Van Jones? Was it Fate?", New Zeal, September 9, 2009; available online at: http://newzeal.blogspot.com/2009/09/obama-file-84-why-was-obamas-brain.html [accessed March 27, 2010].

[56] Fredrick, The Obama Timeline, p. 41.

[57] Jack Cashill, "Did Ayers Help Obama get into Harvard?", American Thinker, September 20, 2009; available online at: http://www.americanthinker.com/2009/09/did_ayers_help_obama_get_into.html [accessed March 26, 2010].

[58] "Bill Ayers and Bernardine Dohrn", The Obama File, copyright 2009; available online at: http://www.theobamafile.com/_associates/BillAyers.htm [accessed March 27, 2010].

[59] Ibid.

[60] "The Wife", The Obama File, copyright 2009; available online at: http://theobamafile.com/ObamaWife.htm [accessed March 27, 2010].

[61] "Bill Ayers and Bernardine Dohrn", The Obama File, op. cit.

[62] Karen Springen, "First Lady in Waiting", ChicagoMag.com, October 2004; available online at: www.chicagomag.com/Chicago-Magazine/October-2004/First-Lady-in-Waiting/ [accessed March 27, 2010].

[63] Obama, The Audacity of Hope, p. 387.

[64] Corsi, The Obama Nation, p. 138.

[65] Brad O'Leary, "The Obama-Ayers Incestuous Money Trail", World Net Daily, October 14, 2008; available online at: http://www.wnd.com/index.php?fa=PAGE.view&pageId=77926 [accessed March 26, 2010].

[66] JB Williams, "Palin Hits Obama – Obama Cries Foul", Canada Free Press, October 6, 2008; available online at: http://www.canadafreepress.com/index.php/article/5412 [accessed June 2, 2010].

[67] John M. Murtagh, "Fire in the Night", City Journal, April 30, 2008; available online at: http://www.city-journal.org/2008/eon0430jm.html [accessed April 29, 2010].

[68] Fredrick, The Obama Timeline, 53.

[69] O'Leary, "The Obama-Ayers Incestuous Money Trail", op. cit.

[70] Brad O'Leary, "Obama's Mentors", World Net Daily, October 17, 2008; available online at: http://www.wnd.com/index.php?fa=PAGE.view&pageId=78217 [accessed March 27, 2010].

[71] Thomas Lifson, "When Barry met Billy", American Thinker, May 1, 2010; available online at: http://www.americanthinker.com/blog/2010/05/when_barry_met_billy.html [accessed May 3, 2010].

[72] Ibid.

[73] Stephen Diamond, "Barack Obama's Visit to the Other Ayers House", King Harvest, September 25, 2009; available online at: http://02ce1ab.netsolhost.com/KingHarvest/?p=1245 [accessed May 3, 2010].

[74] "Obama got Start in Civil Rights Practice", Organizing for America, February 20, 2007; available online at: http://www.barackobama.com/2007/02/20/obama_got_start_in_civil_right.php [accessed March 27, 2010].

[75] "Community Organizing", The Obama File, copyright 2010; available online at: http://theobamafile.com/obamaworks.htm [accessed March 27, 2010].

[76] Steve Diamond, "The Obama-Ayers Top Ten: Highlights of the 20 Year Obama-Ayers Connection", No Quarter, August 12, 2008; available online at: http://www.noquarterusa.net/blog/2008/08/12/the-obama-ayers-top-ten-highlights-of-the-20-year-obama-ayers-connection/ [accessed June 2, 2010].

[77] Fredrick, The Obama Timeline, 50.

[78] Ibid.

[79] Steve Diamond, "Behind the Annenberg Gate: Inside the Chicago Annenberg Challenge Records", Global Labor and Politics, August 20, 2008; available online at: http://globallabor.blogspot.com/2008/08/behind-annenberg-gate-inside-chicago.html [accessed April 29, 2010].

[80] Fredrick, The Obama Timeline, p. 69.

[81] Aaron Klein, "N.Y. Times Whitewashes Obama-Ayers Connection", World Net Daily, October 4, 2008; available online at: http://www.wnd.com/index.php?fa=PAGE.view&pageId=77075 [accessed May 3, 2010].

[82] "Obama's American Socialism: Decades in the Making", Logistics Monster, October 19, 2008; available online at: http://logisticsmonster.com/2008/10/19/obamas-american-socialism-decades-in-the-making/ [accessed March 27, 2010].

[83] Simpson, "The Cloward-Piven Strategy, Part III: Conspiracy of the Lemmings", op. cit.

[84] John Batchelor, "Obama's Plumbers", Human Events, September 12, 2008; available online at: http://www.humanevents.com/article.php?id=28508 [accessed June 2, 2010].

[85] Tom Maguire, "Obama, Ayers, and the Annenberg Challenge Cover-Up", Pajamas Media, August 22, 2008; available online at: http://pajamasmedia.com/blog/obama-ayers-and-the-annenberg-challenge-cover-up/2/ [accessed March 27, 2010].

[86] Steve Diamond, "Who 'Sent' Obama?", Global Labor and Politics, October 13, 2008; available online at: http://globallabor.blogspot.com/2008/04/who-sent-obama.html [accessed June 3, 2010].

[87] Fredrick, The Obama Timeline, p. 69.

[88] Ibid.

[89] Mary Grabar, "Teachers: They're all Bill Ayers now", Pajamas Media, March 10, 2009; available online at: http://pajamasmedia.com/blog/teachers-theyre-all-bill-ayers-now/ [accessed March 27, 2010].

[90] Diamond, "The Obama-Ayers Top Ten: Highlights of the 20 Year Obama-Ayers Connection", op. cit.

[91] Stanley Kurtz, "Obama and Ayers Pushed Radicalism on Schools", Wall Street Journal, September 23, 2008; available online at: http://online.wsj.com/article/SB122212856075765367.html [accessed March 27, 2010].

[92] "Bill Ayers", DiscovertheNetworks.org, op. cit.

[93] Michelle Malkin, "Flashback: Bill Ayers Declares Education 'The Motor-Force of Revolution'", Michelle Malkin, September 2, 2009; available online at: http://michellemalkin.com/2009/09/02/flashback-bill-ayers-declares-education-the-motor-force-of-revolution/ [accessed March 27, 2010].

[94] Meyers, "Obama's Early Years in New York Finally Revealed?", op. cit.

[95] Aaron Klein, "Obama Worked Closely with Terrorist Bill Ayers", World Net Daily, September 23, 2008; available online at: http://www.wnd.com/?pageId=76022 [accessed March 27, 2010].

[96] Ibid.

[97] Fredrick, The Obama Timeline, p. 176-177.

[98] Stanley Kurtz, "Obama's Challenge", National Review Online, September 23, 2008; available online at: http://article.nationalreview.com/print/?q=MTViMGRmMmYxZTgwZTFjYmFj ODU5YzM4Y2MwM2ViMjY [accessed March 27, 2010].

[99] Ibid.

[100] Aaron Klein, "Obama Worked with Terrorist", World Net Daily, February 24, 2008; available online at: http://www.wnd.com/index.php?pageId=57231 [accessed March 27, 2010].

[101] "Woods Fund of Chicago", DiscovertheNetworks.org, op. cit.

[102] Ibid.

[103] "Midwest Academy", DiscovertheNetworks.org, copyright 2009-2009; available online at: http://www.discoverthenetworks.org/groupprofile.asp?grpid=6725 [accessed March 27, 2010].

[104] Ibid.

[105] "Bill Ayers and Bernardine Dohrn", The Obama File, op. cit.

[106] Ibid.

[107] Corsi, The Obama Nation, p. 137.

[108] "Bill Ayers and Bernardine Dohrn", The Obama File, op. cit.

[109] Brenda J. Elliot, "Just Your Everyday Hyde Park Radicals — Obama, Ayers, Dohrn, Young", RBO, October 27, 2008; available online at: http://therealbarackobama.wordpress.com/2008/10/27/just-your-everyday-hyde-park-radicals-obama-ayers-dohrn-young/ [accessed January 23, 2010].

[110] Brenda J. Elliot, "Close, but no Cigar. Webscrub-a-Rub-a-Dub—Ayers-Dohrn-Obama 1995 (Updated)", RBO, October 20, 2008; available online at: http://therealbarackobama.wordpress.com/2008/10/20/close-but-no-cigar-webscrub-a-rub-a-dub-ayers-dohrn-obama-1995/ [accessed March 27, 2010].

[111] Brad O'Leary, "Obama's Money Trail", October 20, 2008; available online at: http://www.wnd.com/index.php?fa=PAGE.view&pageId=78538 [accessed March 27, 2010].

[112] Brenda J. Elliot, "Obama, Ayers and the Leadership for Quality Education", RBO, October 11, 2008; available online at: http://therealbarackobama.wordpress.com/2008/10/11/obama-ayers-and-the-leadership-for-quality-education/ [accessed March 27, 2010].

[113] Ibid.

[114] Ed Morrissey, "Obama's Lobbyist Problem: David Axelrod", Hot Air, May 25, 2008; available online at: http://hotair.com/archives/2008/05/25/obamas-lobbyist-problem-david-axelrod/ [accessed March 27, 2010].

[115] James A. Barnes, "Obama's Inner Circle", NationalJournal.com, March 31, 2008; available online at: http://news.nationaljournal.com/articles/080331nj1.htm [accessed June 3, 2010].

[116] Larry Johnson, "Breaking News: David Axelrod Talking Regularly with Bill Ayers?", No Quarter, August 29, 2008: available online at: http://noquarterusa.net/blog/2008/08/29/breaking-news-david-axelrod-talking-regularly-with-bill-ayers/ [accessed April 3, 2010].

[117] George Neumayr, "Guilt by Agreement", The American Spectator, October 9, 2008; available online at: http://spectator.org/archives/2008/10/09/guilt-by-agreement [accessed March 27, 2010].

[118] Chris Fusco and Abdom M. Pallasch, "Who is Bill Ayers?", Chicago Sun-Times, April 18, 2008; available online at: http://www.suntimes.com/news/politics/obama/902213,CST-NWS-ayers18.article [accessed June 3, 2010].

[119] "Obama has Links to Another '60s Radical", Newsmax.com, November 3, 2008; available online at: http://newsmax.com/InsiderReport/Obama-Has-Links/2008/11/03/id/339950 [accessed April 14, 2010].

[120] Fredrick, The Obama Timeline, p. 193.

[121] "Marilyn Katz", Barack Book, copyright 2008; available online at: http://www.barackbook.com/Profiles/MarilynKatz.htm [accessed March 27, 2010].

[122] Fredrick, The Obama Timeline, p. 93-94.

[123] "Marilyn Katz", The Obama File, copyright 2009; available online at: http://theobamafile.com/_associates/MarilynKatz.htm [accessed March 27, 2010].

[124] Fredrick, The Obama Timeline, p. 89.

[125] Fusco and Pallasch, "Who is Bill Ayers?", op. cit.

[126] Stanley Kurtz, "Chicago Annenberg Challenge Shutdown", National Review Online, August 18, 2008; available online at: http://article.nationalreview.com/366637/chicago-annenberg-challenge-shutdown/stanley-kurtz [accessed March 27, 2010].

[127] Corsi, The Obama Nation, p. 140.

[128] Ibid.

[129] Bill Ayers, "Weather Underground Redux", Bill Ayers, April 20, 2006; available online at: http://billayers.wordpress.com/2006/04/20/weather-underground-redux/ [accessed April 3, 2010].

[130] "William Ayers Stopped Using Bombs, Hired Barack Obama, & now is Orchestrating a Political Takeover of the USA", Global News Daily, copyright 2008-2010; available online at: http://www.globalnewsdaily.com/ [accessed March 27, 2010].

[131] Bernardine Dohrn, "Homeland Imperialism: Fear and Resistance", Volume 55 No. 3, Monthly Review, July-August 2003; available online at: http://www.monthlyreview.org/0703dohrn.htm [accessed March 27, 2010].

[132] Susan UnPC, "The 527's Reply to Obama's Efforts to Quash Ayers Ad", No Quarters, August 25, 2008; available online at: http://www.noquarterusa.net/blog/2008/08/25/the-527s-reply-to-obamas-efforts-to-quash-ayers-ad/ [accessed March 27, 2010].

[133] "Exclusive: Bill Ayers Talks about Election Night in Grant Park", NBC Chicago, updated July 30, 2009; available online at: http://www.nbcchicago.com/news/local-beat/Exclusive-Bill-Ayers-Talks-About-Election-Night-in-Grant-Park.html [accessed March 27, 2010].

[134] Ibid.

[135] Laura S. Washington, "Debunking the 60s with Ayers and Dohrn", In These Times, August 17, 2006; available online at: http://www.inthesetimes.com/article/2785/ [accessed March 27, 2010].

[136] "Weather Underground and Obama Logo – Coincidence or Design?", Quipster, October 27, 2008; available online at: http://quipster.wordpress.com/2008/10/27/weather-underground-and-obama-logo-coincidence-or-design/ [accessed March 27, 2010].

[137] Tarpley, Obama: The Postmodern Coup, p. 315.

[138] Allan H. Ryskind, "Obama and His Weatherman Friends", Human Events, April 29, 2008; available online at: http://www.humanevents.com/article.php?id=26243 [accessed March 27, 2010].

[139] "Obama Weatherman Logo", Total Information Analysis, October 15, 2008; available online at: http://www.total411.info/2008/10/obama-weatherman-logo.html [accessed April 3, 2010].

[140] Rob Raeside, "British Union of Fascists", CRW Flags, modified August 12, 2006; available online at: http://www.crwflags.com/fotw/flags/gb%7Dbfp.html [accessed March 27, 2010].

[141] "Weather Underground and Obama Logo – Coincidence or Design?", Quipster, op. cit.

Chapter Seven

[1] Brian Ross, "FBI: Illinois Governor Sought to 'Sell' Obama's Senate Seat", ABC News, December 9, 2008; available online at: http://abcnews.go.com/Blotter/ConductUnbecoming/story?id=6424985&page=1 [accessed April 3, 2010].

[2] Kevin Robinson, "Rezko 101: The Businessman", Chicagoist, February 20, 2008; available online at: http://chicagoist.com/2008/02/20/rezko_101_the_b.php [accessed March 28, 2010].
[3] Jack Cashill, "The Mansourian Candidate", World Net Daily, September 4, 2008; available online at: http://www.wnd.com/index.php?pageId=74231 [accessed March 28, 2010].
[4] Edward McClelland, "How Close were Barack Obama and Tony Rezko?", Salon, February 1, 2008; available online at: http://www.salon.com/news/feature/2008/02/01/rezko [accessed May, 28, 2010].
[5] Freddoso, The Case Against Barack Obama, p. 221.
[6] Tim Novak, "Broken Promises, Broken Homes", Chicago Sun-Times, April 24, 2007; available online at: http://www.suntimes.com/news/metro/355099,cst-nws-rez24a.article [accessed March 28, 2010].
[7] "Obama Mentor: Slumlord/Felon Tony Rezko – The Facts", CA Political News, August 24, 2008; available online at: http://capoliticalnews.com/blog_post/show/915 [accessed March 28, 2010].
[8] Freddoso, The Case Against Barack Obama, p. 221.
[9] David A. Patten, "Rezko Tie Links Obama and Blagojevich", Newsmax.com, December 9, 2008; available online at: http://newsmax.com/Newsfront/rezko-obama-governor/2008/12/09/id/327012 [accessed March 28, 2010].
[10] Ibid.
[11] Jim Geraghty, "The Obama-Blagojevich Ties-don't Forget Rezko", National Review Online, December 9, 2008; available online at: http://www.nationalreview.com/campaign-spot/8241/obama-blagojevich-ties-dont-forget-rezko [accessed May 29, 2010].
[12] Andrew Walden, "Obama's Syrian Connection", FrontPageMag.com, March 11, 2008; available online at: http://97.74.65.51/readArticle.aspx?ARTID=30175 [accessed May 29, 2010].
[13] "Tony Rezko", Wikipedia, op. cit.
[14] Malkin, Culture of Corruption, p. 96.
[15] "Jury Finds Tony Rezko Guilty on 16 of 24 Charges", CBS 2 Chicago, June 4, 2008; available online at: http://cbs2chicago.com/local/rezko.trial.verdict.2.740375.html [accessed April 30, 2010].
[16] Ibid.
[17] Patten, "Rezko Tie Links Obama and Blagojevich", op. cit.
[18] Evelyn Pringle, "Pringle Cliff Notes: Curtain Time for Barack Obama – Part 2 (Planning Board Scheme)", Rezko Watch, May 27, 2008; available online at: http://rezkowatch.blogspot.com/2008/05/pringle-cliff-notes-curtain-time-for_27.html [accessed March 28, 2010].
[19] Tim Novak, "All Eyes on Rezko Power Ties", Chicago Sun-Times, February 26, 2008; available online at: http://www.suntimes.com/news/metro/812715,CST-NWS-rezko26.article [accessed April 3, 2010].
[20] Fredrick, The Obama Timeline, p. 152.
[21] "Tony Rezko", Wikipedia, op. cit.

[22] Ibid.

[23] Brian Ross and Sara Keingsberg, "Rezko Locked up until Trial Starts Feb. 25", ABC News, January 29, 2008; available online at: http://abcnews.go.com/Blotter/story?id=4211771&page=1 [accessed April 30, 2010].

[24] John Batchelor, "The Obama Files", Human Events, February 25, 2008; available online at: http://www.humanevents.com/article.php?id=25166 [accessed March 28, 2010].

[25] David Freddoso, "He Hoped for Favors from Obama", National Review Online, December 9, 2008; available online at: http://corner.nationalreview.com/post/?q=NjA1MmNlZDUzYWQyZWViOTU4 YmRjMDA4ODUwOWMwMTE [accessed March 28, 2010].

[26] "Rod Blagojevich", Wikiquote, modified June 8, 2009; available online at: http://en.wikiquote.org/wiki/Rod_Blagojevich [accessed March 28, 2010].

[27] "Fitzgerald: 'New Low' in Illinois Politics", Chicago Breaking News Center, December 9, 2008; available online at: http://www.chicagobreakingnews.com/2008/12/us-attorney-fitzgerald-press-conference-blagojevich.html [accessed March 28, 2010].

[28] Sam Feist, "Sources: Jarrett Headed to White House, not Senate", CNN Politics, November 10, 2008; available online at: http://politicalticker.blogs.cnn.com/2008/11/10/sources-jarrett-headed-to-white-house-not-senate/?fbid=ivVY8v3cmqK [accessed March 28, 2010].

[29] David A. Patten, "Blagojevich Scandal: What did Obama Know, and when did He Know it?", Newsmax.com; December 9, 2008; available online at: http://newsmax.com/Newsfront/Blagojevich-Indictment/2008/12/09/id/327018 [accessed March 28, 2010].

[30] Susan Davis, "SEIU's Stern Tops White House Visitor List", Wall Street Journal, October 30, 2009; available online at: http://blogs.wsj.com/washwire/2009/10/30/seius-stern-tops-white-house-visitor-list/tab/article/ [accessed March 28, 2010].

[31] Natasha Korecki and Abdon M. Pallasch, "Illinois Governor Rod Blagojevich Taken into Federal Custody", Chicago Sun-Times, December 9, 2010; available online at: http://www.suntimes.com/news/metro/blagojevich/1321300,rod-blagojevich-illinois-governor-custody-120908.article [accessed March 28, 2010].

[32] Ibid.

[33] "TV Station Reported Obama Met with Blagojevich", World Net Daily, December 10, 2008; available online at: http://www.wnd.com/index.php?pageId=83240 [accessed March 28, 2010].

[34] Ibid.

[35] Ibid.

[36] "Judicial Watch Obtains Documents Re: Blagojevich Contacts with Obama and Transition Team", Judicial Watch, January 5, 2009; available online at: http://www.judicialwatch.org/news/2009/jan/judicial-watch-obtains-documents-re-blagojevich-contacts-obama-and-transition-team [accessed March 28, 2010].

[37] Jake Tapper, "Questions Arise about the Obama/Blagojevich Relationship", ABC News, December 9, 2008; available online at:

http://blogs.abcnews.com/politicalpunch/2008/12/questions-arise.html [accessed April 3, 2010].

[38] Associated Press, "Sen. Obama Dogged by Tony Rezko Connection", Newsmax.com, June 12, 2007; available online at: http://archive.newsmax.com/archives/articles/2007/6/11/154620.shtml [accessed March 29, 2010].

[39] Freedom Fighter, "Obama's Connection with Nation of Islam", Joshuapundit, September 9, 2008; available online at: http://joshuapundit.blogspot.com/2008/09/obamas-connection-with-nation-of-islam.html [accessed March 29, 2010].

[40] Binyamin Appelbaum, "Obama Haunted by Friend's Help Securing Dream House", Boston Globe, March 16, 2008; available online at: http://www.boston.com/news/nation/articles/2008/03/16/obama_haunted_by_frie nds_help_securing_dream_house/?page=1 [accessed April 3, 2010].

[41] Tim Novak, "How Reform-Minded City Hall Critic Became a Cozy Insider", Chicago Sun-Times, November 11, 2007; available online at: http://www.suntimes.com/news/politics/644511,CST-NWS-davis11.article [accessed March 29, 2010].

[42] Ibid.

[43] Ken Timmerman, "Obama's Early Campaigns Financed by Lobbyists", Newsmax.com, September 8, 2008; available online at: http://newsmax.com/KenTimmerman/obama-campaign-lobbyists/2009/12/14/id/342450 [accessed April 3, 2010].

[44] "Tony Rezko", DiscovertheNetworks.org, copyright 2003-2009; available online at: http://www.discoverthenetworks.org/Articles/Rezkoupdate.html [accessed March 28, 2010].

[45] Sammy Benoit, "When Obama/Jarrett and Rezko Faked the Poor into Sub-Standard Real Estate Deals", The Lid, September 30, 2009; available online at: http://yidwithlid.blogspot.com/2009/09/when-obama-jarrett-and-rezko-faked-poor.html [accessed March 29, 2010].

[46] Tim Novak, Chris Fusco, Dave McKinney, and Carol Marin, "More Rezko Dough Found", Chicago Sun-Times, March 16, 2008; available online at: http://www.suntimes.com/news/politics/obama/844455,CST-NWS-obama15.article [accessed March 29, 2010].

[47] Pringle, "Pringle Cliff Notes: Curtain Time for Barack Obama – Part 2 (Planning Board Scheme)", op. cit.

[48] Benoit, "When Obama/Jarrett and Rezko Faked the Poor into Sub-Standard Real Estate Deals", op. cit.

[49] Tim Novak, "Obama and His Rezko Ties", Chicago Sun-Times, April 23, 2007; available online at: http://www.suntimes.com/news/metro/353829,CST-NWS-rez23.article [accessed June 4, 2010].

[50] Andrew Walden, "Obama's Iraqi Oil for Food Connection", American Thinker, March 6, 2008; available online at: http://www.americanthinker.com/2008/03/obamas_iraqi_oil_for_food_conn.html [accessed March 29, 2010].

[51] Aaron Klein, "Obama Tied to Iraqi Government Fraud?", World Net Daily, July 30, 2008; available online at: http://www.wnd.com/?pageId=70972 [accessed June 4, 2010].

[52] Tim Novak & Chris Fusco, "Rezko's $50 Mil. Iraq Deal", Chicago Sun-Times, August 7, 2007; available online at: http://www.suntimes.com/news/metro/499796,CST-NWS-rezko07.article [accessed March 22, 2010].

[53] James Glanz, "Escaped Minister Says He Fled Iraqi Jail 'the Chicago Way'", The New York Times, December 20, 2006; available online at: http://www.nytimes.com/2006/12/20/world/middleeast/20minister.html [accessed March 29, 2010].

[54] Corsi, The Obama Nation, p. 174.

[55] Evelyn Pringle, "Pringle Cliff Notes: Curtain Time for Barack Obama – Part 1 (Iraq Connections)", Rezko Watch, May 27, 2008; available online at: http://rezkowatch.blogspot.com/2008/05/pringle-cliff-notes-curtain-time-for.html [accessed March 31, 2010].

[56] Corsi, The Obama Nation, p. 174.

[57] Aaron Klein, "Obama's 'Fraud' Associate to Run for Iraqi Parliament", World Net Daily, December 13, 2009; available online at: http://www.wnd.com/index.php/%3Chttp://www.wnd.com/The%20http://superstore.wnd.com/store/index.php/index.php?fa=PAGE.printable&pageId=118945 [accessed June 5, 2010].

[58] Chris Fusco, "Obama to Donate Funds Received from Rezko Friend", Chicago Sun-Times, April 29, 2008; available online at: http://www.suntimes.com/news/politics/obama/920701,CST-NWS-obama29WEB.article [accessed March 29, 2010].

[59] Brenda J. Elliot, "Good News for Rezko, Bad News for Obama. Kicking the Rezko Can Further down the Road (Updated)", RBO, August 20, 2008; available online at: http://therealbarackobama.wordpress.com/2008/08/20/good-news-for-rezko-bad-news-for-obama-kicking-the-rezko-can-further-down-the-road/ [March 29, 2010].

[60] Lee Cary, "Obama and Daley's Public Housing Plan", American Thinker, September 23, 2008; available online at: http://www.americanthinker.com/2008/09/obama_and_daleys_public_housin.html [accessed March 29, 2010].

[61] Corsi, The Obama Nation, p. 162.

[62] Novak, "Obama's Letters for Rezko", op. cit.

[63] "Bill Ayers and Bernardine Dohrn", The Obama File, op. cit.

[64] Tim Novak, "Obama Helped Ex-Boss Get $1 Mil. from Charity", Chicago Sun-Times, November 29, 2007; available online at: http://www.suntimes.com/news/watchdogs/672314,CST-NWS-watchdog29.article [accessed April 3, 2010].

[65] "Follow the Money: Obama's Ex-Boss = Rezko Business Partner (Updated)", Rezko Watch, February 7, 2008; available online at: http://rezkowatch.blogspot.com/2008/02/obamas-ex-boss-rezko-business-partner.html [accessed March 29, 2010].

[66] S.S.M., "Sun-Times Omitted Key Information in Suggesting Obama Conflict of Interest", Media Matters for America, November 29, 2007; available online at: http://mediamatters.org/research/200711290009 [accessed March 29, 2010].

[67] Richard Henry Lee, "Obama and the Woods Fund of Chicago", American Thinker, July 7, 2008; available online at: http://www.americanthinker.com/2008/07/obama_and_the_woods_fund_of_ch.html [accessed March 29, 2010].

[68] Ibid.

[69] Tim Novak, "Obama's Letters to Rezko", Chicago Sun-Times, June 13, 2007; available online at: http://www.suntimes.com/news/politics/425305,CST-NWS-obama13.article [accessed March 29, 2010].

[70] Novak, "Obama and His Rezko Ties", op. cit.

[71] Binyamin Appelbaum, "Grim Proving Ground for Obama's Housing Policy", The Boston Globe, June 27, 2008; available online at: http://www.boston.com/news/nation/articles/2008/06/27/grim_proving_ground_for_obamas_housing_policy/?page=1 [accessed March 31, 2010].

[72] Malkin, Culture of Corruption, p. 51-52.

[73] Appelbaum, "Grim Proving Ground for Obama's Housing Policy", op. cit.

[74] M.J. Stephey & Claire Suddath, "Valerie Jarrett", Time, November 11, 2008; available online at: http://www.time.com/time/politics/article/0,8599,1858012,00.html [accessed April 30, 2010].

[75] Tom Fitton, "JW's 'Ten Most Corrupt Politicians' of 2008", January 2, 2009; available online at: http://www.judicialwatch.org/weeklyupdate/2009/01-jws-ten-most-corrupt-politicians-2008 [accessed March 31, 2010].

[76] Chelsea Schilling, "What Happened to Michelle Obama's Law License", World Net Daily, August 4, 2009; available online at: http://www.wnd.com/?pageId=105998 [accessed March 31, 2010].

[77] Brenda J. Elliot, "Did Rezko Help Obama Buy His House (4 Updates)?", RBO, April 21, 2008; available online at: http://therealbarackobama.wordpress.com/2008/04/21/did-rezko-help-obama-buy-his-house-4-updates/ [accessed June 6, 2010].

[78] Lee Cary, "Obama and South Chicago Slum Developers", American Thinker, September 12, 2008; available online at: http://www.americanthinker.com/2008/09/obama_and_south_chicago_slum_d.html [accessed March 31, 2010].

[79] Appelbaum, "Grim Proving Ground for Obama's Housing Policy", op. cit.

[80] Ibid.

[81] Ibid.

[82] Meredith Jessup, "Obama's Olympic Bid: The Chicago Way", Townhall.com, September 29, 2009; available online at: http://townhall.com/blog/g/3847a38b-1202-4645-a8ad-98ca26743c86 [accessed March 31, 2010].

[83] Kim Chipman, "Senator Obama says He has Chosen a Vice President (Update 2)", Bloomberg.com, August 21, 2008; available online at: http://www.bloomberg.com/apps/news?pid=20601087&sid=ab7jy_RX83Do&refer=home [accessed March 31, 2010].

[84] Corsi, *The Obama Nation*, p. 165.

[85] Tim Novak, "8 Things You Need to Know about Obama and Rezko", Chicago Sun-Times, January 24, 2008; available online at: http://www.suntimes.com/news/watchdogs/757340,CST-NWS-watchdog24.article [accessed March 31, 2010].

[86] Ibid.

[87] Ray Gibson and David Jackson, "Rezko Owns Vacant Lot Next to Obama's Home", Chicago Tribune, November 1, 2006; available online at: http://blogs.chicagotribune.com/news_columnists_ezorn/2008/01/obama-gives-rez.html [accessed April 2, 2010].

[88] John Chase, "Tony Rezko", Chicago Tribune, May 26, 2005; available online at: http://articles.chicagotribune.com/2005-05-26/news/0505260217_1_blagojevich-administration-tony-rezko-rod-blagojevich [accessed June 5, 2010].

[89] Jerome R. Corsi, "Rezko Attorney 'Owns' Obama Mansion", World Net Daily, December 25, 2008; available online at: http://www.wnd.com/index.php?pageId=84101 [accessed March 31, 2010].

[90] Ibid.

[91] Jerome R. Corsi, "Fitzgerald Renews Interest in Rezko-Obama Deal", World Net Daily, December 15, 2008; available online at: http://www.wnd.com/index.php?pageId=83760 [accessed March 31, 2010].

[92] Ibid.

[93] Ibid.

[94] Corsi, *The Obama Nation*, p.166.

[95] Appelbaum, "Obama Haunted by Friend's Help Securing Dream House", op. cit.

[96] Fredrick, *The Obama Timeline*, p. 110.

[97] "Follow the Money: The Rezko Lot 2 (Updates/Questions Added)", Rezko Watch, February 10, 2008; available online at: http://rezkowatch.blogspot.com/2008/02/follow-money-rezko-lot.html [accessed March 31, 2010].

[98] Corsi, *The Obama Nation*, p. 172

[99] Ibid.

[100] "Obama Bagman is Sent to Jail after Failing to Declare $3.5M Payment by British Tycoon", Times Online, February 1, 2008; available online at: http://www.timesonline.co.uk/tol/news/world/us_and_americas/us_elections/article3284825.ece [accessed March 31, 2010].

[101] Walden, "Obama's Syrian Connection", op. cit.

[102] Rick Moran, "What You didn't Know about Obama and Rezko", Pajamas Media, February 28, 2008; available online at: http://pajamasmedia.com/blog/what_you_didnt_know_about_obam/ [accessed June 6, 2010].

[103] Ed Morrissey, "Obama Met Auchi through Rezko in 2004", Hot Air, April 14, 2008; available online at: http://hotair.com/archives/2008/04/14/obama-met-auchi-through-rezko-in-2004/ [accessed March 21, 2010].

[104] Evelyn Pringle, "Pringle Cliff Notes: Curtain Time for Barack Obama – Part 3 (Nobody Knows Auchi)", Rezko Watch, May 29, 2008; available online at: http://rezkowatch.blogspot.com/2008/05/pringle-cliff-notes-curtain-time-for_29.html [accessed March 31, 2010].

[105] "Follow the Money: Auchi's Money, Rezko's Lot, Obama's House (Updated)", Rezko Watch, February 25, 2008; available online at: http://rezkowatch.blogspot.com/2008/02/follow-money-auchis-money-rezkos-lot.html [accessed June 6, 2010].

[106] Corsi, *The Obama Nation*, p. 172.

[107] Olandug, "Buying Obama – The Auchi Connection", Best Syndication, April 4, 2008; available online at: http://www.bestsyndication.com/?q=20080407_barack_obama_connections_to_middle_east_commentary.htm [accessed March 31, 2010].

[108] Brenda J. Elliot, "Nadhmi Auchi and the Leaked DoD IG Report", RBO, September 23, 2008; available online at: http://therealbarackobama.wordpress.com/2008/09/23/nadhmi-auchi-and-the-leaked-dod-ig-report/ [accessed March 31, 2010].

[109] "Follow the Money: The Rezko Lot (2 Updates/Questions added)", Rezko Watch, op. cit.

[110] John Chase, "Major Fundraiser for Ex. Gov. Rod Blagojevich Resigns from Bank", Chicago Tribune, February 26, 2009; available online at: http://articles.chicagotribune.com/2009-02-26/news/0902250965_1_mutual-bank-rod-blagojevich-resignation [accessed June 4, 2010].

[111] Ibid.

[112] Malkin, *Culture of Corruption*, p. 162.

[113] "FEC Investigation Confirms Obama Received Discount Mortgage", Judicial Watch, February 9, 2009; available online at: http://www.judicialwatch.org/news/2009/feb/fec-investigation-confirms-obama-received-discount-mortgage [accessed March 31, 2010].

[114] Kenneth Vogel, "No Mortgage Pinch for Obama, Team", CBS News, March 7, 2009; available online at: http://www.cbsnews.com/stories/2009/03/08/politics/politico/main4852092.shtml [accessed April 3, 2010].

[115] "FEC Investigation Confirms Obama Received Discount Mortgage", Judicial Watch, op. cit.

[116] "Complete Transcript of the Sun-Times Interview with Barack Obama", The Chicago Sun-Times, March 15, 2008; available online at: http://www.suntimes.com/news/politics/obama/844597,transcript031508.article [accessed March 31, 2010].

[117] Pringle, "Pringle Cliff Notes: Curtain Time for Barack Obama – Part 2 (Planning Board Scheme)", op. cit.

[118] Ibid.

[119] "Complete Transcript of the Sun-Times Interview with Barack Obama", The Chicago Sun-Times, op. cit.

[120] "Must Read! Do We Really Know Our Democratic Presidential Candidate Barrack (sic) Obama.", Baiganchoka, November 1, 2008; available online at:

http://www.baiganchoka.com/blog/must-read-do-we-really-know-our-democratic-presidential-candidate-barack-obama/ [accessed April 30, 2010].
[121] Fusco, "Obama to Donate Funds Received from Rezko Friend", op. cit.
[122] Evelyn Pringle, "Barack Obama – The Wizard of Oz", Countercurrents.org, March 28, 2008; available online at: http://www.countercurrents.org/pringle280308.htm [accessed March 31, 2010].
[123] David Catron, "Pay-to-Play Politics, the SEIU and Obamacare", American Thinker, January 6, 2009; available online at: http://www.americanthinker.com/2009/01/paytoplay_politics_the_seiu_an.html [accessed March 31, 2010].
[124] Freddoso, The Case Against Barack Obama, p. 213.
[125] Walden, "Obama's Syrian Connection", op. cit.

Chapter Eight

[1] Jim Simpson, "The Cloward-Piven Strategy, Part II: Barack Obama and the Strategy of Manufactured Crisis", American Daughter, September 29, 2008; available online at: http://frontpage.americandaughter.com/?p=1999 [accessed March 31, 2010].
[2] Gary Wood, "Acorn Embraces Marxist Principles", Examiner.com, March 26, 2009; available online at: http://www.examiner.com/x-4285-Salt-Lake-Nonpartisan-Examiner~y2009m3d26-ACORN-embraces-Marxist-principles [accessed March 31, 2010].
[3] "Association of Community Organizations for Reform Now (ACORN)", DiscovertheNetworks.org, copyright 2003-2009; available online at: http://www.discoverthenetworks.org/groupProfile.asp?grpid=6968 [accessed March 31, 2010].
[4] "Cloward-Piven Strategy (CPS)", DiscovertheNetworks.org, copyright 2003-2009; available online at: http://www.discoverthenetworks.org/groupprofile.asp?grpid=7522 [accessed March 31, 2010].
[5] Horowitz and Poe, The Shadow Party, p.106.
[6] Ibid.
[7] Ibid.
[8] Ibid., p. 107-108.
[9] Ibid.
[10] Simpson, "Barack Obama and the Strategy of Manufactured Crisis", op. cit.
[11] "Cloward-Piven Strategy (CPS)", DiscovertheNetworks.org, op. cit.
[12] Horowitz and Poe, The Shadow Party, p. 108-109.
[13] Ibid., p. 109.
[14] "George Alvin Wiley", DiscovertheNetworks.org, copyright 2003-2009; available online at: http://www.discoverthenetworks.org/individualProfile.asp?indid=1769 [accessed April 1, 2010].
[15] Horowitz and Poe, The Shadow Party, p. 110.

[16] "John V. Lindsay", Knowledgerush, copyright 2009; available online at: http://www.knowledgerush.com/kr/encyclopedia/John_V._Lindsay/ [accessed April 5, 2010].

[17] Mary L. Wissler, "Lindsay: Dilemmas of Policy and Politics", The Harvard Crimson, October 3, 1966; available online at: http://www.thecrimson.com/article/1966/10/3/lindsay-dilemmas-of-policy-and-politics/ [accessed April 5, 2010].

[18] Steven Malanga, "The Myth of the Working Poor", City Journal, Autumn 2004; available online at: http://www.city-journal.org/html/14_4_working_poor.html [accessed April 1, 2010].

[19] "Cloward-Piven Strategy (CPS)", DiscovertheNetworks.org, op. cit.

[20] Horowitz and Poe, The Shadow Party, p. 112.

[21] Ibid.

[22] Sol Stern, "ACORNs Nutty Regime for Cities", City Journal, Spring 2003; available online at: http://www.city-journal.org/html/13_2_acorns_nutty_regime.html [accessed April 1, 2010].

[23] Horowitz and Poe, The Shadow Party, p. 113-114.

[24] James Walsh, "Obama, Voter Fraud & Mortgage Meltdown", Newsmax.com, September 22, 2008; available online at: http://newsmax.com/Politics/obama-voter-fraud/2008/09/22/id/325456 [accessed April 1, 2010].

[25] Horowitz and Poe, The Shadow Party, p. 110.

[26] Ibid., p.123.

[27] Ibid.

[28] Ibid., p.124.

[29] "Association of Community Organizations for Reform Now (ACORN)", DiscovertheNetworks.org, op. cit.

[30] John Atlas and Peter Dreier, "Enraging the Right", NHI, Issue #129, May/June 2003; available online at: http://www.nhi.org/online/issues/129/ACORN.html [accessed April 1, 2010].

[31] Horowitz and Poe, The Shadow Party, p. 126.

[32] Ibid.

[33] Ibid.

[34] Ibid., p. 122.

[35] Alinsky, Rules for Radicals, p. 138.

[36] Walsh, "Obama, Voter Fraud & Mortgage Meltdown", op. cit.

[37] "Who is ACORN", ACORN, copyright 1999-2008; available online at: http://www.acorn.org/index.php?id=12342 [accessed April 1, 2010].

[38] "Project Vote (PV)", DiscovertheNetworks.org, copyright 2003-2009; available online at: http://www.discoverthenetworks.org/groupProfile.asp?grpid=6966 [accessed April 1, 2010].

[39] Horowitz and Poe, The Shadow Party, p. 126.

[40] Ibid., p. 127.

[41] Simpson, "Barack Obama and the Strategy of Manufactured Crisis", op. cit.

[42] Horowitz and Poe, The Shadow Party, p.127.

[43] "More ACORN Voter Fraud in Ohio", The Traditional Values Coalition, October 9, 2008; available online at: http://www.traditionalvalues.org/read/3433/more-acorn-voter-fraud-in-ohio/ [accessed April 5, 2010].

[44] McQ, "So that's what Community Organizers do", The QandO Blog, October 8, 2008; available online at: http://www.qando.net/details.aspx?entry=9461 [accessed April 1, 2010].

[45] Nancy Matthis, "The Vote Fraud Chronicles – Mississippi", American Daughter, October 29, 2008; available online at: http://frontpage.americandaughter.com/?tag=registered-voters [accessed April 2, 2010].

[46] "The ACORN Indictments", The Wall Street Journal, November 3, 2006; available online at: http://www.opinionjournal.com/editorial/feature.html?id=110009189 [accessed April 2, 2010].

[47] Michelle Malkin, "The ACORN Obama Knows", National Review Online, June 25, 2008; available online at: http://article.nationalreview.com/361584/the-acorn-obama-knows/michelle-malkin [accessed April 3, 2010].

[48] Oskar Garcia, "Las Vegas ACORN Office Raided in Voter-Fraud Probe", Chron, October 7, 2008; available online at: http://www.chron.com/disp/story.mpl/front/6045904.html [accessed April 3, 2010].

[49] Devvy Kid, "Going to the Polls November 5, 2002", Devvy, October 29, 2002; available online at: http://www.devvy.com/~devvy/polls_20021029.html [accessed April 17, 2010].

[50] Alan Choate, "ACORN Voter Registration Drive Nets Charges", Las Vegas Review-Journal, May 4, 2009; available online at: http://www.lvrj.com/news/breaking_news/44307912.html [accessed April 3, 2010].

[51] Mary Manning, "Criminal Charges Filed against ACORN, Two Employees", Las Vegas Sun, May 4, 2009; available online at: http://www.lasvegassun.com/news/2009/may/04/criminal-charges-filed-against-acorn-two-employees/ [accessed April 3, 2010].

[52] Molly Ball, "Rising Registration: New Voter Sign-Ups Up", Las Vegas Review-Journal, July 7, 2008; available online at: http://www.lvrj.com/news/24004424.html [accessed April 3, 2010].

[53] "Nevada Files New Voter Registration Charges against ACORN", FoxNews.com, May 6, 2009; available online at: http://www.foxnews.com/story/0,2933,519155,00.html [accessed April 3, 2010].

[54] Choate, "ACORN Voter Registration Drive Nets Charges", op. cit.

[55] "Wade Rathke", DiscovertheNetworks.org, copyright 2003-2009; available online at: http://www.discoverthenetworks.org/individualProfile.asp?indid=1773 [accessed April 1, 2010].

[56] Horowitz and Poe, The Shadow Party, p. 125-126.

[57] Ed Barnes, "States' Secretaries of State are Tipping Balance of Power", FoxNews.com, February 1, 2010; available online at:

http://www.foxnews.com/politics/2010/01/29/states-secretaries-state-tipping-balance-power/ [accessed April 5, 2010].
[58] "Secretary of State Project", Ballotpedia, modified January 13, 2010; available online at: http://www.ballotpedia.org/wiki/index.php/Secretary_of_State_Project [accessed April 1, 2010].
[59] Bill Turner, "Secretary of State Project", The Cypress Times, February 24, 2010; available online at:
http://www.thecypresstimes.com/article/Columnists/Bill_Turner/SECRETARY_OF_STATE_PROJECT/27974 [accessed April 1, 2010].
[60] Barnes, "States' Secretaries of State are Tipping Balance", op. cit.
[61] Kevin Hassett, "How the Democrats Created the Financial Crisis", Bloomberg.com, September 22, 2008; available online at:
http://www.bloomberg.com/apps/news?pid=newsarchive&sid=aSKSoiNbnQY0 [accessed April 4, 2010].
[62] Simpson, "Barack Obama and the Strategy of Manufactured Crisis", op. cit.
[63] Ibid.
[64] Ibid.
[65] Ibid.
[66] Stanley Kurtz, "Planting Seeds of Disaster", National Review Online, October 7, 2008; available online at: http://article.nationalreview.com/374045/planting-seeds-of-disaster/stanley-kurtz [accessed April 3, 2010].
[67] Matthew Vadum, "Financial Affirmative Action", The American Spectator, September 29, 2008; available online at:
http://spectator.org/archives/2008/09/29/financial-affirmative-action [accessed April 3, 2010].
[68] Hassett, "How the Democrats Created the Financial Crisis", op. cit.
[69] Tula Connell, "FDL Book Salon Welcomes Wade Rathke, Citizen Wealth", FDL, August 23, 2009; available online at:
http://firedoglake.com/2009/08/23/fdl-book-salon-welcomes-wade-rathke-citizen-wealth-winning-the-campaign-to-save-working-families/ [accessed April 3, 2010].
[70] Stanley Kurtz, "Inside Obama's ACORN", National Review Online, May 29, 2008; available online at: http://article.nationalreview.com/358910/inside-obamas-acorn/stanley-kurtz [accessed April 3, 2010].
[71] Freddoso, The Case Against Barack Obama, p. 149.
[72] Connie Hair, "ACORN Whistleblowers Produce Shocking Testimony on Capitol Hill", Human Events, March 23, 2009; available online at:
http://www.humanevents.com/article.php?id=31172 [accessed April 3, 2010].
[73] Malkin, Culture of Corruption, p. 246.
[74] Hair, "ACORN Whistleblowers Produce Shocking Testimony on Capitol Hill", op. cit.
[75] Publius, "ACORN Oklahoma Document Dump: ACORN's Doorknocking Basics", Big Government, November 24, 2009; available online at:
http://biggovernment.com/publius/2009/11/24/acorn-oklahoma-document-dump-acorns-doorknocking-basics/ [accessed April 4, 2010].

[76] Joshua Rhett Miller, "Arrest Made in Home Foreclosure Civil Disobedience Program", FoxNews.com, February 23, 2009; available online at: http://www.foxnews.com/story/0,2933,498669,00.html [accessed April 3, 2010].

[77] Ibid.

[78] Simpson, "Barack Obama and the Strategy of Manufactured Crisis", op. cit.

[79] Michelle Malkin, "Kill the Bailout: More ACORN Funding?!", Michelle Malkin, September 25, 2008; available online at: http://michellemalkin.com/2008/09/25/kill-the-bailout-more-acorn-funding/ [accessed April 3, 2010].

[80] Bob Unruh, "ACORN 'Shock Troops' Tied to Election Crimes", World Net Daily, October 30, 2008; available online at: http://www.wnd.com/index.php?pageId=79430 [accessed April 3, 2010].

[81] Christopher Chantrill, "Minimum Wage Hits $9.50 in Santa Fe", American Thinker, January 26, 2006; available online at: http://www.americanthinker.com/2006/01/minimum_wage_hits_950_in_santa.ht ml [accessed April 3, 2010].

[82] "Report: Is ACORN Intentionally Structured as a Criminal Enterprise?", Oversight and Government Reform, July 23, 2009; available online at: http://republicans.oversight.house.gov/index.php?option=com_content&view=art icle&id=3%3Areport-is-acorn-intentionally-structured-as-a-criminal-enterprise&catid=21&Itemid=5 [accessed April 5, 2010].

[83] Ibid.

[84] Matthew Vadum, "The Powers that Be", The American Spectator, June 30, 2009; available online at: http://spectator.org/archives/2009/06/30/the-powers-that-be [accessed April 4, 2010].

[85] "ACORN Protected By 'Powers that Be'", Steve King United States Congressman, June 26, 2009; available online at: http://steveking.house.gov/index.cfm?FuseAction=Newsroom.PressReleases&Co ntentRecord_id=1d608177-19b9-b4b1-12af-c4d07a126daa&Region_id=&CFTOKEN=82801898&IsTextOnly=False [accessed April 4, 2010].

[86] "List of 361 ACORN Council Affiliates, Subsidiaries, and Allied Organizations", U.S. Department of Energy, July 23, 2009; available online at: http://management.energy.gov/documents/Flash2010-06Attachment.pdf [accessed April 4, 2010].

[87] John Fund, "More ACORN Voter Fraud comes to Light", Wall Street Journal, May 9, 2009; available online at: http://online.wsj.com/article/SB124182750646102435.html [accessed April 4, 2010].

[88] "Testimony of Heather S. Heidelbaugh, Esquire", Committee on the Judiciary, March 19, 2009; available online at: http://judiciary.house.gov/hearings/pdf/Heidelbaugh090319.pdf [accessed April 5, 2010].

[89] Ibid.

[90] Ibid.

[91] Ibid.

[92] Ibid.

[93] Ibid.

[94] Mr. Harrington, "Folks, the ACORN Fraud is Unraveling", The Harrington Report, May 12, 2009; available online at: http://harringtonreport.com/2009/05/12/folks-the-acorn-fraud-is-unraveling/ [accessed April 4, 2010].

[95] Matthew Vadum, "Huffington Post Covers up Obama's ACORN Roots", Canada Free Press, October 4, 2008; available online at: http://www.canadafreepress.com/index.php/article/5375 [accessed April 4, 2010].

[96] "Barack Hussein Obama", DiscovertheNetworks.org, op. cit.

[97] Corsi, The Obama Nation, p. 134.

[98] Lowell Ponte, "Clever Obama Tries to Bury ACORN Past", Newsmax.com, October 13, 2008; available online at: http://newsmax.com/InsideCover/obama-acorn-organizer/2008/10/13/id/325885 [accessed April 4, 2010].

[99] "Association of Community Organizations for Reform Now (ACORN)", DiscovertheNetworks.org, op. cit.

[100] Julie, "Barack Obama's Involvement with ACORN Unearthed, Missing Article Recovered", The Cleveland Leader, October 9, 2008; available online at: http://www.clevelandleader.com/node/7203 [accessed April 5, 2010].

[101] "Madeline Talbott", BarackBook, copyright 2008; available online at: http://www.barackbook.com/Profiles/MadelineTalbott.htm [accessed April 5, 2010].

[102] Chelsea Schilling, "Unearthed! Obama's Twisted ACORN Roots", World Net Daily, September 18, 2009; available online at: http://www.wnd.com/index.php?pageId=110131 [accessed April 4, 2010].

[103] Richard Poe, "Project Vote: Extended Profile", DiscovertheNetworks.org, 2005; available online at: http://www.discoverthenetworks.org/Articles/pvextprofile.html [accessed June 11, 2010].

[104] "Thomas", The Library of Congress, last major action September 20, 2005; available online at: http://thomas.loc.gov/cgi-bin/bdquery/?&Db=d109&querybd=@FIELD(FLD003+@4((@1(Sen+Obama++Barack))+01763)) [accessed April 4, 2010].

[105] "Congress Tries to Fix what it Broke", Investors.com, September 17, 2008; available online at: http://www.investors.com/NewsAndAnalysis/Article.aspx?id=490605 [accessed April 4, 2010].

[106] Iusbvision, "Obama Sued Citibank under CRA to Force it to Make Bad Loans – Update)", The IUSB Vision Weblog, September 30, 2008; available online at: http://iusbvision.wordpress.com/2008/09/30/obama-sued-citibank-under-cra-to-force-it-to-make-bad-loans/ [April 4, 2010].

[107] Lee, "Obama and the Woods Fund of Chicago", op. cit.

[108] Sammy Benoit, "ACORN, Obama, and the Banking Meltdown", The Lid, September 29, 2008; available online at: http://yidwithlid.blogspot.com/2008/09/acorn-obama-and-banking-meltdown.html [accessed April 4, 2010].

[109] Jerome R. Corsi, "Fannie Mae, Freddie Mac Execs now Offering Advice to Obama", World Net Daily, September 17, 2008; available online at: http://www.wnd.com/index.php?pageId=75586 [accessed April 4, 2010].

[110] Juliana Goldman, "Johnson Quits Obama's Vice Presidential Search Team", Bloomberg.com, June 11, 2008; available online at: http://www.bloomberg.com/apps/news?pid=20601087&sid=auHZ.1T7m1gw [accessed April 5, 2010].

[111] Malkin, *Culture of Corruption*, p. 163.

[112] Simpson, "Barack Obama and the Strategy of Manufactured Crisis", op. cit.

[113] Jack Kelly, "Raines, Obama, and the Media", Real Clear Politics, September 23, 2008; available online at: http://www.realclearpolitics.com/articles/2008/09/how_close_are_raines_and_obama.html [accessed June 11, 2010].

[114] "Text – Obama Speech on Home Mortgage Crisis", Reuters, February 18, 2009; available online at: http://www.reuters.com/article/idUSN1844161820090218 [accessed April 4, 2010].

[115] Horowitz, *Barack Obama's Rules for Revolution*, p. 15.

[116] Murdock, "Obama Squirrels Away His Links to ACORN", op. cit.

[117] Aaron Klein, "Obama Website Lies about ACORN Ties", World Net Daily, October 12, 2008; available online at: http://www.wnd.com/index.php?pageId=77813 [accessed April 4, 2010].

[118] Ibid.

[119] Matt Wolking, "Obama Advised by ACORN Leaders on Foreclosure Solutions Update", Wolking's World, October 14, 2008; available online at: http://mattwolking.com/2008/10/14/obama-advised-by-acorn-leaders-on-foreclosure-solutions/ [accessed April 4, 2010].

[120] Michelle Malkin, "ACORN Watch, PT II: Obama Hid $800,000 Payment to ACORN through 'Citizen Services, Inc.'", Michelle Malkin, August 22, 2008; available online at: http://michellemalkin.com/2008/08/22/acorn-watch-pt-ii-obama-hid-800000-payment-to-acorn-through-citizen-services-inc/ [accessed August 22, 2008].

[121] Malkin, *Culture of Corruption*, p. 237.

[122] Eastan McNeal, "Money Laundering Scandal? (Updated + Thursday Evening Update)", August 20, 2008; available online at: http://www.noquarterusa.net/blog/2008/08/20/money-laundering-scandal/ [accessed April 4, 2010].

[123] Malkin, "ACORN Watch, Pt II: Obama Hid $800,000 Payment to ACORN through 'Citizen Services, Inc.'", op. cit.

[124] Ibid.

[125] Ibid.

[126] Toni Foulkes, "Case Study: Chicago-The Barack Obama Campaign", DiscovertheNetworks.org, copyright 2003-2006; available online at: http://www.discoverthenetworks.org/Articles/Chicago%20The%20Barack%20Obama%20Campaign.html [accessed April 5, 2010].

[127] Obama, *The Audacity of Hope*, p. 124.

[128] "Joseph Stalin", Wikiquote, modified March 16, 2010; available online at: http://en.wikiquote.org/wiki/Joseph_Stalin [accessed April 4, 2010].

[129] Malkin, "The ACORN Obama Knows", op. cit.

[130] Matthew Vadum, "ACORN's Stimulus", The American Spectator, January 27, 2009; available online at: http://spectator.org/archives/2009/01/27/acorns-stimulus [accessed April 5, 2010].

[131] Malkin, Culture of Corruption, p. 233.

[132] Stephen Dinan, "Exclusive: Minn. Lawmaker Vows not to Complete Census", Washington Times, June 17, 2009; available online at: http://www.washingtontimes.com/news/2009/jun/17/exclusive-minn-lawmaker-fears-census-abuse/ [accessed April 5, 2010].

[133] Ibid.

[134] Schilling, "Unearthed! Obama's Twisted ACORN Roots", op. cit.

[135] Ibid.

[136] Ibid.

[137] Ian Urbina, "Acorn on Brink of Bankruptcy, Officials Say", The New York Times, March 19, 2010; available online at: http://www.nytimes.com/2010/03/20/us/politics/20acorn.html [accessed April 30, 2010].

[138] Jonathan D. Salant, "Congress Votes to Cut U.S. ACORN Funds after Video", Bloomberg.com, September 18, 2009; available online at: http://www.bloomberg.com/apps/news?pid=20601087&sid=alHxUmFKCLC8 [accessed April 5, 2010].

[139] Aristotle the Hun, "Obama's 2011 Budget Allocates $4 Billion for ACORN", The Steady Drip, February 12, 2010; available online at: http://thesteadydrip.blogspot.com/2010/02/obamas-2011-budget-allocates-4-billion.html [accessed April 5, 2010].

[140] Peter Orszag, "Memorandum for the Heads of Executive Departments and Agencies", Whitehouse.gov, March 16, 2010; available online at: http://www.whitehouse.gov/omb/assets/memoranda_2010/m10-12.pdf [accessed April 5, 2010].

[141] Kevin Mooney, "ACORN Drops Tarnished Name and Moves to Silence Critics", The Washington Examiner, June 21, 2009; available online at: http://www.washingtonexaminer.com/opinion/blogs/beltway-confidential/ACORN-drops-tarnished-name-and-moves-to-silence-critics-48730537.html [accessed June 21, 2009].

[142] Ben Smith, "ACORN 'Dissolved as a National Structure'", Politico, February 22, 2010; available online at: http://www.politico.com/blogs/bensmith/0210/ACORN_dissolved_as_a_national_structure.html [accessed April 5, 2010].

[143] Matthew Vadum, "ACORN Official: Gangster Group will be Bankrupt Soon but Fake Spinoff Groups will Carry on the Corruption", Big Government, February 22, 2010; available online at: http://biggovernment.com/tag/alliance-of-californians-for-community-empowerment/ [accessed April 30, 2010].

[144] Ben Smith, "ACORN Folds", Politico.com, March 22, 2010; available online at: http://www.politico.com/blogs/bensmith/0310/Acorn_folds.html [accessed April 5, 2010].
[145] "Megyn Kelly – The Truth about A.C.O.R.N. – Interview with Wade Rathke", Youtube, October 2, 2009; available online at: http://www.youtube.com/watch?v=lPSFoxwNKmU&feature=player_embedded [accessed April 5, 2010].
[146] Ibid.
[147] Matthew Vadum, "Wrathful Wade Rathke", The American Spectator, July 16, 2009; available online at: http://spectator.org/archives/2009/07/16/wrathful-wade-rathke [accessed April 5, 2010].

Chapter Nine

[1] Rachel Ehrenfeld, "The Man Who would be Kingmaker, Part I", FrontPageMag.com, October 28, 2004; available online at: http://97.74.65.51/readArticle.aspx?ARTID=10796 [accessed April 7, 2010].
[2] Ralph Hostetter, "U.S. Govt, Soros Fund Offshore Drilling in Brazil", Newsmax.com, February 11, 2010; available online at: http://www.newsmax.com/hostetter/hostetter-Soros-Obama-economy/2010/02/11/id/349645 [accessed April 5, 2010].
[3] David Horowitz and Richard Poe, "The Shadow Party: Part I", FrontPageMag.com, October 6, 2004; available online at: http://97.74.65.51/readArticle.aspx?ARTID=11100 [accessed April 5, 2010].
[4] "Move On (MO)", DiscovertheNetworks.org, copyright 2003-2009; available online at: http://www.discoverthenetworks.org/groupProfile.asp?grpid=6201 [accessed April 5, 2010].
[5] Richard Poe, "Media Matters' Attack on the Shadow Party", FrontPageMag.com, October 30, 2006; available online at: http://97.74.65.51/readArticle.aspx?ARTID=1826 [accessed April 5, 2010].
[6] Lisa Smith, "George Soros: The Philosophy of an Elite Investor", Investopedia, copyright 2010; available online at: http://www.investopedia.com/articles/financial-theory/09/how-soros-does-it.asp [accessed April 5, 2010].
[7] Horowitz and Poe, The Shadow Party, p.87.
[8] Ibid.
[9] "The Greatest Investors: George Soros", Investopedia, copyright 2010; available online at: http://www.investopedia.com/university/greatest/georgesoros.asp [accessed April 4, 2010].
[10] "George Soros", Wikipedia, modified April 7, 2010; available online at: http://en.wikipedia.org/wiki/George_Soros [accessed April 7, 2010].
[11] Allen R. Myerson, "Currency Markets; When Soros Speaks, World Markets Listen", The New York Times, June 10, 1993; available online at:

http://www.nytimes.com/1993/06/10/business/currency-markets-when-soros-speaks-world-markets-listen.html?pagewanted=1 [accessed April 6, 2010].
[12] Ibid.

[13] Gretchen Morgenson, "International Business; Soros's Quantum Fund Losses in Russia Put at $2 Billion", The New York Times, August 27, 1998; available online at: http://www.nytimes.com/1998/08/27/business/international-business-soros-s-quantum-fund-losses-in-russia-put-at-2-billion.html?pagewanted=1 [accessed April 6, 2010].

[14] Horowitz and Poe, The Shadow Party, p. 5.

[15] Jim O'Neill, "Soros: Republic Enemy #1", Canada Free Press, September 15, 2009; available online at: http://www.canadafreepress.com/index.php/article/14700 [accessed April 6, 2010].

[16] Horowitz and Poe, The Shadow Party, p. 21.

[17] O'Neill, "Soros: Republic Enemy #1", op. cit.

[18] Ibid.

[19] "U.S. Financier behind Attacks on Asian Currencies", Google News, July 25, 1997; available online at: http://news.google.com/newspapers?nid=1370&dat=19970725&id=zJgVAAAAIBAJ&sjid=9woEAAAAIBAJ&pg=2533,2574428 [accessed April 6, 2010].

[20] Kyle-Anne Shiver, "George Soros and the Alchemy of 'Regime Change'", American Thinker, February 27, 2008; available online at: http://www.americanthinker.com/2008/02/george_soros_and_the_alchemy_o.html [accessed April 5, 2010].

[21] O'Neill, "Soros: Republic Enemy #1", op. cit.

[22] Dr. Vera Butler, "George Soros – Mr. Lucifer", Northstar Compass, n.d.; available online at: http://www.northstarcompass.org/nsc0209/soros.htm [accessed April 6, 2010].

[23] Horowitz and Poe, The Shadow Party, p.67.

[24] Ibid., p. 67-68.

[25] Horowitz and Poe, The Shadow Party, p.68.

[26] "The Open Society and its Enemies", Wikipedia, modified February 7, 2010; available online at: http://en.wikipedia.org/wiki/The_Open_Society_and_Its_Enemies [accessed April 7, 2010].

[27] Horowitz and Poe, The Shadow Party, p.68.

[28] Ibid.

[29] Ibid., p.3.

[30] Brother Nathanael Kapner, "The Obama/Soros Plan to Destroy America", Real Zionist News, June 29, 2009; available online at: http://www.realzionistnews.com/?p=411 [accessed April 7, 2010].

[31] Ibid.

[32] Horowitz and Poe, The Shadow Party, p.22.

[33] "George Soros", DiscovertheNetworks.org, copyright 2003-2009; available online at: http://www.discoverthenetworks.org/individualProfile.asp?indid=977 [accessed April 6, 2010].

[34] George Soros, *George Soros on Globalization*, (New York: Public Affairs, 2002), p. 10.

[35] Ibid.

[36] Horowitz and Poe, *The Shadow Party*, p.218.

[37] "Guide to the George Soros Network", DiscovertheNetworks.org, copyright 2003-2009; available online at: http://www.discoverthenetworks.org/viewSubCategory.asp?id=589 [accessed April 6, 2010].

[38] Horowitz and Poe, *The Shadow Party*, p. 177-178.

[39] Ibid., p.178.

[40] Ibid., p.179.

[41] Ibid.

[42] David Horowitz and Richard Poe, "The Shadow Party: Part II", FrontPageMag.com, October 7, 2004; available online at: http://97.74.65.51/readArticle.aspx?ARTID=11084 [accessed April 6, 2010].

[43] Ibid.

[44] "George Soros Biography and Political Campaign Contributions", CampaignMoney.com, copyright 2010; available online at: http://www.campaignmoney.com/biography/george_soros.asp [accessed April 6, 2010].

[45] Horowitz and Poe, *The Shadow Party*, p.90.

[46] Ibid., p. xii.

[47] Kapner, "The Obama/Soros Plan to Destroy America", op. cit.

[48] Horowitz and Poe, "The Shadow Party: Part I", op. cit.

[49] Ibid.

[50] Horowitz and Poe, *The Shadow Party*, p. 203.

[51] Robert B. Bluey, "Unlike Kerry, Obama Covets Soros' Support", Newsmax.com, July 28, 2004; available online at: http://archive.newsmax.com/archives/articles/2004/7/28/164147.shtml [accessed April 6, 2010].

[52] "Timothy Geithner", Wikipedia, modified April 4, 2010; available online at: http://en.wikipedia.org/wiki/Timothy_Geithner [accessed April 6, 2010].

[53] Fredrick, *The Obama Timeline*, p. 42.

[54] Dr. Kate, "Obama, Brzezinski, and Pakistan", Dr. Kate's View, October 19, 2009; available online at: http://drkatesview.wordpress.com/2009/10/19/obama-brzezinski-and-pakistan/ [accessed April 6, 2010].

[55] Janny Scott, "Stanley Ann Dunham Obama Soetoro", Hand Maid Stale, March 13, 2008; available online at: http://handmaidstale.blogspot.com/2008/03/stanley-ann-dunham-soetoro.html [accessed April 6, 2010].

[56] John D. McKinnon and Bob Davis, "IMF Informed Geithner on Taxes", The Wall Street Journal, January 15, 2009; available online at: http://online.wsj.com/article/SB123194884833281695.html [accessed April 6, 2010].

[57] Julia A. Seymour, "Like a Mama Bear, Networks Protect Obama from His Down Market", Business and Media Institute, March 11, 2009; available online

at: http://businessandmedia.org/printer/2009/20090311161342.aspx [accessed April 6, 2010].

[58] Bud Meyers, "Occidental Recalls Barry Obama", Bud's Blog, September 10, 2009; available online at: http://tobuds.com/blogs/blog1.php/2009/09/10/occidental-recalls-barry-obama [accessed April 6, 2010].

[59] David Quam, "The Trilateral Commission", LizMichael.com, n.d.; available online at: http://www.lizmichael.com/trilat.htm [accessed April 23, 2010].

[60] "Zbigniew Brzezinski", Wikipedia, modified March 28, 2010; available online at: http://en.wikipedia.org/wiki/Zbigniew_Brzezinski [accessed April 12, 2010].

[61] Richard Baehr and Ed Lasky, "Samantha Power and Obama's Foreign Policy Team", American Thinker, February 19, 2008; available online at: http://www.americanthinker.com/2008/02/samantha_power_and_obamas_fore_1. html [accessed April 7, 2010].

[62] Webster Griffin Tarpley, "Confirmed: Obama is Zbigniew Brzezinski Puppet", Rense.com, March 21, 2008; available online at: http://www.rense.com/general81/abig.htm [accessed April 7, 2010].

[63] Tarpley, *Obama: The Postmodern Coup*, p. 167.

[64] Ibid., p. 81.

[65] Kapner, "The Obama/Soros Plan to Destroy America", op. cit.

[66] Stephen Laughlin, "George Soros in Tune with the Zeitgist", Stephen Posterous, February 1, 2009; available online at: http://stephenlaughlin.posterous.com/?tag=kynikosassociates [accessed April 7, 2010].

[67] Ibid.

[68] Bluey, "Unlike Kerry, Obama Covets Soros' Support", op. cit.

[69] Tarpley, *Obama, the Postmodern Coup,* p. 135.

[70] Obama, *The Audacity of Hope*, p. 418.

[71] Ibid., p. 420.

[72] Juanita Gonzales, "Obama Fake Senator in Illinois", Stop Barack Obama, March 29, 2008; available online at: http://www.stop-obama.org/?p=148 [accessed April 7, 2010].

[73] "Emil Jones an Early Backer of Obama White House Bid", Chicago Defender, November 5, 2008; available online at: http://www.chicagodefender.com/article-2394-emil-jones-an-early-backer-of-obama-white-house-bid.html [accessed April 7, 2010].

[74] Todd Spivak, "Barack Obama and Me", Houston Press, February 28, 2008; available online at: http://www.houstonpress.com/2008-02-28/news/barack-obama-screamed-at-me/print [accessed April 7, 2010].

[75] Gonzales, "Obama Fake Senator in Illinois", op. cit.

[76] "U.S. Senator", The Obama File, copyright 2010; available online at: http://www.theobamafile.com/ObamaSenate.htm [accessed April 7, 2010].

[77] Jon Christian Ryter, "Obamination", Jon Christian Conservative World, August 9, 2008; available online at: http://www.jonchristianryter.com/2008/080908.html [accessed April 7, 2010].

[78] "Barry Davis Obama Section", Shattering Denial, October 30, 2008; available online at: http://www.shatteringdenial.com/obama2.html [accessed April 7, 2010].

[79] Shailagh Murray and Chris Cillizza, "Obama Jumps into Presidential Fray", The Washington Post, January 16, 2007; available online at: http://www.washingtonpost.com/wp-dyn/content/article/2007/01/16/AR2007011600529.html [accessed April 7, 2010].

[80] "Guide to the George Soros Network", DiscovertheNetworks.org, op. cit.

[81] Judy Woodruff: "The Financial Crisis: An Interview with George Soros", The New York Review of Books, May 15, 2008; available online at: http://www.nybooks.com/articles/21352 [accessed April 7, 2010].

[82] "Barry Davis Obama Section", Shattering Denial, op. cit.

[83] Ibid.

[84] Pam Martens, "Obama's Money Cartel", Counter Punch, May 5, 2008; available online at: http://www.counterpunch.org/martens05052008.html [accessed April 7, 2010].

[85] Bill Dedman, "Obama Names 110 White House Visitors", MSNBC, November 4, 2009; available online at: http://www.msnbc.msn.com/id/33556933/ [accessed April 7, 2010].

[86] Fredrick, The Obama Timeline, p.179.

[87] Michelle Malkin, "Hope, Change, & Peddling Access", New York Post, October 31, 2009; available online at: http://www.nypost.com/p/news/opinion/opedcolumnists/item_L9zp49BohuxP8ep ZFWXehO [accessed April 7, 2010].

[88] Malkin, Culture of Corruption, p. 168.

[89] Michelle Malkin, "People in 'Fat Cat'-Infested Houses Shouldn't Throw Stones", Michelle Malkin, December 14, 2009; available online at: http://michellemalkin.com/2009/12/14/people-in-fat-cat-infested-houses-shouldnt-throw-stones/ [accessed April 7, 2010].

[90] Ibid.

[91] Horowitz and Poe, The Shadow Party, p. 190.

[92] Eric Boehlert, "Rush's Forced Conscripts", Salon, May 26, 2005; available online at: http://www.salon.com/news/feature/2004/05/26/rush_limbaugh [accessed April 7, 2010].

[93] Horowitz and Poe, The Shadow Party, p. 191.

[94] Horowitz, Unholy Alliance, p. 230.

[95] Horowitz and Poe, "The Shadow Party: Part I", op. cit.

[96] Horowitz and Poe, The Shadow Party, p. 186.

[97] "MoveOn (MO)", DiscovertheNetworks.org, op. cit.

[98] Clark Hoyt, "Betraying It's Own Best Interest", The New York Times, September 23, 2007; available online at: http://www.nytimes.com/2007/09/23/opinion/23pubed.html [accessed April 7, 2010].

[99] Fredrick, The Obama Timeline, p. 560.

[100] Rondi Adamson, "George Soros, Movie Mogul: 'Social Justice' Cinema and the Sundance Institute", Capital Research Center, March 2008; available online at: http://www.capitalresearch.org/pubs/pdf/v1204311857.pdf [accessed June 5, 2010].

[101] Ibid.

[102] Ibid.

[103] Ibid.

[104] Ibid.

[105] "George Soros", DiscovertheNetworks.org, op. cit.

[106] Lowell Ponte, "The ABC's of Media Bias", FrontPageMag.com, October 14, 2004; available online at: http://97.74.65.51/readArticle.aspx?ARTID=10987 [accessed April 30, 2010].

[107] Alexander Burns, "Halperin at Politico/USC Conf.: 'Extreme Pro-Obama' Press Bias", Politico, November 22, 2008; available online at: http://www.politico.com/news/stories/1108/15885.html [accessed June 5, 2010].

[108] Marie Magleby, "Democratic Leader is 'Sure' ABC will cover GOP's Comments on Obama's Primetime Townhall", CNSNews.com, June 16, 2009; available online at: http://www.cnsnews.com/news/print/49633 [accessed April 7, 2010].

[109] "Updated: Beck, Drudge, WND, Fox Nation Falsely Accuse Dunn of Admitting White House 'Control' Over News Media", Media Matters, October 19, 2009; available online at: http://mediamatters.org/research/200910190025 [accessed April 7, 2010].

[110] "Did Fox News Vanquish Anita Dunn?", The Week, November 11, 2009; available online at: http://theweek.com/article/index/102696/Did_Fox_News_vanquish_Anita_Dunn [accessed April 7, 2010].

[111] Suzanne Malveaux, "Obama Aide Fires Back at Beck over Mao Remarks", CNNPolitics.com, October 16, 2009; available online at: http://www.cnn.com/2009/POLITICS/10/16/beck.dunn.index.html [accessed April 7, 2010].

[112] Brian Stelter, "TV News Winds down Operations on Iraq War", AV Science Forum, December 29, 2008; available online at: http://www.avsforum.com/avs-vb/showthread.php?t=838060&page=905 [accessed April 7, 2010].

[113] Michael Barker, "The Soros Media Empire", Swans.com, July 14, 2008; available online at: http://www.swans.com/library/art14/barker02.html [accessed April 7, 2010].

[114] McChesney, "Journalism, Democracy,…and Class Struggle", op. cit.

[115] Glenn Beck, "Net Neutrality Pits Free Speech against Free Press", FoxNews.com, April 6, 2010; available online at: http://www.foxnews.com/story/0,2933,590506,00.html [accessed April 7, 2010].

[116] Ibid.

[117] Vincent Fiore, "Barack Obama and the Making of a Vice President", Enter Stage Right, January 8, 2007; available online at: http://www.enterstageright.com/archive/articles/0107/0107obamavp.htm [accessed April 7, 2010].

[118] Ibid.

[119] Deepak Chopra, "Obama and the Call: 'I am America'", The Huffington Post, January 5, 2008; available online at: http://www.huffingtonpost.com/deepak-chopra/obama-and-the-call-i-am-a_b_80016.html [accessed April 7, 2010].

[120] "April 2008- The Secret Life of Barack Obama", WND SuperStore, April 2008; available online at: http://superstore.wnd.com/store/item.asp?ITEM_ID=2329 [accessed April 7, 2010].

[121] Ibid.

[122] Kyle Drennen, "Newsweek's Evan Thomas: Obama is 'Sort of God'", NewsBusters, June 5, 2009; available online at: http://newsbusters.org/blogs/kyle-drennen/2009/06/05/newsweek-s-evan-thomas-obama-sort-god [accessed April 7, 2010].

[123] Cathryn Friar, "'The Truth' Painting is Obama as Jesus Christ", RightPundits.com, April 25, 2009; available online at: http://www.rightpundits.com/?p=3810 [accessed April 7, 2010].

[124] Fredrick, The Obama Timeline, p. 157-158.

[125] Ibid.

[126] Ibid.

[127] Ibid.

[128] "America Coming Together (ACT) Backgrounder", DiscovertheNetworks.org, March 2005; available online at: http://www.discoverthenetworks.org/Articles/Z%20-%20AMERICA%20COMING%20TOGETHER%20ONE%20PAGER.htm [accessed April 7, 2010].

[129] Kenneth Vogel, "Soros-Linked Group Hit with Huge Fine", Politico, August 29, 2007; available online at: http://www.politico.com/news/stories/0807/5555.html [accessed April 7, 2010].

[130] Phil Kerpen, "The Apollo Alliance: Unifying Activists on the Left", Capital Research Center, October 2009; available online at: http://www.capitalresearch.org/pubs/pdf/v1254459150.pdf [accessed April 7, 2010].

[131] Fred Lucas, "SEIU PAC Spent $27 Million Supporting Obama's Election, FEC Filing Says", CNSNews.com, December 18, 2008; available online at: http://www.cnsnews.com/news/article/40959 [accessed April 7, 2010].

[132] Ibid.

[133] "ACORN Part I: Rathke, ACORN, SEIU, the Tides Foundation, Oh My!", Liberty Chick, May 8, 2009; available online at: http://libertychick.com/2009/05/08/rathke-acorn-seiu-the-tides-foundation-oh-my/ [accessed April 7, 2010].

[134] Evan McMorris-Santoro, "Andy Stern Appears Most Often on WH Logs Released Tonight", TPM, October 30, 2009; available online at: http://tpmdc.talkingpointsmemo.com/2009/10/andy-stern-appears-most-often-on-wh-logs-released-tonight.php [accessed April 7, 2010].

[135] Ben Smith, "Saturday Reading: Dede", Politico, October 31, 2009; available online at: http://www.politico.com/blogs/bensmith/1009/Saturday_reading_Dede.html [accessed April 7, 2010].

[136] Matthew Vadum, "Communist-Linked Apollo Alliance Dictates to Congress", Canada Free Press, July 31, 2009; available online at: http://www.canadafreepress.com/index.php/article/13274 [accessed April 7, 2010].

[137] "Van Jones", DiscovertheNetworks.org, copyright 2003-2009; available online at: http://www.discoverthenetworks.org/individualProfile.asp?indid=2406 [accessed April 7, 2010].

[138] Kerpen, "The Apollo Alliance: Unifying Activists on the Left", op. cit.

[139] Ibid.

[140] "Progressive States Network (PSN)", DiscovertheNetworks.org, copyright 2003-2009; available online at: http://www.discoverthenetworks.org/groupProfile.asp?grpid=7339 [accessed April 7, 2010].

[141] Kerpen, "The Apollo Alliance: Unifying Activists on the Left", op. cit.

[142] Ibid.

[143] Ibid.

[144] "George Soros", DiscovertheNetworks.org, op. cit.

[145] Ibid.

[146] Ehrenfeld, "The Man Who would be Kingmaker, Part I", op. cit.

[147] Steve Clemons, "George Soros has it Right on America's History and Accountability Problem", The Washington Note, February 3, 2007; available online at: http://www.thewashingtonnote.com/archives/001922.php [accessed April 7, 2010].

[148] Cliff Kincaid, "The Hidden Soros Agenda: Drugs, Money, the Media, and Political Power", Accuracy in Media, October 27, 2004; available online at: http://www.aim.org/special-report/the-hidden-soros-agenda-drugs-money-the-media-and-political-power/ [accessed April 7, 2010].

[149] Emily Miller, "On Obama White House Visitor Log: Lobbyists, Movie Stars and Bailed out CEOs", Politics Daily, November 2, 2009; available online at: http://www.politicsdaily.com/2009/11/02/on-obama-white-house-visitor-log-lobbyists-movie-stars-and-bai/ [accessed April 7, 2010].

[150] "George Soros", DiscovertheNetworks.org, op. cit.

[151] Ibid.

[152] Ibid.

[153] Horowitz and Poe, The Shadow Party, p. 220-227.

[154] Ibid.

[155] Ibid.

[156] "George Soros", Wikipedia, op. cit.

[157] Horowitz and Poe, The Shadow Party, p. 222.

[158] Heather Stewart, "G20 Summit Recovery Package: 'A Global Plan on Unprecedented Scale'", Guardian.co.uk, April 3, 2009; available online at:

http://www.guardian.co.uk/world/2009/apr/03/g20-recovery-package [accessed April 7, 2010].

[159] Eben Esterhuizen, "Will Obama Trash the Dollar and Support a Global Currency?", The Huffington Post, April 7, 2009; available online at: http://www.huffingtonpost.com/eben-esterhuizen/will-obama-trash-the-doll_b_184118.html [accessed April 7, 2010].

[160] Joe Weisenthal, "Soros Calls the G20 a Success", Business Insider, April 2, 2009; available online at: http://www.businessinsider.com/soros-calls-the-g20-a-success-2009-4 [accessed April 7, 2010].

[161] "London Summit Communique", The Pittsburg Summit, April 2, 2009; available online at: http://www.pittsburghsummit.gov/resources/125131.htm [accessed April 7, 2010].

[162] "Declaration of Principles", Socialist International, June 2009; available online at: http://www.socialistinternational.org/viewArticle.cfm?ArticleID=31 [accessed April 7, 2010].

[163] "Carol Browner", Wikipedia, modified June 6, 2010; available online at: http://en.wikipedia.org/wiki/Carol_Browner [accessed June 6, 2010].

[164] Fredrick, The Obama Timeline, p. 181.

[165] Pamela Gellar, "Right before the Election of President Hussein: 'A $550 Billion Electronic Run on the Banks'", Atlas Shrugs, February 11, 2009; available online at: http://atlasshrugs2000.typepad.com/atlas_shrugs/2009/02/tight-before-the-election-of-president-hussein-an-electronic-run-on-the-banks.html [accessed April 7, 2010].

[166] Noel Sheppard, "'I'm Having a Good Crisis': Will Soros be Attacked for His Profits?", NewsBusters, March 26, 2009; available online at: http://newsbusters.org/blogs/noel-sheppard/2009/03/26/having-good-crisis-will-soros-be-attacked-his-profits [accessed June 6, 2010].

[167] Ibid.

[168] Alice Thomson and Rachel Sylvester, "George Soros, the Man Who Broke the Bank, Sees a Global Meltdown", Times Online, March 28, 2009; available online at: http://www.timesonline.co.uk/tol/news/uk/article5989163.ece [accessed April 7, 2010].

[169] Michelle Kung, "Hedge Fund Managers Score Biggest-Ever Payday", The Huffington Post, April 16, 2008; available online at: http://www.huffingtonpost.com/2008/04/16/hedge-fund-managers-score_n_96912.html [accessed April 7, 2010].

[170] Sheppard, "'I'm Having a Good Crisis': Will Soros be Attacked for His Profits?", op. cit.

[171] "Obama Underwrites Offshore Drilling", The Wall Street Journal, August 18, 2009; available online at: http://online.wsj.com/article/SB10001424052970203863204574346610120524166.html [accessed April 9, 2010].

[172] Michelle Malkin, "Obama, Soros, Petrobras, Brazil & Offshore Drilling Double Standards", Michelle Malkin, August 19, 2009; available online at:

http://michellemalkin.com/2009/08/19/obama-soros-petrobras-brazil-offshore-drilling-double-standards/ [accessed April 9, 2010].

[173] O'Neill, "Soros: Republic Enemy #1", op. cit.

[174] George Soros, *The Bubble of American Supremacy: Correcting the Misuse of American Power* (New York: Public Affairs, 2004) p. 159.

[175] Ibid.

[176] Horowitz and Poe, *The Shadow Party*, p. 69.

[177] Ibid., p. 242-243.

[178] Cliff Kincaid, "Obama Endorses Soros Plan to Loot America", GOPUSA, April 3, 2009; available online at:
http://www.gopusa.com/commentary/ckincaid/2009/ck_0403p.shtml [accessed April 9, 2010].

[179] D.B. & S.S.M., "Echoing Lyndon LaRouche, Horowitz and Poe Smear 14-Year-Old George Soros as Nazi 'Collaborator', New Book Features Doctored Quotes, Factual Errors", Media Matters, August 2, 2006; available online at:
http://mediamatters.org/research/200608020003 [accessed April 9, 2010].

[180] Arnold Kling, "Milton Freidman on Big Business vs. Freedom", Library of Economics and Liberty, February 9, 2007; available online at:
http://econlog.econlib.org/archives/2007/02/milton_friedman_8.html [accessed April 9, 2010].

[181] "Barack Obama", Encyclopedia of World Biography, 2007; available online at: http://www.notablebiographies.com/newsmakers2/2007-Li-Pr/Obama-Barack.html [accessed June 6, 2010].

[182] Peter Stine, *The Sixties*, (Detroit: Wayne State University Press, 1995), p. 222.

[183] Ibid.

[184] A.M. Siriano, "The Dark Lord Soros", Intellectual Conservative, January 26, 2004; available online at:
http://www.intellectualconservative.com/2004/01/26/the-dark-lord-soros/ [accessed April 9, 2010].

[185] Ibid.

[186] Ken LaRive, "Drill Now: Goldman Sachs, the Federal Reserve, and George Soros is the Source", Examiner.com, October 15, 2009; available online at:
http://www.examiner.com/x-/x-17078-Lafayette-Political-Buzz-Examiner~y2009m10d15-Drill-Now-Goldman-Sachs-The-Federal-Reserve-and-George-Soros-is-the-source [accessed April 9, 2010].

[187] Brian Montopoli, "Obama: Only Government Can Save the Economy", CBS News, February 9, 2009; available online at: http://www.cbsnews.com/8301-503544_162-4788181-503544.html [accessed April 9, 2010].

[188] Ibid.

[189] "Benito Mussolini Quotes", Liberty-Tree.ca, copyright 1998-2005; available online at: http://quotes.liberty-tree.ca/quotes_by/benito+mussolini [accessed April 9, 2010].

[190] Fredrick, *The Obama Timeline*, p. 317.

[191] "Quote from Zbigniew Brzezinski", Liberty-Tree.ca, copyright 1998-2005; available online at: http://quotes.liberty-tree.ca/quote/zbigniew_brezhinsky_quote_1f9d [accessed April 9, 2010].

[192] Department of Homeland Security, "Rightwing Extremism", p.9, Federation of American Scientists, April 7, 2009; available online at: http://www.fas.org/irp/eprint/rightwing.pdf [accessed April 9, 2010].

[193] Ibid., p.2.

[194] Ibid.

[195] "American Legion to DHS: We're Not Terrorists", World Net Daily, April 14, 2009; available online at: http://www.wnd.com/index.php?fa=PAGE.view&pageId=94939 [accessed April 9, 2010].

[196] John Hinderaker, "The Friends of Barack Obama, Part I", Free Republic, April 24, 2008; available online at: http://www.freerepublic.com/focus/f-news/2006227/posts [accessed June 6, 2010].

Chapter Ten

[1] Joseph Farah, "The Day Socialism Comes to America", World Net Daily, February 17, 2008; available online at: http://www.wnd.com/index.php?pageId=56620 [accessed April 6, 2010].

[2] Glenn Beck, "Rewriting our History, Changing Our Traditions", FoxNews.com, December 16, 2009; available online at: http://www.foxnews.com/story/0,2933,580414,00.html?loomia_ow=t0:s0:a4:g4:r3:c0.000000:b0:z5 [accessed April 6, 2007].

[3] Mark Steyn, "Obama, Political Viagra", National Review Online, June 7, 2008; available online at: http://article.nationalreview.com/360082/obama-political-viagra/mark-steyn [accessed April 6, 2010].

[4] Horowitz, *Barack Obama's Rules for Revolution*, p. 1.

[5] Brian Montopoli, "Obama: Taxes Can't be 'Monopoly Money'", CBS News, February 1, 2010; available online at: http://www.cbsnews.com/8301-503544_162-6162902-503544.html [accessed April 10, 2010].

[6] Ralph R. Reiland, "Hopelessly Naïve", The American Spectator, March 30, 2009; available online at: http://spectator.org/archives/2009/03/30/hopelessly-naive [accessed April 20, 2010].

[7] "Putin Speaks at Davos", Wall Street Journal, January 28, 2009; available online at: http://online.wsj.com/article/SB123317069332125243.html [accessed April 6, 2010].

[8] "Thomas Jefferson Quotes", Brainy Quotes, copyright 2010; available online at: http://www.brainyquote.com/quotes/quotes/t/thomasjeff157220.html [accessed April 6, 2010].

[9] "Glenn Beck: Manufacturing Czar Says 'The Free Market is Nonsense'", The Glenn Beck Program, October 20, 2009; available online at: http://www.glennbeck.com/content/articles/article/198/32133/ [accessed April 6, 2010].

[10] Obama, *The Audacity of Hope*, p. 25.

[11] Corsi, *The Obama Nation*, p. 252.

[12] Horowitz and Poe, *The Shadow Party*, p. 218.

[13] Obama, *The Audacity of Hope*, p. 209.

[14] Ibid., p. 152.

[15] "A 40-Year Wish List", Wall Street Journal", January 28, 2009; available online at: http://online.wsj.com/article/SB123310466514522309.html [accessed April 7, 2010].

[16] Matthew Vadum, "Hillary Clinton: 'Never Waste a Good Crisis'", The American Spectator, July 3, 2009; available online at: http://spectator.org/blog/2009/07/03/hillary-clinton-never-waste-a [accessed April 6, 2010].

[17] Timothy P. Carney, "Secretary Loophole", The American Spectator, May 2009 issue; available online at: http://spectator.org/archives/2009/05/15/secretary-loophole/print [accessed April 6, 2010].

[18] John Mauldin, "Debt Crisis Economic End Game, Future Evolution of the Debt-to-GDP Ratio", The Market Oracle, May 19, 2009; available online at: http://www.marketoracle.co.uk/Article10743.html [accessed April 6, 2010].

[19] James Shott, "Potential New Tax Threatens to Keep the U.S. Economy in a Crisis", Annuit Coeptis, April 13, 2010; available online at: http://news-political.com/2010/04/13/potential-new-tax-threatens-to-keep-the-u-s-economy-in-a-crisis/ [accessed May 2, 2010].

[20] Pedro Nicolaci da Costa, "Bernanke says Prompt Action Needed on Deficit", Reuters, April 27, 2010; available online at: http://uk.reuters.com/article/idUKTRE63Q2KH20100427?feedType=RSS&feedName=everything&virtualBrandChannel=11708 [accessed May 3, 2010].

[21] Obama, *The Audacity of Hope,* p. 83.

[22] Ibid., p. 223.

[23] Steve Dinan, "CBO: Obama Stimulus Harmful Over Long Haul", The Washington Times, February 4, 2009; available online at: http://www.washingtontimes.com/news/2009/feb/04/cbo-obama-stimulus-harmful-over-long-haul/ [accessed April 7, 2010].

[24] Mike, "Biden: We have to Spend More Money Faster so We don't Run out of Money", Save the GOP, July 17, 2009; available online at: http://www.savethegop.com/?p=8005 [accessed April 7, 2010].

[25] "Transcript: George Stephanopoulos' Exclusive Interview with President Obama", ABC News, January 20, 2010; available online at: http://blogs.abcnews.com/george/2010/01/transcript-george-stephanopoulos-exclusive-interview-with-president-obama.html [accessed April 10, 2010].

[26] Lisa Snell, "Failing Public Schools Wipe out any Preschools Gains", Reason Foundation, June 6, 2008; available at: http://reason.org/news/show/failing-public-schools-wipe-ou [accessed April 7, 2010].

[27] Paul Sperry, "Obama's Stealth Reparations", FrontPageMag.com, October 28, 2008; available online at: http://97.74.65.51/readArticle.aspx?ARTID=32892 [accessed April 7, 2010].

[28] Ibid.

[29] Ibid.

[30] Jeanne Sahadi, "$4.8 Trillion – Interest on U.S. Debt", CNNMoney, December 20, 2009; available online at:

http://money.cnn.com/2009/11/19/news/economy/debt_interest/index.htm
[accessed April 7, 2010].
[31] L. Brent Bozell III, "Breathtakingly Bold Barack", Media Research Center,
March 4, 2009; available online at:
http://www.mrc.org/BozellColumns/newscolumn/2009/col20090304.asp
[accessed April 7, 2010].
[32] Jerome R. Corsi, "Federal Obligations Exceed World GDP", World Net Daily,
February 13, 2009; available online at:
http://www.wnd.com/index.php?pageId=88851 [accessed April 7, 2010].
[33] Jake Tapper, "Obama's New Attack on those Who don't Want Higher Taxes:
'Selfishness'", ABC News, October 31, 2008; available online at:
http://blogs.abcnews.com/politicalpunch/2008/10/obamas-new-atta.html
[accessed April 10, 2010].
[34] Ed Morrissey, "Obama: I do Think at a Certain Point You've Made Enough
Money", Hot Air, April 29, 2010; available online at:
http://hotair.com/archives/2010/04/29/obama-i-do-think-at-a-certain-point-youve-
made-enough-money/ [accessed May 31, 2010].
[35] "Biden Calls Paying Higher Taxes a Patriotic Act", MSNBC, September 18,
2008; available online at: http://www.msnbc.msn.com/id/26771716/ [accessed
April 10, 2010].
[36] Ned Barnett, "Senator Obama's Four Tax Increases for People Earning under
$250K", American Thinker, October 27, 2008; available online at:
http://www.americanthinker.com/2008/10/senator_obamas_four_tax_increa.html
[accessed April 7, 2010].
[37] Ibid.
[38] Steve Dennis, "Obama's Backdoor Tax Increase (Letting the Bush Tax Cuts
Expire)", America's Watchtower, February 23, 2009; available online at:
http://americaswatchtower.com/2009/02/23/obamas-backdoor-tax-increase-
letting-the-bush-tax-cuts-expire/ [accessed April 7, 2010].
[39] Robert J. Herbold and Scott S. Powell, "Chasing Corporations out of the U.S.",
Investors.com, November 16, 2009; available online at:
http://www.investors.com/NewsAndAnalysis/Article.aspx?id=512549 [accessed
April 7, 2010].
[40] Ed Morrissey, "EPA Declares Air a Danger to Human Health", Hot Air,
December 7, 2009; available online at:
http://hotair.com/archives/2009/12/07/epa-declares-air-a-danger-to-human-
health/ [accessed April 7, 2010].
[41] Christopher Monckton, "Christopher Monckton's Destruction of
Anthropogenic Global Warming to the US House of Representatives", Milton
Conservative, April 14, 2009; available online at:
http://miltonconservative.blogspot.com/2009/04/christopher-monctons-
destruction-of_17.html [accessed April 7, 2010].
[42] Gregory Young, "Global Warming? Bring it On!", American Thinker,
November 21, 2008; available online at:
http://www.americanthinker.com/2008/11/global_warming_bring_it_on.html
[accessed April 7, 2010].

[43] "Fred Singer and Global Warming: Everyone is out of Step but Him and His Cosmic Rays", See Different, November 16, 2007; available online at: http://seesdifferent.wordpress.com/2007/11/16/fred-singer-and-global-warming-everyone-is-out-of-step-but-him-and-his-cosmic-rays/ [accessed April 7, 2010].

[44] Ed Morrissey, "The Age of Obama: Heat for Me, but not for Thee", Hot Air, January 29, 2010; available online at: http://hotair.com/archives/2009/01/29/the-age-of-obama-heat-for-me-but-not-for-thee/ [accessed April 7, 2010].

[45] Ibid.

[46] David Horowitz, "Boring from Within: Alinsky, Beck, Satan and Me, Part III", FrontPageMag.com, August 18, 2009; available online at: http://97.74.65.51/readBlog.aspx?BLOGID=1050 [accessed April 7, 2010].

[47] Ken Shepherd, "Network Shows Ignore Copenhagen's Warm Reception for Anti-Capitalist Rhetoric from Chavez", NewsBusters, December 17, 2009; available online at: http://newsbusters.org/blogs/ken-shepherd/2009/12/17/network-shows-ignore-copenhagens-warm-reception-anti-capitalist-rhetor [accessed April 7, 2010].

[48] Jonah Goldberg, "Does Obama Support Largest Middle Class Tax Increase in History?", National Review Online, March 16, 2009; available online at: http://corner.nationalreview.com/post/?q=YzFmODFjNjA5ODUxODE1ZDZhZWVjODBjY2M0MmM1Y2Q [accessed April 7, 2010].

[49] "Obama Caps Exec Pay for Bailout Firms", US News, February 5, 2009; available online at: http://www.usnews.com/usnews/politics/bulletin/bulletin_090205.htm [accessed April 7, 2010].

[50] Michelle Malkin, "Newsflash: Wonderboy Treasury Secretary is in over His Head", Michelle Malkin, March 4, 2009; available online at: http://michellemalkin.com/2009/03/04/newsflash-wonderboy-treasury-secretary-is-in-over-his-head/ [accessed April 7, 2010].

[51] Neal Boortz, "Charlie Rangel gets a Pass", Boortz, October 8, 2009; available online at: http://boortz.com/nealz_nuze/2009/10/charlie-rangel-gets-a-pass.html [accessed April 7, 2010].

[52] "Glenn Beck: Congressman Jason Chaffetz", The Glenn Beck Show, December 11, 2009; available online at: http://www.glennbeck.com/content/articles/article/196/34124/ [accessed April 7, 2010].

[53] Dr. Richard Swier, "100 Economists Say Obama Plan Wrong for Economy", Red County, October 7, 2008; available online at: http://www.redcounty.com/sarasota/2008/10/100-economists-say-obama-plan/ [accessed April 7, 2010].

[54] Ibid.

[55] Martina Stewart, "Gregg: 'This Country will go Bankrupt'", Political Ticker, March 22, 2009; available online at: http://politicalticker.blogs.cnn.com/2009/03/22/gregg-this-country-will-go-bankrupt/?fbid=11t4bsu2Eks [accessed April 7, 2010].

[56] "Millionaires Flee Maryland Taxes", The Washington Examiner, May 27, 2009; available online at:

http://www.washingtonexaminer.com/local/Millionaires-flee-Maryland-taxes-46138062.html [accessed April 7, 2010].

[57] William Ahern, "Can Income Tax Hikes Close the Deficit", Tax Foundation, October 22, 2009; available online at: http://www.taxfoundation.org/publications/show/25415.html [accessed April 7, 2010].

[58] Juhana Rossi, "McDonald's Deemed More Credit-Worthy than U.S. Government", Watching America, September 26, 2008; available online at: http://watchingamerica.com/News/7016/mcdonalds-deemed-more-credit-worthy-than-the-us-government/ [accessed April 8, 2010].

[59] Sara Goss, "Obama Said He Would Bankrupt the Coal Industry", American Thinker, February 27, 2009; available online at: http://www.americanthinker.com/blog/2009/02/obama_said_he_would_bankrupt_t.html [accessed April 8, 2010].

[60] "New Video: Obama Vows Electricity Rates would 'Necessarily Skyrocket' Under His Plan", Breitbart TV, November 3, 2008; available online at: http://www.breitbart.tv/?p=211663 [accessed April 8, 2010].

[61] "Lost in an Energy Wilderness", National Center for Policy Analysis, April 1, 2009; available online at: http://www.ncpa.org/sub/dpd/index.php?Article_ID=17803 [accessed April 8, 2010].

[62] Obama, *The Audacity of Hope*, p. 199-200.

[63] Ibid., p. 201.

[64] Adam Summers, "China Worried Over the Value of the Dollar (with Good Reason)", Reason Foundation, March 31, 2009; available online at: http://reason.org/blog/show/china-worried-over-the-value-o [accessed April 8, 2010].

[65] Ambrose Evans-Pritchard, "A 'Copper Standard' for the World's Currency System?", Telegraph.co.uk, April 15, 2009; available online at: http://www.telegraph.co.uk/finance/comment/ambroseevans_pritchard/5160120/A-Copper-Standard-for-the-worlds-currency-system.html [accessed May 3, 2010].

[66] Hemant Parikh, "US Greenback is Doomed! – Now or Never", Mudraa.com, December 7, 2009; available online at: http://www.mudraa.com/trading/31456/0/us-greenback-is-doomed-now-or-never-hemant-.html [accessed May 3, 2010].

[67] Clarice Feldman, "Chavez and Fidel to Obama's Right?", American Thinker, June 3, 2009; available online at: http://www.americanthinker.com/blog/2009/06/chavez_and_fidel_to_obamas_rig.html [accessed April 8, 2010].

[68] "Treasury Limits Pay at Five Companies", Celebrifi, March 23, 2010; available online at: http://celebrifi.com/gossip/Treasury-limits-pay-at-five-companies-1944546.html [accessed April 10, 2010].

[69] Stuart Varney, "Obama Wants to Control the Banks", Wall Street Journal, April 4, 2009; available online at:

http://online.wsj.com/article/SB123879833094588163.html [accessed April 8, 2010].

[70] "Fascism/Nazism", Ayn Rand Lexicon, copyright 1986, available online at: http://aynrandlexicon.com/lexicon/fascism-nazism.html [accessed April 8, 2010].

[71] Larry Kudlow, "A 'Truly Breathtaking' Departure", National Review Online, March 30, 2009; available online at: http://article.nationalreview.com/390040/a-truly-breathtaking-departure/larry-kudlow [accessed April 8, 2010].

[72] Montopoli, "Obama: Only Government Can Save the Economy", op. cit.

[73] Phil Izzo, "Secondary Sources: Taxpayer Robbery, Corporate Taxes, Geithner Notes", Wall Street Journal, March 25, 2009; available online at: http://blogs.wsj.com/economics/2009/03/25/secondary-sources-taxpayer-robbery-corporate-taxes-geithner-notes/tab/article/ [accessed April 8, 2010].

[74] Warner Todd Houston, "Obama's Faith-Based Programs Pushing Global Warming, Climate Change, Green Issues", Big Government, May 16, 2010; available online at: http://biggovernment.com/wthuston/2010/05/16/obamas-faith-based-programs-pushing-global-warming-climate-change-green-issues/ [accessed June 1, 2010].

[75] Obama, The Audacity of Hope, p. 142.

[76] William Tate, "Obama, the PAC-Man", American Thinker, July 10, 2008; available online at: http://www.americanthinker.com/2008/07/obama_the_pacman.html [accessed April 9, 2010].

[77] Brian Johnson, "A Lobbyist by any Other Name: SEUI and the Obama White House", Big Government, December 3, 2009; available online at: http://biggovernment.com/brjohnson/2009/12/03/a-lobbyist-by-any-other-name-seiu-and-the-obama-white-house/ [accessed April 9, 2010].

[78] Neal Boortz, "Here They Come for Your Retirement!", Boortz, March 24, 2010; available online at: http://boortz.com/nealz_nuze/2010/03/here-they-come-for-your-retire.html [accessed June 1, 2010].

[79] Malkin, Culture of Corruption, p. 197.

[80] "National Council of La Raza, Miami, FL", Ask Sam, July 22, 2007; available online at: http://www.asksam.com/ebooks/releases.asp?file=Obama-Speeches.ask&dn=National%20Council%20of%20La%20Raza [accessed April 9, 2010].

[81] "Senator Barack Obama's Remarks at the 2008 Annual Conference", National Council of La Raza, copyright 2010; available online at: http://www.nclr.org/content/viewpoints/detail/52978/ [accessed April 9, 2010].

[82] Don Fredrick, The Obama Timeline, p. 531.

[83] Associated Press, "Obama: U.S. Troops in Afghanistan Must do More than Kill Civilians", FoxNews.com, August 14, 2007; available online at: http://www.foxnews.com/story/0,2933,293187,00.html [accessed April 9, 2010].

[84] Jim Meyers, "Obama Bow to Saudi King Labeled 'Shocking'", Newsmax, April 8, 2009; available online at: http://newsmax.com/InsideCover/Obama-bow-king/2009/04/08/id/329349 [accessed April 9, 2010].

[85] Clifford Bryan, "Barack Obama Bows to Emperor Akihito and Empress Michiko", Examiner, November 14, 2009; available online at:

http://www.examiner.com/x-19673-Michelle-Obama-Examiner~y2009m11d14-Barack-Obama-bows-to-Emperor-Akihito-and-Empress-Michiko [accessed April 9, 2010].

[86] Byron York, "Obama's Bad Night", National Review Online, July 24, 2007; available online at: http://article.nationalreview.com/322555/obamas-bad-night/byron-york [accessed April 9, 2010].

[87] Michelle Malkin, "Yes! The Ultimate Obama Endorsement! (Updated)", Michelle Malkin, June 22, 2008; available online at: http://michellemalkin.com/2008/06/22/yes-the-ultimate-obama-endorsement/ [accessed April 9, 2010].

[88] Ed Morrissey, "Sarkozy: Obama an Empty Suit on Foreign Policy", October 28, 2008; available online at: http://hotair.com/archives/2008/10/28/sarkozy-obama-an-empty-suit-on-foreign-policy/ [accessed April, 9, 2010].

[89] Pamela Gellar, "French President Sarkozy Calls Obama Insane", Atlas Shrugs, April 11, 2010; available online at: http://atlasshrugs2000.typepad.com/atlas_shrugs/2010/04/french-president-sarkozy-calls-obama-insane.html [accessed May 3, 2010].

[90] Reverend Amy, "'He's Done Everything Wrong' – Hell hath no Fury", No Quarters, January 22, 2010; available online at: http://www.noquarterusa.net/blog/2010/01/22/hes-done-everything-wrong-hell-hath-no-fury/ [accessed April 9, 2010].

[91] John Noonan, "Lech Walesa Slams Obama's Foreign Policy", WeeklyStandard.com, February 5, 2010; available online at: http://www.weeklystandard.com/blogs/lech-walesa-slams-obamas-foreign-policy [accessed April 9, 2010].

[92] Dick Morris and Eileen McGann, "Asking the Bombers to Try Again", DickMorris.com, June 19, 2008; available online at: http://www.dickmorris.com/blog/2008/06/23/asking-the-bombers-to-try-again/ [accessed April 9, 2010].

[93] Ed Morrissey, "Webb: Criminal Trials for 9/11 Terrorists a Bad Idea", Hot Air, November 13, 2009; available online at: http://hotair.com/archives/2009/11/13/webb-criminal-trials-for-911-terrorists-a-bad-idea/ [accessed April 9, 2010].

[94] Neo-neocon, "Obama on Afghanistan: Victory is a Four-Letter Word", American Thinker, July 25, 2009; available online at: http://www.americanthinker.com/2009/07/post_23.html [accessed June 3, 2010].

[95] "Senate Confirms Sonia Sotomayor to U.S. Supreme Court", FoxNews.com, August 6, 2009; available online at: http://www.foxnews.com/politics/2009/08/06/senate-confirms-sonia-sotomayor-supreme-court/ [accessed April 9, 2010].

[96] Michelle Malkin, "SCOTUS Pick: Sonia Sotomayor", Michelle Malkin, May 26, 2009; available online at: http://michellemalkin.com/2009/05/26/scotus-pick-sonia-sotomayor/ [accessed April 9, 2010].

[97] Aaron Klein, "Obama's Supreme Pick has Love Affair with Socialism", World Net Daily, May 10, 2010; available online at:

http://www.wnd.com/index.php?fa=PAGE.view&pageId=152133 [accessed June 3, 2010].

[98] Obama, *The Audacity of Hope,* p. 109-110.

[99] Ibid., p. 108.

[100] John Perazzo, "Obama's 'Diversity Chief' and the End of Talk Radio", FrontPageMag.com, September 16, 2009; available online at: http://97.74.65.51/readArticle.aspx?ARTID=36280 [accessed April 9, 2010].

[101] Matt Cover, "Acting FCC Chair Sees Government Role in Pushing 'Media Diversity'", CNSNews.com, February 12, 2009; available online at: http://www.cnsnews.com/news/print/43414 [accessed April 9, 2010].

[102] Ibid.

[103] Lowell Ponte, "Obama may Consider Nonprofit Status for Newspapers", Newsmax.com, September 22, 2009; available online at: http://www.newsmax.com/LowellPonte/nonprofit-pbs-npr-obama/2009/09/22/id/335153 [accessed April 9, 2010].

[104] Pamela Geller, "Obama Open to State Run Media: Newspaper Bail-out", Atlas Shrugs, September 20, 2009; available online at: http://atlasshrugs2000.typepad.com/atlas_shrugs/2009/09/obama-open-to-state-run-media-newspaper-bailout.html [accessed April 9, 2010].

[105] Brad O'Leary, "U.S. Regulatory Czar Nominee Wants Net 'Fairness Doctrine'", World Net Daily, April 27, 2009; available online at: http://www.wnd.com/index.php?pageId=96301 [accessed April 9, 2010].

[106] Ibid.

[107] Malcolm Kline, "Anatomy of an Activist", Canada Free Press, May 13, 2010; available online at: http://canadafreepress.com/index.php/article/23128 [accessed May 31, 2010].

[108] "Upton Sinclair", Wikiquote, modified March 10, 2010; available online at: http://en.wikiquote.org/wiki/Upton_Sinclair [accessed April 9, 2010].

[109] "Fact Sheet Regarding President Obama's Education Investments", Democratic Policy Committee, n.d.; available online at: http://dpc.senate.gov/docs/fs-111-1-70.html [accessed April 11, 2010].

[110] Bob Unruh, "New Law to 'Manage' 8 Million 'Volunteers'", World Net Daily, April 21, 2009; available online at: http://www.wnd.com/index.php?fa=PAGE.view&pageId=95674 [accessed April 9, 2010].

[111] Jerome R. Corsi, "'Mandatory Youth Service' Bill Advances", World Net Daily, March 25, 2009; available online at: http://www.wnd.com/index.php?pageId=92902 [accessed April 9, 2010].

[112] Robert Farley, "'Mandatory Volunteerism'? Not in this Bill", PolitiFact.com, March 31, 2009; available online at: http://www.politifact.com/truth-o-meter/article/2009/mar/31/mandatory-volunteerism-nope/ [accessed April 10, 2010].

[113] Nice Deb, "A Version of Obama's Civilian Service Corps Approved by House", Nice Deb, March 21, 2009; available online at: http://nicedeb.wordpress.com/2009/03/21/a-version-of-obamas-civilian-service-corps-approved-by-house/ [accessed April 9, 2010].

[114] "Glenn Beck: Obama's Radical Followers", The Glenn Beck Program, September 5, 2008; available online at: http://www.glennbeck.com/content/articles/article/198/14846/ [accessed April 9, 2010].
[115] Ibid.
[116] Ibid.
[117] "Obama Wants You", Investors.com, July 31, 2008; available online at: http://www.investors.com/NewsAndAnalysis/Article.aspx?id=495249 [accessed April 9, 2010].
[118] David Boaz, "Our Collectivist Candidates", Cato Institute, May 28, 2008; available online at: http://www.cato.org/pub_display.php?pub_id=9429 [accessed April 9, 2010].
[119] Pamela Geller, "Atlas Exclusive: Obama Organizing in High School", Atlas Shrugs, January 30, 2010; available online at: http://atlasshrugs2000.typepad.com/atlas_shrugs/2010/01/atlas-exclusive-obama-organizing-for-communism-and-youth-corps-in-the-public-school-1.html [accessed April 11, 2010].
[120] Ibid.
[121] Ibid.
[122] Berit Kjos, "The Mind-Changing Dialectic Process", Kjos Ministries, n.d.; available online at: http://www.crossroad.to/articles2/Reinventing2.htm [accessed April 9, 2010].
[123] "Quote from Aldous Huxley", Liberty-Tree.ca, copyright 1998-2005; available online at: http://quotes.liberty-tree.ca/quote/aldous_huxley_quote_57b0 [accessed April 9, 2010].
[124] Berit Kjos, "Mind Change and Collective Service", Kjos Ministries, October 2008; available online at: http://www.crossroad.to/articles2/08/2-service.htm [accessed April 9, 2010].
[125] Ibid.
[126] Ibid.
[127] Duane Lester, "HR 1388 or the Obama Youth Brigade Bill – Update", All-American Blogger, March 26, 2009; available online at: http://www.allamericanblogger.com/6886/hr-1388-or-the-obama-youth-brigade-bill-update/ [accessed June 5, 2010].
[128] Obama, The Audacity of Hope, p. 188.
[129] Ibid., p. 210-213.
[130] Ken Watts, "The Closing Gap between the Right and Left", The Daily Mull, January 14, 2009; available online at: http://dailymull.com/1284/The-Closing-Gap-Between-Right-and-Left [accessed April 20, 2010].
[131] P.J. O'Rourke, "The Liberty Manifesto", Cato Institute, May 6, 1993; available online at: http://www.cato.org/pub_display.php?pub_id=6857 [accessed April 9, 2010].
[132] "Marxist Quotes", New England Freedom, copyright 2010; available online at: http://nefreedom.ning.com/page/marxist-quotes [accessed April 10, 2010].
[133] Ibid.

[134] Kyle-Anne Shiver, "Obama's Politics of Collective Redemption", American Thinker, February 11, 2008; available online at: http://www.americanthinker.com/2008/02/obamas_politics_of_collective.html [accessed April 10, 2009].

[135] Lee Cary, "Obama's Civilian National Security Force", American Thinker, July 20, 2008; available online at: http://www.americanthinker.com/2008/07/obamas_civilian_national_secur.html [accessed April 10, 2010].

[136] Obama, *The Audacity of Hope*, p. 375.

[137] "About Barack Obama", Global News Daily, copyright 2008-2010; available online at: http://www.globalnewsdaily.com/ [accessed April 10, 2010].

[138] "Agenda – Service", Change.gov, n.d.; available online at: http://change.gov/agenda/service_agenda/ [accessed June 5, 2010].

[139] "Gun Quotations", Brainy Quote, copyright 2010; available online at: http://www.brainyquote.com/words/gu/gun171055.html [accessed June 5, 2010].

[140] Malkin, *Culture of Corruption*, p. 141.

[141] Chelsea Schilling, "Obama Czar Pick: 'Raving Animal Rights Nut'", World Net Daily, July 24, 2009; available online at: http://www.wnd.com/index.php?pageId=104820 [accessed April 10, 2010].

[142] Joseph Abrams, "Obama's Science Czar Considered Forced Abortions, Sterilization as Population Growth Solutions", FoxNews.com, July 21, 2009; available online at: http://www.foxnews.com/politics/2009/07/21/obamas-science-czar-considered-forced-abortions-sterilization-population-growth/ [accessed April 10, 2010].

[143] Michael Zak, "The Healthcare Bill would be Obama's 'Enabling Act'", Big Government, March 13, 2010; available online at: http://biggovernment.com/mzak/2010/03/13/the-healthcare-bill-would-be-obamas-enabling-act/#more-88118 [accessed April 11, 2010].

[144] Tarpley, *Obama: The Postmodern Coup*, p. 315.

[145] Shiver, "Obama's Politics of Collective Redemption", op. cit.

[146] Huntwork, "The 99 Most Memorable, Interesting and Outrageous Political Quotes of 2008", op. cit.

[147] John Marini, "Our Enemy, the State?", Claremont Institute, Winter 2002; available online at: http://www.claremont.org/publications/crb/id.1151/article_detail.asp [accessed April 10, 2010].

[148] "Abraham Lincoln Quotes", ThinkExist.com, copyright 1999-2010; available online at: http://thinkexist.com/quotation/we_the_people_are_the_rightful_masters_of_both /221236.html [accessed April 10, 2010].

[149] James A. Leggette and Michael W. Funk, "Ronald Reagan and the Opening Salvos in the War on Terror", American Thinker, June 7, 2005; available online at: http://www.americanthinker.com/2005/06/ronald_reagan_and_the_opening.html [accessed April 10, 2010].

[150] M. More, "House Joint Resolution No. 26", February 17, 2009; available online at: http://data.opi.mt.gov/bills/2009/BillHtml/HJ0026.htm [accessed April 10, 2010].

[151] Jim O'Neill, "Scott Brown: 'It's the People's Seat!'", Canada Free Press, January 13, 2010; available online at: http://www.canadafreepress.com/index.php/article/18942 [accessed April 10, 2010].

[152] Muckabin Thomas Owens, "The Case against Secession", Claremont Institute, copyright 2002-2009; available online at: http://www.claremont.org/publications/pubid.171/pub_detail.asp [accessed April 10, 2010].

[153] "Martin Luther King, Jr. Quotes", Brainy Quote, copyright 2010; available online at: http://www.brainyquote.com/quotes/quotes/m/martinluth134767.html [accessed April 11, 2010].

[154] "Edmund Burke", Wikiquote, modified March 23, 2010; available online at: http://en.wikiquote.org/wiki/Edmund_Burke [accessed April 10, 2010].